Automatic Society

Automatic Society

Volume 1
The Future of Work

Bernard Stiegler

Translated by Daniel Ross

polity

First published in French as *La Société automatique. 1. L'Avenir du travail*, © Librairie Arthème Fayard, 2015

This English edition © Polity Press, 2016

Polity Press
65 Bridge Street
Cambridge CB2 1UR, UK

Polity Press
350 Main Street
Malden, MA 02148, USA

ISBN-13: 978-1-5095-0630-9
ISBN-13: 978-1-5095-0631-6 (pb)

A catalogue record for this book is available from the British Library.

Names: Stiegler, Bernard, author.
Title: Automatic society / Bernard Stiegler.
Other titles: Société automatique. English
Description: Cambridge, UK ; Malden, MA : Polity Press, [2016]– | "First published in [French] as La Société automatique." | Includes bibliographical references and index.
    Contents: Volume 1. The future of work –
Identifiers: LCCN 2016023994 (print) | LCCN 2016046717 (ebook) | ISBN 9781509506309 (v. 1 : hardcover : alk. paper) | ISBN 1509506306 (v. 1 : hardcover : alk. paper) | ISBN 9781509506316 (v. 1 : pbk. : alk. paper) | ISBN 1509506314 (v. 1 : pbk. : alk. paper) | ISBN 9781509506330 (mobi) | ISBN 9781509506347 (epub)
Subjects: LCSH: Automation–Economic aspects. | Automation–Social aspects. | Technological innovations–Social aspects. | Technology and civilization–Philosophy.
Classification: LCC HD6331 .S73513 2016 (print) | LCC HD6331 (ebook) | DDC 338/.064–dc23
LC record available at https://lccn.loc.gov/2016023994

Typeset in 10.5 on 12 pt Sabon by Toppan Best-set Premedia Limited

For further information on Polity, visit our website: politybooks.com

Contents

Rational objectivity, technical objectivity and social objectivity are now tightly connected. To neglect one of these aspects of modern scientific culture is to enter the sphere of utopia.

Gaston Bachelard[1]

We untiringly construct the world in order that the hidden dissolution, the universal corruption that governs what 'is' should be forgotten in favor of a clear and defined coherence of notions and objects, relations and forms – the work of tranquil man. A work that nothingness would be unable to infiltrate and where beautiful names – all names are beautiful – suffice to make us happy.

Maurice Blanchot[2]

These motors must be very different from all the others. It seems logical to suppose that Morel designed them so that no one who came to this island would be able to understand them. But the difficulty in running the green motors must stem from their basic difference from the other motors. As I do not understand any of them, this greater difficulty disappears. [...] And what if Morel had thought to photograph the motors –

Adolfo Bioy Casares[3]

Introduction
Functional Stupidity, Entropy and Negentropy in the Anthropocene

The strangest thing about this remarkable return of 'humankind' into history is that the Anthropocene provides the clearest demonstration that, from an environmental point of view, humanity as a whole does not exist.

Christophe Bonneuil and Jean-Baptiste Fressoz[1]

1. What occurred between 23 June and 23 October 2008

In an analysis of Google's business model in *Wired* on 23 June 2008, Chris Anderson showed that the services provided by this company – which are based on what Frédéric Kaplan has called *linguistic capitalism*[2] – operate without any reference whatsoever to a theory of language.[3]

Continuing with a form of reasoning similar to that which he applies to the epidemiology of Google, Anderson comes to the conclusion that what is referred to today as 'big data',[4] consisting of gigabytes of data that can be analysed in real time via high-performance computing, no longer has any need for either theory or theorists – as if data 'scientists', specialists in the application of mathematics to very large databases through the use of algorithms, could replace those theoreticians that scientists always are in principle, regardless of the scientific field or discipline with which they happen to be concerned.

Four months later, on 23 October 2008, Alan Greenspan appeared before a Congressional hearing to explain the reasons behind so many financial catastrophes that were unleashed after the subprime crisis of August 2007. Challenged for having failed to anticipate or prevent the systemic crisis, he defended himself by arguing that the scale of the crisis was due to the misuse of financial mathematics and automated calculation systems to assess risk, mechanisms established by digital trading in its various forms (from subprime to high-frequency trading): 'It was the failure to properly price such risky assets that precipitated the crisis. In recent decades, a vast risk management and pricing system has evolved, combining the best insights of mathematicians and finance experts supported by major advances in computer and communications technology.'[5] Greenspan also stressed that such approaches had been legitimated through the Nobel Prize for economics[6] – his intention being to assert that, if there is blame to be apportioned, it ought not to fall only upon the president of the US Federal Reserve: the whole apparatus of computerized formalization and automated decision-making undertaken by financial robots was involved, as well as the occult economic 'theory' that gave it legitimacy.

If until August 2007 this had managed to function (this paradigm having 'held sway for decades'), if computerized formalization and automated decision-making had been imposed *in fact*, this 'whole intellectual edifice, however, collapsed [that summer] because the data inputted into the risk management models generally covered only the past two decades, a period of euphoria'.[7] I would add to Greenspan's statement that the ideologues of this 'rational risk management' were undoubtedly not unaware of the limitations of their data sets. But they assumed that 'historic periods of stress' had occurred *only because these financial instruments did not exist during these periods*, or because competition was *not yet* 'perfect and undistorted'. Such was the concealed theory operating behind these robots, robots that supposedly 'objectify' reality and do so according to 'market rationality'.

Not long after the publication of Chris Anderson's article on Google, Kevin Kelly objected that, behind every automated understanding of a set of facts, there lies a hidden theory, whether there is awareness of it or not, and, in the latter case, it is a theory *awaiting formulation*.[8] What this means for us, if not for Kelly himself, is that *behind and beyond every fact, there is a law*.

Science is what goes beyond the facts by *making a claim for an exception* to this law: it posits that there *can always be an exception* (and this is what '*exciper*' means in law: to plead for, or to claim, an exception to the law) to the *majority* of facts, even to the *vast majority* of facts, that is, to virtually all of them, an exception that *invalidates them in law* (that invalidates their apparent coherence).

This is what, in the following chapters, we will call, alongside Yves Bonnefoy and Maurice Blanchot, the *improbable* – and this is also the question of the black swan, which Nassim Nicholas Taleb has posed in a way that remains closer to the epistemology of statistics, probability and categorization.[9]

2. Bottling Paris

The ideology of perfect and undistorted competition was and remains today the discourse of neoliberalism, and this includes the discourse of Alan Greenspan, who concluded his 2008 Congressional testimony by expressing himself in such terms: 'Had instead the models been fitted more appropriately to historic periods of stress, capital requirements [for funds held in financial institutions] would have been much higher and the financial world would be in far better shape today, in my judgment.' But what this comment obscures is the fact that 'with *ifs*, one could bottle Paris'.[10] For had these capital requirements 'been much higher', the model would simply never have developed. For this model developed precisely in order to paper over the systemic insolvency of *consumer capitalism* (that is, of 'growth'), a form of capitalism afflicted for over thirty years by the drastic reduction in the purchasing power of workers, as demanded by the conservative revolution – and by financialization, in which the latter fundamentally consists, and which made it possible for countries to become structurally indebted, and hence subjected to an unprecedented form of blackmail that indeed resembles a racket (and which we can therefore refer to as mafia capitalism).[11]

The application of this model based on the 'financial industry' and its automated computer technologies was intended both to capture *without redistribution* the capital gains generated by productivity and to conceal, through computer-assisted financial fraudulence operating on a worldwide scale, the fact that the conservative revolution had broken the 'virtuous circle' of the Fordist-Keynesian 'compromise'.[12]

With the conservative revolution, then, capitalism becomes *purely computational* (if not indeed 'purely mafiaesque'). Max Weber showed in 1905 that, on the one hand, capitalism was originally related to a form of incalculability the symbol of which was Christ as the cornerstone of the Protestant ethic, the latter constituting the spirit of capitalism.[13] But he showed, on the other hand, that the transformative dynamics of the society established by this 'spirit' consisted in a secularization and rationalization that irresistibly thwarts it – what might be called the *aporia of capitalism*.[14]

We shall see that as contemporary capitalism becomes *purely* computational, concretized in the so-called 'data economy', this aporia is exacerbated, this contradiction is 'realized', and in this way it succeeds in accomplishing that becoming without future referred to by Nietzsche as *nihilism* – of which Anderson's blustering assertions and Greenspan's muddled explanations are symptoms (in the sense given to this term by Paolo Vignola).[15]

3.   What is hidden in *France Ten Years From Now*?

Anderson's storytelling belongs to a new ideology the goal of which is to hide (from itself) the fact that with total automatization a new explosion of generalized insolvency is readying itself, far worse than that of 2008: the next ten years will, according to numerous studies, predictions and 'economic assessments', be dominated by automation.

On 13 March 2014 Bill Gates declared in Washington that with the spread of software substitution, that is, as logical and algorithmic robots come increasingly to control physical robots – from 'smart cities' to Amazon, via Mercedes factories, the subway and trucks that deliver to supermarkets from which cashiers and freight handlers are disappearing, if not customers – employment will drastically diminish over the next twenty years, to the point of becoming the exception rather than the rule.

This thesis, which in the last few years has been explored in depth, has recently come to the attention of European newspapers, firstly in Belgium in *Le Soir*, which in July 2014 warned of the risk of the loss of half of all the jobs in the country 'within one or two decades', then in France. It was taken up again by *Journal du dimanche* in October 2014, in an article based on a study the newspaper commissioned from the firm Roland Berger. This warned of the destruction by 2025 of three million jobs, equally affecting the middle classes, management, the liberal professions and the manual trades. Note that the loss of three million jobs represents an increase in unemployment of about eleven points – an unemployment level of 24%, in addition to the rise of 'part-time' or 'casual' under-employment.

Ten years from now, and regardless of how it is counted, French unemployment is likely to shift to between 24% and 30% (the Roland Berger scenario being relatively optimistic compared to the forecasts of the Brussels-based think tank Bruegel, as we shall see). Furthermore, each one of these studies predicts the eventual demise of the Fordist-Keynesian model, which had hitherto organized the redistribution of the productivity gains obtained through Taylorist automation in the form of purchasing power acquired through wages.

Hence this portends an *immense transformation*. Despite this, the report submitted by Jean Pisani-Ferry to the French president in the summer of 2014 as part of a 'government seminar' had *not one word to say* about these literally overwhelming prospects – which represent an upheaval for any macroeconomics to come.

Pisani-Ferry's France Stratégie report, *France Ten Years From Now?*, does, of course, discuss employment, but in a wheedling tone more or less amounting to the injunction, 'Let us set modest, realistic goals: in terms of employment, let's aim to be in the top third of similar countries.'[16] And it goes on and on in these tepid terms for two hundred pages, never deigning to mention the prospect of a drastic reduction in employment, on the contrary asserting:

> [T]he goal must be full employment. As far as we can see today, this is the normal way in which the economy functions. Any other social condition becomes pathological and involves an unsustainable waste of skills and talents. There is no reason to give up on reaching this, given that for a long time we experienced a situation of very low unemployment and that some of our neighbours have today returned to such a situation.[17]

According to Pisani-Ferry, Commissioner General of France Stratégie, then, the goal of full employment should be reaffirmed, but in a 'credible' way – but the reasoning behind this argument turns out to be extraordinarily tenuous:

> To set this target today for 2025 would not be deemed credible by the French public, which has suffered decades of persistent mass unemployment. A goal that is perceived, rightly or wrongly, as being too high can have a demotivating effect. It is better, as the Chinese proverb says, to cross the river by feeling the stones. Furthermore, the problem with setting goals in absolute terms lies in not taking into account the global and European economic situation. Reasoning in relative terms avoids this pitfall. In this spirit, we can aspire to return sustainably to the top third of European countries in terms of employment.[18]

The claims of *France Ten Years From Now?* are contradicted by Bruegel, the Brussels-based policy research institute that had been headed by Pisani-Ferry himself until his May 2013 appointment as Commissioner General of France Stratégie. Bruegel argues, through Jeremy Bowles and by taking note of the figures provided by Benedikt

Frey and Michael Osborne,[19] that Belgium could see 50% of its jobs disappear, England 43%, Italy and Poland 56% – and all this, according to *Le Soir*, 'within one or two decades'.

At the time he submitted his report (in June 2014), Pisani-Ferry could not have been unaware of these forecasts made by the very institute he helped found in 2005. How did he allow himself to so dissimulate? The reality is that, like Greenspan, he internalized a calamitous situation that he continues to misunderstand thanks to a deeply flawed analysis, thereby preventing France from taking stock of a highly dangerous situation: '[C]ashiers, nannies, supervisors, even teachers [...], by 2025 a third of jobs could be filled by machines, robots or software endowed with artificial intelligence and capable of learning by themselves. And of replacing us. This is a vision of the future prophesied by Peter Sondergaard, senior vice president and global head of research at Gartner.'[20] We shall see that this 'vision' is shared by dozens of analysts around the world – including the firm Roland Berger, which released a study arguing that 'by 2025, 20% of tasks will be automated. And more than three million workers may find themselves giving up their jobs to machines. An endless list of sectors is involved: agriculture, hospitality, government, the military and the police.'[21] To conceal such prospects is a serious mistake, as noted by an associate of Roland Berger, Hakim El Karoui:

> 'The tax system is not set up to collect part of the wealth generated (by the digital), and the redistribution effect is therefore very limited.'
>
> Warning against the risk of social explosion, [El Karoui] calls for 'anticipating, describing, telling the truth [...], to create a shock in public opinion now'. Otherwise, distrust of the elites will increase, with serious political consequences.[22]

4.   Entropy and negentropy in the Anthropocene

To anticipate, describe, alert, but also to propose: such are the goals of this book, which envisages a completely different way of 'redistributing the wealth generated by the digital', to put it in Hakim El Karoui's terms. Is a different future possible, a new beginning, in the process of complete and generalized automatization to which global digital reticulation is leading?

We must pose this as the question of the passage from the Anthropocene, which at the end of the eighteenth century established the conditions of generalized proletarianization (something that Adam Smith himself already understood), to the *exit* from this period, a period in which anthropization has become a 'geological factor'.[23] We will call this exit the *Neganthropocene*. The escape from the Anthropocene constitutes the global horizon of the theses advanced here. These theses posit as first principle that the *time saved by automatization must be invested in new capacities for dis-automatization*, that is, for the *production of negentropy*.

Analysts have been predicting the end of wage labour for decades, from Norbert Wiener in the United States to Georges Friedmann in France, after John Maynard Keynes himself foreshadowed its imminent disappearance. Marx, too, explored this hypothesis in depth in a famous portion of the *Grundrisse* on automation, known as the 'fragment on machines'.

This possibility will come to fruition over the next decade. What should we do over the course of the next ten years in order to make the best of this *immense transformation?*

Bill Gates has himself warned of this decline in employment, and his recommendation consists in reducing wages and eliminating various related taxes and charges. But lowering yet again the wages of those who still have jobs can only increase the global insolvency of the capitalist system. The true challenge lies elsewhere: the time liberated by the end of work must be put at the service of an automated culture, but one capable of producing new value and of reinventing work.[24] Such a *culture of dis-automatization, made possible by automatization,* is what can and must produce negentropic value – and this in turn requires what I have previously referred to as the *otium* of the people.[25]

Automation, in the way it has been implemented since Taylorism, has given rise to an immense amount of entropy, on such a scale that today, throughout the entire world, humanity fundamentally doubts its future – and young people especially so. Humanity's doubt about its future, and this confrontation with unprecedented levels of youth worklessness, are occurring at the very moment when the Anthropocene, which began with industrialization, has become 'conscious of itself':

> Succeeding the Holocene, a period of 11,500 years marked by a rare climatic stability [...] a period of blossoming agricultures, cities and civilizations, the swing into the Anthropocene represents a new age of the Earth. As Paul Crutzen and Will Steffen have emphasized, under the sway of human action, 'Earth is currently operating in a *no-analogue state.*'[26]

That the Anthropocene has become 'conscious of itself'[27] means that human beings have become more or less conscious of belonging to the Anthropocene era, in the sense that they feel 'responsible'[28] – something that became visible in the 1970s. After the Second World War and the resultant acceleration of the Anthropocene, there was a growing 'common consciousness' of being a geological factor and the collective cause of massive and accelerated entropization via mass anthropization. This occurred even before the formulation (in 2000) of the concept of the Anthropocene itself – a fact that Bonneuil and Fressoz highlight by referring to a speech delivered by Jimmy Carter in 1979: 'Human identity is no longer defined by what one does, but by what one owns. But we've discovered that owning things and consuming things does not satisfy our longing for meaning. We've learned that piling up material goods cannot fill the emptiness of lives which have no confidence or purpose.'[29] It is striking that an American president here declares the end of the American way of life. Bonneuil and Fressoz recall that this runs counter to the discourse that would subsequently appear with Ronald Reagan: 'If Carter's defeat by Ronald Reagan in 1980, who called for a restoration of US hegemony and the deregulation of polluting activities, shows the limits of this appeal, his speech does illustrate the influence [...] that criticism of the consumer society had acquired in the public sphere.'[30] In recent years, and especially since 2008, this 'self-consciousness' of the Anthropocene has exposed the *systemically and massively toxic* character of contemporary organology[31] (in addition to its insolvency), in the sense that Ars Industrialis and the Institut de recherche et d'innovation (IRI) give to this term within the perspective of general organology.[32]

There is now a general awareness of this pharmacological toxicity, in the sense that factors hitherto considered progressive seem to have inverted their sign and are instead sending humanity on a course of generalized regression. With this in mind, the Anthropocene, whose history coincides with that of capitalism, presents itself as a process that begins with organological industrialization (including in those countries thought of as 'anti-capitalist'), that is, with the industrial revolution – which must accordingly be understood as an *organological revolution*.

5. The completion of nihilism and the entry into the Neganthropocene

The Anthropocene era is that of industrial capitalism, an era in which *calculation prevails over every other criteria of decision-making*, and where algorithmic and mechanical becoming is concretized and materialized as logical automation and automatism, thereby constituting the advent of nihilism, as computational society becomes a society that is automated and remotely controlled.

The confusion and disarray into which we are thrown in this stage – a stage that we call 'reflexive' because there is a supposedly 'raised consciousness' of the Anthropocene – is a historical outcome in relation to which new causal and quasi-causal factors can now be identified that have not hitherto been analysed. This is why Bonneuil and Fressoz rightly deplore 'geocratic' approaches that short-circuit political analyses of that history which begins to unfold with what they call the Anthropocene *event*.[33]

To Bonneuil and Fressoz's historical and political perspective, however, we must add that, as a result of this event, what philosophy had denied in a structural way for centuries has now become clear, namely, that the artefact is the mainspring of hominization, its condition and its destiny. It is no longer possible for anyone to ignore this reality: what Valéry, Husserl and Freud posited between the two world wars as a new age of humanity, that is, as its pharmacological consciousness and unconsciousness of the 'world of spirit',[34] has become a *common, scrambled and miserable* consciousness and unconsciousness. Such is ill-being [*mal-être*] in the contemporary Anthropocene.[35]

What follows from this is an urgent need to redefine the noetic fact in totality – that is, in every field of knowledge (of how to live, do and conceptualize) – and to do so by integrating the perspectives of André Leroi-Gourhan and Georges Canguilhem, who were the first to posit the artificialization of life as the starting point of hominization.[36] This imperative presents itself as a situation of extreme urgency crucial to politics, economics and ecology. And it thereby raises a question of *practical organology*, that is, of *inventive* productions.

We argue that this question and these productions necessarily involve (and we will show why) a complete reinvention of the world wide web – *the Anthropocene having since 1993 entered into a new epoch* with the advent of the web, an epoch that is as significant for us today as were railways at the beginning of the Anthropocene.

We must think the Anthropocene with Nietzsche, as the geological era that consists in the devaluation of all values: it is in the Anthropocene, and as its vital issue, that the *task of all noetic knowledge becomes the transvaluation of values*. And this occurs at the moment when the noetic soul is confronted, through its own, organological putting-itself-in-question, with the *completion of nihilism*, which amounts to the *very ordeal of our age* – in an Anthropocene concretized as the age of planetarizing capitalism.

It is with Nietzsche that, after the Anthropocene event, we must think the advent of the Neganthropocene, and it must be thought as the transvaluation of becoming into future. And this in turn means reading Nietzsche with Marx, given that, in 1857, the latter reflects upon the new status of knowledge in capitalism and the future of work, in the section of the *Grundrisse* on automation known as the 'fragment on machines', in which he also discusses the question of the *general intellect*.

Reading Marx and Nietzsche together in the service of a new critique of political economy, *where the economy has become a cosmic factor on a local scale (a dimension of the cosmos)* and therefore an ecology, must lead to a process of *transvaluation*, such that both *economic values* and those *moral devaluations* that result when nihilism is set loose as consumerism are *'transvaluated' by a new value of all values, that is, by negentropy* – or negative entropy,[37] or anti-entropy.[38]

Emerging from thermodynamics about thirty years after the advent of industrial technology and the beginning of the *organological revolution* lying at the origin of the Anthropocene, both with the grammatization of gesture by the first industrial automation and with the steam engine,[39] the theory of entropy succeeds in redefining the question of *value*, if it is true that the *entropy/negentropy relation is the vital question par excellence*. It is according to such perspectives that we must think, organologically and pharmacologically, both what we are referring to as the *entropocene* and what we are referring to as *neganthropology*.

6. The question of fire and the advent of thermodynamics

The *kosmos* is conceived at the dawn of philosophy as identity and *equilibrium*. Through this opposition posited *in principle* between an equilibrium of ontological origin and the disequilibrium of corruptible beings, technics, which in fact constitutes the organological condition, is relegated to the sublunary as the world of contingency and of 'what can be otherwise than it is' (*to endekhomenon allōs ekhein*), and thereby finds itself as such excluded from thought.

The Anthropocene, however, makes such a position untenable, and consequently constitutes an epistemic crisis of unprecedented magnitude: the advent of the thermodynamic *machine*, which reveals the human world as being one of *fundamental disruption,*[40] inscribes processuality, the irreversibility of becoming and the instability of equilibrium in which all this consists, at the heart of physics itself. All *principles* of thought as well as action are thereby overturned.

The thermodynamic machine, which posits in *physics* the new, specific problem of the dissipation of energy, is also an industrial technical object that fundamentally disrupts *social* organizations, thereby radically altering 'the understanding that being there has of its being'[41] and establishing the era of what is referred to as 'technoscience'. As it consists essentially in a *combustion*, this technical object, of which the centrifugal 'flyball' governor will be a key element at the heart of the conception of cybernetics, introduces the *question of fire and of its pharmacology* both on the plane of astrophysics (which replaces cosmology) and on the plane of human ecology.

The question of fire – that is, of combustion – is thereby inscribed, from the standpoint of physics but also from the perspective of anthropological ecology, at the heart of a renewed thought of the cosmos *as cosmos* (and beyond 'rational cosmology' as it was conceived by Kant[42]): the Anthropocene epoch can appear as such only starting from the moment when the question of the cosmos itself becomes the question of combustion in thermodynamics and in astrophysics – and, via the steam engine, in relation to that eminent *pharmakon* that is domestic fire as the artifice par excellence brought to mortals by Prometheus, and watched over by Hestia.[43]

As a question of physics, the techno-logical conquest of fire[44] puts anthropogenesis – that is, organogenesis that is not just organic but organological – at the heart of what Whitehead called *concrescence*, and does so as the *local technicization of the cosmos*. This local technicization is relative, but it leads to *conceiving of the cosmos in its totality on the basis of this position* and on the basis of this *local opening of the question of fire* as the *pharmakon* of which we must *take care* – where the question of *energy* (and of *energeia*) that fire (which is also light) harbours, posed on the basis of the organological *and epistemological* revolution of thermodynamics as reconsidered by Schrödinger, constitutes *the matrix of the thought of life as well as information, and does so as the play of entropy and negentropy.*

Establishing the *question* of entropy and negentropy among human beings as the *crucial problem* of the everyday life of human beings and of life in general, and, finally, of the universe in totality for every form of life, *technics* constitutes the matrix of all thought of *oikos*, of habitat and of its law. Is it not striking from such a standpoint that at the very moment when Schrödinger was delivering the lectures in

Dublin that would form the basis of *What is Life?*, Canguilhem was asserting that the noetic soul is a technical form of life that requires new conditions of fidelity in order to overcome the shocks of infidelity caused by what we ourselves call the *doubly epokhal redoubling?*[45]

7. The Anthropocene as a succession of technological shocks and the neganthropic role of knowledge

What Canguilhem described as the infidelity of the technical milieu[46] is what is encountered as an *epokhal technological shock* by the organological and pharmacological beings that we are qua noetic individuals – that is, as intellectual and spiritual individuals. This shock and this infidelity derive fundamentally from what Simondon called the phase shifting of the individual. This de-phasing of the individual in relation to itself is the dynamic principle of individuation.

We have developed the concept of the 'doubly epokhal redoubling' in order to try to describe how a shock begins by destroying established circuits of transindividuation,[47] themselves emerging from a prior shock, and then gives rise to the generation of new circuits of transindividuation, which constitute new forms of knowledge arising from the previous shock. A techno-logical *epokhē* is *what breaks with constituted automatisms*, with automatisms that have been socialized and are *capable of producing their own dis-automatization* through appropriated *knowledge*: the *suspension of socialized automatisms* (which feeds stupidity in its many and varied forms) occurs when *new, asocial automatisms are set up*. A second moment of shock (the second redoubling) then produces new capacities for dis-automatization, that is, for negentropy to foster new social organizations.

Knowledge always proceeds from such a double shock – whereas *stupidity* always proceeds from automaticity. Recall here that Canguilhem posits in principle the more-than-biological meaning of *epistēmē*: *knowledge of life* is a specific form of life conceived not only as biology, but also as *knowledge of the milieus, systems and processes of individuation*, and where *knowledge is the condition and the future* of life exposed to return shocks from its vital technical productions (organogenetic productions, which it secretes in order to compensate for its default of origin).

Knowledge [*connaissance*] is what is constituted as the therapeutic knowledges [*savoirs*] partaking in the *pharmaka* in which consist the artificial organs thus secreted. It is immediately social, and it is always more or less transindividuated in social organizations. Knowledge *of pharmaka* is also knowledge *through pharmaka*: it is constituted in a thoroughly organological way, but it is also wholly and originally internalized – *failing which it is not knowledge, but information*. This is why it does not become diluted in 'cognition': hence cognitive science, which is one such form, is incapable of thinking knowledge (that is, of thinking *itself*).

We must relate the organo-logical function of knowledge such as we understand it on the basis of Canguilhem, and as necessitated by the technical form of life, to what Simondon called the knowledge of individuation: to know individuation is to individuate, that is, it is to *already no longer know* because it is to *de-phase*.

Knowledge [*connaissance*], as the knowledge [*savoir*] that conditions both the psychic and collective individuation of knowing, 'always comes too late', as Hegel said, which means that it is not self-sufficient: it presumes life-knowledge [*savoir-vivre*, knowledge of how to live] and work-knowledge [*savoir-faire*, knowledge of how to do] that always exceed it and that are themselves always exceeded by technical individuation, which generates the technological shocks that constitute epochs of knowledge.

The socialization of knowledge increases the complexity of societies, societies that individuate and as such participate in what Whitehead called the concrescence of the cosmos, itself conceived as a cosmic process that generates processes of individuation wherein entropic and negentropic tendencies play out differently each time.

In the Anthropocene epoch, from which it is a matter of escaping as quickly as possible, the questions of life and negentropy arising with Darwin and Schrödinger must be redefined from the organological perspective defended here, according to which: (1) natural selection makes way for artificial selection; and (2) the passage from the organic to the organological displaces the play of entropy and negentropy.[48]

Technics is an *accentuation of negentropy*. It is an agent of *increased differentiation*: it is 'the pursuit of life by means other than life'.[49] But it is, equally, an *acceleration of entropy*, not just because it is always in some way a process of the combustion and dissipation of energy, but also because *industrial standardization* seems to be leading the contemporary Anthropocene to the possibility of a destruction of life as the burgeoning and proliferation of differences – as the biodiversity, sociodiversity ('cultural diversity') and psychodiversity of singularities generated *by default* as psychic individuations and collective individuations.

The destruction of social diversity results from short-circuits of the processes of transindividuation imposed by industrial standardization. We shall see in the conclusion of this work that anthropology understood as entropology is the problem that Lévi-Strauss succeeds in recognizing but not in thinking – he fails to pose this as the question of neganthropology, that is, as the question of a *new epoch of knowledge* embodying the task of entering into the Neganthropocene. This is what leads him to abandon the political dimension implied in any anthropology.

The Anthropocene is a singular organological epoch inasmuch as it engendered the organological question itself. It is in this way retroactively constituted through its own recognition, where the *question* this period poses is how to make an *exit* from its own toxicity in order to enter the curative and care-ful – and in this sense economizing – epoch of the Neganthropocene. What this means in practical terms is that in the Neganthropocene, and *on the economic plane, the accumulation of value must exclusively involve those investments that we shall call neganthropic.*

We call *neganthropic* that human activity which is explicitly and imperatively governed – via processes of transindividuation that it implements, and which result from a criteriology established by retentional systems – by negentropic criteria. The neganthropization of the world breaks with the care-less and negligent anthropization of its entropic effects – that is, with the essential characteristics of the Anthropocene. Such a rupture requires the overcoming of the Lévi-Straussian conception of anthropology by a neganthropology that remains entirely to be elaborated.

The *question* of the Anthropocene, which bears within it its own overcoming, and bears the structure of a *promise*, is emerging at the very moment when, on the other hand, we are witnessing the establishment of that *complete and general automatization* made possible by the *industry of reticulated digital traces*, even though the latter seems to make this promise untenable. To hold fast, that is, to hold good to this promise, means beginning, precisely, from those neganthropic possibilities opened up by *automation* itself: it is to think this industry of reticulation as a new epoch of work, and as the end of the epoch of 'employment', given that the latter is ultimately and permanently compromised by *complete and general automatization*. And it is to think this industry as the 'transvaluation' of value, whereby 'labour time ceases and must cease to be its measure, and hence exchange value [must cease to be the measure] of use value',[50] and where *the value of value becomes neganthropy.* Only in this way can and must the passage from the Anthropocene to the Neganthropocene be accomplished.

8. Smartification

Since 1993, a new global technical system has been put in place. It is based on digital tertiary retention and it constitutes the infrastructure of an automatic society to come. We are told that the data economy, which seems to be concretizing itself as the economic dynamic generated by this infrastructure, is the inevitable destiny of this society.

We shall show, however, that the 'destiny' of this society of hyper-control (chapter 1) is not a destination: it leads nowhere other than to nihilism, that is, *to the negation of knowledge itself* (chapter 2). And we will see, first with Jonathan Crary (chapter 3), then with Thomas Berns and Antoinette Rouvroy (chapters 4 and 5), why this automatic society to come will be able to constitute a future – that is, a destiny of which the negentropic destination is the Neganthropocene – only on the condition of overcoming this 'data economy', which is in reality the diseconomy of a 'dis-society'[51] (chapter 6).

The current system, founded on the industrial exploitation of modelled and digitalized traces, has precipitated the entropic catastrophe that is the Anthropocene qua destiny that leads nowhere. As 24/7 capitalism and algorithmic governmentality, it hegemonically serves a *hyper-entropic* functioning that accelerates the rhythm of the consumerist destruction of the world while installing a structural and unsustainable insolvency, based on a generalized stupefaction and a functional stupidity that destroys the neganthropological capacities that knowledge contains: unlike mere competence, which does not know what it does, *knowledge is a cosmic factor that is inherently negentropic.*

We intend in this work to show that the reticulated digital infrastructure that supports the data economy, put in place in 1993 with the world wide web and constituting the most recent epoch of the Anthropocene, can and must be inverted into a neganthropic infrastructure founded on *hermeneutic* digital technology in the service of dis-automatization. That is, it should be based on *collective investment* of the productivity gains derived from automatization in a culture of knowing how to do, live and think, insofar as this knowledge is essentially neganthropic and as such produces new value, which alone is capable of establishing a new era bearing a new solvency that we call the Neganthropocene (chapters 7 and 8).

The current infrastructure is rapidly evolving towards a society of hyper-control founded on mobile devices such as the 'smartphone', domestic devices such as 'web-connected television', habitats such as the 'smart house' and 'smart city', and transport devices such as the 'connected car'.

Michael Price showed recently that the connected television is a tool for automated spying on individuals:

> I just bought a new TV. [...] I am now the owner of a new 'smart' TV [...]. The only problem is that I'm now afraid to use it. [...] The amount of data this thing collects is staggering. It logs where, when, how and for how long you use the TV. It sets tracking cookies and beacons designed to detect 'when you have viewed particular content or a particular email message.' It records 'the apps you use, the websites you visit, and how you interact with content.' It ignores 'do-not-track' requests as a considered matter of policy. It also has a built-in camera – with facial recognition. The purpose is to provide 'gesture control' for the TV and enable you to log in to a personalized account using your face.[52]

What will occur with the connected clothing that is now appearing on the market?[53]

In addition, Jérémie Zimmermann highlighted in an interview in *Philosophie magazine* that the smartphone has led to a real change in the hardware of the digital infrastructure, since the operations of this handheld device, unlike either the desktop or laptop computer, are no longer accessible to the owner:

> The PCs that became available to the broad public in the 1980s were completely understandable and programmable by their users. This is no longer the case with the new mobile computers, which are designed so as to prevent the user from accessing some of the functions and options. The major problem is the so-called baseband chip that is found at the heart of the device. All communications with the outside – telephone conversations, SMS, email, data – pass through this chip. More and more, these baseband chips are fused with the interior of the microprocessor; they are integrated with the main chip of the mobile computer. Now, none of the specifications for any of these chips are available, so we know nothing about them and cannot control them. Conversely, it is potentially possible for the manufacturer or the operator to have access, via these chips, to your computer.[54]

For his part the physicist Stephen Hawking, in a co-authored article appearing in the *Independent*, stated that 'AI may transform our economy to bring both great wealth and great dislocation.'[55] The authors observe that, if we undoubtedly have a tendency to believe that, 'facing possible futures of incalculable benefits and risks, the experts are surely doing everything possible to ensure the best outcome', then we are wrong. And they invite us to measure what is at stake by considering one question: 'If a superior alien civilisation sent us a message saying, "We'll arrive in a few decades," would we just reply, "OK, call us when you get here – we'll leave the lights on"? Probably not – but this is more or less what is happening with AI.' They point out that the *stakes are too high to not be given priority and urgency at the core of research*: 'Although we are facing potentially the best or worst thing to happen to humanity in history, little serious research is devoted to these issues outside non-profit institutes.'

Referring to the work of Tim O'Reilly, Evgeny Morozov talks about 'smartification' based on 'algorithmic regulation' that amounts to a new type of governance founded on cybernetics, which is above all the science of government, as Morozov recalls.[56] I have myself tried to show, provisionally, that in a way this constitutes the horizon of Plato's *Republic*.[57]

Morozov quotes O'Reilly: 'You know the way that advertising turned out to be the native business model for the internet? [...] I think that insurance is going to be the native business model for the internet of things.'[58] Morozov's central idea is that the way we currently organize the collection, exploitation and reproduction of what we are here calling *digital tertiary retention*[59] rests on the structural elimination of conflicts, disagreements and controversies: '[A]lgorithmic regulation offers us a good-old technocratic utopia of politics without politics. Disagreement and conflict, under this model, are seen as unfortunate byproducts of the analog era – to be solved through data collection – and not as inevitable results of economic or ideological conflicts.'

We shall see how Thomas Berns and Antoinette Rouvroy have from a similar standpoint analysed what they themselves call, in reference to Foucault, algorithmic governmentality – wherein the insurance business and a new conception of medicine based on a transhumanist program both have the goal of 'hacking' (that is, 'reprogramming') not only the state, but the human body.[60] Google, which along with NASA supports the Singularity University, has invested heavily in 'medical' digital technologies based on the application of

high-performance computing to genetic and also epigenetic data –
and with an explicitly eugenic goal.[61]

9.   The goal of the present work

Morozov points out that net activists, who have become aware of
the toxicity of 'their thing', are nevertheless manipulated and recuperated by 'algorithmic regulation' through non-profit organizations
that intend to 'reprogramme the state': '[T]he algorithmic regulation
lobby advances in more clandestine ways. They create innocuous
non-profit organisations like Code for America which then co-opt the
state – under the guise of encouraging talented hackers to tackle civic
problems. Such initiatives aim to reprogramme the state and make
it feedback-friendly, crowding out other means of doing politics.'[62]
Morozov calls for the elaboration of a new politics of technology –
one that would serve left-wing politics: 'While many of the creators
of the internet bemoan how low their creature has fallen, their anger
is misdirected. The fault is not with that amorphous entity but, first
of all, with the absence of robust technology policy on the left.'[63]
We fully share this analysis: the goal of this work is to contribute to
establishing the conditions of such a politics through its two volumes
on the neganthropic future of work and of knowledge as the conditions of entry into the Neganthropocene – where this is also a matter
of *redesigning the digital architecture* and *in particular the digital
architecture of the web,* with the goal of creating a digital hermeneutics that gives to controversies and conflicts of interpretation their
negentropic value, and constitutes on this basis an economy of work
and knowledge founded on intermittence, for which the model must
be the French system designed to support those occasional workers
in the entertainments industry called '*intermittents du spectacle*'.

1

The Industry of Traces and Automatized Artificial Crowds

We might, then, also refer to a sort of panic that is on the verge of replacing the assurance we had of being able to conduct our affairs under the sign of freedom and reason.

Robert Musil[1]

10. The automatization of existences

The rise of so-called 'social' digital networks brought with it a new kind of economy, based on personal data, cookies, metadata, tags and other tracking technologies through which is established what Thomas Berns and Antoinette Rouvroy have called *algorithmic governmentality*.[2] It was this context, too, that saw the rise of 'big data' – that is, those technologies connected to what is referred to as high-performance computing[3] – which utilizes methods derived from applied mathematics, placing them in the service of automated calculation and forming the core of this algorithmic governmentality.

Digital tracking technologies are the most advanced stage of a process of grammatization that began at the end of the Upper Palaeolithic age, when humanity first learnt to discretize[4] and reproduce, in traces of various kinds, the flux and flow running through it and that it generates: mental images (cave paintings), speech (writing), gestures (the automation of production), frequencies of sound and light (analogue recording technology) and now individual behaviour, social relations and transindividuation processes (algorithms of reticular writing).

These traces constitute hypomnesic tertiary retentions.[5] Having become digital, they are today generated by interfaces, sensors and other devices, in the form of binary numbers and hence as *calculable* data, forming the base of an automatic society in which *every* dimension of life becomes a functional agent for an industrial economy that thereby becomes thoroughly *hyper-industrial*.

The outlines of the hyper-industrial epoch first appear when the analogue technologies of the mass media set up those modulation processes characteristic of what in 1990 Gilles Deleuze called 'control societies'.[6] But it is only when digital calculation integrates this modulation in the form of algorithmic governmentality[7] that hyper-industrial society is fully accomplished as the *automatization of existences*.

11.   The proletarianization of sensibility

With the conservative revolution and the neoliberal turn, the dissolution of everyday life as described by Henri Lefebvre[8] (the analysis of which was taken up again by Guy Debord) leads in the last quarter of the twentieth century to the reign of symbolic misery:[9] the analogue, audiovisual apparatus of the mass media is then essentially subjected to strategic marketing via the privatization of radio stations and television channels.

Symbolic misery results from the proletarianization of sensibility that commenced in the early twentieth century. This de-symbolization leads in a structural way to the destruction of desire, that is, to the ruin of libidinal economy. And it ultimately leads to the ruin of all economy whatsoever when, at the beginning of the 1980s, speculative marketing, under direct shareholder control, becomes hegemonic and systematically exploits the drives, which are thereby divested of all attachment.[10]

Symbolic misery follows from the mechanical turn of sensibility[11] that proletarianizes the sensible realm by subjecting symbolic life to the industrial organization of what then becomes 'communication' between, on the one hand, professional producers of symbols and, on the other hand, proletarianized and de-symbolized consumers, deprived of their life-knowledge. Individual and collective existences are thereby subjected to the permanent control of the mass media,[12] which short-circuits the processes of identification, idealization and transindividuation that would otherwise weave the thread of inter-generational relations and so form the fabric of desire by 'binding' the drives.[13]

Elementary *savoir-vivre*, elementary life-knowledge, is formed and transmitted through processes of identification, idealization and transindividuation, constituting the attentional forms[14] that lie at the basis of any society. These forms metastabilize the psychosocial ability to bind the drives by diverting their goals towards social investments.

As the industrial deformations and diversions of attention that short-circuit these processes, the de-symbolization in which consists the symbolic misery imposed by *consumer capitalism* inevitably leads to the destruction of all investment, and to the subsequent annihilation of libidinal economy.[15]

The object in which desire invests is what libido *economizes*. The object is *desired* to the point of inverting the goals of the drives that support it[16] only because, thus economized, that is, *saved and retained*, it *no longer exists*: it *consists*. And, as such, it is *infinitized* – that is, it *exceeds* all calculation.[17] This is also the question of excess in the 'general economy' of Georges Bataille.

The simultaneous destruction of desire, of investment in its object and of the experience of its consistence results in the liquidation of all attachment and all fidelity – that is, of all confidence, without which no economy is possible – and ultimately *of all belief*, and therefore of all *credit*.[18]

12. The original artificiality of traces in noetic life

In 1905, Freud's investigation of fetishistic perversion led him to what he would later call the 'libidinal economy'. Love, as everyone knows, is in the strictest and most immediate sense the experience of artifice: to fetishize the one we love is essential.[19] When we cease to love someone we had formerly loved, the artificiality of the amorous situation falls back brutally into everyday ordinariness. Desire, as that which economizes its object, as what takes care of it by idealizing it and transindividuating it (by socializing it, that is, by making it an object of social relations), arises only with the artificialization of life – with what Georges Canguilhem described as technical life. This is why Pandora, the wife of Epimetheus, the 'first woman', that is, the first being to become an object of desire, is originally bejewelled.

Two or three million years ago, when life began to pass *essentially* through non-living artifice (which means that it cannot do without its prostheses, which is the human characteristic, as Rousseau already understood[20]), there first arose what Aristotle referred to as the noetic soul, which desires and loves, that is, which idealizes – as we are taught by Diotima.

Hence it is that this soul projects 'consistences', which are sublime objects of desire. In so doing it infinitizes itself by passing through the artefacts that support this libidinal economy – which is the economy of *nous*. As such, it is a noetic soul. *Nous* was translated from Greek into Latin as *intellectus* and *spiritus*: a noetic soul is intellective and spiritual. This means that it is always and essentially inhabited and possessed by revenances, fantasies, obsessions and apparitions, supported by the artifices in which consist the artificial organs with which the human being is covered (including the jewels of Pandora, but also clothes and shoes, which can become the organs of a shoe fetish – a 'perversion' that has been extensively studied).[21]

Through its artefacts, this soul can generate intellectual technologies via which it accedes to the intellect inasmuch as it is analytical. The spiritual soul can be haunted by spirits (by that which returns and those who return) only because technical life, by augmenting itself prosthetically, by thereby amplifying and intensifying its powers of sublimation, equips itself with a transindividual artificial memory that makes possible what Simondon called psychic and collective individuation. Biological economy is what in Simondon is referred to as vital individuation,[22] whereas the noetic life formed by libidinal economy belongs to psychosocial individuation.

Because it does not transindividuate its traces, vital individuation is not yet an economy of drives diverted into social investment: it is an economy of the instincts, which control animal behaviour with the rigour of automatism.[23] With the appearance of fetishizable artificial supports, objects of adoration characteristic of the noetic soul insofar as it is dedicated to cults, worship and rituals, *the instincts are relatively dis-automatized*: they can be displaced, they can change object. They become detachable, as artificial organs that are the supports of fetishization, and as such they are no longer instincts but, precisely, drives.

In this way, vital individuation gives way to psychic and collective individuation, wherein we must constantly *contain* and *retain* these drives, which, because they can change object, are called 'perverse'. They are perverse inasmuch as they are structurally detachable, since they too are artificial organs. This means that they are structurally fetishistic and 'objectal'. In this libidinal economy that is no longer just biological but thanatological and organological, the detachability of the drives, induced by that of artifices themselves, installs an economy of ambiguity symbolized by that jar which is Pandora's box.

13.   The industry of traces

With modernity and capitalism, artifice manifests itself as such – this is Baudelaire – at the heart of what Paul Valéry described as a *political economy* of spirit, founded on commerce and industrial technology, and leading to what the latter called a fall in 'spirit value'.

In the current, hyper-industrial epoch, we shall see that this is now an *absolutely* and *totally* computational capitalism. And it is so essentially starting from the conservative revolution initiated in the 1980s – this economy having structurally become a libidinal *diseconomy*, that is, an *absolute* lack of care for its objects.

In this diseconomy that a dissociety becomes,[24] objects can no longer constitute supports of investment: they are no longer infinitizable since they have become *fully* calculable, that is, *totally futile*. They become no-things: *nihil*. Fully computational capitalism is as such the *completion of nihilism*. The structural effect of full and generalized automatization is that capitalism becomes a computerized nihilism, which seems to be giving rise to a new form of totalitarianism.

It is this threat that we now all feel and perceive, in a more or less muffled way. Such is the great malaise experienced throughout the world – beginning with the 'net blues'[25] that has afflicted 'hacktivists' since the appearance of 'social networking'. The absolutely computational contemporary libidinal diseconomy no longer economizes its objects and so destroys and dissipates its subjects – who destroy themselves by conforming to the automated prescriptions of computational capitalism.

This is so because this libidinal diseconomy has become a computerized industry of traces, traces that had formerly been the condition of possibility of libidinal economy and investment. At the dawn of consumerism, however – in the first half of the twentieth century, when the proletarianization of consumers first commenced – singularities began to be progressively subjected to calculability. As Jonathan Crary stresses, in this period intimate areas still remained that were protected from these calculations, and this was so for a long time.[26] But today this is no longer the case.

The economy of traces (or of data) nevertheless claims to be overcoming what, especially since 2008, is increasingly perceived as carelessness and negligence: this claim is what is sometimes called 'digital utopianism'.[27] But for almost ten years Ars Industrialis has argued that digitalization, which made the industry of traces possible, does bear within it a new industrial model constitutive of an economy of contribution – that is, an economy that reconstitutes knowledge of how to live, do and conceptualize, and that thereby forms a new age of care.

The question is therefore the following: if this computational and industrial traceology presents itself today and in fact, through algorithmic governmentality, as the acceleration, crystallization and in a way the precipitation of insolvency, discredit, disindividuation and the generalized entropy that inevitably results from this headlong flight, *is it nevertheless possible to effect a reversal, through which the trace could again become an object of social investment?* To answer this question, we must begin by analysing how and why the industry of traces conjoins with the psychopower of the mass media.

14.   Automatic decision-making, stupor, sideration – 'net blues'

The conservative revolution, which is the historical reality of financialization, has globalized consumerism and taken it to extreme levels by destroying the processes of binding the drives in which investments in sublime objects of all kinds consist. But if so, the current and very recent hegemony of the industry of traces *is what attempts* to control these unbound drives through automatisms founded on social networks while at the same time functionalizing *them*, that is, making them serve a 'personalized' stimulation of the consumerist drive, via mimetic mechanisms that, however, only end up making these drives more uncontrollable, contagious and threatening than ever.

The channelling of the drives through the application of mathematical algorithms to automatized social control can do nothing but push these drives to a highly dangerous level, by *dis-integrating them* – and in so doing creating what Félix Guattari called 'dividuals'.[28] With the advent of reticular reading and writing[29] via networks made accessible to everyone through the implementation, beginning in 1993, of the technologies of the world wide web, digital technologies have led hyper-industrial societies towards a new stage of proletarianization – through which the hyper-industrial age becomes the era of systemic stupidity, which can also be called functional stupidity.[30]

Remote-action networks make it possible to massively de-localize production units, to form and remotely control huge markets, to structurally separate industrial capitalism and financial capitalism, and to permanently interconnect electronic financial markets, using applied mathematics to automate the 'financial industry' and control these markets in real time. Through the implementation of such mechanisms, *processes of automated decision-making* become *functionally* tied to *drive-based automatisms*, controlling consumer markets through the industry of traces and the economy of personal data.

Such mathematics is applied twenty-four hours a day, seven days a week: everyday life is thereby subjected to reticular standards and calculations, while at the same time consumer markets are 'personalized'. According to Jonathan Crary, this economy of personal data aims 'to reduce decision-making time [and] to eliminate the useless time of reflection and contemplation'.[31] Digital automatons shortcircuit the deliberative functions of the mind, and systemic stupidity, which has been installed across the board from consumers to speculators, becomes *functionally drive-based* as soon as ultra-liberalism begins to privilege speculation and discourage investment, thereby crossing a threshold beyond that described by Mats Alvesson and André Spicer as functional stupidity.[32] In recent years (post-2008 and especially since the revelations of Edward Snowden) a state of *generalized stupefaction*[33] has accompanied this functional stupidity, itself boosted by total automatization.

This stupor has been caused by a *series of technological shocks* that emerged from the digital turn of 1993, which, as their main features and consequences have become manifest, have brought about a state that now verges on stunned paralysis – in particular in the face of the hegemonic power of Google, Apple, Facebook and Amazon.[34] The fact that these four companies have been referred to as the 'four horsemen of the Apocalypse' reflects that they are literally *disintegrating the industrial societies* that emerged from the *Aufklärung*.

From this state of fact there results a feeling of 'net blues', which is spreading among those who believe in the promise of the digital era. The industrial societies that emerged from the *Aufklärung* are now being disintegrated by hyper-industrial societies, because the latter constitute the third stage of accomplished proletarianization.

After the loss of work-knowledge in the nineteenth century, then of life-knowledge in the twentieth century, there arises in the twenty-first century the age of the loss of theoretical knowledge – as if the cause of our being stunned was an *absolutely unthinkable* becoming. With the *total automatization* made possible by digital technology, theories, those most sublime fruits of idealization and identification, are deemed obsolete – and along with them, scientific method itself. We saw in the introduction that this is the conclusion Chris Anderson reaches in 'The End of Theory',[35] and it is a proposition we will examine in greater detail in the following chapter.

15. Ill-being and the goddess of intermittence

Founded on the self-production of digital traces, and dominated by automatisms that exploit these traces, hyper-industrial societies are undergoing the proletarianization of theoretical knowledge, just as broadcasting analogue traces via television resulted in the proletarianization of life-knowledge, and just as the submission of the body of the labourer to mechanical traces inscribed in machines resulted in the proletarianization of work-knowledge. The decline in 'spirit value' thereby reaches its peak: it now strikes *all* minds and spirits.

This new ill-being [*mal-être*], which occurs in the context of the stupefaction generated by the doubly epokhal redoubling that occurred in 1993, is not just a case of the 'blues': it amplifies what I had described in *Technics and Time, 3*, that is, the deafness and suffering provoked by the culture industries, not just as a negative *Stimmung* afflicting the end of the twentieth century like the black bile that struck the end of the nineteenth, from Baudelaire's 'spleen' to the Austro-Hungarian empire, but as the experience, recognized and felt by everyone, of the *futility of the criteriology of truth in every sphere of 'what is'* and of the 'values' deriving from the history of philosophy as discourse on being – as ontology.

Algorithmic ill-being, which is characteristic of the age of hyper-control, radicalizes this disorientation. All the grand promises of the Enlightenment epoch have been inverted and seem inevitably destined to become poisonous. It is this pharmacological ill-being as absolute devaluation that was foreshadowed by Nietzsche, and this depletion leads us back to the *tragic question* that constituted Pre-Socratic thought[36] as precisely the individual and collective experience of the *putting in question of being by becoming* – insofar as it is the becoming *of the pharmakon* through which the experience of the question is opened up *as such*.[37]

This renewal constitutes the question of what, in the course conducted for pharmakon.fr and by referring to the Freudian allegory of facilitation [*Bahnung*], I have described as a return to the tragic sources of the West.[38] It leads us to confront the irreducibility of the organological and pharmacological condition, to which the sacrificial practices of the Greeks bore witness by celebrating *Persephone* as the *goddess of intermittence*:[39] Vernant showed that the mysteries practised by the mystics (which the Greeks are as a whole) primordially refer to the inaugural conflict of every mythic tension, that is, to the tragic tensions arising from the conflict between Zeus the Olympian and Prometheus the Titan.[40]

16.   From control societies to full automatization (from Angela Merkel to the 'bum on the corner')

The proletarianization of theoretical knowledge is more precisely that of the noetic functions, conceived by Kant as intuition, understanding and reason – and the fall of 'spirit value' here reaches its zenith, which means that it strikes *all* minds and spirits, because it strikes *the spirit (that is, revenance) as such*. Given that stupidity is always more or less what results from stupor and stupefaction,[41] we all become more or less stupid, if not quite beasts.

But, *striking the spirit*, it can also engender and therefore *must* also engender a new epoch of the spirit. It can thus strike it as a coin is struck, in a *second* moment of shock and stupefaction, pioneering the *new circuits of transindividuation* of the doubly epokhal redoubling. To confront this question, we must return to the genesis of the first shock of the doubly epokhal redoubling at the origin of the hyper-industrial era.

The stunning and stupefying hyper-industrial epoch was already foreshadowed in what Deleuze called 'control societies'. This is why, concerning the end of the twentieth century, Crary can write: 'As disciplinary norms [...] lost their effectiveness, television was crafted into a machinery of regulation, introducing previously unknown effects of subjection and supervision. This is why television is a crucial and adaptable part of a relatively long transition [...], lasting several decades, between a world of older disciplinary institutions and one of 24/7 control.'[42] The destructive capture of attention and desire is what occurs with the non-coercive power of modulation exerted on consumers by television. These control societies arise along with the conservative revolution, at the end of the consumerist epoch. It is through them that the transition to the hyper-industrial epoch takes place.

In the automatic society that Deleuze was never to know, but which with Félix Guattari he anticipated, in particular when they referred to *dividuals*, control passes through the *mechanical liquidation of discernment*, the liquidation of what Aristotle called *to krinon* – from *krino*, a verb that has the same root as *krisis*, 'decision'. The discernment that Kant called understanding (*Verstand*) has been automatized as the *analytical* power delegated to algorithms executed through sensors and actuators operating according to formalized instructions that lie outside any intuition in the Kantian sense – that is, outside any experience.

We will see later that, in a dialogue with Serge Daney, Deleuze envisaged that the epoch of control societies would give birth to an 'art of control' – which would be the *quasi-causality forming the second moment of shock* and of the doubly epokhal redoubling. Might an 'art of hyper-control' be similarly conceived within the economy of traceability – which would necessarily also be an art of the *automaton* that the *pharmakon* has become?[43]

This is the question of total proletarianization and of the total disintegration of the spirit. But what is proletarianization in general? Proletarianization is what constitutes an exteriorization without return, that is, without interiorization in return, without 'counter-thrust' [*choc en retour*],[44] and the first to question and problematize the *pharmakon* in this sense was Socrates.

Just like written traces, in which Socrates already saw the risk of proletarianization contained in any exteriorization of knowledge – the apparent paradox being that *knowledge can be constituted only through its exteriorization*[45] – digital, analogue and mechanical traces are tertiary retentions. The automatic society of hyper-control is a society founded on the industrial, systemic and systematic exploitation of digital tertiary retentions. All aspects of behaviour thereby come to generate traces, and all traces become objects of calculation – from Angela Merkel to the 'bum on the corner'.[46]

17. Crisis, metamorphosis, stupefaction

Almost a decade after the collapse of 2008, it is still not clear how best to characterize this *event*: as *crisis, mutation, metamorphosis?* All these terms are *metaphors* (including the 'concept' of crisis, however overused it may be in economics) that are still too little thought, if not unthinkable.

Krisis refers in Hippocrates to a decisive bifurcation or turning point in the course of an illness and is the origin of all critique, of all decision exercised by *to krinon* as the power to judge on the basis of criteria. *Mutation* is understood today primarily in relation to biology – even if, in French, to be '*muté*' generally refers in everyday life to being transferred to another posting. And *metamorphosis* is a zoological term that comes from the Greek, by way of Ovid.

Almost ten years after this major event, it seems that the *proletarianization of minds*, and, more precisely, the *proletarianization of the noetic faculties of theorization*, and, in this sense, of *scientific, moral, aesthetic and political deliberation* – combined with the proletarianization of sensibility and affect in the twentieth century, and with the proletarianization of the gestures of the worker in the nineteenth century – is both the *trigger for* and the *result of* this continuing 'crisis'. As a result, no decisions are taken, and we fail to arrive at any bifurcation. In the meantime, *all of the toxic aspects that lie at the origins of this crisis continue to be consolidated.*

When a triggering factor is also an outcome, we find ourselves within a spiral. This can be very fruitful and worthwhile, or it can enclose us – *absent new criteria* – in a vicious circle that we can then describe as a 'downward spiral'.

The *post-larval state* in which the 2008 crisis has been left implies we should refer to it in terms of metamorphosis[47] rather than mutation: what is going on here is not biological, even if biology comes into play via biotechnology, and, in certain respects, in an almost 'proletarianized' way.[48] This does not mean there is no *krisis*, or that we need not take account of the critical labour for which it calls. It means *that* this work of critique is precisely what this metamorphosis seems to render impossible, thanks precisely to the fact that it consists above all in the proletarianization of theoretical knowledge – which is critical knowledge.

This apparent impossibility is what must be fought against – and therein lies the limit of the allegory of metamorphosis: the latter may suggest the completion of a natural, relentless and predetermined process, to which it would be a matter of submitting and 'adapting oneself'. What is at stake, however, involves organological multidimensionality, or play between the somatopsychic organs, artificial organs and social organizations, which ideology – that is, that narrative which justifies the established order – conceals in order to *legitimate the proletarianizing tendency* that leads to the 'end of theory'.

This tendency is the pharmacological expression of a process of grammatization of which digital technology is the most advanced stage. Grammatization, as noted above, is itself a technical tendency[49] that goes back to at least the end of the Upper Palaeolithic, consisting in the duplication and discretization of mental experiences (that is, temporal experiences) in the form of hypomnesic tertiary retentions.

After Socrates, we know that hypomnesic tertiary retention, of which alphabetic writing is a case, tends always to replace what it 'amplifies' by substituting itself.[50] This amplification opens new possibilities of individuation and de-proletarianization, constituting a therapy or therapeutics in the second moment of the doubly epokhal redoubling, of which technological shock is the first moment. All this results from the technical exteriorization that lies at the origin of hominization, of human evolution, which was conceived as an organological becoming for the first time in *The German Ideology*.[51]

In *Ce qui fait que la vie vaut la peine d'être vécue*,[52] I argued that in the *industrial stage of grammatization and proletarianization*, which capital tends always to take advantage of, ideology tends to treat the technical system (which is the organological level wherein the artificial organs form a system) as a *second nature* that duplicates, absorbs, replaces and short-circuits the social systems between which and within which psychic individuals form and connect the circuits of transindividuation through which and within which they form collective individuals.

As full and generalized automatization, the current stage of grammatization systematizes, on a global scale, this absorption, these short-circuits and the resulting disintegration, which constitutes algorithmic governmentality. The unprecedented critical effort that must now be undertaken consists in *conceiving the specific rational criteria of digital tertiary retention* – which is today conjoining with the *biological retentions* that are *physiological automatisms*: this is what neuroeconomics strives to impose.[53] It is on the basis of these new criteria that new social rules can reconfigure a *noetic arrangement* – *that is, a negentropic arrangement* – between psychic individuals, technical individuals and collective individuations.

In the current stage of metamorphosis, which would be that of the chrysalis (with the appearance of new forms and a new organization), the *stupefying and narcotizing state of fact* in which the present experience of automatic society consists sets up a new mental context – stupefaction – within which systemic stupidity proliferates. The result is a significant increase in functional stupidity, drive-based capitalism and industrial populism.

But this extreme planetary disturbance can also be considered in terms of a *new concern* – which, *if it does not turn into a panic*, and can instead become a fertile *skepsis*, could become the *origin of a new intelligence or understanding of the situation*, in fact generating *new criteria*, that is, new *categories*: this is the question of what I will call, in the second volume of this work, *categorial invention*.

This new understanding would be that which, inverting the toxic logic of the *pharmakon*, would give rise to a new hyper-industrial age constituting *an automatic society founded on de-proletarianization*[54] – and which would provide an exit from the chrysalis of *noetic hymenoptera*.[55] In the following chapters, therefore, I will continue to pursue this allegory of metamorphosis by introducing a *noetic bifurcation*: the latter is what, through *critique*, intervenes in the metamorphic process that is life so that it is *de-naturalized* and *dis-automatized*, and, through that, *neganthropized*.

18. Pharmacology of 'big data'

The proletarianization of the gestures of work (of producing works) amounts to the proletarianization of the conditions of the worker's *subsistence*.

The proletarianization of sensibility and the affects and, *through that*, the proletarianization of the social relation[56] – which is thus being replaced by conditioning – amounts to the proletarianization of the conditions of the citizen's *existence*.

The proletarianization of minds and spirits, that is, of the noetic faculties enabling theorization and deliberation, is the proletarianization of the conditions of *consistence* of the life of the rational spirit in general, and of scientific life in particular (including the human and social sciences) – through which rationality becomes what Weber, Adorno and Horkheimer described as rationalization. It is the final culmination of nihilism.

In the hyper-industrial stage, *hyper-control* is established through a process of generalized automatization. This represents a step beyond the control-through-modulation discovered and analysed by Deleuze (we will return to this question in chapter 3 by commenting on Crary's commentary on the Deleuzian thesis on control societies). In the hyper-industrial stage, the noetic faculties of theorization and deliberation are short-circuited by the *current operator of proletarianization*, which is *digital tertiary retention* – just as analogue tertiary retention was in the twentieth century the operator of the proletarianization of life-knowledge, and just as mechanical tertiary retention was in the nineteenth century the operator of the proletarianization of work-knowledge.

Tertiary retention, whatever its form or material may be, *artificially retains something through the material and spatial copying of a mnesic and temporal element*, and thereby modifies – in a general way, that is, for *all* human experience – the relations between the psychic retentions of perception that Husserl referred to as *primary* retentions, and the psychic retentions of *memory* that he called *secondary* retentions.[57]

As consequences of the evolution of tertiary retention, these changes in the *play* between primary retentions and secondary retentions, and therefore between memory and perception, that is, between imagination and reality, produce *processes of transindividuation* that are each time different, that is, specific epochs of what Simondon called the *transindividual*.

In the course of processes of transindividuation, founded on the successive epochs of tertiary retention,[58] meanings [*significations*] form that are shared by psychic individuals, thereby constituting collective individuals themselves forming societies. Shared by psychic individuals within collective individuals of all kinds, the meanings formed in the course of transindividuation processes constitute the transindividual as an ensemble of collective secondary retentions within which collective protentions form – which are the *expectations* typical of an epoch.

If, according to the Chris Anderson article to which we previously referred, 'big data' heralds the 'end of theory' – big data technology designating what is also called 'high-performance computing' carried out on massive data sets,[59] whereby the treatment of data in the form of digital tertiary retentions occurs *in real time* (at the speed of light), on a *global scale* and at the level of billions of gigabytes of data, operating through data-capture systems that are located everywhere around the planet and in almost every relational system that constitutes a society[60] – it is because digital tertiary retention and the algorithms that allow it to be both produced and exploited thereby also enable *reason as a synthetic faculty to be short-circuited* thanks to the *extremely high speeds at which this automated analytical faculty of understanding* is capable of operating.[61]

This proletarianization is a *state of fact*. Is it inevitable and unavoidable? Anderson claims it is (like Nicholas Carr, who less gleefully suggests that the destruction of attention is fatal).[62] I argue the contrary: the *fact of proletarianization* is *caused* by the digital, which, like *every* new form of tertiary retention, constitutes a new age of the *pharmakon*. It is *inevitable* that this *pharmakon* will have toxic effects, *as long as new therapies or therapeutics are not prescribed* – that is, as long as *we* do not take up our responsibilities.

The therapeutic prescription of *pharmaka* for an epoch constitutes knowledge in general as rules for taking care of the world. This is, indeed, the responsibility of the scientific world, the artistic world, the legal world, the world of the life of the spirit in general, and of citizens, whoever they may be – and, in the first place, of those who claim to represent them. Much courage is required: it is a struggle that must confront countless interests, including those who in part suffer from this toxicity and in part feed off it. It is this period of suffering that is akin to the stage of the chrysalis in the allegory of metamorphosis.

Any tertiary retention is a *pharmakon* in that, rather than creating *new transindividual arrangements* between psychic and collective primary retentions and secondary retentions, and therefore between retentions and protentions – which constitute the expectations through which objects of attention appear, objects that are as such the sources of desire[63] – rather than creating new *attentional forms* by spawning new circuits of transindividuation, new meanings and new projective capabilities bearing those horizons of meaning that are consistences, this *pharmakon* may on the contrary *substitute itself* for psychic and collective retentions.

Psychic and collective retentions, however, can produce meaning and sense (that is, desire and hope) only as long as they are *individuated by all and hence shared by all* on the basis of processes of psychic individuation that form, from out of relations of co-individuation,[64] social processes of transindividuation, creating relationships of solidarity that are the basis for sustainable (and intergenerational) *social systems.*[65]

As tertiary retention, the *pharmakon* is the condition of the production and metastabilization of those circuits of transindividuation that enable psychic individuals to ex-press themselves to each other, via their *psychic* retentions and with this *pharmakon*, thereby forming collective individuals founded on these traces and facilitations, that is, on the *collective* retentions and protentions emerging from this pharmacology. But when a new *pharmakon* appears, it may always short-circuit, and *always begin* by short-circuiting, the established circuit of transindividuation that had issued from a prior tertiary retention, pharmacology and organology. Hence there is in this sense nothing unusual about the situation we see unfolding today with the digital.

Nevertheless, when psychic and collective individuation is short-circuited by digital processes of *automatized* transindividuation, founded on automation in real time, it becomes a process of trans*dividuation* – the extent of which is immeasurable. This poses *absolutely unprecedented* problems and therefore requires highly specific analyses capable of taking account of the *remarkable novelty* of the digital *pharmakon*. It is to this that the present chapter and the following two chapters are dedicated.

The destructive effects of these digital forms of automatized and reticulated tertiary retention call for a *complete social reorganization*, the main features of which will be outlined in the final two chapters of this work on the basis of an attempt to reconceptualize the conditions of right and law and the character and content of work (chapters 4–7) with respect to the 'challenge of the century' that is the Anthropocene, as a conflict between entropy and negentropy produced by the anthropized milieu, which nowadays extends across the planet.

Rethinking work and right in this context, in which digital tertiary retention constitutes a new form of grammatization, presupposes the elaboration of a new *epistemology*, a new *philosophy* and a new *organology*, in turn elaborating *a reconceptualization and a transformation of the digital as such* and on another basis than that of the computational ideology that took hold after the Second World War. This will be the subject of *The Future of Knowledge*, the second volume of *Automatic Society*.

19.   Ultra-liberalism as the dis-integration of individuals into 'dividuals'

In order to achieve socialization, that is, a collective individuation, any new *pharmakon* – in this case, a new form of tertiary retention – always requires the formation of *new knowledge*, which means new *therapies or therapeutics* for this new *pharmakon*, through which are constituted new ways of doing things and reasons to do things, of living and thinking, that is, of projecting consistences, which constitute at the same time new forms of existence and, ultimately, new conditions of subsistence.

This new knowledge is the result of what I call the second moment of the epokhal redoubling emerging from the technological shock that is always provoked whenever there appears a new form of tertiary retention.[66] If Anderson claims that the contemporary fact of proletarianization is insurmountable, which is to claim that there is *therefore no way to bring about its second moment*, the reason he does so lies in another fact: he himself happens to be a businessman who defends an ultra-liberal, ultra-libertarian perspective[67] that amounts to the ideology of our age – an ideology faithful to the ultra-liberalism implemented in all industrial democracies after the conservative revolution implemented at the beginning of the 1980s.

The problem with this, for Anderson, as for us, and as for the global economy, is that the becoming that leads to this stage of proletarianization is *inherently entropic*: it *depletes* the resources that it exploits – resources that in this case are psychic individuals and collective individuals: in the strict sense of the term, it leads to the stage of their *dis-integration*.

The dis-integration of psychic individuals and collective individuals begins with the exploitation of the drives, when, the consumerist libidinal economy having destroyed the processes of idealization and identification by submitting all singularities to calculability (these are the stakes of what Deleuze and Guattari describe as the becoming dividual of individuals), marketing was forced to *directly* solicit and exploit the drives – being incapable of capturing desires that *no longer exist* because, *all their objects* having been turned into *ready-made commodities*, they *no longer consist*.

Automatic society is now attempting to channel, control and exploit these *dangerous automatisms* that are the drives, by subordinating them to *new retentional systems that are themselves automatic*, which capture drive-based automatisms *by outstripping and overtaking them*: formalized by applied mathematics, concretized by algorithms designed to capture and exploit the traces generated by individual and collective behaviour, *reticular interactive automatisms* are systems for capturing behavioural expressions.

20.   That by which the world holds

A behavioural expression is prompted by a field of primary retentions that, having been perceived in a present become past, are internalized in the form of memories, thereby becoming bound secondary retentions. The personality of a psychic individual is composed *exclusively*[68] of such primary retentions that have become secondary, that is, *bound* to the secondary retentions that preceded them.[69]

In the course of this becoming secondary of primary retentions, protentions form – that is, expectations and attentions that more or less de-phase (and affect) the psychic individual, in relation to itself and in relation to others: behavioural expressions are the protean exteriorizations (attitudes, gestures, speech, actions) of these expectations, and these exteriorizations are produced when favourable circumstances arise.

Since at least the Upper Palaeolithic age, the noetic souls that are psychic individuals have expressed their expectations by tertiarizing them, that is, by projecting their retentions and their protentions outside themselves, between themselves and other psychic individuals, and in the form of traces through which they *spatialize* what they are living through or have lived through *temporally* (temporally meaning psychically, in the past, present or future). These traces are the hypomnesic tertiary retentions with which and through which these psychic individuals transindividuate themselves according to specific modalities – modalities specified by the characteristics of the tertiary retentions thereby engendered.

These expressive behaviours (like the much older production of tools, organologically augmenting and amplifying the organic capabilities of noetic bodies[70]) are *transformations of the sensorimotor loops* that Jacob von Uexküll described in living beings equipped with a nervous system – including the famous tick[71] – and they belong to the cycle of images analysed by Simondon in *Imagination et invention*.[72]

These transformations cause *bifurcations* and *withholdings*, that is, *différances* (from processes of temporalization that are at the same time processes of spatialization – which allows the putting in reserve that Derrida called différance): they are *put in reserve* and therefore *withheld from reacting*, whereby the 'response' of the animal's nervous systems to a *stimulus* instead becomes the *action* of the psychic individual, and through which the process of individuation undergoes bifurcations, that is, *singular* and strictly *incommensurable differentiations* of a kind not found in *vital différance*.[73]

This psychic individual, who is thus no longer the vital individual[74] who is subject to Uexküll's sensorimotor loop, participates in collective individuation[75] by exteriorizing him- or herself in the world formed by this collective individuation. In so doing, he or she transforms this world by forming *him- or herself*, which means that *his or her expressions participate in the formation of the transindividual by which this world holds* – holds up, holds its own, and holds those who form it: by which this world '*holds on*' (confronted with the successive technological shocks from which it comes), and through which life is worth the *pain and effort* (that is, the *coup*[76]) of being lived.

21.   The automated capture of behavioural expressions as the automated formation of new kinds of 'conventional crowds'

In automatic society, those digital networks referred to as 'social' channel these expressions by subordinating them to mandatory protocols, to which psychic individuals bend because they are drawn to do so through what is referred to as the *network effect*,[77] which, with the addition of *social networking*, becomes an *automated herd* effect, that is, one that is highly mimetic. It therefore amounts to a new form of *artificial crowd*, in the sense Freud gave to this expression.[78]

The constitution of groups or crowds and the conditions in which they can pass into action were subjects analysed by Gustave Le Bon, cited at length by Freud:

The most striking peculiarity presented by a psychological crowd (in German: *Masse*) is the following. Whoever be the individuals that compose it, however like or unlike be their mode of life, their occupations, their character, or their intelligence, the fact that they have been transformed into a crowd puts them in possession of a sort of collective mind which makes them feel, think, and act in a manner quite different from that in which each individual of them would feel, think, and act were he in a state of isolation. There are certain ideas and feelings that do not come into being, or do not transform themselves into acts except in the case of individuals forming a crowd. The psychological crowd is a provisional being formed of heterogeneous elements, which for a moment are combined, exactly as the cells which constitute a living body form by their reunion a new being which displays characteristics very different from those possessed by each of the cells singly.[79]

On the basis of Le Bon's analyses,[80] Freud showed that there are also 'artificial' crowds, which he analyses through the examples of the Church and the Army.

In the twentieth century, and starting in the 1920s, the audiovisual programme industries, too, also form, every single day, and specifically through the mass broadcast of programmes, such 'artificial crowds'. The latter become, as masses (and Freud refers precisely to *Massenpsychologie*), the permanent, everyday mode of life in the industrial democracies, which are at the same time what I call industrial tele-cracies.[81]

Unlike Walter Benjamin in 1935, in 1921 Freud was unable to see the possibility – which would be systematically exploited via the radio by Goebbels and Mussolini – of constituting artificial crowds through the use of relational technologies: radio stations expanded widely in Europe starting from 1923, and the first radio station was created in the United States by RCA in 1920 (which in 1929 became RCA Victor, acquiring a catalogue of gramophone discs that would transform the musical destiny of humankind). And Freud would never know television, which makes powerful use of the *scopic drive* by combining it with the regressive power of artificial crowds.

As for us, what we find is that an *automatized mimetism*, based on the network effect and the feedback loops produced in real time by 'big data', lies at the core of *reticulated* artificial crowds. Generated by digital tertiary retention, *connected* artificial crowds constitute the economy of 'crowdsourcing', which should be understood in multiple senses[82] – dimensions of which include the so-called 'cognitariat'[83] and digital labour.[84] To a large degree, 'big data' is utilized by technologies that exploit the potential of crowdsourcing in its many forms, engineered by social networking and data science.

Through the network effect, through the artificial crowds that it creates (more than a billion psychic individuals on Facebook), and through the crowdsourcing that it can exploit through 'big data', it is possible:

- *to generate the production and self- and auto-capture* by individuals of those tertiary retentions that are 'personal data', spatializing their psychosocial temporalities;
- *to intervene in the processes of transindividuation* that are woven between them by utilizing this 'personal data' at the speed of light via circuits that are formed automatically and *performatively;*[85]
- through these circuits, and through the collective secondary retentions that they form automatically, and no longer transindividually, *to intervene in return, and almost immediately, on psychic secondary retentions*, which is also to say, on protentions, expectations and ultimately personal behaviour: it thus becomes possible *to remotely control, one by one*, the members of a network – this is so-called 'personalization' – while subjecting them to mimetic and 'viral' processes of a kind never before seen.

Self-produced in the form of personal data, transformed automatically and in real time into circuits of transindividuation, these digital tertiary retentions short-circuit every process of *noetic différance*, that is, every process of collective individuation conforming to relational, intergenerational and transgenerational knowledge of all kinds.[86]

As such, these digital tertiary retentions *dis-integrate* these psychic secondary retentions of social reality insofar as the latter constitutes an associated milieu, that is, *a milieu individuated through those who live within this milieu by transindividuating themselves*. And, as such, they *annihilate the protentions* borne by these psychic as well as collective secondary retentions.[87]

22. Pharmacology of associated milieus

In addition to those occasions when the concept of associated milieu is used by Simondon to refer to the memory of the psychic individual insofar as it is constantly associated with this individual and as such constitutes his or her psychic milieu,[88] he uses this concept to describe a technical milieu of a highly specific kind: a natural milieu (called a techno-geographical milieu) is referred to as 'associated' when the technical object of which it is the environment structurally and functionally 'associates' with the energies and elements of which this natural milieu is composed, in such a way that nature becomes functional for the technical system. This is the case for the Guimbal turbine, which, in tidal power plants, assigns to seawater, that is, to this natural element, a threefold technical function: providing the energy, cooling the turbine and, through water pressure, sealing the bearings.

With digital tertiary retention, techno-geographical milieus of a new kind arise, where it is the *human element* of geography that is associated with the becoming (that is, the individuation) of the technical milieu, so that this element itself acquires a technical function: such is the specificity of the internet network when it becomes 'navigable' via the technologies of the world wide web. And it is for this reason that the 'web' makes possible the *contributory economy* typified by free software.

More generally, the internet is indeed a technical milieu in which the receivers are in principle placed in the position of being senders, which forms the basis of the contributory economy that to a large extent is at work in, and supports, the business models of the data economy. The economy of contribution requires, in other words, a *pharmacological* critique of contribution, that is, a critique of the digital economy: today, the contributory is concretized above all as a new stage of proletarianization, even if the free software model amounts, on the contrary, to an industrial economy founded on de-proletarianization.

Even before the appearance of the web, the internet, which is its infrastructural framework, was already a contributory and dialogical associated milieu, because it enabled the development of a new industrial model of algorithmic software production, wherein the 'users' of programs are in principle and by right (if not in fact) its *practitioners*, in that they contribute to the individuation of the software: it is their practices – which are therefore no longer simply usages – that bring about the evolution of the software itself.

Hence the economy of free software, like the technical milieu constituted by the IP standard that makes all digital networks compatible and through which can form the network of networks called the internet, constitutes a factor giving rise to the contributory economy and providing the concepts for a new industrial model. But the internet is a *pharmakon* that is obviously capable of doing just the opposite, of becoming a technics of hyper-control, that is, of dissociation, of dis-integration and of the proletarianization of the social itself.

Since the appearance of 'social engineering', the automated treatment of personal data mined from social networks has *short-circuited all singularity that could form at the level of the collective individual* – a collective singularity that constitutes *idiomatic differentiation*, which is the condition of any meaning and any significance – and has transformed individual singularities into individual *particularities*:

unlike the singular, which is incomparable, the particular is calculable, that is, manipulable, and soluble into these manipulations.[89]

Without a new politics of individuation, that is, without a *formation of attention geared towards the specific tertiary retentions*
that make possible the new technical milieu,[90] digital and reticulated
tertiary retention will inevitably become an agent of dissociation
through which contribution will become the operator of hyper-
proletarianization. For this reason, today we must elaborate a new
critique of political economy that must also be a pharmacology of
contribution, calling for therapies and therapeutics, that is, for new
knowledge, where the challenge is to totally reshape the academic
sphere in the epoch of digital tertiary retention. Such is the object of
what we call 'digital studies'.[91]

2

States of Shock, States of Fact, States of Law

Brucker finds it ridiculous for the philosopher to assert that a prince will never govern well unless he participates in the ideas. But we would do better to pursue this thought further, and (at those points where the excellent man leaves us without help) to shed light on it through new endeavors, rather than setting it aside as useless under the very wretched and harmful pretext of its impracticability.

Immanuel Kant[1]

23. From the common origin of law and science to the ruin of theory

Since the industrial revolution, the diversification of technical objects has continued to intensify. In the twentieth century, the war between technological innovations became the basic principle of 'economic evolution',[2] in the form of 'creative destruction'.[3] And this has not ceased to affect social organizations and to create more or less disruptive states of shock, in which generally new economic actors seize 'opportunities'. The positions attained by the social actors who had emerged from the preceding state of shock are thereby destroyed, and a state of fact 'in advance' of law – so to speak – comes to be established. In this way the technical system 'disadjusts' the social systems.

The state of shock provoked in 1993 by the creation of the web, spreading reticular writing throughout the solvent inhabitants of the earth, has immeasurably amplified the 'shock doctrine' that in 1979 asserted that there is no alternative to the destruction of public power, that is, to the unlimited expression of computational logic as induced and required by the total market.

With the constitution of automatized artificial crowds and the globalization of the industry of traces, and through the complete commodification of existence and everyday life, the dis-integration of the retentions and protentions of psychic and collective individuals has destroyed noetic faculties – and, with them, the theories that emerge from them, those theories whose end is pronounced by Chris Anderson.

Overcoming this state of fact through the constitution of *a state of law of digital tertiary retention* presupposes the *reconsideration of the difference of fact and law* itself.[4] This is so inasmuch as this difference, as a specific regime of psychic and collective individuation, is the *common origin of the state of law, philosophy and science* insofar as they (philosophy at its origin merging with science) distinguish, originally and in principle, the theoretical and the empirical. And this distinction coalesces with the constitution of a positive law, that is, an experience of *alētheia* as the fruit of disputation, and no longer as oracular or divine utterance.

What must be reconsidered with respect to the juridical, philosophical and epistemological tradition is that the *differentiation of law and fact is conditioned by tertiary retention* – and it is *theorized*, precisely, starting from the shock (the challenge, the putting in question) resulting from the appearance of *literal* (lettered) tertiary retention, which opened up a crisis from which arose critique.

Maiandrios can put *kratos en mesoi* – put *power* in the centre[5] – only because the *knowledge* constituting collective individuation as the creation of circuits of transindividuation has been literalized, and because this *retention in letters* of the common past corrodes it while assimilating the previous forms of the process of individuation, which therefore become archaic and feed into the mythologies of the origin. This becoming, which passes through the geometrization of space,[6] results in the formation of what Gilbert Murray and E. R. Dodds called the 'inherited conglomerate'.[7]

This inherited conglomerate both forms the preindividual funds of the *political* psychic and collective individuation process, emerging from the new retentional condition of which Hesiod and Thales were contemporaries, and enters into structural conflict with the new *epistēmē*. This is what Dodds described as a Greek *Aufklärung*.[8]

At its political origin, and *as* this origin, law (*nomos*), stemming fundamentally from a transindividuation *in letters*, such that it is alphabetically tertiarized, literalizes and spatializes the *epistēmē*, forming the rules (as the *explicit* circuits of transindividuation) on the basis of which conflict (*polemos*) can become the dynamic principle of a society within which History appears as such (as *Geschichte* and as *Historie*) – starting from the agora.[9]

This is why the *skholeion* is the primordial political institution: citizens are those who read and write these literal traces – which thus form *new kinds of associated milieus*, which, as we shall see, also constitute *regimes of parities*[10] establishing *regimes of truth*.[11] And this is why *today*, and *as the condition of any new constitution of knowledge*, the retentional condition of all knowledge must be thematized and elucidated, and particularly that of the apodictic forms of knowledge that nourish the Western experience of rationality.

24. Phenomenotechnics, automatism and catastrophe

It is in this sense that we should interpret Bachelard's phenomenotechnics as analysed by François Chomarat: 'Writing would be the first phenomenotechnics, since it involves passing from a description to a production, by "inverting the axis of empirical knowledge".'[12] The theoretical critique of the state of fact that Anderson claims is insurmountable presupposes a critique of digital tertiary retention. This critique would itself be founded on a pharmacological critique of the history of knowledge in its totality, that is, founded on an epistemology that takes full account, through a general organology that is the condition of this pharmacology, of the role of tertiary retention in general in the genesis of work-knowledge and of theoretical knowledge, as in that of the law governing life-knowledge in political – and as such civil-ized [*policée*] – society. This new critique amounts to the programme of what we call digital studies – taking up here the perspective defended by Franck Cormerais and Jacques Gilbert in the journal *Études digitales*, which they have founded with Éditions Garnier.[13]

The *desirable* in general is what *consists*, and this consistence, in the psychic and collective individuation that constitutes the *polis*, presents itself as:

- the just, which does not exist, but the idea of which is *practically* managed and conserved by law, which prescribes social ways of living in common, and promises a liveable and polite [*poli*],[14] if not actually just, world;
- the true, of which geometry, in the Western experience of rationality, is the matrix and the canon, constituted through the ideality of the point, which does not exist, but which *trans-forms the world*

through being contemplated theoretically, and through the practical consequences of this contemplation;

- the beautiful, which is improbable, as Kant said, that is, unprovable, and as such 'imaginary' and 'dreamed', *allowing us to dream*, but which, *experienced* by the subject who judges aesthetically, puts to the test the singularity of his or her judgement and the object of this judgement, allowing this subject to *individuate him- or herself* and to do so as this dreamer – sometimes to the point of becoming an artist.[15]

Consistence is experienced in desire: in the desire for any object in which this desire invests by diverting the drives, on the basis of which this object is expected, and presents itself by projecting itself towards another plane that does not exist, but consists. This consistence of the object is its infinitization. The drives amount to arche-retentions that are also arche-protentions, that is, primordial sensorimotor schemas that Simondon described as 'driving tendencies' [*tendances motrices*], founded on '*a priori* images',[16] and that the infinitization of their non-existent objects diverts, effecting singular – that is, negentropic – bifurcations.

Since the *objects of such consistences are also those of theories*, the latter *presuppose* the learning and apprenticeship of affective and erotic idealization. It is for this reason that Diotima relates all knowledge to the experience of desire.

Consequently, *when the libidinal economy lies in ruin, so too does theory*. Now that the dis-integration of individuals is liquidating desire itself in all its forms, as well as the infinite variety of idealizations in which all knowledge consists (knowledge of how to live, do and conceptualize), the theoretical enterprise itself seems to have reached its end. This liquidation of desire unbinds the drives, which cease to be the dynamic source of the retentions (as that which is contained and retained) and protentions of ideality, becoming on the contrary the source of so many evils emerging from Pandora's box.[17]

Technological automatisms, however, can in no way *contain* these evils (in the sense of controlling them – and which they contain also in the sense that they harbour them): these evils are expressions of the drives that are themselves *biopsychic automatisms*. Far from controlling them, technological automatisms can on the contrary only *exacerbate them* – because they *intensify their unbinding* by dis-integrating psychic and collective retentions and protentions. This is why hyper-control in reality leads to a *total loss of control* (well beyond the disaffection that I earlier described in *Uncontrollable*

Societies of Disaffected Individuals[18]), that is, to an immeasurable catastrophe that is an entropic cataclysm.

Avoiding this catastrophe by bringing about the inaugurating *katastrophē* of a new *différance*: such is the challenge of a redefinition of the difference of law and fact in the digital epoch, and in the age of libertarian ideology, whose best representative is undoubtedly Chris Anderson.

25.   The duty of every non-inhuman being[19]

Differentiating law from fact means engaging in a political struggle, but also an economic and epistemic struggle. And if it is true that the law is what conserves the consistence of the just, just as science conserves that of the true and art that of the beautiful and the sublime,[20] the conception of a new state of law, which would also be a new age of theory as what distinguishes states of fact and states of law, is the cornerstone of any reconstitution of an *economy* of the drives and a rearming of desire – that is, of economy in all its forms.

Theory and law are notions inseparable from the processes of idealization wherein form objects of desire and, with them, consistences. The passage from the proletarianization of the mind by automatons as *state of fact* to a new stage of noetization rediscovering what Kant called the subjective principle of differentiation,[21] and through that the difference of law and fact, or in other words *the passage to automatic society as the constitution of a new age of mind and spirit* (in Paul Valéry's sense), is the passage from a toxic stage in which the digital *pharmakon* destroys the social systems that engendered it, and, along with them, destroys the processes of idealization they make possible, to a therapeutic stage in which this *pharmakon* becomes *the tertiary retention of new circuits of transindividuation*.

This passage from the current toxic state of fact to a curative state of law requires both:

- new notions of what constitutes *law in any rational discipline* – in the sense that each discipline defines the criteria of scientific law, certified by peers, through which states of fact are transformed into states of law, that is, empirical data into theoretical data, while advances in any science consist in inventions of *new criteria*, effecting paradigm shifts, and constituting *categorial invention*;[22] and
- new notions of what constitutes the *law common to all citizens* as psychic individuals who are supposed to be capable of

implementing political and rational criteria of judgement in their everyday life, in relation to themselves, those close to them, and others – which constitutes the *political* question of law.

'Why must we rediscover the difference of law and fact?', some may ask. 'Has this difference not been surpassed? Has not law itself become outmoded – just as people say, for example, that religious beliefs are outmoded?'

Besides the fact that this last suggestion in fact remains far from clear,[23] and in any case does not belong to the same order of questions, given that *the difference of law and fact conditions apodictic judgement*, and therefore demonstrative judgement, I posit as starting principles for all the theses presented here (as in all my work):

- that there are *omnitemporal structures* (valid at any time) outside of which the just, the true, the beautiful and the sublime could not *consist*;
- *that the difference of fact and law is one such omnitemporal structure*;
- *that the regression in which, in particular, the unbinding of the drives consists is always not only possible but imminent* for the non-inhuman being, and this can lead this being to forget,[24] for example, the subjective principle of differentiation that provides access to the difference of law and fact, and thus it is always possible for the non-inhuman being to sink into inhumanity;
- that the duty of reason and of every reasonable being – and every non-inhuman being is *reason-able, that is, affected and pained by injustice, falsehood and ugliness* – is to *always struggle to be worthy of the non-inhuman* that we must try to be, no matter what.[25]

No matter what happens. *Inshallah*.

26. The common obsolescence of the scientist and the soldier in the age of total automatization

The theoretical and practical capacity to *make* the difference between fact and law constitutes what Kant called reason.[26] This is why *law is ruined by the proletarianization of the life of the mind and spirit as a whole* – which can lead only to barbarism.

There is no doubt that this is now clearly taking place, as drones combine with and utilize 'big data' in the service of the automatic detection of 'suspects', that is, people whose behaviour corresponds, according to statistically calculated correlations, to that of potential terrorists, whom these *new automatic weapons*, drones, can then eliminate, perpetrating a state violence that, adhering to no law of war, diffuses the lawlessness of a deterritorialized and blind automatic police. As Grégoire Chamayou observes:

> The modern art of tracking is based on an intensive use of new technologies, combining aerial video surveillance, the interception of signals, and cartographic tracking. [...] In this model the enemy individual is no longer seen as a link in a hierarchical chain of command: he is a knot or 'node' inserted into a number of social networks. [...] [T]he idea is that by successfully targeting its key 'nodes', an enemy network can be disorganized to the point of being practically wiped out. [...] This claim to predictive calculation is the foundation of the policy of prophylactic elimination, for which the hunter-killer drones are the main instruments. [...] In the logic of this security, based on the preventive elimination of dangerous individuals, 'warfare' takes the form of vast campaigns of extra-judiciary executions.[27]

In relation to the current use of drones in Pakistan, Somalia and Yemen, Chamayou quotes Mary Ellen O'Connell: ' "International law does not recognize the right to kill with battlefield weapons outside an actual armed conflict. The so-called 'global war on terror' is not an armed conflict." These strikes therefore constitute grave violations of the laws of war.'[28]

The thesis of the end of theory and the obsolescence of science proclaimed by Anderson is the counterpart of this liquidation of law by these new forms of automatic weapon.[29] This liquidation of law is in turn directly tied to the elimination of sacrifice – without which there can be no warrior, and through which the conquering soldier receives his greater share [*solde*]: he is in principle glorious. His life, steeped in the test of mortal combat, is also, and, according to Hegel, *firstly*, one that knows consistence (this is the issue in the first moment of the master/slave dialectic in the *Phenomenology of Spirit*).[30]

Knowledge too, however, presupposes the capacity for self-sacrifice, no longer just the death that covers one in glory but an intermittent noetic sacrifice and a wrenching away that confers, like death, what the Greeks called *kleos* (of which the contemporary wish to be 'known', to have a reputation, which social networks claim to provide for their contributors, is the disintegrated version – a disintegration of the transindividuation networks themselves to the benefit of the 'reputation' of advertisers).

The experience of knowledge is the experience of what, in this knowledge, teaches, through being learned, the history of the 'deaths' and 'rebirths' of knowledge. Knowledge is par excellence what, opening knowing to what is not yet known, 'kills off' what had hitherto been considered knowledge – yet in this, and with the death of what had hitherto been considered knowledge, knowledge finds itself reborn, in the course of what was described by Socrates (in *Meno*) as an *anamnesis*,[31] and by Husserl (in 'The Origin of Geometry') as a *reactivation*,[32] which is the individuation of knowledge through the individuation of the knower. We shall see in *Automatic Society, Volume 2: The Future of Knowledge* that what we are here metaphorically calling the 'death' and 'rebirth' of knowledge refers to the acquisition of knowledge as *automatization* and to its rebirth as *dis-automatization*.

As for *full* automatization, made possible by digital tertiary retention through the integration of all automatisms and by short-circuiting all *therapeutic possibilities for dis-automatization*, it disintegrates in the field of battle as in the epistemic field this dual sacrificial experience of the struggle for freedom and the struggle against what is *in itself*, and not *for itself*, as Hegel said – as what prevents, as 'well known', the expression of what remains to come for the self and as its *for itself* (these are Hegel's terms).

Full automatization effects this disintegration, at once and in the same movement, for both warriors and scientists.

According to Anderson, this disintegration foreshadows the death of the scientist by proclaiming the end of science in a world where the 'scholar', who has been proletarianized just as has Alan Greenspan, no longer fights for anything or knows anything. He or she no longer fights *for any consistence*, or *against any inconsistence*: he or she *no longer knows anything consistent*.[33] Such is the price of total nihilism, of nihilistic totalization, of the disintegration in which consists *the accomplished nihilism that is totally computational capitalism*, in which there is no longer anything worth anything – since everything has become calculable.

27.   The uselessness of knowledge and the obsolescence of taxonomy, hypotheses and experiments: the power of Google according to Chris Anderson

It is not necessary to know anything, writes Anderson, to be able to work with applied mathematics in an age where the petabyte becomes the unit of measurement of mass storage,[34] and it is this *uselessness of knowledge, whatever it may be,* that, according to him, constitutes Google's power, and its fundamental 'philosophy':

> Google's founding philosophy is that we don't know why this page is better than that one: If the statistics of incoming links say it is, that's good enough. No semantic or causal analysis is required. That's why Google can translate languages without actually 'knowing' them (given equal corpus data, Google can translate Klingon into Farsi as easily as it can translate French into German). And why it can match ads to content without any knowledge or assumptions about the ads or the content.[35]

In the epoch where digital tertiary retention is the medium supporting the use of applied mathematics to treat 'big data' in high-performance computing, '[f]orget taxonomy, ontology, and psychology'. And not only that, science now has little room for *hypotheses, models* or *experiments*: '[F]aced with massive data, this approach to science – hypothesize, model, test – is becoming obsolete.'

The result:

- science is not knowledge but *a self-sufficient and unalterable automatic system*, that is, finite and *closed off from any individuation,* the latter being essentially singular, interminable in fact and infinite by law;
- or science *is* knowledge but knowledge that *no longer needs experts or scientists* – just as drones no longer need soldiers but only operators;
- or *there is no longer any science at all* but *a state of fact maintained by a system of capture that renders obsolete the difference of fact and law.*

This final thesis is Anderson's – who today runs a start-up that manufactures drones and promotes a 'new industrial revolution' founded on 'fab labs' and 'makers'.[36]

The automated 'knowledge' celebrated by Anderson no longer needs to be *thought.* In the epoch of the algorithmic implementation of applied mathematics in computerized machines, *there is no longer any need to think:* thinking is *concretized in the form of algorithmic automatons that control data-capture systems* and hence make it obsolete. As automatons, these algorithms no longer require it in order to function – *as if thinking had been proletarianized by itself.* Later, we will read the *Grundrisse* and return to *the question of the general intellect, and the question of work, from the perspective of tertiary retention* in order to clarify this possibility.[37]

A similar proletarianization is at work for a soldier who no longer needs to fight, who is therefore no longer a soldier, and who becomes the controller of those automated systems of remotely controlled murder that are military drones. This is also in some ways what Paul Valéry, Edmund Husserl and Sigmund Freud each foresaw in the development of knowledge after the First World War.[38]

Soldiers who operate drones disappear into the weapon that replaces them, just as workers disappear into the machines that turn them into proletarians. The machine becomes the technical individual, which hitherto workers had been qua tool-bearers, individuating themselves via practices that embody the knowledge derived from the practice of these tools, tools that are themselves thereby also individuated: 'Humankind centralized technical individuality within itself, in an age when only tools existed.' For Simondon, far from being a pure disintegration, the advent of the machine that replaced the worker qua tooled individual is an achievement that brings about a new age of individuation, in that 'the machine takes the place of humans because the human had been performing a function that became the machine's – to bear tools.'[39]

Simondon does not reason pharmacologically. He affirms in principle and immediately the positive necessity of machinic becoming. This shortcut is for us a weakness, but we should also and firstly understand its force. If, for a threefold psychic, collective and technical individuation, the machine fulfils a need, it is because it is the bearer of a new possibility of individuation.

Does this becoming occur in the same way for the soldier and the scientist as for the worker? In the epoch of generalized automatization, the fully automatic weapon is totally detached from and independent of the bearer of the weapon, who hitherto was the warrior, just as, according to Anderson, fully automatic (if not absolute) knowledge would be totally detached from the scientist, that is, from his or her individuation.

We shall see that the disappearance of the worker, resulting from an initial automatization that gave rise to the proletariat, leads to the disappearance of the proletariat itself, with the new wave of full and generalized automatization, and that this new economic but also epistemic and moral rationality can and must lead:

- to a strengthening of knowledge, of the sharing of knowledge and of its interiorization, and of the individuation of knowledge facilitated by automatons;

- to a *rebirth of work* made possible by the *disappearance of employ-ment*, employability, wage labour and governance according to the imperative to increase purchasing power – which since Keynes has been called 'growth'.[40]

Only a new jurisdiction for work in the service of an increase of negentropy and a reduction of entropy can lead to a legitimate extension of global security through the creation of new juridical conditions for peace – in what should become an 'internation', in the sense we can give to this term deriving from Marcel Mauss,[41] and of which the web should become the contributory infrastructure. Such is our proposal in response to Tim Berners-Lee's initiative, 'The Web We Want', launched at W3C, to write a Magna Carta for the world wide web.

28. The computational becoming of language as the standardization of enormity

Kevin Kelly reformulates Anderson's observations in the following terms:

> When you misspell a word when googling, Google suggests the proper spelling. How does it know this? How does it predict the correctly spelled word? It is not because it has a theory of good spelling, or has mastered spelling rules. In fact Google knows nothing about spelling rules at all.
>
> Instead Google operates a very large dataset of observations which show that for any given spelling of a word, x number of people say 'yes' when asked if they meant to spell word 'y'. Google's spelling engine consists entirely of these datapoints [...]. That is why the same system can correct spelling in any language.[42]

Hence Google effects a statistical and probabilistic *synchronization* that on average *eliminates diachronic variability*.

This idiomatic standardization derived from 'large numbers', however, poses the same problems as Quételet's average man, as understood by Gilles Châtelet: 'For Quételet, there is a certain *excel-lence of the average as such* [...]: the most beautiful face is that obtained by taking the average features of the whole population, just as the wisest conduct is that which best approaches the set of behaviours of the average man.'[43] If it is true that linguistic genius is this *poïesis* that proceeds from gaps through which the singularly enormous transindividuates the norm, and if linguistic prescription makes law after the fact in 'enormity becoming normal' [*énormité devenant norme*],[44] then this is the very possibility of a linguistic prescription founded on a poetic art – constituting as such a *quasi-causal legitimacy of the becoming* of language, opening its future as the necessity of the artificial 'arbitrariness of the sign' and the individuation of singularities. It is all this that the statistical analysis of average written expression eliminates *in advance* and as a process of automatic transindividuation that, as we shall see, in reality amounts to a trans*dividuation*.

Given that a language evolves, as we have known since Humboldt, in what sense must it evolve? Must it do so according to the dominant practices, that is, in an entropic sense, or on the basis of exceptional interpretations of the preindividual funds in which it consists? Obviously the statistical prescription practised by the Google spelling engine leads to the reinforcement of dominant practices. In so doing, it eliminates at a single stroke all linguistic prescription put in place in the *skholeion* since the origin of civilization. And it invalidates in advance and eliminates in fact any linguistic prescription founded on:

- a theory of language describing the dynamic and necessary relationships between diachrony and synchrony on the basis of such an art;
- a theory of collective individuation via a theory of these diachronic and synchronic relationships and of the tendencies in which they consist as the irreducible tension between the 'bottom up' and the 'top down';[45]
- a theory of *negentropy* – and of its *improbable* condition – becoming the *quasi-cause that reverses entropy*.

It is all this that this statistical analysis of average written expression renders impracticable and unthinkable, by establishing a literally disintegrated relation to language. And this clearly concerns not only the Google spelling engine but also Google Translate, the algorithmic 'engine' for translating between languages, in relation to which 'Peter Norvig, head of research at Google, once boasted to me [Kevin Kelly], "Not one person who worked on the Chinese translator spoke Chinese." There was no theory of Chinese, no understanding. Just data.'[46] But what results from this is a *generalized and global degradation* of the processes of psychic, collective and technical individuation that are all the written languages on earth, and a destruction of the associated milieus[47] in which these languages consist, individually and as a whole – through the work of those *interpreters* that good translators must always be.[48]

Speakers, who themselves are always in the final reckoning inter-preters whenever in their interlocution they *say* something and are not content simply to engage in chatter, are in this instance short-circuited – and with them their transindividual relations of the constitution of diversified and idiomatic metastabilities. This is how I interpret Frédéric Kaplan's analysis of the business models of Google's linguistic capitalism,[49] which reaches its limits in the dys-orthography brought about by the auto-completion function of its spelling engine, and in the semantic impoverishment inevitably gener-ated by AdWords.

These questions are crucial because they are generic for knowledge in general: they concern all forms of noetic life insofar as the latter rests on its analytical exteriorization – which enables the apprehen-sion and the categorization of the exterior as such, and in its various aspects. As such, these questions concern techniques that are now being implemented in every field of scientific knowledge:

> Many sciences such as astronomy, physics, genomics, linguistics, and geology are generating extremely huge datasets and constant streams of data in the petabyte level today. They'll be in the exabyte level in a decade. Using old fashioned 'machine learning', computers can extract patterns in this ocean of data that no human could ever possibly detect. These patterns are correlations. They may or may not be causative, but we can learn new things. Therefore they accomplish what science does, although not in the traditional manner.[50]

I have argued, however, that the understanding implements schemas so that, for example, the analytical fact of counting in thousands requires a passage through the outside, an exteriorization and a tertiary retention constituting a system of numeration on the basis of which it is possible to perform operations on symbolic exteri-orizations (not on the things they 'represent'). These are analytical operations that have been carried out mentally on the basis of inte-riorizations of the system of numeration,[51] and been formalized and themselves exteriorized in the form of rules that may subsequently be utilized *without having to make them conscious*, that is, without having to again actively internalize them, without reactivating the neuromnesic circuits that lie at their origin. If this is true, then what Kelly describes here, commenting on Anderson, is what happens as a result of delegating such rules to analytical automatons as operations of understanding and cerebral dis-interiorization, that is, of mental dis-integration.

This is what results from short-circuiting the operation of organo-logical integration on which the knowledge of a scholar or a scientist is based. By short-circuiting interiorization, such a delegation discon-nects the understanding as analytical formalism and reason, the latter being, as we shall argue in what follows, the capacity for interpreta-tion. Yet we have known since Kant that the analytical operations of the understanding are not self-sufficient, not just when it is a matter of producing theory, but also when it comes to producing truth.

29.   End of theory or new age of theories?

Digital tertiary retention constitutes a new epoch of knowledge and of theories. If a theory is constituted by the possibilities it opens up through the retentional modalities of its exteriorization, its transindi-viduation and its re-interiorization, that is, its individuation *in return*, after the fact, always late, and if it is tertiary retention that enables this analytical discretization and this interpretative synthesis, then it follows that digital tertiary retention transforms knowledge.

New forms of knowledge arise from a new relationship between the understanding, transformed by a new tertiary retention (itself having always been made possible by a form of tertiarization and grammatization), and reason, as the interpretation of the play of retention and protention enabled by their tertiarization.

When Anderson claims there is no longer a theoretical model, Kelly responds that there is one, but that it is not known as such, as if it were generated by an automated analytical function. And he concludes that we are witnessing the beginning of a *new epoch* of theory rather than its end:

> I think Chris [Anderson] squander [*sic*] a unique opportunity by titling his thesis 'The End of Theory' [...]. I am suggesting Correlative Analytics rather than No Theory because I am not entirely sure that these correlative systems are model-free. I think there is an emergent, unconscious, implicit model embedded in the system that generates answers. [...] The model may be beyond the perception and under-standing of the creators of the system, and since it works it is not worth trying to uncover it. [...] It just operates at a level we don't have access to.[52]

This inadequation between theory and comprehension, or the late-ness of the understanding produced by tertiarization (for this is indeed what is involved), is what leads theory and its functional definition (as what Whitehead called the function of reason[53]) to again be *called into question* – and Kelly mentions here a remark attributed to Picasso: 'In this part of science, we may get answers that work, but which we don't understand. Is this partial understanding? Or a different kind of understanding? Perhaps understanding and answers are overrated. "The problem with computers", Pablo Picasso is rumored to have said, "is that they only give you answers." '[54] Kelly concludes that in the epoch of 'big data' and correlative systems, the 'real value of the rest of science then becomes asking good questions'. This is indeed how things seem to strike us when reading Greenspan's response to members of Congress on 23 October 2008, to which it is interesting to add this comment by Sean Carroll:

> Sometimes it will be hard, or impossible, to discover simple models explaining huge collections of messy data taken from noisy, nonlinear phenomena. But it doesn't mean we shouldn't try. Hypotheses aren't simply useful tools in some potentially outmoded vision of science; they are the whole point. Theory is understanding, and understanding our world is what science is all about.[55]

I argue, however, by introducing the question of controversy and debate, without which there is no theory, that more than under-standing, more than a comprehension, science seeks what I call a surprehension – what Socrates called *aporia*,[56] a discomfiting and perplexing impasse [*embarras*] that would provoke in him and his interlocutors an anamnesis, and what Aristotle called a *thaumasmos*, a surprise.

30. Technology, science, politics and dis-automatization

The worker's loss of individuation as described by Simondon, deprived of his or her knowledge by the machine, seems to anticipate the sci-entist's loss of individuation, deprived of his or her knowledge by intensive computing.

That there is *loss* here does not mean that Simondon is *hostile* to the machine. It means that humankind must *rediscover the site of its psychic individuality*, and that, as tool-bearer, the human was itself only *provisionally* a technical individual, awaiting the transfer of this tooling to *the more accomplished technical individual that is the machine.*[57] The power of these tools, then, is amplified in order to benefit the human being's own individuation, and not just the individuation of the technical system as what destroys psychic systems and social systems (but also geographical and biological systems) for the sole benefit of capital as entropic economic system.

The Simondonian perspective on the human and the machine means that the human, as *psychic individual*, and the machine, as *technical individual*, must *constitute a new relation* where thought, art, philosophy, science, law and politics form *a new understanding of their technical condition*, a new form of knowledge that Simondon called 'mechanology', which would allow 'awareness to be raised of the significance of technical objects'.[58] It is in this context that he referred to a process of concretization inherent in technical individuation and more generally in the creation of what he called technical lineages.

In the next chapter we will see how Jonathan Crary questions the relationship between technical becoming and social becoming – that is, the future. The analysis of these relationships is the precise goal of general organology, but at the same time significantly displaces them on several points.

Simondon himself never posed the question of pharmacology. And, probably thanks to the highly necessary critique he undertook of cybernetic metaphysics,[59] but also because he failed to see that the question of the *pharmakon* is always the question of the *automaton*, he greatly underestimated the question of automatism and the consequences of automatization – as the integration of biological, psychic, social and technical automatisms, an integration carried out by digital retention, and carried out as the disintegration of psychic and social individuals.

The goal of the present work (and its second volume) is to project the conditions of a general organology and a philosophy of automaticity by taking up and displacing such Simondonian questions in the epoch of *full automatization* and of the proletarianization of the mind and spirit that results from it, and by posing as a *first principle* (in the wake of Simondon) that *the issue is not the toxicity of algorithms* (any technics being inherently toxic), but *the absence of thinking, by philosophy, science and the law, about what makes this possible, namely, tertiary retention*. Taking account of and overcoming this state of fact forms the programme of 'digital studies'.[60]

Following Jean-Pierre Vernant and Marcel Detienne, I have repeatedly argued that literal tertiary retention is the *sine qua non* of the co-emergence of political *nomos* and of the *epistēmē* as rational knowledge reconfiguring all knowledge, which is thereafter conceived on the basis of the experience of truth, argued according to the canon of geometrical demonstration.[61] Literal tertiary retention *constitutes public* space as such – that is, constitutes it as the space of publication, the space of expression via spatialized traces accessible to all those who form 'the public' (in the form of letters, in the Greek epoch) – and such that the *law*, as public political space and as in principle constitutive of the *polis*, is submitted to this *new criterion*, for every process of transindividuation that is *alētheia*.

It is only because of this common origin of the *polis* and the apodictic *epistēmē* that we can refer to scientific 'law'. And this is also why, in proclaiming the end of theory and science, *Anderson is in fact asserting the end of political psychic and collective individuation* – which is not without an echo in the initiative of Peter Thiel, founder of PayPal:

> [O]ne of Facebook's earliest backers [...], he believes that artificial countries built in international waters on oilrig-type platforms could hold the key to humanity's future.
>   The aim is to create communities that would be run according to extreme laissez faire ideals [...]. The first step will involve a pilot project, off the coast of San Francisco.[62]

The individuation of political public space is conditioned by the formation[63] of each citizen in the *skholeion*, where citizens accede to the letter (that is, as we shall see,[64] where they *organologically re-organize* their *organic* cerebral organ). Citizens, by forming themselves *à la lettre* – through this *interiorization* of the letter (by reading) and through its *exteriorization* (by writing), an internalization and externalization that require the acquisition of this competence as a *new automatism written into the cerebral organ through learning, through an apprenticeship – can access the consistences* that theoretical knowledge forms, and *thereby dis-automatize* automatic behaviours, whether biological, psychic or social: if consistence is what makes dis-automatization possible, it is accessible only on the basis of an automatization.

Tertiary retention is now digital, and literal as well as analogue tertiary retention have themselves been *integrated and reconfigured* digitally, thereby opening up another experience of both reading and writing. Given this, to think automatic *society* – that is, a digital *automaton* placed in the service not of calculations that disindividuate and disintegrate both the social and the psychic, but of a calculation leading the *subjects* of this calculation to *dis-automatization*[65] *by expanding the experience of individuation beyond all calculation,*[66] that is, *always passing through a form of sacrifice*[67] – presupposes *rethinking law as such*. That is, it presupposes rethinking the *constitution* of the law, in the sense that we refer to the law in constitutional assemblies, and in the sense that a constitution constitutes *the basis and the promise of a new process of psychic and collective individuation*.

31.   The 'Robot Apocalypse' and the true meaning of the revelations of Edward Snowden

The hyper-industrial state of fact takes what Deleuze called control societies, founded on modulation by the mass media, into the stage of *hyper-control*. The latter is generated by self-produced personal data, collected and published by people themselves – whether knowingly or otherwise – and this data is then exploited by applying intensive computing to these massive data sets. This *automatized modulation* establishes algorithmic governmentality in the service of what Crary calls 24/7 capitalism.[68]

Automatized modulation and algorithmic governmentality are an issue for debate in all manner of forums and under many other names and in very different terms, whether it is the Organization for Economic Cooperation and Development, the European Union or in France at the Commission nationale de l'informatique et des libertés or the Conseil national du numérique, and so on. Parliamentary commissions have been set up in Germany and France on these subjects. Many themes emerge, problems that arise one after another from the growth of the data economy, crowdsourcing and automatized artificial crowds, amounting to so many problems posed by hyper-control.[69]

The coming integration of traceability and robotization remains greatly under-anticipated, and its global consequences remain seriously underestimated, despite recent studies that show that

> robots could take over half of our jobs [...] within two decades [...].
> According to two researchers from Oxford, Carl Frey and Michael
> Osborne, [...] 47% of American jobs are in the next two decades
> likely to be occupied by robots [...]. Most workers in transport and
> logistics, as well as most administrative jobs and factory workers,
> are likely to be replaced by machines. This is also the case [...] for a
> substantial proportion of jobs in the service sector [...]. [For] Jeremy
> Bowles, in Belgium, 50% of jobs could be affected. The percentages
> are similar for our European partners.[70]

Indeed, Jeff Bezos, founder and head of Amazon, announced in May 2014 that his company would be filling its warehouses with ten thousand robots, manufactured by Kiva Systems, which it acquired two years earlier.

Despite these facts, and the declarations of Bill Gates, whose statements on 13 March 2014 to the American Enterprise Institute led to the headline, 'People Don't Realize How Many Jobs Will Soon Be Replaced by Software Bots',[71] which the *International Business Times* chose to refer to as the 'Robot Apocalypse',[72] we in France and Europe continue to reaffirm unemployment reduction targets – an *omerta* on reality that can lead only to political discredit, to the collapse of the confidence that is considered so precious, and to serious social conflicts.

Given that the consequences of robotization in the digital context of full and generalized automatization have not been properly anticipated, the risk is that these things may occur very quickly and in disastrous conditions. The Pisani-Ferry report in particular is highly negligent on this level – despite the warnings from *Le Journal du dimanche* of the likelihood that in France three million jobs will be destroyed in the next ten years.[73]

By revealing the illegal practices of the National Security Agency (NSA), Edward Snowden has exposed a global and subterranean logic and put into perspective the imperative need for an alternative, by *sounding the alarm* about this situation, *dominated as it is by lawlessness*. He has thus placed into its true context the question of traceability and of the automatization that it requires, and that it immeasurably amplifies. But if with these revelations the state suddenly returned to the forefront of consciousness – an American federal government that appears to systematically operate outside of any law – they also and immediately functioned as a smokescreen concealing the true situation and the real question of law.[74]

More than the surveillance conducted by military and police authorities, the fundamental issue is the privatization of data: this is what makes it possible to give up on the rule of law in the name of reasons of state. The NSA network surveillance scandal was possible because *there is no law* that truly governs the treatment and management of digital traces by platforms, and because in the final analysis it is law in general, in all its forms and as distinct from fact, that is dis-integrated in its very foundations by full and generalized automatization – which the issue of big data makes clear.

These questions cannot continue to be avoided and evaded for long, because full and generalized automatization is leading in an inevitable way to a decline in employment and to the effective collapse of the model of economic rationality that was established by Roosevelt and Keynes in 1933 on the base of the technological shock that was the Taylorist and partial automatization implemented by Ford in the early twentieth century.

32.   What is to be done?

Generalized disintegration – of knowledge, power, economic models, social systems, basic psycho-relational structures, intergenerational relations and the climate system – is engendered by the *automatized integration of the technical system, which is now thoroughly digitalized* via compatibility and other standards, exchange formats, data formats, bridges, plug-ins, platforms, and so on, and including the whole set of elements of the hyper-industrial milieu, via radio-frequency identification (RFID) tags and other identification, tagging and auto-traceability systems.

The digital enables the unification of all technological automatisms (mechanical, electromechanical, photoelectrical, electronic, and so on) by installing sensors and actuators, and intermediating software, between the producer and the consumer. Computer-aided design (CAD) systems produce simulations and prototypes via computer-generated imagery and 3D printing on the basis of cognitive automatisms; robots are controlled by software that can handle separate parts tagged by RFID[75] technology; design integrates crowdsourcing just as marketing is founded on network technologies and network effects; logistics and distribution have become remotely controlled systems operating on the basis of digital identification via the 'internet of things';[76] consumption is based on social networking; and so on.

It is this complete integration of the technical system, via the digital, that enables the functional integration of biological, psychic and social automatisms – and it is this context that has seen the development of neuromarketing and neuroeconomics. This functional integration leads on the side of production to a *total robotization* that disintegrates not just public power, social and educational systems, intergenerational relations and consequently psychic structures: it is *the industrial economy itself*, based on wage labour as the criterion for distributing purchasing power, and for the formation of mass markets capable of absorbing the ready-made commodities of the consumerist model, which is in the course of dis-integrating – becoming *functionally insolvent* because *fundamentally irrational*.

All this seems overwhelming and hopeless. Is it possible, nevertheless, to invent, on the basis of this *state of fact* that is *total disintegration*,[77] an '*ars* of hyper-control' – for example, by updating Deleuze's position in terms of his support for an 'art of control'?

In 'Optimism, Pessimism and Travel', Deleuze's letter to Serge Daney about control societies and the new powers of control that make them possible, he stated that we must 'get to the heart of the confrontation'.[78] This should consist in an inversion: 'This would almost be to ask whether this control might be inverted, harnessed by the supplementary function that opposes itself to power: to *invent* an art of control that would be like a new form of *resistance*.'[79]

To invent or *to resist*? We shall return to this hesitation. The supplementary function involved in this statement by Deleuze comes from Daney's reference to the Derridean notion of the supplement, applying it to television.[80] And this is indeed a matter of a politics and a philosophy of the supplement, which, as we will try to show in the second volume, also passes, and now more than ever, through a philosophy of automaticity as well as of invention – much more than of 'resistance'.

Invention is in Deleuze what creates an event and bifurcation starting from a quasi-causality that inverts a situation of default.[81] Here, it is art that invents – an 'art of control'. Quasi-causality is clearly a kind of therapeutics within a pharmacological situation: the 'supplement' capable of 'inverting' through its 'quasi-causal' logic is obviously a *pharmakon*. And I have recently recalled that *Difference and Repetition* thinks in terms that are fundamentally pharmacological.[82]

33. Supplementary invention

Invention is today the challenge of the struggle against the state of fact that is a total dis-integration of the 'dividuals' that we will have become, a situation about which Edward Snowden sounded the alarm, according to Glenn Greenwald, who declared on 27 December 2013, at a meeting of the Chaos Computer Club of Hamburg:

> It is possible that there will be courts that will impose some meaningful restrictions [on NSA and American espionage conducted via digital networks]. It's much more possible that other countries around the world who are truly indignant about the breaches of their privacy security will band together and create alternatives [...]. Even more promising is the fact that large private corporations, Internet companies and others will start finally paying a price for their collaboration

> with this spying regime. [...] *But I ultimately think that where the greatest hope lies is with the people in this room and the [technical] skills that all of you possess.*[83]

Greenwald is declaring, then, that the answer lies in the hands of the hacktivists. This assertion is only *partially* right. *What is absolutely correct* is to posit that today the question of *organological invention* constitutes the *categorical imperative* common to all those struggles – juridical, philosophical, scientific, artistic, political and economic – that must be carried out against this state of fact and for a state of law, and where this is a matter not of resisting, but of inventing. *What is not correct* is to believe that this organological question is an issue only for hackers – even if it is clear that they have in this regard been pioneers and important contributors.

In addition, there is no doubt that art has a distinct role to play with respect to invention in relation to the organological in general. But Deleuze is far from clear about this, and he conceives this art of control much more in terms of resistance than of invention – where the latter is always, in the aesthetic field, in one way or another, organological. In other words, it is always a question of inventing technically or technologically, and not just artistically. But Deleuze is generally unconcerned with thinking technicity, or cinema, or the *pharmakon*, and even in his reading of Foucault he has little interest in technologies of power.[84]

In the field of art, and of cinema, of this industry of dreams that art becomes with cinematography, it is with Jean Renoir that we must think organological invention – for example, when he analyses in the history of cinema the artistic meaning of the passage from orthochromatic film to panchromatic film, concluding that 'artistic discoveries are almost a direct result of technical discoveries'.[85] The question of cinema and of its technicity is a *jumbled patchwork*, in a way typical of the metaphysical traps that arise whenever technics is in question – including in Deleuze and in Derrida.

Cinema is a becoming that is *obviously technical*. But cinema is also the very possibility of dreaming: it is an *essentially psychic* becoming.[86] And socialization always presupposes the convergence and projection of psychic desires via technical inventions, that is, via new forms of tertiary retention, which form stages in a process of grammatization – of which full automatization is a bifurcation of unprecedented scope.

These questions are those of arche-cinema,[87] which lie at the heart of my interpretation of the allegory of the cave.[88] As Jean-Louis

Comolli recalls, André Bazin stated that 'the cinema is an idealist phenomenon',[89] referring both to *L'invention du cinéma* by Georges Sadoul, a Marxist and materialist film historian, and to Plato's *Republic*: 'The concept men had of it existed so to speak fully armed in their minds, as if in some platonic heaven.'[90]

Now, this is *totally confused*:

- Bazin presumes that cinema falls from the heaven of ideas, whereas
- Plato's cave is an allegorical yet precise description of cinema as an illusory projection from which we must absolutely escape in order to reach the ideas ... and that says we must stop 'making cinema' so as finally to be able to contemplate the pure and true light, namely, the light of the sun.

This metaphysics, which is both Marxist and Platonic, relates to what Daney called photology.[91] It results from a complete misunderstanding of what is at stake in grammatization and, more generally, in organological becoming, a question posed for the first time in *The German Ideology* – a text that must be revisited in relation to Derrida's theory of the trace. But the Derridean theory of the trace is not itself sufficient to effectively and concretely think organology and the *supplementary invention* from which it proceeds as the historical becoming of a threefold individuation that is inextricably psychic, technical and social.

Cinema is what, as arche-cinema, begins as soon as technical life starts to *assemble* gestures, which are already signifying chains, gestures through which it metastabilizes, by what it makes, ways of doing things, forms of *savoir-faire*, work-knowledge – whatever is thus *made* being a tertiary retention, that is, a *mnesic exteriorization* that operates through the *spatialization of the time of a gesture*.

It is obvious that this assemblage or montage is anticipated in dreams (and this is what so clearly disturbs the thinking of both Bazin and Sadoul). Arche-cinema is the inaugurating regime of desire, consisting in a dis-automatization of instinct that, becoming detachable – like technical organs, which are themselves always in some way fetishes – is generated from the drives *contained* by desire. This is so in two senses of this word 'contain': the drives are borne within desire as its dynamic element, but their completion is curtailed or limited by being 'diverted from their goals'.

What occurred in 1895 was the culmination of this primordial technology of the dream that is arche-cinema, and the analogical continuation of a process of grammatization that has not yet come to completion, which probably began in the Upper Palaeolithic, and which has allowed (from 1895 until today) this arche-cinema to enjoy a new epoch, that of the so-called cinemato*graphic* art and of the film industry – which then shapes the twentieth century, as seen and reflected upon by Jean-Luc Godard in his highly organological studio.[92]

What is missing in Deleuze, as in all philosophy, epistemology and most of so-called aesthetics, is an understanding of the stakes of tertiary retention, *that is, of technics*. But this absence is also found among jurists, and is yet more common among economists – and even anthropologists. It is towards conceiving the role of tertiary retention in the formation of knowledge, and doing so starting from the crucible constituted by total dis-integration, and towards thinking the quasi-causal inversion that all this requires, that we must now devote ourselves – and sacrifice (time).

3

The Destruction of the Faculty
of Dreaming

It is still only in a dream state, but I really long to delve deeper into
this idea.

Gustave Flaubert[1]

34. Full synchronization through 'online correlates'

In *24/7: Late Capitalism and the Ends of Sleep* Jonathan Crary
shows how the industry of traceability creates *doubles* of psychic
individuals through user profiling technologies, not only by making
digital puppet models, but in the sense that they *outstrip and overtake
them*.[2]

By producing their 'profiles' on the basis of their reticulated activity, and by 'personalizing' them – beyond the statistical calculation
of phrases, requests and other linguistic acts that Google produces
– the traceability industry leads to their *functional integration* as consumers in '24/7 markets and a global infrastructure for continuous
work and consumption'.[3] After the organization of production facili-
ties into three daily eight-hour shifts in the early twentieth century,
and then the connection of worldwide stock exchanges operating
twenty-four hours a day in the second half of the twentieth century,
'now a human subject is in the making to coincide with these more
intensively'.[4]

By means of this synchronization operating through functional economic integration, full and generalized automatization
is directly sustained by psychic individuals themselves, at the cost
of social disintegration – and therefore of psychic disintegration,
given that psychic individuation can be achieved only as collective
individuation.

These 24/7 infrastructures that never stand still, where there is never a pause, and where it is a matter of eliminating the 'useless' time of decision-making and reflection,[5] keep individuals continuously connected to online resources in a manner that short-circuits 'everyday life'[6] by emptying it of its everydayness, that is, its familiarity: anonymizing it.

The interactive consultation of these resources, which systematize the constant recording and archivization of movements, the paths followed by and expressions used by connected psychic individuals,[7] both feeds these online resources and allows behavioural profiles to be traced along the paths followed within them. Hence a final integration of marketing and ideology takes place, the completion of a process that began in the 1980s with psychopower.[8] 'Hence': that is, through the *grammatization of relations* in which consists that traceability implemented by social networking.

All political questions are dissolved into economics, since ideology is no longer about collective choices but about 'individual' relations to products: 'There is an ever closer linking of individual needs with the functional and ideological programs in which each new product is embedded.'[9] These programmed relations give rise to *dividuation* in Guattari's sense, that is, to the destruction of in-dividuation in Simondon's sense – which forms the basis of 'algorithmic governmentality'.

This is so only because espionage and marketing have themselves been functionally integrated. In 'data marketing', the 'most advanced forms of surveillance and data analysis used by intelligence agencies are now equally indispensable'.[10]

In the 1980s the neoliberal turn began to rely on the combined exploitation of the mass media, the nascent personal computer and telematics. Any technological innovation is then placed into the service of the infrastructure of the 24/7 regime, where it is 'impossible that there might be a clearing or pause in which a longer-term time frame of transindividual concerns and projects might come into view'.[11] In this way it is diachrony that is 'switched off' [*mise hors circuit*], just as social processes of transindividuation in general are short-circuited – precisely insofar as they articulate the diachronic and the synchronic.

This structural and permanent short-circuiting of diachrony operates through computational automatons in 'real time', that is, through an interactivity in which the individual act is integrated with the algorithmic operation that anticipates it, pushes it towards conforming to a behavioural standard, dividualizes it, and of which it becomes a function.[12]

Hence a new calendarity is established, founded on behavioural homogenization and the importation of work procedures into leisure time and everyday life.[13] Emerging from the rationalization of the service sector, imported into all the routines that constitute the rhythms of society on the basis of what Leroi-Gourhan called 'socio-ethnic programmes', the *grammatization of existences* established through these computerized generic procedures dissolves 'everyday life' by diluting it into 'administered life': 'one's bank account and one's friendships can now be managed through identical machinic operations and gestures'.[14]

All aspects of existence have seen the development of 'online cor-relates'[15] for every kind of individual and collective activity, enabling the short-circuiting of everyday life, that is, of local life: life *precisely insofar as it is social.*

This results in the 'absolute abdication of responsibility for living'.[16]

35. Accelerated transformations of calendarity by innovation in the service of 24/7 capitalism and the liquidation of intermittence

If from the early nineteenth century modernity tends to eliminate 'unadministered'[17] everyday life, nevertheless large zones of pre-modern 'everydayness' remained intact well into the first half of the twentieth century, as Fredric Jameson has shown: until then, 'only a minute percentage of the social and physical space of the West could be considered either fully modern in technology or production or substantially bourgeois in its class culture'.[18]

Starting from the Second World War, with those innovations that will lead to the mass media and to the constitution of telecratic psychopower, and to information and computer technologies, the process of dissolving everydayness into standardized 'modern life' rapidly accelerates[19] – and eventually it is the bourgeoisie itself that disappears, while capitalism expresses with ever greater ferocity its tendency to become mafiaesque and illiterate, although this last point is not one made by Crary himself.

At the end of the 1960s, social movements arise with the aim of 'reclaiming the terrain of everyday life'[20] – which will eventually lead, in the 1980s, to what Crary calls a 'counter-revolution',[21] that is, to the conservative 'revolution' in which the individual is 'redefined as a full-time economic agent, even in the context of "jobless capitalism"'.[22] Thus begins a series of transformations of everyday life, firstly with the 'sudden and ubiquitous reorganization of human time and activity accompanying [the rise of] television'.[23]

These transformations then lead into an acceleration and complexification that starts in 1983 with the videocassette recorder – which suspends the hegemony of the television broadcast schedule – and with micro-computing, that is, with interactivity:

> [This enables] the mobilization and habituation of the individual to an open-ended set of tasks and routines, far beyond what was asked of anyone in the 1950s and '60s. Television had colonized important arenas of lived time, but neoliberalism demanded that there be a far more methodical extraction of value from television time, and in principle from every waking hour.[24]

As we saw in the previous chapter, this becoming occurred as a result of what Deleuze described as the rise of control societies that 'effectively operated 24/7'.[25]

Micro-computing then leads to a significant dismantling of the linear calendarity of the programme industries[26] – but this does not really occur until after the appearance of the web in 1993. (Crary does not mention this date, which is nevertheless crucial, and to which I will return in *Automatic Society, Volume 2: The Future of Knowledge*.) The full and perpetual establishment of this system, however, occurs only after the introduction of so-called 'smart' devices that have the 'capacity to integrate their user more fully into 24/7 routines'.[27]

This 'integration' of psychic individuals into standardized and grammatized routines – and thereby into the *technical system* of which these individuals become a *technical function* as *crowds*, that is, as digital artificial and conventional crowds within a techno-geographical milieu[28] in which the human becomes less a resource (what Heidegger called *Bestand*, standing reserve) than a functional organ – in fact *dis-integrates* them.

The functional becoming of individuals in turn dis-integrates social systems (in the sense of Bertrand Gille and Niklas Luhmann[29]) and collective individuals, because there can be no psychic individuation that does not participate in a collective individuation, and vice versa: no collective individuation is possible without the *diachronic nourishment* brought by psychic individuals – a 'nourishment' consisting of what Simondon called 'quantum leaps' in psychic individuation,[30] the adjective 'quantum' referring in processes of individuation to an *incalculable intermittence*. We will come back to this.

This reciprocal participation of the psychic and the collective is possible only on the condition that psychic individuation cannot be reducible to collective individuation, that is, on the condition that the *singular* cannot be reduced to the *particular* (to the *calculable*),[31] that it cannot be short-circuited, pre-empted and denied through the calculation of its traces. Real individuation requires a dynamic tension between psychic individuation and collective individuation, a tension that is their mutual and transductive condition of individuation (through a transductive amplification).[32]

It is precisely such a dissolution of the psychic into the collective that occurs with social networking technology, that is, in digital conventional crowds.

Nevertheless, I will argue at the end of this book that it is not only possible but absolutely necessary to *change digital organology in order that digital tertiary retention becomes a differentiating factor for these individuations and for the transductive amplification*[33] *of their potentials for individuation*, and in order to turn the entropic becoming of the Anthropocene into a negentropic becoming establishing the Neganthropocene.

36.   Intermittences of the improbable

What is at stake here is the *progressive elimination by 24/7 environments of those intermittences* that are *states of sleep* and of *daydream*: 'One of the forms of disempowerment within 24/7 environments is the incapacitation of daydream or of any mode of absent-minded introspection.'[34] It is worth noting that Simone Weil described her own experience of proletarianized manual labour in an Alstom factory in terms that were different but comparable.[35]

The theme of nocturnal as well as diurnal dreaming, which was the theme of the 2014 summer academy at pharmakon.fr, is of interest with respect to this book for two reasons. On the one hand, we take note of an observation by the archaeologist Marc Azéma at the beginning of his *Préhistoire du cinéma*, in which he analyses cave paintings of the Upper Palaeolithic by taking as his starting point that 'man has always "dreamed". He shares this faculty with many animals. But his brain is a machine for producing far more advanced images [...] capable of being projected outside of his internal "cinema".'[36] We argue, following many others (in particular Valéry), that this *ability to dream* lies at the origin of all *thinking* – the latter being defined as the *capacity to dream the conditions of its own realization, organology thus being constituted by a power to realize its dreams* (a power that is that of *tekhnē* in all the meanings, past and present, of this very old word that in Latin is written as *ars*, and in French as *technique*, then *technologie*).[37]

On the other hand, and consequently, the power to *dream possibilities* in which the *realizable* dream consists – possibilities that appear *firstly, always and structurally* as *impossibilities* (and it is for this reason that it is so difficult and paradoxical to paint dreams[38]) – relates to the fact of an experience and a projection of what both Bonnefoy and Blanchot name, in a strict sense, the *improbable*,[39] and this is a *power to dis-automatize the automatisms* that *constitute* this power.

The power of dreaming can dis-automatize its own automatisms – just as the drives constitute desire, even though the latter contains, retains and defers them, and as such also constitute the 'sublime', *by quasi-causally inverting the accident in which they consist* as blind and fatal necessity.[40] 'There is a profound incompatibility of anything resembling reverie with the priorities of efficiency, functionality, and speed'[41] imposed by 24/7 capitalism, that is, by the data economy and its automatic, interactive and instantaneous traceability: 'Within 24/7 capitalism, a sociality outside of individual self-interest becomes inexorably depleted, and the interhuman basis of public space is made irrelevant to one's fantasmatic digital insularity.'[42] Crary in this way describes a state of fact, but one that must, however, be strongly qualified: he fails ever to mention any therapeutic aspects of this reticularity, such as the formation of new processes of collective and deliberative individuation.[43]

Now, just as the application of high-performance computing to big data, which leads Chris Anderson to conclude that theory has become obsolete, occurs in the form of a state of fact that can and must be inverted into a state of law constituting the therapeutics of this *pharmakon* that is digital tertiary retention, so too an account of 24/7 capitalism implies the question of the passage from fact to law, the question of 'how existing technical capabilities and premises could be deployed in the service of human and social needs, rather than the requirements of capital and empire'.[44] We must see 'current arrangements, in reality untenable and unsustainable, as anything but inevitable and unalterable', and we should 'articulate strategies of living that would delink technology from a logic of greed, accumulation, and environmental despoliation'.[45]

37. Dream, fact and law

Questioning and challenging this state of fact is the precise political programme of Ars Industrialis. It presumes that the techno-logical challenge that is the contemporary state of shock should be understood as a doubly epokhal redoubling founded on tertiary retention as artificiality in general, and as trace. The passage from the first moment to the second moment of this redoubling requires a supplementary organological invention, and this is the scientific and technological programme of the Institut de recherche et d'innovation.

This state of shock, which *always begins* with the installation of a state of fact, can and must, through the work of transindividuation – that is, of binding (the drives, but also psychic secondary retentions and collective secondary retentions) – constitute a new state of law. But the subject of the verb *constitute* here is the state of shock, which means that it is the specificity of the tertiary retentions involved that must be thought, because tertiary retention is the operator of the shock and it is what must become constitutive of the new law.

For centuries, the constitution of law by tertiary retention (in this case, literal tertiary retention) remained concealed behind the reference to the law of divine authorities. In the West, the constitution of the law was founded on the Book, but the capitalization of this founding element is a clear indication of the character of the relationship it had to the *pharmakon*: sacralized and theocratized.

Today, unlike previous epochs, this need to think the *pharmakon as such* can no longer be concealed, not just because 'God is dead', but also because this pharmacological unbinding is now perceived and experienced by everyone (including those for whom God is not dead[46]) – and, in France, this is beginning with those who vote for the National Front.

To put it another way, it is now a matter of working to develop *noetic* circuits of digital transindividuation, which are currently still severely lacking, on the basis of a recognition and an analysis of the specificities of the first moment of improbable epokhality into which we must enter – by analysing not only the state of *fact*, but also the state of *shock*, that is, the *epokhal specificity* of digital (intrinsically and thoroughly computational) tertiary retention separated out from its ideological-consumerist slag.

Such a programme is a dream, say the sceptics. Indeed: the sceptics are lucid, and this moment of *skepsis* is necessary because from it we learn something essential. This *dream programme* posits that *tertiary retention proceeds primordially from dreaming*, and from a specific type of dream: the *noetic dream* such that it *may* become thought, and such that it is always the beginning of *any true thinking*, which is always negentropic – in passing through reverie – that is, insofar as it *can dream the conditions of its own realization* in the course of a neganthropological process.

The *dream that thinks* leads to *realizations* (technical inventions, artistic creations, political institutions, economic enterprises, movements of all kinds and social bricolages, all of these being inaugurations of new processes of transindividuation, frequently participating in what Patricia Ribault and Thomas Golsenne call 'bricology'[47]), which themselves become automatisms, and which thus lose their oneiric force, that is, their noetic force – until a new intermittence revives them, rediscovering the power of dreaming by dis-automatizing them.

38.   Confronting the power of totalization – the right and duty to dis-automatize by dreaming

I argue in the next chapter that what I believe to be the passage from fact to law awaited and claimed by Crary (though these are not his terms) must be not only *theoretical*, as is the case for the epistemic therapeutics of 'big data', but also *practical and functional* in relation to *data behaviourism*, which, in the words of Antoinette Rouvroy, opposes itself to 'due process',[48] that is, to procedural regulation and to questions of the *interpretation* of the law.

In affirming that this passage from fact to law must be *both practical and functional*, I am referring firstly to Kant and to his question of *practical reason*, and secondly to Marx, who posits that the law is always that of a *political economy* of which it is a question of making a critique – which posits that the law is always and above all an economic law, a question that with Foucault becomes that of biopower and biopolitics.

24/7 capitalism is totally computational and it is, more precisely, capitalism conceived in terms of the power of totalization. In other words, it aims through its operations to impose *an automatic society without the possibility of dis-automatization, that is, without the possibility of theory* – without thinking, given that all thinking is a power effectively exerted to dis-automatize and, as such, *a power of dreaming exerted through exercises*,[49] related to technics of the self in general, and to disciplined practices of *hypomnēmata* in particular,[50] but also those *scientific dreams* dreamed, conceived and practised by Bachelard.

To critique, in the philosophical sense of the word, always means *to take account of the necessity at work* in that which it is a matter of critiquing, and against which it is a matter of struggling. To struggle here means (from a pharmacological and organological perspective) to make oneself capable of becoming the quasi-cause of such a necessity.[51]

The automatic becoming of society *requires* – both *rationally*, that is, from the perspective of theoretical and practical reason, and *functionally*, that is, from the perspective of economic rationalization:[52]

- a refunctionalization of the possibility of dis-automatizing automatisms;
- that this possibility become accessible to everyone by right, if not in fact;
- that it constitute the heart of economic activity and the industrial future, in a context where automatization tends increasingly to eliminate employment and to exacerbate the entropic threats brought by the Anthropocene.

The challenge is to effect a *massive redistribution of thinking time* [*temps de songer*] on the basis of the *temporal benefits made possible by automatons*. Only through such a redistribution can solvency be reconstituted – that is, a credit supported by a *credo* – and the reconstitution of values and 'value chains' that would be not just economic, but social and practical, in a context of generalized automatization and robotization, that is, of the *disappearance of the kind of redistribution that took the form of purchasing power mediated through wage labour*.

All this presupposes a *fundamental* reconceptualization of political and economic rights and in France a re-writing of the constitution, which itself requires a redefinition of the goals and practices of scientific research and education, in a new general epistemological framework, and a new digital organology (these will be the issues addressed in the second volume of *Automatic Society*).

All these points fall within the compass of a *transvaluation* and they can and must be seen as contemporary aspects of a *fundamental intermittence* of which dreams and sleep are the elementary conditions (and this is how we should hear Prospero in *The Tempest*).[53] This intermittence constitutes noetic life, according to Aristotle[54] as according to Socrates.[55]

This is why, totally unlike what the current French government or the current president of the Mouvement des entreprises de France

(MEDEF) would do, and following on from the analyses initiated in *For a New Critique of Political Economy*, we advocate the *generalization of the law of the 'intermittents du spectacle'*[56] instituted in 1936 in France: only a complete redefinition of work and value starting from the consideration of *intermittence qua source of all noetic life*, that is, as power of dis-automatization, and therefore as source of all production of value (of negentropy), will open up prospects beyond 24/7 capitalism and the nihilism it accomplishes.

39. The organological bases of sleep, dream and intermittence

Crary's reflections on sleeping and dreaming are a meditation on intermittence, of which sleeping and dreaming are the most elementary experiences, themselves founded on a cosmology of diurnal and nocturnal alternations embedded in an organology of sleep, that is, founded on the fact that this elementarity of sleep – which is our element, says Prospero[57] – just like that of the dream that is its supplement, derives from an *elementary supplementarity*.

Crary points out that in Mauss techniques of the body affect sleep itself.[58] This organology of sleep is inscribed in a programmatology[59] that is an organology of the cosmos,[60] an arrangement of cosmic, planetary and stellar programmes with socio-ethnic and socio-technical programmes, of which astrology is an ancient manifestation lying at the origin of astronomy but also at the origin of those hypomnesic calendarities that are the calendars that emerge from the various forms of writing. These calendarities found civilizations by establishing civil and urban regimes composed of synchronizing and diachronizing tendencies that crisscross the processes of psychic and collective individuation that have succeeded one another since the birth of humanity.

All calendarities have always involved – and this is so long before the appearance of the hypomnesic calendrical forms of Antiquity – the engagement of intermittences, which are their very foundations, that is, the sources of their authority, the commemoration on various registers of their point of origin.[61] There is no everyday life in Lefebvre's sense, that is, in the sense of existence (distinguished from and in subsistence by its relation to consistences), without calendarity opening the temporality of an epoch – and there is no calendarity without intermittence.

From the beginning of human society insofar as we are aware, and until the advent of 24/7 capitalism, which brought it to an end, programmatology and calendarity have articulated the various forms of intermittence with the commonplace tasks of subsistence, and have done so in a more or less therapeutic way.[62] As a moment of exception, intermittence is what ensures the possibility of existence and the necessity of consistence within the necessity of subsisting – a kind of subsistence that the so-called 'needy' and 'derelicts' are unable to access.

With Sunday as the *otium* of the people[63] within the experience of the sacred and for the religious, as well as with the secular *otium* of the people in which consists the right and duty of a public education for all, committed to the elevation of everyone, well before it is an economic function of production, with what Hegel called the 'Sunday of life', which is also the subject of the eponymous novel by Raymond Queneau,[64] with all of this, it is intermittence as the foundation of social life that the festival or the celebration reaffirms – and with it the noetic dimension of any society (as experience and event of what Roberto Esposito calls '*delinquere*'[65]).

There is an *organology* of intermittence, including the totem, which is one of its elementary forms, and which for Aboriginal Australians combines with 'the Dreaming' to form a common, primordial resource for dis-automatization, normalized by socio-ethnic programmes.[66]

40. The interpretation of dreams and organology

Interpreting Chris Marker's *La Jetée* as a premonitory film or dream (or as a kind of nightmare *within which* we still dream[67]) concerned with the question, 'How does one remain human in the bleakness of this world?',[68] passing through Robert Desnos' practices of dreaming and sleeping,[69] and more generally through the epoch of surrealism, Crary's reading suggests to my thinking (to my dreaming) that, in its fundamental freedom, poetic and artistic reverie establishes an intermittence (that is, a kind of *epokhē*) between the two moments of a doubly epokhal redoubling, which weaves itself between the psychic level and the collective level of emerging transindividuation (and here again we should read *Imagination et invention*).[70]

The poet and the artist, exteriorizing their dreams and reveries, make us dream and hallucinate a world in a state of shock, under the influence of a shock more or less close or distant, and sometimes very distant (the shock of the letter, a shock first received almost three thousand years ago, affects us still), often deeply repressed, systematically and socially concealed and denied. And the shockwaves emanating from this more or less close or distant shock are thus trans-formed by the poet and the artist into inaugurating bifurcations of new circuits of transindividuation.

The artist, especially since the dawn of the modern age and the acceleration of technical individuation from which this age proceeds, is a psychic individual whose individuation coincides with that of his or her epoch as an ensemble of collective individuations – and it is this specific feature of Marcel Duchamp that becomes clear when we confront the process of generalized proletarianization, the advent of which he foresaw in the early twentieth century.[71]

This was the consideration to which I was led by Crary's interpretation of *La Jetée*: 'Marker [...] situated a utopian moment, not in the future yet to be made but in the imbrication of memory and the present, in the lived inseparability of sleep and waking, of dream and life, in a dream of life, as the inextinguishable promise of awakening.'[72] On the basis of this interpretation Crary outlines a concise history of dreaming, a history at the end of which (that is, today) one finds the increasingly widespread idea 'that dreams are objectifiable, that they are discrete entities that, given the development of applicable technology, could be recorded and in some way played back or downloaded',[73] as if the dream has, in its turn, become *Bestand*.

And indeed, a 2013 article published in *Science* entitled 'Neural Decoding of Visual Imagery During Sleep'[74] describes a technology for tracing dreams, based yet again on predictive machine-learning that there is every reason to believe empties dreams of what constitutes their very power: what is predictable about a dream in such conditions (if in fact there is anything predictable whatsoever) can only be what constitutes its *automatic stuff*.[75]

Now, that in which the dream *consists*, that by which it can nourish the projection to come of any consistency whatsoever through which this dream *could* work, that is, think, is precisely what is not only unpredictable, but *utterly improbable*, and therefore strictly *the fruit of dis-automatization* – the name of which is also, in Greek, *epokhē*.

The dream would thus be what articulates an *epoch made of inherited automatisms* – forming a preindividual fund (and emerging from the unconscious, which is always, as Freud showed, 'in itself collective'[76]) – with the *most improbable powers of individuation and invention*. In this way it produces turns, changes of epoch, bifurcations deriving from the quasi-causal logic of desire, which is to say the unconscious. It is this improbable – that is, incalculable – quasi-causality that totally computational capitalism tends to *systemically* eliminate, thereby sawing off, as we shall see, the very branch that bears it.

If there is a historicity of the dream, as Crary emphasizes,[77] and if in this history its fundamental facticity can become what leads to the *nihilistic dream of the denial of the dream*, and if 'dreaming will always evade such [computerized] appropriation [and even if, moreover], it inevitably becomes culturally figured as software or content detachable from the self, as something that might be circulated electronically or posted as an online video',[78] this is because *the dream is organological through and through*.

Such a perspective obviously presupposes a critique of Freud in particular and psychoanalysis in general, and this is perhaps why Crary can write that 'we have been in the post-Freudian era for some time',[79] which to me seems a highly doubtful proposition. *On the contrary, we still dwell within a pre-Freudian era*, and this is so firstly because *Freud himself did not allow his own thinking to go all the way* – or his own dreaming, which it remains up to us to interpret.

To interpret. The organology of dreams (and of the unconscious) is *the interiorization and the exteriorization* of the *never finally resolvable* consequences of the detachability of artificial organs and of the resulting tensions between the somatic and social organs, within the psychic individual and within society, and as the *experience of the individual and collective retention and protention of the drives, which these individuals can bind into desire only by unbinding them* – that is, only if they can dis-automatize the social automatisms that bind these neurobiological automatisms.

Desire is constitutively transgressive – and there is an organology of transgression:[80] organology itself proceeds from this transgressivity. This is also why it shocks and stupefies.

41. Against the ideological naturalization of technics and noesis

Crary posits as a principle that our state of fact can and should be transformed into a state of law. We agree, adding that to produce such a passage from fact to law (a passage through *epimētheia* as the reflective *après-coup* of this *promētheia* that is shock), we must in our epoch specify the unprecedented aspects (that are as such shocking and stupefying) of digital tertiary retention, and place this analysis in the service of a supplementary invention as we have advanced the idea through a reading of the exchange between Daney and Deleuze on technologies of control.

At this point we should return to Crary's brief reflections on technical development and innovation, in particular where he challenges historical periodizations based on inventions, innovations and technological mutations that he invokes so as to characterize our own age as a transitional situation.

Crary shows that such a discourse on transition serves an ideology of adaptation[81] to what would then amount to an autonomous development of technics, an idea he rejects, and that he rejects because it is based on naturalizing technics: 'The idea of technological change as quasi-autonomous, driven by some process of auto-poiesis or self-organization, allows many aspects of contemporary social reality to be accepted as necessary, unalterable circumstances, akin to facts of nature.'[82] And indeed the theory of self-organization, just like the 'bottom-up' technologies[83] that seem orchestrated as its exemplification and concretization, often serves a libertarian ideology – such as, for example, that defended by Jimmy Wales, founder of Wikipedia. In this context such a theory leads to a Darwinian conception of the social (which is not that of Darwin himself – nor of course is it the conception of the theoreticians of autopoiesis, Umberto Maturana and Francisco Varela) that is inherent in the 'naturalistic' (that is, biocentric and neurocentric) tendency of the cognitive sciences.

The theory of self-organization, when it is interpreted from a cognitivist perspective, leads to denying any role for heteronomy, and notably for the artefact (that is, for tertiary retention) as a primordial heteronomous factor in noetic individuation. And, in the data networks of data behaviourism, the automatization of the system is based on a hidden heteronomy that is applied as a 'top-down' system to a 'bottom-up' material, treating it at near-light speed, so that this treatment in a way *precedes* it, and makes it submit to a technological performativity of a very specific kind, through which it naturalizes itself or providentializes itself (just as the invisible hand of the market can seem like Providence – which it is for the industry of totally computational data, but we should here recall Greenspan's defence when he faced the US Congress).

The naturalization of the conditions of psychic and collective individuation – that is, of noetic life – is characteristic of the cognitivist programme in its dominant version. This is what makes it possible to deny the need, imposed by the organological and pharmacological situation, for therapeutic prescriptions and decisions: to naturalize technology is also to naturalize the market. It is in *this* way that cognitive science (and with it, and in the first place, Noam Chomsky, who 'naturalizes' Descartes) is made to 'spontaneously' serve a technology of management and marketing that is ever more toxic.

This is also the case for evolutionary understandings of tech-nics, which tend to naturalize it by concealing the social, economic and political dimensions at work: 'In the false placement of today's most visible products and devices within an explanatory lineage that includes the wheel, the pointed arch, movable type, and so forth, there is a concealment of the most important techniques invented in the last 150 years: the various systems for the management and control of human beings.'[84] Beyond the fact that this comment merits further explanation (what is being referred to here as 'tech-niques' should be specified, as well as what is meant by 'important'), the question is that of knowing *why* this managerial technology is *effective*.

My thesis is that *its effectiveness stems firstly from taking advan-tage of a state of fact that has received no critique*, starting from a state of shock that it provokes and that, in the absence of the work of producing new circuits of transindividuation, does not produce the new state of law that it requires.

Crary shows that the 24/7 capitalism that is totally computational capitalism always moves faster than this law. What he then adds, which is very original and useful, is that 24/7 capitalism precedes us and is always there before us, precisely by depriving us *in fact* of the right to dream, and even to sleep, that is, *by annihilating every form of intermittence*, and therefore of any time for thinking. It imposes 'the calculated maintenance of an ongoing state of transition',[85] all in the name of technological development and innovation.

We will nevertheless try to show in the following chapters that *there is still time to think* – to dream the conditions of the realization of dreams – in the contemporary world, and that this possibility passes through a new thinking of automatisms and dis-automatization, whereby automatons will come to serve dis-automatization, which is a matter of conceiving systems and infrastructure founded on digital tertiary retention.

It is necessary for this to occur because *totally computational capitalism is structurally self-destructive, that is, absolutely entro-pic* – and it is the responsibility of everyone, from Crary to our-selves, to create the conditions for establishing a negentropic dynamic starting from the contemporary potential for automatization and dis-automatization.

42. Pharmacology of functional integration

To think this we must combat the 'explanatory lines' ideologized by functional stupidity in the service of speculative financialization. But this means we must always rethink and critique attempts to *rigorously* conceptualize technical evolution and its effects on society – for example, the concept of *technical lineage* put forward by Simondon to think what he called *concretization* as *functional integration* and *transductive amplification*.

All these concepts are quite amenable to a libertarian reading that would interpret them as describing a fundamental autonomy of technics – and Simondon could be utilized in the service of the ideology of marketing, just as Foucault was used by neoliberals and just as Darwin is today being systematically instrumentalized.

A reinterpretation of Simondon's thought with respect to contemporary realities is essential. And it is all the more essential given that what gives rise to techno-geographical milieus in which psychic individuals become, through functional integration, functions of the apparatus of production and consumption is a process of the *concretization* (in the Simondonian sense) of the technical system that the 24/7 infrastructure itself forms qua functional integration of biological, psychic, sociological and technological automatisms. This forms what Simondon called an associated milieu,[86] but in this case of a new type, and one he did not envisage.

Simondon's concepts can be used by libertarian ideology because, like those of Freud (and like *all* concepts – which are concepts only because they are not divine), they are incomplete: they demand that *their individuation be continued* through the process of transindividuation made both possible and impossible by the digital artefacts of functional integration and disintegration that constitute the organological and pharmacological basis of algorithmic governmentality. This should be undertaken by drawing the consequences of the following problems:

- *Simondon never theorized the process of technical individuation*, even though he posited, on the one hand, that the machine is a technical individual that replaces the individual tool-bearer that was the worker, and, on the other hand, that no individual can appear or be conceived outside the process of individuation from which it emerges.
- As we have already pointed out, *in Simondon's mechanology*, which is the study of the concretization of technical individuals, *there is no pharmacology*.
- All this adds up to the fact that the *arrangement between the psychic, the technical and the social is not problematized*.

In forging the concepts of mechanology, functional integration, concretization, associated milieu and transductive amplification, Simondon provided a theoretical apparatus singularly pregnant for an understanding of automatic society. But the latter, insofar as it constitutes a new stage of the threefold process of psychic, collective and technical individuation, also gives rise to new problems that call for new concepts.

43.   Transitions and phase shifts

Having posited all this, let us return to Crary's comment concerning the imposition of an ongoing – that is, permanent – state of transition. This indubitable state of fact hurtles forward, yet it is also a fable (and more precisely a 'storytelling'[87]) that is all the more effective inasmuch as it is auto-suggestive, having its source in what Joseph Schumpeter described as 'creative destruction'[88] – and of which the welfare state as conceived by Roosevelt and Keynes was a state of law consolidated on an international scale via the Philadelphia Declaration, as Alain Supiot explains.[89]

It is this state of law that has been liquidated by the neoliberalism of the conservative revolution, and it has done so in order to restore a state of fact and to improve a rate of profit that by the early 1970s was in significant decline.[90] This *restoration* was imposed in order to create a global economic war between nations, a war called globalization – and it was effected by exploiting the audiovisual media, which have themselves been globalized. In the preceding period, these 'industries of the imaginary', as they were called by Patrice Flichy,[91] constituted an industry of dreams in the service of capital: Hollywood, factory of dreams.

The neoconservative and ultra-liberal turn creates an industry of bad dreams and nightmares by systematically exploiting the drives – and the destructive drives – which can no longer be bound by desire. Then, starting in 1993 with digital reticulation, and after the final collapse of the Eastern bloc, the 'old-fashioned' conservative revolution makes way for an ultra-liberal libertarianism[92] that exploits mimetism, exhibitionism and voyeurism via a digital media that forms new artificial crowds, but that also constitutes a laboratory of new forms of individuation, which arise as alternatives to disindividuating consumerism and which make the critique of new conservatism highly complex.

During this time, however, creative destruction turns into destructive destruction, something that becomes visible, even if it does not become totally clear (far from it), with the crisis of 2008. And it is as an alternative to the exhausted consumerist model that the data economy and more generally the 'iconomy' (as Michel Volle calls it[93]) is imposed on the basis of a new shock caused by the appearance of the web – leading, with social networking and big data, to the dissolution of everyday life via the automatized grammatization of existences.

Marc Giget has shown that the first question raised by this economy, which awaits its state of law, is another state of fact – one that accompanies that state of fact which Anderson claims is insurmountable, in terms of the 'end of theory'. This other state of fact is largely occluded in France: the fact that the destruction of employment by the digital seems in this economy to always be more important than the creation of new jobs.[94]

It is starting from this question that we must critique the 'storytelling' of the permanent transition. This story assumes that the model of creative destruction could continue to infinity, which is absolutely false, not only because the finitude of resources clearly constrains 'growth' (which is the current name for 'creative destruction'), not only because it produces negative externalities that are ever more costly and toxic for the entire system, but also because, in addition to the speculative pressure on purchasing power exerted since the 1980s that ultimately led to the subprime mortgage system, it is now destroying the functional pair 'employment/purchasing power', that is, production/consumption.

It is difficult to decide whether Crary himself takes seriously the auto-suggestive and self-fulfilling fable of permanent transition – as he seems to suggest when he writes that 'there never will be a "catching up" on either a social or individual basis in relation to continually changing technological requirements'[95] – or if, on the contrary, he denounces it. If what he is saying here is that technics will always continue to individuate, or (and for us this is the same thing) that the *de-phasing* of the noetic soul that is the psychic individual's phase shift with itself (which for Simondon constitutes the dynamic of psychic individuation) lies in its individuating itself collectively, and in the fact that this collective is organologically and therefore technically constituted, and that technical individuation is what leads to the resolution of phase shifts only at the cost of instigating new phase shifts,[96] and that individuation is thus *always* in relative transition, that is, in *metastable* equilibrium (hence in relative disequilibrium) – if he is saying all this, then we can only agree.

But if he is suggesting that this individuation will *always and forever* run counter to psychic individuation and counter to social individuation, then we must disagree: such a becoming (which would be the linear extension of the current curve of technological innovation qua destructive destruction) is inevitably self-destructive because technical individuation can continue only *with* psychic and collective individuation – and it is at present destructive in the very short term, and not just on the environmental and mental planes, but also on the economic plane. Failing the occurrence of a historical bifurcation, it will become *militarily* self-destructive – 'big data' being designed for the purpose of dataveillance in relation not just to marketing but also to military 'intelligence', whose endpoints now include drones as well as missiles.

The fable of permanent transition would have us believe that a constant, accelerated transformation of the world by technological innovation, itself controlled by speculative marketing, is unavoidable. It would have us believe that *there is no alternative*. To oppose this fable is to affirm that we are indeed living through a transition – which can be understood on the basis of the metaphor of 'metamorphosis' as the appearance of new somatopsychic, technical and social forms and organizations – but that this is not merely a technological transition (firstly because nothing is ever merely technological), and is instead *an organological chrysalis in three dimensions* constituting *three correlated individuations*, that is, occurring through a process of psychic, technical and social transindividuation, even though there are conflicts between and within these three dimensions.

It is a question of knowing what exactly is in transition. And more precisely it is a matter of knowing to which processes of individuation one is referring. To investigate this question, the organological approach analyses the evolution of the transductive relations that connect the somatic organs, artificial organs and social organizations, these organs being formed *through* these relations and through their evolution, so that they are constituted by what Simondon called transductive amplifications.[97]

44.   Transition, dreaming and transindividuation – towards the Neganthropocene

Clearly a transition is underway, and it is between two industrial models:

- consumerism, founded on Taylorism, the culture industries (as described by Adorno) and the welfare state designed to directly and indirectly redistribute productivity gains in the form of the wages of employees who are not just producers but consumers, that is, equipped with purchasing power;

- a fully automatized society where employment has disappeared, and hence where wages are no longer the source of purchasing power, in turn implying the disappearance of the producer/ consumer, which clearly requires the *institution of a new process of redistribution* – redistributing not purchasing power, but *time*: the time to constitute forms of knowledge (including purchasing knowledge, that is, knowledge of social practices governing use values and exchange values according to practical values and societal values).

Knowledge takes time. It takes nighttime to sleep and dream, and daytime to think, reflect and act by determining the contents of good and bad nightdreams and daydreams in order to materialize and transmit them and to receive them from others, and also to struggle: to learn what results from dreams and reveries, the reflections, theories and inventions of others. It takes time to confront the time of realized and de-realized dreams, time perhaps for what the Australian Aborigines called 'Dreaming': time to deliberate and decide, by *inscribing* oneself in new circuits of transindividuation formed by these dreams, and by *pursuing* them through *bifurcations* that disautomatize them.

This transition, which is also a specific time of intermittence, if it is to lead *positively* to its end, requires the supplementary invention of a *political organology*, given that what is at stake and what is emerging at the end of this 'metamorphosis' is *another social organization supported by new digital organs* – producing a new 'technical system' in Bertrand Gille's sense.[98] The origin of this metamorphosis lies in the initial shock of this transition, which must be socialized and configured through a new social organization, itself transindividuated through therapeutic invention and stimulated by the new *pharmakon*.

There are technological transformations, and among them, some provoke changes of the technical system. This is the case with digital technology. And among the changes of the technical system, some provoke civilizational change: this was the case for writing by hand and for printing, and it is clearly also the case for the digital technical system. But when this kind of transformation occurs, it in fact gives rise to a new form of human life, as happened in the epoch of the Upper Palaeolithic and then the Neolithic.

A transformation of this magnitude is telluric in the sense that, shifting the soil on which the most solid and most ancient edifices have been built, it overturns every aspect of the foundations of life, and not just of the life of human beings. It is a transformation of this magnitude, so extraordinary that it seems to go beyond the limits of History and Proto-History, that we refer to as the Anthropocene.

What is at stake in the new social organization that we must dream, conceive and realize – that is, establish and institute as the *therapeia* of the new *pharmakon* – is the time of knowledge that can and must be *gained* by and through automatization, time that it is a question of *redistributing*. To do so we must make an exit from Taylorism, Keynesianism and consumerism by *organizing the economy and society differently, including the elaboration and transmission of knowledge itself.* And achieving this requires a *supplementary invention* leading to a *categorial invention*, that is, to a fundamental epistemic change itself opening onto a reinvention of academic institutions as well as the editorial and publishing industry.[99]

To anticipate and prepare this, that is, to *mobilize and form* the social forces capable of bearing and inventing it, we must anticipate the new shock that will soon happen – and that will be extremely brutal, because it bears within it the end of employment. We must engage resolutely and without delay in the social change called for by the current period of transition that passes through this new technological shock of generalized automatization and therefore of robotization. The mutation of the conditions of production currently underway means that the exit from the industrial world founded on employment and redistribution via wages is going to occur no matter what. Failure to anticipate and negotiate this change will only provoke an explosion of violence.

Either *generalized* automatization – the effects of which are being felt in all dimensions of existence and in all sectors of the economy, dis-integrating the one (existence) as well as the other (the economy) – will occur through the sheer force of fact, unleashing a clash of particular and national interests, or it will lead to the establishment of a new state of law that must become the object of a global negotiation at all local levels and as the constitution of what, borrowing a term from Mauss, we call the *internation*.[100]

It is the absolute role and interest and the urgent priority of Europe to advocate for this other path at the level of the international organizations that are the United Nations, the International Labour Organization, the World Trade Organization, the World Bank and the International Monetary Fund, but also within the World Wide Web Consortium.

Before examining this subject in greater detail, which is the heart of this book, and before further analysing, from the perspective of a *government of the future*, the concept of algorithmic governmentality that describes the general framework within which the conditions of shock have been set in place, we should recall some elementary principles with respect to the technical evolution of noetic life, in order to analyse the functional possibilities of articulating the evolutions of technics with the time of dreaming.

The algorithmic governmentality imposed by computational 24/7 capitalism will become an automatic *society* (rather than a 'dis-society') only if it makes technics serve arrangements between the times of intermittence and the times submitted to subsistence, between automatisms and their dis-automatization, the latter projecting consistences. In a society where knowledge becomes the primary productive function (and the first if not the only one to have seen this was Marx), the *new value* that will re-found the economy and politics will no longer be the time of employment, but the time of knowledge, that is, *negentropy*, constituting a *neganthropy* and opening the age of the *Neganthropocene*.

45. Expression of tendencies and digital madness

To think the functionality of such neganthropic arrangements between the time of automatons (that is, of technics) and the time of dreams (that is, the time of knowledge – consider the dream of d'Alembert[101]), we must mobilize the concepts of André Leroi-Gourhan and Bertrand Gille and coordinate them with Simondonian concepts.

Leroi-Gourhan showed why and how, when we observe evolution in the field of technics, we must always distinguish between *technical tendencies* and *technical facts* – facts that are quite often expressions of counter-tendencies. For example, when a large energy producer, such as an oil or electricity corporation, buys a renewable energy company, it is generally a negative expression of the tendency borne by these new types of energy: the operator buys the new operator, if not to 'kill' it (an expression commonly used in these operations), at least to control it and hold back the evolutionary tendency that it expresses, that is, in order to subject this tendency to the retrograde logic and dynamic of the historical interest of the purchaser – retrograde in that what hitherto *was* innovative, through which a secure income could previously have been generated, has become archaic.

Many potential technological developments are thereby diverted and inverted by market realities (which are today the major if not the only prescribers of technical facts). From the perspective of general organology, the play of technical tendencies and counter-tendencies as technical facts is always transductively arranged with the play of psychic tendencies and counter-tendencies (such as the pairs Eros/Thanatos, libido/drives, reality/pleasure, sublimation/ regression, and so on) and with that of social tendencies (forming metastable equilibriums composed of synchronic tendencies and dia-chronic counter-tendencies).

The neoliberal current is imposed by taking control of these arrangements via the economic system, by directly and functionally articulating and integrating it with the evolution of the technical system, and by thus short-circuiting the other social systems (which concretize and metastabilize the processes of collective individuation) at the risk of destroying them, which is also to say, of disintegrating psychic individuals. But at the same time, far from liberating the evolutionary potential borne by the technical system in the form of technical tendencies in Leroi-Gourhan's sense, it has bridled and repressed its expression in the direction of its own interests, some-thing that is particularly noticeable in the evolution of the web.[102]

In general, the play of psychic individuation and collective individ-uation, which weaves itself by writing a history composed of circuits of transindividuation, is made possible by technical individuation[103] that conditions the conservation of traces in all their forms, and, consequently (and through what I have called retentional systems), conditions both the metastabilization of the diachronic and the syn-chronic and the sharing out of the transindividual.

The technical 'supplement' is in a general way a tertiary retention insofar as it constitutes a third functional memory (as a vital condi-tion) for the technical living thing that is the noetic being. Noesis occurs only intermittently[104] by distinguishing, within ordinary time, those extraordinary times when consistences form. Noesis enters into its current fullness, as we have known it since *Homo ludens*,[105] and as we recognize ourselves in it, only with the commencement of the prehistory of grammatization that begins with the appearance of rup-estral hypomnesic tertiary retentions, which Marc Azéma presented as dream projections (such would be the specificity of *Homo ludens*), and which will engender the *hypomnēmata* that lie at the foundation of the powers of the great proto-historical and historical civilizations.

With respect to these epochs of grammatization, the contemporary history of the industrial exploitation of hypomnesic tertiary reten-tions via the digital and the data economy is exceptional in that it functionally articulates them with the psychic secondary retentions of individuals in the service of purely industrial and economic purposes, thereby taking computerized control of the formation of collective secondary retentions that are the basis of transindividuation – this is unprecedented and cannot last: it leads to madness.

It leads to madness because it is based on an automated repression of what, in the noetic soul – that is, the desiring and idealizing soul, trans-forming its drives into investments – individuates potentials for individuation concealed in preindividual funds in the form of trauma-types, that is, of defaults and accidents engendered from wounds awaiting liberation via an individuation capable of becoming a quasi-cause. We will see in the next two chapters how algorithmic govern-mentality represses (in both senses) these potentials for individuation.

Traumatypes are wounds that the noetic soul treats by dream-ing. Individuation is what transforms this oneiric care into social-ized care through relations with other noetic souls affected by other traumatypes that create an echo. Technical tendencies, which are organological tendencies, are themselves carriers of potentials for the liberation of such traumatypes. But they may also be diverted into technical facts that, far from contributing to the expression of these traumatypes, repress them. In the contemporary context this repres-sion occurs by taking control of these relations, as we will see with Berns and Rouvroy.

46. Technical facts and the end of work

Everything described by Crary in his analysis of 24/7 capitalism amounts to what Leroi-Gourhan called technical facts. But beneath these facts there are technical tendencies that compose with psychic tendencies and social tendencies – which in turn compose with them. These compositions form the transductive relations to which we referred previously.

To constitute a state of law beyond the contemporary state of fact is to institute the possibility and the obligation to *deliberate* about these tendencies – and it is *to re-found knowledge*, as the transindi-vidual framework of such deliberations, on taking account of supple-mentary invention (on the organological dimension of any *epistēmē*) and on categorial invention (as constitutive of 'regimes of truth' established through processes of individuation), as will be seen later.

Through the composition and the amplifying transductivity of the three spheres, tendencies find expression in the form of facts that, most of the time, conceal these tendencies. This is so because market-ing seizes hold of these tendencies, diffracting them. The diffraction of tendencies began not with marketing but with the first known human groups – this is what Leroi-Gourhan established, initially by studying the Asiatic tribes of the Pacific that he visited in the late 1930s.

Marketing today has the goal of facilitating the penetration of technical tendencies by 'diffracting' them (that is, by limiting or even inverting them, as we have seen) into *social milieus* so that they constitute *politically and territorially unified local syntheses* of what Bertrand Gille called social systems. As such, strategic marketing, whose aims are worldwide, is an avatar of what we conceive more generally in the history of technics as the innovation process but on a global level and ignoring local constraints.

Innovation consists in adjusting the individuation of the technical system (what Gille called technical evolution) and the individuation of the social systems (collective individuation, and the psychic individuation of those who contribute to the formation and maintenance of these social systems). The strategies of the conservative revolution, and of ultra-liberalism more generally, have consisted in short-circuiting the political processes governing innovation – that is, of social change envisaged as based on the deliberative taking account of technological change: what we call progress.

This elimination of political power, which is normally derived from political debate, both having been discredited (made useless, reduced to nothing – *nihil*), and which is also called governance, has been effected by ensuring that strategic marketing dictates the directions and conditions of innovation, and does so in the name of economic war, presented (and inverted in the political discourses justifying this war) as the 'battle for jobs'.

Political discourse would therefore supposedly need to adapt to this war in order to 'save jobs', even though the lords of this war are in fact engaged in a war against employment, that is, to reduce payrolls by 'downsizing' and by pitting national and regional territories against one another. This often leads these territories to bankruptcy, and not just in Europe,[106] even though the latter is undoubtedly the big loser in this turn of capitalism – and this is the primary significance of the European election results of 25 May 2014.

In this way the innovation that produced the creative destruction of the consumerist capitalism of the twentieth century became the functional destroyer of the social systems, and did so through a functional disintegration in which it is not only psychic individuals who are transformed into divided segments: regions and territories, where collective individuations had hitherto been produced and synthesized, are also being disintegrated. But this kind of asocial (that is, anomic) functioning obviously cannot last, and cannot last because it will reach its endpoint: soon there will no longer be any jobs left to eliminate.

47. The quasi-causality of capital itself

As creative destruction becomes destructive destruction, technological becoming and the bifurcations that it produces provide competitive advantages to businesses in the war they are undertaking on a planetary scale, but at the cost of mobilizing and destroying all available earthly resources – physical, biological, mental and retentional (heritage).

In this context the regular mutations of the now-global technical system continue to accelerate, and the resulting technological shocks occur at an increasing rhythm that totally computational capitalism aims to exploit economically, just as it aims to produce a state of stupor that will leave it free to undo the circuits of transindividuation that are the legacy of several thousand years of civilization. It is a singular page of the doubly epokhal redoubling that is here being written, a sorrowful page, where everyone feels that the entire future of humanity is at stake.

What Gille described as the succession of disadjustments and readjustments that occur in the course of human history between technical systems and social systems at an accelerating rhythm – a succession that becomes dramatized, conscious and thematized after the industrial revolution – corresponds on each occasion to what occurs between the two forms of *epokhē* that are, on the one side, the technological shock that interrupts and suspends established social practices, and, on the other side, the new social practices that arise in its aftermath, generating circuits of transindividuation constitutive of a new epoch. This corresponds to the passage from a supplementary invention to a categorial invention that forms new retentional systems.

For twenty years, the precipitation of innovation has had two aspects: Western capitalism's strategic attempt to maintain control of its worldwide extension; and a technological factuality whose time came via digital grammatization, when industrialized and automatized reticular writing was generalized with the web. The ability of global capitalism to make what it neither planned nor wanted into its own necessity[107] is here both astounding and admirable: in a few years what Fred Turner called 'digital utopia'[108] has become the new regime of global capitalist governance via algorithmic governmentality, and notably through those who John Doerr, 'manager of the Kleiner Perkins venture capital fund, called the "four horsemen of the apocalypse"'.[109] This was possible only because there is also a quasi-causal force at work in capital itself (a quasi-causality of capital), through which it seizes hold of the accidental events that it provokes and turns them, in an *après-coup*, performatively and retroactively into a quasi-cause – as when it seized hold of critiques made of it by the theories that emerged from its dis-automatization.[110]

This is so because totally computational capital transindividuates technical individuation in a profoundly irrational way, which it transforms into social individuation. The problem is that this 'individuation' is entropic and leads to disindividuation.

Until now it has compensated for and 'corrected' its irrationality by integrating the critique to which it itself gave rise. Now, however, algorithmic governmentality tends to structurally eliminate this critique, by replacing it with *automatic correction in real time*, and we will see how Berns and Rouvroy describe this process. This becoming is a loss of the spirit of capitalism, as analysed by Weber and then by Boltanski and Chiapello, and which I myself have attempted to describe in *The Lost Spirit of Capitalism*.

Up until it completely loses its mind and spirit, the force of capitalism is quasi-causal, and it consists in transforming the unwanted effects it generates into necessities, that is, into quasi-causes of its power. Hence we cannot follow Crary when he writes that television and other related apparatus 'are part of larger strategies of power in which the aim is not mass-deception, but rather states of neutralization and inactivation, in which one is dispossessed of time'.[111] The apparatus in question – especially those devices that arise with the reticularity of 24/7 capitalism – was not the fruit of strategies of power, but the concretization of a process of exteriorization that is as old as humankind, which is fundamentally accidental, artefactual and artificial, which becomes at the end of prehistory a process of grammatization, and the question of which is raised for the first time in the history of thought by Marx, in *The German Ideology* and then in the *Grundrisse*.

The strategies of power that seize hold of this dynamic and its apparatus do not have as their fundamental goal the 'neutralization and inactivation' of those masses that we also call 'crowds'. This state of fact is not a *goal* of capital: it is a *functional consequence* of compensatory processes resulting from the current innovation of defaults generated by past innovations – defaults that today fundamentally consist in a destruction of libidinal economy. The neutralization and inactivation of the masses are in a way an ideological and functional *windfall* that concretizes and systematizes capital's ability to make a virtue out of necessity – and through which it establishes algorithmic governmentality by seizing hold of this accident.

Clearly there are strategies and programmes directing and pre-scribing research and development in order to reinforce this potential, which is the result of a technical tendency. But the tendency precedes the strategy, while the latter tends to divert it and thereby turn it into a social fact beneficial to the interests of computational capitalism – which at the same time becomes 24/7 capitalism, and introduces a new form of governmentality that will now be examined more closely.

4

Overtaken: The Automatic Generation of Protentions

The knowledge of life must take place through unpredictable conversions, as it strives to grasp a becoming whose meaning is never so clearly revealed to our understanding as when it disconcerts it.

Georges Canguilhem[1]

48. Overproduction, anomie and neganthropy

Over the past decade, digital tertiary retention has brought an unprecedented power to integrate automatisms as well as to disintegrate individuals (psychic and collective), profoundly transforming the organization of consumption through 'crowdsourcing', itself founded on cloud computing,[2] social networking that exploits the network effect, and high-performance computing that exploits 'big data'.

With the IPv6 standard[3] this reticulation, which will be inscribed much more deeply into the internet of things,[4] will constitute the infrastructure of the 'smart cities' that will soon become commonplace. More importantly, over the next ten years digital integration will lead to a *generalization of robotization* in all economic sectors.

Amazon is at the forefront of this evolution:

By the end of the year, Amazon will increase the number of robots on its warehouses tenfold. A cohort that should surpass ten thousand valiant little soldiers, in the words of Jeff Bezos. [...]

The BBC journalist Adam Littler, who as part of a journalistic investigation took an agency job and infiltrated an Amazon warehouse in Swansea in the UK, said of his experience: 'We are machines, we are robots, we plug our scanner in, we're holding it, but we might as well be plugging it into ourselves.' [...] Disgruntled employees may soon be tempted by a cheque of between $2,000 and $5,000 to leave the business. This is one means, according to Jeff Bezos, of 'retaining only the most motivated'. A new programme called 'Pay to leave'.

The robots are manufactured by Kiva Systems, a subsidiary purchased by Amazon two years ago for $775 million.[5]

Fully automated production involves the computerized control of robots integrating design, development, production, logistics and consumption in a loop that functions twenty-four hours a day, seven days a week, and on a global scale. But with the organization of this fully automated production the Fordist-Keynesian model based on wage labour as the operator redistributing purchasing power is itself now disintegrating – after the first 'staggering blow' that was the crisis of 2008.

Full automation in the service of hyper-productive generalized robotization will require a complete reconsideration of redistribution processes, without which the result will be catastrophic overproduction. Increasing productivity enables time to be saved, and it is then a question of knowing how this time should be redistributed. It has been known for some time that the main production function is becoming knowledge. The time saved must therefore consist in time for knowledge, in turn conceived as time for de-proletarianization: as an augmentation and a generalization of the capacities for dis-automatization made possible (the augmentation and the generalization) and necessary (the dis-automatization) by new automatisms.

This presupposes the *rethinking of knowledge itself*, and engaging in research into digital studies through an organological and pharmacological approach that reconsiders the relationship between automatism and autonomy, which philosophy has until now mostly seen as an opposition.

It also presupposes reconsidering the question of right and law from an epistemological and philosophical perspective (as the differentiation of fact and law), from a political perspective (as the constitution of a subject of law and of a public lawful power) and from an economic perspective (as the right to work).

Generalized automatization is a challenge to the right and duty to work, which in the twentieth century became questions of employment, wages and the constitution of purchasing power guaranteeing the sustainability of a system of production founded on the Taylorist model. Taylorism is a specific stage of automatization effected by *mechanical tertiary retention*. With the advent of full and generalized automatization, functionally integrating production and consumption via the mediation of those new artificial crowds provided by 'crowdsourcing', the division of labour of the transformation of matter and information leads to the concretization (in Simondon's sense[6]) of tasks and specializations by robotic technical individuals.

In his analysis of the division of labour, Émile Durkheim highlights that this notion, which describes functional specialization, is also relevant in biology and zoology: '[T]he law of the division of labour applies to organisms as well as to societies. It may even be stated that an organism occupies the more exalted a place in the animal hierarchy the more specialised its functions are.'[7] Everything occurs today as if this division of labour, concretizing a functional specialization that we already find between organisms and within a single organism (as their organs), and that will be specialized by human beings and organized in societies, is now drifting towards a technological differentiation of ever more autonomous technical individuals – becoming with digital technology *almost* totally autonomous... but *not quite*.

And the entire issue lies here – what Greenspan claimed in defending himself before Congress, for example, in fact showed that total automatization is an ideological fact. If this is of course not what he said, it is nevertheless what he made clear.

The evolution that led to *almost* total autonomization of the organs of production expresses what Leroi-Gourhan called technical tendencies, concretized in the form of what he called technical facts. To constitute a law is to constitute the quasi-causality of tendencies so that the technical facts coincide as strictly as possible (almost) with the tendencies and with the best conditions of psychic individuation and collective individuation, thereby constituting what Durkheim called organic solidarity.[8]

In other words, it is a question of creating functional solidarity for psychic, collective and technical individuations against the anomic tendencies clearly borne by almost total automatization. Truly total automatization is impossible: it could occur only by destroying the conditions of its own functioning, namely, in this instance, the psychic individuals and social individuals without which some *purely* automatic functioning could do nothing other than turn the earth into a desert – that is, entropize it.

The best conditions for psychic individuation here are those that allow the *valorizing* of the time of psychic individuals so that their knowledge, that is, their capacity to produce bifurcations with automatons and the instruments that they are, and which are spontaneously entropic factors, instead becomes an agent of neganthropy, through a solidarity that we prefer to call organological rather than organic, that is, through a structural reduction of anomie.

49.   The improbable, technics and time

To think the role of technics in knowledge is firstly to think the role of technology in contemporary society on a basis other than that which currently predominates – in particular because there is confusion about the relationship between technical tendencies and technical facts.

At the start of the becoming that is totally computational capitalism, no strategies are involved, neither to deceive the masses through the use of algorithmic machines, nor to 'neutralize and inactivate' them by these means. This occurs *de facto*. But this fact is an outcome of the appropriation of diffracted universal technical tendencies, tendencies that *precede* all such strategies. I insist on this point because it is only through the *rational, that is, neganthropic*, appropriation of these tendencies, and by collective individuations instituting a process of transindividuation, and thereby constituting psychic individuals, that the outcome can be a *state of law*.

In the first moment of the epokhal redoubling induced by a change in the technical system – causing a suspension of the existing behavioural programmes – capital *always* exploits the resulting short-circuits in circuits of transindividuation, circuits that have themselves emerged from the previous epoch of the epokhal redoubling. In this way systems of proletarianization are created, which allow for a large amount of surplus value to be captured and productivity gains to be thereby achieved. But the organization of these short-circuits is not undertaken deliberately: they are the result of technological evolution, that is, organological and pharmacological evolution.

It was not 'capitalists' who conceived Vaucanson's automatons or the steam engine. It was two noetic individuals (Jacques Vaucanson and James Watt) who dreamed up these supplementary inventions, Vaucanson continuing a concatenation of technical inventions dating back to ancient Egypt, and Watt individuating work dating back to Hero of Alexandria, via Denis Papin and Thomas Newcomen – and conjoining it with capital through his encounter with Matthew Boulton, just as Vaucanson would pave the way for a similar arrangement between his automatons and industrial production via Marie-Joseph Jacquart.

It is because critical theory – this term often referring in America and the Anglophone world today more or less to political thought – is yet to elaborate a theory of the *technicity* of *all* noetic life (that is, its *own* technicity) that this becoming in which 24/7 capitalism and algorithmic governmentality encloses us, absurd and without future as it may be, can become hegemonic – and suicidal. Here it is striking to note the impasse that Hartmut Rosa reaches, on this question as on many others, when he claims to re-found the Frankfurt School project on a theory of social time by criticizing 'the "forgetfulness of time" in twentieth-century social-scientific theory, which notoriously preferred "static" models of society', and by proposing to rebuild critical research on 'a systematic theory of social acceleration'.[9]

Rosa aims to follow on from previous works that had, at the heart of their critical propositions, 'the *relations of production* (the approach of the older critical theory), the *relations of understanding* (Habermas), or the *relations of recognition* (Honneth), all of which involve normative criteria and empirical anchorings that seem to be increasingly problematic'.[10] After these founding perspectives of contemporary critique, work is needed that 'emphasizes a critical diagnosis of *temporal structures*'.[11] Such a perspective is entirely in accord with our own. But it is not possible to invest in this perspective without completely re-elaborating the question of time, starting from the technical fact and its transformation into law (in the broad sense, and not just as positive and political law) under pressure from tendencies and related evolutionary processes. Such an analysis of temporalization must reconstitute the processes of psychic individuation and collective individuation on the basis of the technological shocks that punctuate the prehistoric, proto-historic and historical ages.

Law defines the rules of the social temporality of decision-making, and it is itself constrained by retentional and technical systems that, in the absence of theory and critique, sink into the formalism denounced in particular by Marxists – which is also to say by the Frankfurt School, at least in the initial version of its project.

Digital machines, algorithms and infrastructures participate *after the fact* in strategies that aim in the first place not at mass-deception, nor at 'neutralizing or inactivating' the masses, but at *exploiting them as resources of which they take no care*, and, from this perspective, exploiting them without any biopolitics, inasmuch as biopower also consists, to an extent at least, in 'taking care' of life so as to be able to exploit it. Indeed, the strategies analysed and denounced by Crary lead to a carelessness that could be called '(a)biopolitical'.

Nevertheless, this carelessness is not a *goal* – and the issue is not, first of all, evil but stupidity, which clearly engenders evil – but a *contradiction*, or, if one prefers, a *limit*. This limit, which is a passage to the limits in the sense that it is the system in its totality that finds itself invalidated by its *careless functioning* (based on carelessness), results from the fact that these after-the-fact strategies utilized by 24/7 capitalism to appropriate digital artefactuality consist in the attempt to integrate it into a consumerist model that is based on the functional pair 'production/consumption', itself founded on the redistribution of purchasing power. To concretize the technical tendencies borne by automatization by utilizing such factual strategies (conducted without any care to establish a state of law) is, however, to make this redistribution and therefore this functional pair *strictly impossible*.

To combat this state of fact and establish a state of law is to oppose to this economic irrationality an integrated rationality, that is, to invent a new epoch of care,[12] at a moment when the earth and earthlings have need of this as never before, a care that could only be a new epoch of and therefore *a redefinition of rationality*, in such a way that it would not be limited to calculability and scientific apodicticity: *taking care above all of the improbable*.[13]

50.   The truth of the digital and its denial

In this respect, algorithmic 'governmentality', as it *exists* today in facts but *does not consist in law*, is no doubt still not a regime of truth in Foucault's sense, and what Thomas Berns and Antoinette Rouvroy argue at the beginning of their analysis, namely that 'the new regime of digital truth is embodied in a multitude of new automated systems modeling the "social"',[14] is a promise, or a potential law, more than a reality. The reality is the state of fact, and this, on the contrary, amounts to the *denial* of this promise: *this is to say in effect that this state of fact no longer has any need for the 'truth'*. It just needs 'results' – and they are performative. But this is not openly declared, still less analysed.

There is no doubt that the digital, insofar as it constitutes a new regime of tertiary retention and promises unprecedented and more consistent possible arrangements of psychic and collective retentions and protentions, bears within it a new regime of truth. But, firstly, the digital is not reducible to what is here described as governmentality, that is, the computational data economy. And, secondly, what Foucault called a regime of truth produces 'truth' through *alethurgy*,[15] that is, knowledge founded in one way or another on a heuristic process, however historically determined and therefore limited it may be.

The digital as Berns and Rouvroy describe it in their article is on the contrary *devoid of any heuristic*, as is also the case in Chris Anderson's cynical discourse – which assumes in turn that this state of fact has definitively abolished any differentiation between fact and law.

The way in which Berns and Rouvroy characterize algorithmic governmentality therefore describes a transition – and I will try to show in the second volume of *Automatic Society* that the formation of a regime of truth is precisely the weaving of new circuits of transindividuation, based on new retentional systems, themselves controlling new conditions of certification. All this occurs in the gap, the interruption or the intermittence opened up by a doubly epokhal redoubling, that is, by *a technological shock that always begins by destroying socially recognized intermittences* and that leads the noetic souls who suffer this shock to dream *otherwise*, and to create bad dreams as well as sweet dreams, always at the risk of provoking new nightmares.

Algorithmic 'governmentality' will be capable of *producing any truth whatsoever* – that is, *not lead to pure anomie* – only in and through a profound transformation. What is a regime of truth? And what is the truth of the digital? This is also a question of knowing in what knowledge today consists, that is: what is its *necessity?*

Today, knowledge must formalize, in the form of new circuits of transindividuation, the tendencies borne by the doubly epokhal redoubling, so that it expresses *social* facts, that is, *non-anti-social facts*. Hence knowledge must struggle against the anti-sociality and anomie marked and noted by Berns and Rouvroy with quotation marks, when they refer to the 'multitude of new automated systems modeling the "social"', which would thereby constitute the possibility of a new regime of algorithmic truth.

Anti-social facts are those that destroy social systems (in Gille's sense). This is what occurs when the economic system – which exceeds the territorial limits of the social systems, so that in this respect it is not a social system like the others – tends to take control of the other social systems in order to indenture them to a technical system that this economic system itself, having become essentially international, totally controls, and by diffracting technical tendencies exclusively for its own benefit.

For centuries knowledge has *completely ignored* technical tendencies – and it did so because of a metaphysical repression that I have tried to analyse in *The Fault of Epimetheus*,[16] and that continued up until Deleuze and Derrida. (Foucault and Simondon, inspired greatly by Canguilhem, in this respect bring totally new prospects and perspectives, even if they cannot be considered sufficient for us today.)

Algorithmic governmentality urgently requires a retrospective analysis of the technical constitutivity of the social fact in general and of technical life in general, that is, of hominization, the latter conceived by Canguilhem, like Leroi-Gourhan, as the production of artificial milieus. This 'organalysis' must make it possible to anticipate crossing a threshold through which the digital doubly epokhal redoubling *would provide* the *improbable* time of the constitution of a *new epoch of non-inhumanity conceived as neganthropology.*

From such a perspective the question of innovation must be taken very seriously – and not just treated as an ideological discourse based on the storytelling of marketing. Innovation clearly has a real economic function: it evidently constitutes a production of negentropy. But what has now become obvious is that this negentropy produced in the short term generates far higher entropy in the long term.

The whole question of organology and its pharmacology in the neganthropic field resides in the fact that the *pharmakon* can be toxic and curative only to the extent (and in the excess) that it is both entropic and negentropic. If innovation is a negentropic factor that has become massively entropic, especially since the conservative revolution, how could a new industrial political economy lead to a new production of negentropy – and to new terms for thinking innovation, that is, technological differentiation?

In the context of full and generalized automatization, neganthropy must proceed from a *social innovation* that reinvents the adjustments between the social systems and the technical system, and does so according to a model where it is no longer the economic system, and the technological innovation it requires, that prescribe the social. It must on the contrary be a model in which social innovation, founded on different economics – on a contributory economy – and on a reinvention of politics, conceived as therapeutics, prescribes technological innovation, that is, organological evolution, and does so by *interpreting* technical tendencies.

Such a becoming is highly improbable. Yet it alone is the bearer of the future, that is, of the rational. This means that the rational, far from being that which is more probable, is on the contrary that which is more *improbable* (the most probable is by nature entropic). We will see in the second volume of *Automatic Society* what consequences should be drawn from this, not only for regimes of truth but also for the truth at which these regimes all aim (unlike Anderson, and unlike algorithmic governmentality in the way that it currently and generally functions), and which, *through this aiming alone*, constitutes them *as* regimes *of truth.*

51. Retentions, promises, protentions

We must have time to decide: this is what we say, as does Crary and as do Berns and Rouvroy, and what they show is that everything is being done so that *this is no longer able* to take place. Like Crary, Berns and Rouvroy posit that in algorithmic governmentality a kind of doubling occurs, of which they analyse the conditions of production. And like Crary, but in other ways, they show that intermittence, that is, the time of individuation, has been suspended, and that this occurs through the constitution of a technology that automatically and performatively generates protentions.

Within algorithmic governmentality, there is no longer any time to dream because the *oneiric soul*, which the psychic and noetic individual had hitherto been, is now always *preceded* by its digital double, derived from the industrial traceology that is the data economy. This digital double in effect *functionally* short-circuits the desires in which dreams consist – and replaces them with individual and collective interactive operating sequences. And we will see that these operating sequences amount to what, fashioning an allegory, we may call *digital pheromones*.[17]

Berns and Rouvroy conduct their analyses by mobilizing concepts from Foucault (governmentality and regime of truth), Simondon (individuation, transindividual, disparation), Deleuze (rhizome) and Guattari (machinic unconscious). But they do so by putting the interpretation of Simondon and Deleuze to the test of digital facts and the tendencies that are expressed within them – and in the service of thinking a state of law that could very improbably but very rationally arise from the *disparation*[18] induced by this state of fact.

It is a matter of putting *facts to the test*, in the sense undertaken by Laurent Thévenot in his analysis of *government by standards and things*, an analysis that

> dismantles the transformations effected by these instruments of government. The first is the replacement of legitimate political authorities with systems for setting standards and the supposedly independent regulation of authorities that are largely beyond any policy or critique.
>
> The profusion of instruments for identifying standards, then the standardization and certification of objects and services, from those most commonly used to global benchmarking, highlights the importance of government by standards in our contemporary political economy.[19]

This puts to the test the critical function of the social sciences in the twentieth century and today. As a result,

> legitimate authority has been displaced and distributed into things, making it difficult to apprehend or to question since it is imposed in the name of realism and loses its political visibility. Critique is paralysed because it seems to have been overtaken and rendered obsolete.[20]

In Berns and Rouvroy's highly rigorous and well-documented analysis of algorithmic governmentality, the digital, which intensifies to an immeasurable extent this *outstripping and overtaking*, and the *abandoning of critique* to which it leads, *might* yet constitute in law a new age and a new democratic promise.

Algorithmic governmentality, however, has proven in fact to be the annihilation of this promise that has been borne and proclaimed since the earliest days of the digital,[21] and the annihilation of everything that goes along with it, and more generally the annihilation of political promise and of politics insofar as it promises.[22] Here more than anywhere we must investigate Nietzsche's thinking of nihilism, which is also and fundamentally a thinking of the promise, with respect to memory (retention), and this is also what is at stake in the 'Second Essay' of the *Genealogy of Morality*.

The algorithmic destruction of the promise is an an*nihil*ation, which leads back to the fact that we live in the epoch[23] of the *completion* of nihilism, if not of *fully* accomplished nihilism: we are living through the phase in which the nihilistic *katastrophē* is in the course of unfolding. *Katastrophē* here refers to the moment of a turn or an outcome, a denouement, that may indeed, as in the structure of the stories of the *Scheherazade*, revive the desire for history and for stories (that is, desire *tout court*), rather than lead to the fulfilment of the death drive.[24]

Under what conditions can a state of law (which would be the culmination of such a *katastrophē*, that is, the denouement of the doubly epokhal redoubling – a state of law that would be founded not necessarily or not only on a rule of law, but on an *internation*[25] and a *new public thing* that would not *only* be related to the state) be envisaged in the digital state of fact, and even *founded* on and *as* this algorithmic governmentality, that is, as an *algorithmic state of law* and, as such, *in effect* as a *regime of digital truth*?

Here it is less a question of knowing under what conditions the digital could reconstitute a subject – a subject of law, that is, a political individual, a noetic psychic individual who has the right and the ability to implement apodictic criteria of truth – than of the *possibility of the reconstitution of a collective individuation* within which alone, in law and in fact, a psychic individuation of the citizen would be possible.

52. Performativity in light-time as the flattening of the world

24/7 capitalism and algorithmic governmentality are the economico-political features characteristic of the automatic society that Berns and Rouvroy also understand as a new regime of truth characterized by *its technological performativity*. This regime of truth is founded on the permanent capture of data, on the computational operations performed on this data, and on the digital doubles that are formed as a result. These digital doubles interact in real time with those whom they double, and with the new data these doubles generate and extract by going faster than those they double – hence producing an immediate retroactive effect on the operating sequences of populations.

The performativity of algorithmic automatisms leads to the destruction of those circuits of transindividuation formed in concert by psychic individuals, and it ends in the liquidation of a process that Simondon described as being founded on what he called 'disparation'. In the physiology of optical perception, disparation refers to the difference between the retinal images of each eye, this difference between two bi-dimensional sources forming a third dimension through which the visual organ perceives depth, constituting a faculty of the projection of volume on the basis of what, in monocular vision, remains flat. We will see how this *putting into relief* is *essential* to processes of collective individuation, and more generally to the formation of what Simondon called the transindividual.

This analysis of disparation in the digital age, and of its effacement, leads thematically to the question of law as such, in particular in Rouvroy. I will argue in what follows that to invest in this question of law, as derived also from the Kantian principle of the subjective differentiation between fact and law, today means starting from the question of *work*, and not just on the basis of a juridical order or a regime of legal truth, which the rational disciplines in general form in the name of an apodictic truth that constitutes their canon.

In a society where employment is in decline and where the main economic value is knowledge, we must rethink the right to know and the law of knowledge as a function of the conception of any productive function, that is, as the *power of dis-automatization.*

These considerations call for detailed analysis of the relationships between law and work in Marx and Foucault in debate with Alain Supiot and Mikhaïl Xifaras.[26] We will only begin to broach this question, which leads to the *prior* question of the *right to interpretation*, constituting a *new question of work* as the *work of interpretation* – of juridical dreams and other fictions, without which there would be no *difference* between states of fact and states of law, that is, between subsistence and existence, and therefore between existence and consistence,[27] as well as between dreams and the realization of dreams inasmuch as they may always become nightmares.

53.   Algorithmic governance and digital territories

Berns and Rouvroy, then, posit above all that algorithmic governmentality amounts to a new regime of truth – while we say it is such a regime only in potential, and not in actuality, the question being that of the passage to the *veridical* act. The new regime of truth 'is embodied in a multitude of new automated systems modelling the "social", both remotely and in real time, highlighting the automatic contextualization and personalization of interactions to do with security, health, administration and business'.[28]

Algorithmic governmentality is based on 'ubiquitous', territorial and environmental spatial technologies, through which the programs of 'smart cities' are today being designed, based on 'autonomic computing' and 'ambient computing', on technologies whose invisibility just makes them all the more active and efficient, as Mark Weiser states: 'The most profound technologies are those that disappear. They weave themselves into the fabric of everyday life until they are indistinguishable from it.'[29]

Computational urbanism is promoted by large equipment manufacturing firms who become at the same time its service providers, and they are currently designing the new infrastructure that will be built and managed regionally. Algorithmic governmentality will thus be exploited and managed on a regional scale and in a systemic and systematic way at all levels of space and time.

According to Saskia Sassen:

> The best known example of an instant smart city is Songdo International Business District, an intelligent city near Seoul that's equipped with advanced sensors and monitors from Cisco Systems, features that

are humorously described by John Kasarda and Greg Lindsay in the new book *Aerotropolis: The Way We'll Live Next*. The city's multi-tasking devices are able to open and close, turn on and off, or stop and start everything from the toaster to the videoconference with your boss to the video camera view of your child at play. All of this can be done from both your home and your office, though the distinction between the two becomes increasingly fuzzy in a fully 'sensored' city. Songdo is also about recycling and greening. It is built on reclaimed land and deploys all the latest green technologies.[30]

Another such city is Masdar City in Abu Dhabi. It has a more specifically commercial vocation and it is 'a laboratory, or what social scientists refer to as a natural experiment [...] that we cannot replicate in the university laboratory'. Beyond even these exceptional cases, Sassen expects that new cities being built in China 'will need to house well over 300 million people in the next few years. Its new cities will be planned and intelligent but they will not be little Masdars, [they] will be giant cities.'[31]

Beyond these examples and in the context of the development of 'open data', digital territories, which all spaces inhabited by people equipped with smartphones and the other apparatus of 24/7 capitalism have become (and there are now very few regions on earth that are not digital in this sense), raise immense questions for regional politics. In this regard, Ars Industrialis posits as a first principle that such regions must develop a *contributory* algorithmic governmentality in the service of *reflexive* digital territories.

This is a key question that all politicians and all local, regional, national and European public servants must pose, given that the digitalization of space and time is a fact on the basis of which we must now think all local life, at a moment when open data has become a standard, and when, in such a context, we cannot and must not reduce a city, or a region, which are territorial and transindividuated syntheses of diverse processes of collective individuation, to the sum of the data collected about them – for all manner of things are *not* collected, fortunately, and are therefore not treated, are not 'given', and therefore do not constitute data, even though it is undoubtedly true that it is those things or entities or information that remain *uncalculated* which constitute the profound and secret dynamism of every territory, and which harbour the future of these territories.

It is also from these perspectives and in these contexts of mobile and immobile, urban and rural property, which are therefore colossal in terms of the issues of economics and power, that we must study the 'automatic [...] personalization of interactions to do with security,

health, administration and business' that are being accomplished in
the form of 'smart marketing', for which smart cities are 'ideal' cities,
and of which Masdar City is the prototype.

54. Algorithmic governmentality as anormative automatic transindividuation

Algorithmic governmentality operates via 'three moments [that] feed
into each other'[32] and through the *automatized confusion* that *calculation outstrips*, and in the form of automatized understanding.
This is an automatized understanding *not just of reason* in its scientific forms, as we saw in analysing the effects of high-performance
computing on *big data, but also will, law and the administration of
decision-making in general* – in the most basic dimensions of everyday life[33] as well as in the military field.

Like any form of governmentality in Foucault's sense, algorithmic
governmentality implements technologies of power founded on statistics. But unlike the conception of statistics coming from Bayes or
Quételet,[34] these continuously traced and collected statistics constitute and mobilize an '(a)normative and (a)political rationality based
on the harvesting, aggregation and automatic analysing of data in
massive quantities in order to model, anticipate and affect in advance
possible behaviours'.[35] This *affecting in advance* – which is, it should
be emphasized, a *new regime of affect* within this 'new regime of
truth' – affects all 'powers to act' as the *automatic production of
the possible reduced to the probable*. It is based on a 'passage from
statistical government to algorithmic government', which is also the
passage from a *public governmentality of the state* – statistics is
the science of the state and of governmentality strictly conceived as
the administration of the public thing, of the *res publica* – to *governmentality as governance by generalized privatization*, which is the
destruction, by a 'hypertrophied private sphere', of 'private life' as
well as of the public thing.

For, indeed, the private and the public constitute a polarity, a transductive pair embodied in Greek mythology in the figures of Hermes
and Hestia: the dis-integration of public space by its privatization is
equally a dis-integration of private life (and of what Crary calls, with
Lefebvre, everyday life).[36]

This new regime of truth – which is therefore a new regime of
statistics and, as such, a technology of power that perhaps invites
us on this basis to take up once again the question of the relations
between power and technology[37] – leaves 'social normativities [...]

mute, since they are not translatable into a digital form',[38] which is to say they are *not calculable*, and are therefore eliminated and short-circuited as well as fixed and substantialized. What results is the 'a-normative character of algorithmic governmentality', which is an *annihilation of transindividuation* (as a process of the everyday realization of normative life in the sense of Canguilhem), insofar as the latter results from constant interpersonal co-individuations, consolidated by impersonal retentional systems, but ones that are *visible and open to critique* – but that are also *internalized* by *instituted* knowledge (such as through primary and secondary schools where they teach the common law of the Republic as well as the 'laws' in general of all knowledge).[39]

The 'datamining' in which consists the treatment of the data constantly collected by algorithmic governmentality – and the constant collection of which replaces the constancy of the interpersonal relations of co-individuation in public and private everyday life – is composed of 'self-learning algorithmic systems [...]. Organized for the purposes of profiling [...], they reconstruct, according to a logic of correlation, the singular cases that are crushed by coding, without relating them to a general standard.'[40]

In other words, this statistics, founded on automatic and personalized traceability, is freed from 'any medium': this *autonomic computing* that is analytically produced *datamining* statistically collects and gathers dividuals, who are scattered like atomic elements emerging from a de-composition (and from a dis-integration[41]), and hence constitutes a process of *automatic transdividuation*.

This automatization of the collection and treatment of data, based on the automatic extraction of correlations, which we examined in the first chapter under the name of 'big data', short-circuits all social normativity in that it *'shunts' or 'bypasses' categories and conventions*. And it does so regardless of whether these categories and conventions are derived from modelling hypotheses, or from public political debate,[42] or from the social organizations implicitly conforming to these norms and standards that, since the nineteenth century, anthropologists have studied in all human societies insofar as they produce their normativity without necessarily being conscious of doing so (and that they support all the more strongly the less conscious they are – critique being a form of the becoming-conscious of these norms).

'Algorithmic governmentality breaks with the conventional origin of statistical information, as described by Alain Desrosières.'[43] This a-normativity makes impossible, functionally and in advance, the critique of this probabilistic and atomic statistics: 'The specific uses of statistics involved in datamining, because they are no longer anchored in any convention, are not [...] generators of public space,'[44] that is, of transindividuation. Here, Berns and Rouvroy describe the process analysed in other terms by Laurent Thévenot, whom they cite. It is this liquidation of critical spaces, enabling the 'colonization of public space by a hypertrophied private sphere', as already mentioned, that is the *basis* of algorithmic governmentality,[45] and that leads to the 'disappearance of common experience', and to the regression of everyday life in Lefebvre's sense (but Rouvroy emphasizes the common more than the everyday, establishing between everyday life and administered life the question of the common that links them as law or right – this is something to which we will return).

As we have seen via Saskia Sassen, the colonization of public space by major players of the 'private sector' passes through the promotion of *digital regions* based on the infrastructures of this algorithmic governmentality, from 'smart cities' to the management of household and domestic space by home automation and ambient computing, but more generally the 'internet of things'[46] as a totally integrated environment of hyper-control, made 'reactive and intelligent [...]' by the proliferation of sensors [...] in order to adapt constantly to specific needs and dangers'.[47]

55.　Automatic immanence and the obsolescence of categories

By referring to governmentality and to a regime of truth, Berns and Rouvroy convoke the concepts forged by Foucault throughout the 1970s and the beginning of the 1980s – concepts which are undoubtedly necessary in order to think the algorithmic and ubiquitous hyper-control that constitutes the confinement-through-modulation that is characteristic of 24/7 capitalism. Here, and without doubt as never before, it is a question of a power of technology to form 'meshes'[48] that are not just extremely fine, but whose size and shape vary according to the 'fish' at the very moment when it approaches – as if they themselves set the parameters of the device that captures them, woven by the implementation of algorithms into these multitudinous sensors. This 24/7 capitalism constituted by the functional integration of consumers precisely realizes what Deleuze anticipated in 1990 when he distinguished the moulds of disciplinary societies from the modulations of control societies: 'Confinements are molds, distinct moldings, but controls are a modulation, like a self-deforming cast that will continuously change from one moment to the next, or like a sieve whose mesh will change from one point to another.'[49] Deleuze is here taking up concepts both from Foucault (for example, the mesh) and from Simondon (modulation).

Conceiving the question of power starting from the concepts of biopolitics and governmentality, Foucault posited as a preliminary consideration that we must 'envisage power from a [...] point of view [that is] technological'.[50] He added that we should distinguish two great classes of such technologies. *Disciplinary* technologies aim 'to control the social body in its finest elements, through which we arrive at the very atoms of society, which is to say individuals'.[51] But there is also 'another family of technologies of power [...] that did not target individuals as individuals, but which on the contrary targeted the population [...,] living beings, traversed, commanded, ruled by processes and biological laws'.[52] This other family of technologies of power includes statistics as a science of the state,[53] whose purpose is 'to utilize this population as a machine for producing [...]. And, from this, a whole series of techniques of observation, including statistics, [...] are charged with this regulation of the population.'[54]

Just as Foucault said of biopower that it aims at populations rather than individuals, in algorithmic governmentality 'subjects are in fact avoided, to the point of creating a kind of statistical double of the subjects',[55] but here the technologies of control of individuals qua individuals (which Foucault called disciplinary) are no longer in play. All this occurs as if disciplinary technologies and statistical technologies have been functionally integrated while functionally dis-integrating individuals in order to produce dividuals, that is, atomic elements on the basis of which it becomes possible, through profiling, to create these doubles (to which Crary, too, refers).

To overcome the conventionalist statistics that Desrosières describes,[56] observation and modulation (rather than discipline) had to be functionally integrated, where it is both individuals (but reduced *in real time* to the status of dividuals) and populations (but addressed in terms that go *beyond the limits of the average* as it has been understood since Quételet[57]) that are functionally and invisibly involved in setting the parameters of their own control, forming an associated milieu of a very specific kind. Hence we see an 'apparent individualization of statistics (with the obvious contradiction this expresses), which no longer passes through (or no longer seems to pass through) references to the average person, giving way to the idea that we ourselves become our own profile, assigned automatically and evolving in real time'.[58] This layer of 'personalization' based on user profiling and social networking, in addition to the probabilistic models that are the foundation of Google's business model, was promoted first by Amazon and its profiling technique, then by social networks, which are fundamentally based on the traceability of their 'users' by themselves – exploiting what Laurence Allard and Olivier Brooks have referred to as expressivism.[59]

The 'individualized' normativity engendered by this technology of power is *a-normative* in the sense that it is never debated, which means that it is *immanent*: 'The mode of government by algorithms claims to address itself to everyone through their profile [...], adhering by default to an immanent normativity rather than that of life itself.'[60]

It is subjectivity and its reflexivity that this *affecting in advance of the subject by its double* renders obsolete, the 'subject' always arriving too late, and never having 'to take account by itself for what it is or what it could become'.[61] It is therefore legitimacy as well as critique that *in fact* become 'obsolete', just as does theory, according to Anderson, and with it its criteria and categories of experiment, hypothesis, model, and so on: 'Algorithmic government has no room for and takes no account of any active, consistent or reflexive statistical subject, capable of legitimating it or resisting it.'[62]

56. Automatic government

Algorithmic governmentality no longer has any need to appeal to subjects because it 'focuses [...] on relations':

> The object of algorithmic government [...] is precisely relations [...]. The knowledge generated consists of relations of relations [...]. As such, this would be [...] a government of relations about which we want now to try to determine what in this algorithmic government is really new.[63]

In so doing, algorithmic governmentality substantializes these relations by reducing them to *correlations* that are thus 'obstacles to processes of individuation' because they dis-integrate the potentials with which these relations were charged, reducing them to nothing, *nihil* – to nothing other than *formalizable and calculable* correlations, that is, defusing in advance the potentials carried by the *disparities* with which psychic individuation abounds and that are *integrated* by collective individuation (which *transindividuates* them in the form of metastable collective protentions):

The becoming and the processes of individuation required for 'disparation', that is, for processes of the integration of disparities or differences in a coordinated system, [...] require the 'disparate': a heterogeneity of orders of magnitude, a multiplicity of regimes of existence that algorithmic governmentality constantly stifles by closing the (digitalized) real in upon itself.[64]

Correlationist calculations and formalizations form three 'moments' of algorithmic governmentality. The first is that of the 'massive harvesting [...] of unsorted data [...], the dataveillance constitutive of big data'.[65]

The second moment is the treatment of this data, that is, an extraction of traits common to these dividuals – thereby 'dividualized' (disindividuated) on the basis of these traits extracted qua *relations* (that is, as statistical *correlations*) formed between these dividuals. Psychic individuals and collective individuals are thereby disintegrated in the course of this extraction of correlations inasmuch as the latter constitutes, as we shall see in greater detail, a performative and self-fulfilling production of *automatic protentions* that liquefy and ultimately liquidate[66] the difference between the performative and the constative.[67]

The second moment, the treatment, is that of

datamining properly speaking [...], knowledge whose objectivity could seem absolute, since it would be kept far from any subjective intervention [...]. The norms and standards seem to emerge from reality itself. These norms or 'knowledges' are, however, constituted only from correlations [and we should] be wary of the auto-performative 'effects' of correlations (their retroactive capacity).[68]

I would go further than just saying that we should be wary: the system *is based* on these 'effects', and only through them does it achieve its efficiency, by means of the intensive computing involved in this battery of algorithmic technologies of power that function at near-light speed.

This performativity, caused by correlations in real time – implementing *feedback loops without perceptible delay* – is what destroys 'the essence of politics [that] is to refuse to act solely on the basis of correlations'.[69] This treatment proceeds by algorithmic profiling 'behind the back' of those who are being profiled: 'The knowledge produced at the level of profiling [...] is usually no longer available to individuals, nor is it perceptible to them, but [it is] still applied to them.'[70] This is so even though the results of the calculations performed upon them, and with which they interact *without knowing it*, modify the trajectories of their individuation. In other words, this treatment calculates them in advance, and remotely controls them, and does so in a way that resembles the way in which a drug may change someone's metabolism, which is why pharmaceutical companies are required to mention these changes and their 'side-effects', failing which they are open to prosecution.[71]

An understanding – if not a consciousness – of the effects of interactive environments on the behaviour of those who live within them is quite conceivable, through which the automatic manipulation and disintegration of psychic and collective individuals would give way to a new process of psychic, collective and technical individuation, based on *a new state of law*, itself *constituted by new forms of tertiary retention*. But this would firstly require certification procedures that do not yet exist in the digital field.

Several authors, such as Viktor Mayer-Schönberger and Kenneth Cukier, have argued that this certification should be provided by specialists – expert data scientists.[72] I, on the other hand, believe that, without excluding the constitution of such bodies, it is through a *massive spread of new ways of certifying* – from secondary school education onwards – that this law and right could find its basis, and could *on this juridical basis become the foundation of a new era of industrial economy*.

It is through the treatment of profiling and the transformation of the relations between dividuals into correlations that the third moment becomes possible, which is that 'of the use of statistical probabilistic knowledge in order to anticipate behaviour', which reveals the fundamental function of algorithmic technologies of power: it is a matter of automatically producing immanent protentions in the reticulated and automated system formed by interconnected networks, thereby integrating them into these procedures. 'The field of action of this "power" is situated not in the present, but in the future.'[73] The *power over individual and collective* protentions acquired through the production of automatic, dividual protentions destroys any collective *outstripping or overtaking by psychic protentions* that could come from psychic and collective secondary retentions. And this also amounts to a mutation of the relation to the possible, to the possible *itself*, so that it is *de-realized in advance*, that is, emptied of its potential bifurcations and disparations:

> This form of government is essentially focused on what might happen, on propensities rather than on actions that are committed

[...]. Algorithmic government does not just see the possible in the actual, producing an 'augmented reality', an actuality endowed with a 'memory of the future', but also gives substance to the dream of a systematized serendipity: our real would become the possible, our norms and standards want to correctly and immanently anticipate the possible, the best way being indeed to present ourselves with a possible to which we correspond and which subjects would need only to slip into.[74]

The logical distinction of these three moments is not chronological at the scale of our own existence: all this, on our scale, that is, our order of magnitude, occurs *at the same time*. And it is precisely this 'same time' that constitutes the specificity of algorithmic governmentality, founded on self-realizing performativity operating through the disintegration of psychic individuals and the outstripping of collective individuals.

The result is an endlessly emerging 'normativity', presupposing the emergence of crowds themselves, crowds that form the 'bottom-up' movements emerging from reticular *horizontalization* and *flattening*, and having no need for categories, that is, for authorities – in perpetual transformation, *constantly still emergent* and, in this sense too, a-normative:

Where [juridical normativity] was given, discursively and publicly, before any action on behaviour [...], statistical normativity is precisely what is never given in advance.[75]

Algorithmic government [that] incites 'needs' or desires for consumption [...] depoliticizes the access criteria to certain places, goods or services [and] devalues politics (since there would no longer be anything to decide, in uncertain conditions where decisions have been defused in advance).[76]

What is at stake here is transindividuation – and, more precisely, the *destruction of the permanent oscillation between synchronizing and diachronizing tendencies*, which must play out together just as normativities are born from the play between the 'top down' and the 'bottom up', that is, between, on the one hand, metastable categorizations that are inherited and/or synchronically instituted, and, on the other hand, categorial invention that continuously places them into question.

Algorithms, which are quicker than reason and which therefore amount to automated understanding, short-circuit the work of creating the *more or less* discursive and deliberative nomenclatures, categorizations and indexations in which any work of transindividuation always consists, in those political, 'lawful' societies[77] – which statistics formalizes and quantifies in various ways according to the currents of thought lying behind it, as noted by Alain Desrosières:

> [S]tatistics is connected with the construction of the state, with its unification and administration. All this involves the establishment of general forms, of categories of equivalence, and terminologies that transcend the singularities of individual situations, either through the categories of *law* (the judicial point of view) or through *norms* and *standards* (the standpoint of economy of management and efficiency).[78]

> Creating a political space involves and makes possible the creation of a space of common measurement, within which things may be compared, because the categories and encoding procedures are identical. The task of standardizing the territory was one of the essential labors of the French Revolution of 1789.[79]

This outstripping or overtaking [*prise de vitesse*], which is an *abandoning or taking-apart of form* [*déprise de forme*],[80] creates a performativity inasmuch as it generates automatic protentions by liquidating conventional categories and normativity. Here we find the functional integration of marketing and ideology operating through the functional integration of consumers into the infrastructures of 24/7 capitalism.

Algorithmic government is an automatic government that claims to be able to function on autopilot, that is, without pilots or thinking (this is Anderson's argument). It 'dispenses with institutions and public debate; it replaces prevention (in favour only of preemption)'.[81] In short, it installs an automatic society – in which there develops a computational, technological performativity, itself *supposedly totally autonomized*.

57. The imperturbable power of algorithmic governmentality and the improbability of the default that is necessary in the incessant

The differentiation of fact [*fait*] and law/right [*droit*] would be that of the accident, on the one hand, and of what becomes the quasi-cause, on the other. The law, or the one who acts by right, would be what or who can say: I am by right and duty making this accident my necessity – by taking care of *that which is necessary*.[82]

But the law is a collective individuation, and not just a psychic individuation, which means that the law would be that of *those* who tell *us* of our transindividuating to ensure it happens to us without our having *seen* it coming, or without our *wanting* to see it coming, as what happens to us *by accident, through a supplementary invention that nobody expected, not even the one who invented it* – since he or she discovers that he or she is surely also the invented as well as the inventor – we want to ensure this happens to us *because it is precisely what we want.*

What we want is, here, not simply the category of the autonomous subject of modernity: it is what, on the basis of the shock of this supplementary invention, is softened and amortized into the categorial invention of its curative necessity. The *default*, the accident, is that of which we *must* categorically invent the necessity (but not the essence), in order to do what we must – and to *make* what is necessary (and which is still missing [*fait encore défaut*]).

The annihilation of processes that put into relief and that three-dimensionalize immanence through disparation, however, leads to the *liquidation of defaults* – that is, in reality, to their massive, industrial and automatic repression, and this is yet more disturbing than the burial of nuclear waste, and is undoubtedly more explosive in the short term.

> Algorithmic governmentality, by its perfect 'real time' adaptation, its 'virality' (the more it is used, the more the algorithmic system is refined and perfected, since every interaction between the system and the world results in a record of digitalized data, a corresponding enrichment of the 'statistical base' and an improvement in the performance of the algorithms) and its plasticity, makes the very notion of 'failure' meaningless: if, in other words, a 'failure' can throw the system into 'crisis', it is immediately *reintegrated* in order to further refine the models or profiles of behaviour.[83]

In other words, there is no longer time for the *maturation* of the necessary (de)fault, for supplementary invention, through any categorial invention whatsoever, that is, through the *deferred time* of a transindividuation. Deferred time always arrives too late, faced with this real time that generates a kind of (trap of) automatic quasi-causality. This trap is in reality, however, a *structural elimination of any quasi-causality*, that is, of every event, given that an event is an occurrence that disrupts or perturbs a system, just as for Simondon 'information' is that which generates a transductive amplification.[84]

Here, the digital technology of power appears to be invincible, because the power of the algorithmic system seems to be *literally and structurally im-perturbable* – imperturbable *by the improbable*, which must be understood in a sense that does not simply refer to what mathematical calculation and modelling cannot *prove*, that is, certify beyond what would be merely probable, but in the sense of what always escapes any calculation, any probability and any demonstration:

> The improbable escapes proof, not because it cannot be demonstrated for the time being but because it never arises in the region where proof is required. [...] The improbable is not simply that which, remaining with the horizon of probability and its calculations, would be defined by a greater or lesser probability. The improbable is not what is only very slightly probable. It is infinitely more than the most probable.[85]

If everything was made of gold, says Plato in the *Timaeus*, gold would be the one thing we could never see. And water is the one thing that a fish cannot see, according to Aristotle. Gold would then be im-probable, as is water for the fish, in the sense that it is not soluble into the calculation of probabilities:[86] '[W]ere there a meeting point between possibility and impossibility, the improbable would be this point.'[87]

Understood in this way, the improbable cannot perturb algorithmic, anormative probabilities and statistics because they make those who might have been affected by this improbable *totally deaf* to its imperious improbability. This is so precisely because, as 24/7 capitalism, algorithmic governmentality disintegrates in advance any intermittence, and therefore liquidates the impossible (unpredictable and unanticipatable) possibility of the improbable that it can neither correlate nor identify.

Like gold in the *Timaeus*, we can imagine the improbable as resembling the way that water constitutes the fish's *element*. We can call this improbable element *elementary supplementarity*, which is the milieu of the noetic soul that Plato called the *khōra*. We can, however, experience [*éprouver*] the improbable (but never prove it [*prouver*]) only intermittently – just as the flying fish can regard its milieu only by leaving it and then ceaselessly returning to it – and as within the incessant.[88]

We can now say:

• that 24/7 capitalism, as an economic system for which algorithmic governmentality is the (a)political reality, tends *to annihilate the very possibility of dreaming as the primordial and most common form of experiencing and testing [faire l'épreuve] the improbable*, and as what can never be proven;

- that the experience of the improbable in which this elementary supplementarity *consists* is an experience of an intermittence comparable to that of the flying fish,[89] which leaves the water only briefly, and which at the precise moment it leaves the water is able to perceive it, but must return to it almost immediately – forgetting it almost as quickly as it returns there.

It is this intermittence that constitutes the noetic soul. And it is because 24/7 capitalism and algorithmic governmentality structurally tend to eliminate this intermittence – that is, this noesis – through an automatic performativity that is always outstripping it that it seems no law can ever arise from this fact, and that it seems to us that functional stupidity and generalized stupefaction can only forever confine this improbable within a flat and narrow immanence that digital reticulation imposes as governmentality.

58. Immanence and perturbation – eliminating failure

If this were the case, then there would be no 'regime of truth' for algorithmic governmentality. Is this indeed the case?

This elimination of failure, that is, of the structural and originary default of the origin, generator of individual and collective experiences of the improbable, and as *necessity itself*, is a direct and *unavoidable* consequence of (dis)integrating and im-perturbable performativity – but it is unavoidable and imperturbable *only if we remain within this organology*. For we shall see that a supplementary invention will, on the contrary, enable this situation to be overturned from its very foundations. This can be realized and concretized only by making it the object of a battle that must be at the same time theoretical, political and economic.

Faced with this imperturbability that remotely controls every decision by consolidating mediatic governmentality, which has still been little thought, and the algorithmic governmentality referred to by Berns and Rouvroy, public power has become impotent and incapable – and by public power I mean states, Europe, international organizations and non-governmental organizations. David Cameron has transferred responsibility for the production of public statistics to Facebook, and it is clear that Google and the data scientists gathered there and elsewhere are preparing to take *total* control of the science of the state that hithertofore was statistics, and to do so in order to create a science of the liquidation of the state – including by imposing a model of 'open data', control of which they will retain via data centres. At the same time, floating cities are being planned on which there would be no state, no police, no justice, nor any social dimension, and an absolute oligarchy composed of a post-human nobility and immortal singularities.[90]

Today there seems to be no power or authority capable of reflecting on this situation, or of overcoming it in the political milieu, or the intellectual, artistic or spiritual milieus (those milieus within which we dream and where we learn to realize our dreams), milieus that are expected to conceive the *res publica*, the public power that any *politeia* constitutes. Nor does this capability seem to exist within the spheres emerging from 'internet democracy' as conceived by Dominique Cardon, or in the political spheres that emerge from the mediatic democracy secreted by Nicolas Sarkozy, or by Ségolène Royal and François Hollande, or in the politico-administrative spheres that have emerged from the literate and literal democracy secreted by the left and the right during the French Revolution, who become, in France, a left and right fabricated by the École nationale d'administration, or in other words by a machine for producing nihilism and cynicism of a highly specific kind, or in the academic realm, which emerges from similar spheres and feeds back into them, something I have attempted to describe in *States of Shock: Stupidity and Knowledge in the 21st Century*.

The digital reticulation that Berns and Rouvroy describe as algorithmic governmentality imposes a flat and narrow immanence that is two-dimensional and one-eyed, as I have said, which Berns and Rouvroy describe as a destruction of disparation. We will examine more closely how this destroys *the third dimension of any psychic and collective individuation, namely, the depth or the relief* from which what Simondon called key-points[91] can arise and hold sway, and which are the saliences constitutive of any value, in the sense both of Nietzsche and of Marx read alongside Weber.[92]

As a technology of automatic protentions generated on a collective scale, algorithmic governmentality eliminates any rough edges, anything unexpected, anything improbable. There is, however,

> failure, conflict, the monstrous, of the limit and exceeding the limit, with the deviations and displacements that this leads to in life, as Canguilhem showed. With algorithmic government, we tend to consider social life as organic life, but by understanding the latter as if the adaptations that occur within it no longer relate to displacements and failures, as if these can therefore no longer produce any crisis or interruption.[93]

It is as if no epokhal moment, no agent of bifurcation, of transgression and of individuation, that is, of the quantum leap, 'could any longer compel anyone to appear before it, or put any subjects to the test, or norms themselves'.[94] As we will see, this means that the *computational model* of this algorithmic governmentality combines with the *naturalistic model* of current cognitivism, so that noetic life as well as biological life is reduced to a calculation.[95]

The elimination of failure is the outcome of extracting correlations from relations, as relations of relations, and from the overtaking [*prise de vitesse*] and outstripping of relations themselves by the taking-apart [*déprise*] of form that is the performative structure of reticulation in real time. Berns and Rouvroy recall that in Simondon, 'the relation is what has the "rank of being", always exceeding or going beyond what it ties together, [and] can never be reduced to an interindividual society'.[96]

Now, this excess of the relation over what it ties together only exists because there are failures,[97] and *compensations* for these failures (by supplementary and categorial inventions, that is, organological inventions in every sense) that always engender new failures, new missteps and remediations for these missteps in the form of new missteps (in the manner of Gribouille, as discussed by Lacan): it is *in this sense* that the noetic milieu constitutes an organological noetic différance that engenders a constantly reconfigured elementary supplementarity.

This is so because there is a *third* term in this relation that 'always goes beyond what it ties together', and that provokes these 'failures'. It is this third term that is *the* factor in the phase shift, in failure and in default, which constitutes the relation but which can always also *ruin* the relation – but this is what Simondon never thematizes.[98] The default is the *pharmakon*, which is the origin of the relation (which Blanchot ultimately tried to think in terms of the relation without relation[99]), as this impossible and improbable possibility that is the originary default of origin.

If the digital *pharmakon*, as implemented by algorithmic governmentality, 'continues to absolutize the individual [...] and at the same time de-realize him/her',[100] this is firstly because it makes the individual incapable of dreaming, of leaving the water, of suspending the effects of probability calculations, and through that of realizing *his or her* dreams. It anticipates what cannot be anticipated, and it destroys what it anticipates by the mere fact of anticipating it, namely, the dreams and reveries of noetic souls insofar as they are intermittently oneiric, in a way 'cutting the grass beneath their feet'.[101]

The question of the possible, which is both that of the dream in
Valéry's sense, and that of a mutation of physics and science into
technoscience, must be completely reconsidered on the basis of the
primordial organological situation as the inaugural power to realize
dreams, and as the power to dream arising out of the phase shifts
produced by realized dreams – such that they constitute funds both
transindividual and preindividual. The new thought of the individual
conceived by Simondon on the basis of individuation, and not the
reverse,

> was a matter [...] of no longer making it an abstraction [...], of pre-
> cisely the fact that 'the possible does not contain the already actual',
> and therefore that 'the individual, which arises, differs from the pos-
> sible which led to its individuation' (Debaise, 2004).[102]

We find here the questions of the quantum leap, the phase shift and
dis-automatization, as they are constituted by the default of origin:

> Failure or deviation [...] therefore seems to be precisely that on the
> basis of which alone there is a relation, understood as what cannot be
> assigned to that which it ties together [...] in that what it ties together
> are realities which are, precisely, asymmetrical, partially incompatible
> or disparate.[103]

This is also what Blanchot referred to as the 'Riemann curvature'.[104]
But for this to be possible, and inasmuch as it concerns noetic souls,
that is, psychic and collective individuation, it is necessary that these
asymmetrical realities share a 'default of community' and a *fundamental delinquence*, a primordial *delinquere*[105] – of which every sacrificial form is the revenance that tries to quasi-causally invert it into
a promise.[106] Quasi-causality is the issue here at every level.

The systemic, systematic and automatic 'evasion' of 'failure or
deviation' by algorithmic governmentality 'operates as the denial of
every "disparation"':

> Algorithmic governmentality presents a form of totalization [...] from
> which any form of the power to make a future has been expurgated,
> any dimension of 'otherness', any virtuality. Making failure fail [...]
> removes the possibility that within the *world* there might arise [...]
> its power of interruption, of putting into crisis.[107]

That is, its epokhality. In this way algorithmic governmentality
presents itself as a power without authority, but imperturbable and

continually emerging. But this is also why this governmentality cannot create an epoch.

59.   The epoch of the absence of epoch and the ill-educated boors that we are

This absence of epoch is an *epokhē*, the first moment of a doubly epokhal redoubling – the great shock caused in 1993 by the advent of the web and generalized digital reticulation. The absence of epoch, which necessarily occurs between two epochs (to a greater or lesser extent), can give rise to a *new epoch* as long as it makes room (space and time, *khōra* and advent) for a second epokhal moment through which it reconstitutes the connective tissues that produce real organological solidarities, by writing (that is, tracing), recording and interiorizing infinitely long, anamnesic circuits of transindividuation.[108]

To this is opposed, today, the structural incapacitation imposed by full and generalized automatization, of which algorithmic governmentality and 24/7 capitalism are the worldwide and total concretization. No one escapes this incapacitation, not even those who cause and exploit (or who believe they can exploit) this situation: this is the lesson of Alan Greenspan.

The *liquidation of capacities – that is, of every form of apprenticeship*, the latter founded on the transmissibility to others of individual experiences and of the lessons acquired through familial and institutional education – results from automatization in general, given that in its most commonplace forms the latter engenders, in all aspects of human existence, a widespread process of dis-apprenticeship. One day, as I was passing through a motorway tollbooth, I stopped my car at the barrier, but the ticket I needed was not released automatically. Since I was in a rush, I found this annoying, complaining and swearing under my breath – and what annoyed me was that to obtain the ticket it was necessary for me to press a button.

Sometimes I take advantage of the specific moments of intermittence and reverie that occur during driving in order to make observations of my own behaviour. Motorists often completely change their mood and behaviour as a result merely of having to control these powerful mechanical objects, and to do so in perpetual competition with other, faster or slower mechanical-mobile beings, in order to traverse public space.

Starting up again after having had to press the button to receive my ticket, which prevented things happening in the normally fluid and rapid way one has come to expect on a motorway, where the ticket is usually released before I even move my arm to grab it – because a photo-electric cell has detected my vehicle – I observed that this extra time allowed me to reflect on my own behaviour, and to see an illustration of the process of dis-apprenticeship inevitably caused by any automatism, from automatic sliding doors in shops and public places to GPS navigation systems, and so on.

And I said to myself that if it is true that we *become* what we are, and if it is true that we exist only through the fact of *doing* things, then all these things that automatisms dispense with us having to do, and as a result of which we unlearn how to do them, are so many lost opportunities to encounter ourselves through the encounter with the world. If it is true that we develop ourselves through our practices, and if it is true that automation takes all kinds of practices out of our hands,[109] then automatization is in the course of profoundly stultifying us: making us rough, uncouth and coarse, brutish and, as one used to say, *ill mannered, ill educated* [*malappris*].

We shall soon see how Guattari's observations concerning the machinic unconscious can in turn be observed in the behaviour of motorists. But we will also see that Guattari himself emphasizes (but without drawing all the consequences) that the arrangement of the driver's unconscious body with the mechanical body of the car puts him or her, under favourable circumstances, into a state of daydream, and that what is lost on one plane may be gained on another – so long as this mental intermittence originating from the machine is *cultivated*, as a new practice of apprenticeship and dis-automatization.

Become what you are: this Pindarian motto, which underpins Nietzsche's entire thinking, is what becomes unthinkable within the generalized brutalization resulting from the massive dis-apprenticeship generated by technological automatisms of all kinds (mechanical, electro-mechanical, electronic and digital) as the techno-*logical* becoming that seems not to open any future, but, on the contrary, to confine us between walls within which everything hurtles along. The generalized dis-apprenticeship imposed on each of us by full automatization, and at the most everyday level, causes an ill-being thanks to which the being that I can be only by becoming what I am *no longer becomes anything*: in this becoming there arises only the experience of nothing, of emptiness, of the desertification of the self.

What results is a nameless and unprecedented feeling that existence has become insipid: to lose one's knowledge, in whatever forms, the knowledge of how to live and do but also how to conceive, is to discover that the an*nihil*ation of the world in which all this fails to consist, as it were, is the deprivation of every gesture, every act and every 'being in the world' or 'being together' of that knowledge through which alone the world consists, and does so as all those forms of knowledge that we know to be there and to become there, that is, to project there what, beyond entropic becoming, opens up a negentropic and neganthropological future.

And yet, many of the books I published between 2004 and 2009 were written while driving a car between Paris and Compiègne on the A1 motorway, in this mental state of diurnal dreaming that is provoked by both the fluidity of the motorway and the subjugation of the body to the mechanics through which it augments its automobility – which, according to Aristotle in *Peri Psūkhês*, is constitutive of any soul whatsoever. I did so by creating for myself a literary practice, through an arrangement between my vehicle and the state of my soul, while driving at 130 kilometres per hour with a digital voice recorder, from which my wife Caroline would later retrieve the audio files and turn them into text files with the help of an automatic transcription software called Dragon, thereby providing me with the materials for books that I would finish writing during the summer.

The noetic stakes of mechanical automobility become, then, a question of ensuring that automatization (of my technical devices as well as the automatic gestures that they require me to interiorize as neural circuits and to perform, for example, in the situation of driving a car) is *designed, studied and cultivated* in order to *free up time for intermittences that are richer in experience and learning than the practices for which they are an automated substitute*.[110] This freeing up must in some way be a release from the behavioural constraints of learning in one epoch so that they may be replaced by others that are richer and that yet preserve the memory of lost practical experiences, transforming them into a new experience, proper to the new epoch.

Without such a culture, that is, such an *investment*, automatization can lead us only into a desert of desperate and brutalized beings – and in every case beings who are absolutely uncontrollable other than through the systematic destruction of their very autonomy, that is, of the *capacity for peaceful transgression* in which knowledge in general consists, as the art of creative controversy and as the power of dis-automatization.[111]

All this raises the question of an *integrated politics of automatization* that would be at the same time a politics of education, a cultural politics, a politics of science, an industrial politics, a *politics of non-employment*, a politics of *intermittence* (in the service of the culture of realizable dreams – what some call 'creativity') and a constitutional politics, that is, defining the elementary knowledge conditioning the basic exercise of citizenship. And all of this implies the question of a *constitutional right* the heart of which should be the right and the duty to dream.

What Berns and Rouvroy show, however, is that algorithmic governmentality, in diametric opposition to these imperatives, systematically destroys what Amartya Sen calls capabilities, and does so through the very fact that *individuals* are no longer of interest to this technology of economic power, whose advocates still claim that it is inspired by liberalism and based on the unconditional defence of the rights of the individual: 'Whatever their capabilities [...] it is no longer primarily through these capabilities that [individuals] are interpellated by "power", but rather through their "profiles".'[112]

60.   (Dys)functional incapacitation and the legal vacuum

It is psychic individuals but also collective individuals (including the state itself) that are thereby totally proletarianized, and that are structurally considered to be in-capable, and rendered such by im-perturbable power. And with reason: it is a matter of doing away with their capabilities, here as in production. It is a question of a system *based* on the *incapacitation* and destruction of every form of knowledge – as Anderson makes clear.

This algorithmic governmentality – inasmuch as it is a state of fact producing and exploiting an ever-widening *juridical vacuum*, generalizing a condition of non-law (as Grégoire Chamayou has shown) – has led to the decline of all power to act. This is so for everyone, including for those who still believe in 'governing': instead of the improbable that makes us dream – that is, invent, discover, create – this imperturbable power begets the uncontrollable[113] that everyone can feel is leading us to a war of all against all, conducted with automatic weapons that are themselves uncontrollable.

Just as there is functional stupidity, so, too, there is functional incapacitation of the 'milieus' that are 'associated' through functional integration, but which are thereby associated with and involved in their own disintegration, leading to generalized dys-functionality.

According to IBM, personalization and 'smart marketing' are 'transforming marketing and advertising into "consumer services"'.[114] Berns and Rouvroy show that these 'consumer services' in reality consist in adapting 'individual desire to supply'. It would be better, however, to avoid referring to the adaptation of *desire*: the assumption here is that desire would be 'adaptable', whereas desire is always the expression of, precisely, a non-adapted singularity, always more or less shifting phase, however slightly, in so doing individuating itself, participating in transindividuation in myriad ways.

Rather than the adaptation of desire to supply, we should refer to a destruction of desire by self-fulfilling anticipations of drive-based fantasies of every kind (voyeurism, exhibitionism, the mimetism of conventional (artificial) crowds in general and through profiling that precedes all of this by promoting reinforcements of every kind, that is, by short-circuiting, via the calculation of correlations, the *social* processes of trans-individuation, and replacing them with the *automatic* processes of trans-dividuation).

Here it is a question not of anticipating desire, but of destroying it *by* anticipating it, and short-circuiting it by automatically triggering drive-based behaviour, channelled through the self-fulfilling protentions induced by the feedback loops that constitute the fundamental basis of totally computational 24/7 capitalism. This *transdividual trafficking of data*, operating as a kind of trafficking of 'dividuated' psychic organs, is something that requires more detailed description.

Psychic organs that have been decomposed into dividuals, and the disintegrated psychosocial elements of the psychic apparatus and social systems (in Gille's sense), have become the non-objects and non-subjects of this trafficking between operators, who exploit this data on their own behalf, while still often selling it to their competitors, or exchanging it with other players in conglomerates supported by cloud computing.

'It is indeed market segmentation that we should refer to here,'[115] and not personalization and individualization: the alleged 'individualization' is a dividuation, that is, an *infra*-individual division and a decomposition of individuation. This destruction of desire by an automatization that unleashes the drives, triggering herd-like automatisms that combine with the drives via the network effect, is utterly comparable with the models of neuromarketing and neuroeconomics.[116]

'Utterly', since in the case of neuromarketing 'it is a matter of producing the passage into action without the formation or formulation of desire'.[117] And, as in Crary, this is based on the destruction of intermittence, that is, on a de-noeticization through a return to a *sensorimotor loop in which there is neither delay nor social différance*: this is a return to the sensorimotor loop described by Jacob von Uexküll (forming what he called the 'functional circle'[118]) in his analysis of the tick. In the case of the feedback loop introduced by algorithmic governmentality qua 24/7 capitalism, the time interval (the delay) that separates the reception from the effect is reduced to nothing, *nihil*.

The functional integration of psychic individuations by an automatic associated milieu functioning in light-time thereby constitutes a *factual naturalization* of the technical milieu and, if we can put it like this, an 'artificial naturalization' through which psychic and collective individuation becomes a psychic and collective disindividuation that functions like a kind of 24/7 insect society – via ersatz digital pheromones,[119] and where it is a matter of 'accelerating the flows – wherever possible saving on any "detour" or subjective "reflexive suspension" between the "stimuli" and their "reflex responses"'.[120]

5

Within the Electronic Leviathan in Fact and in Law

Knowledge [...] is one of the ways by which humanity seeks to take control of its destiny and to transform its being into a duty.

Georges Canguilhem[1]

61. Disparation and signification

Berns and Rouvroy relate the automated processes implemented by algorithmic governmentality to Félix Guattari's concepts of *molecular machinic unconscious* and *machinic enslavement*. The example used by Guattari for machinic enslavement is, in fact, 'driving in a state of reverie'.[2] But he *does not elaborate on the reverie* that accompanies this kind of enslavement.

Driving my car 'automatically', that is, 'without thinking' and in this sense 'unconsciously', one 'part' of 'me' is totally enslaved to an engine and a mechanical vehicle that it 'serves' by 'using it' [*en 's'en servant'*], while an 'other' part of 'me' – which is, however, perhaps not completely me or my ego, but rather *also* this obscure zone of intermittences that is the *id* – finds itself in a greatly dis-automatized mode: the mode of reverie, akin at times to floating attention, which is always at the origin of thinking that goes off the beaten track.

The automatisms that accompany this dis-automatization thus belong to what Guattari called the machinic unconscious, where the latter is 'a-signifying', as Berns and Rouvroy recall by citing a commentary of Maurizio Lazzarato, and by emphasizing that in algorithmic governmentality, as in the machinic unconscious and in the enslavement through which it is carried out, 'everything happens as if signification was not absolutely necessary'.[3]

Signification [*signification*], that is, *semiosis* as engendering signs, significations and significance (making-signs), is the transindividual made possible by the process of transindividuation woven between psychic systems, technical systems and social systems – that is, between psychic individuations, technical individuation and collective individuations.[4]

The destruction of signification by the digital technical system results from the technology of power deployed by the algorithmic governmentality of 24/7 capitalism, and it is founded on eliminating processes of disparation. The latter is a concept that Simondon introduces in the following terms:

> Each retina surveys a two-dimensional image; the left image and the right image are disparate; they represent the world seen from two different perspectives [...]; some details hidden from view in the left image are, on the contrary, revealed in the right image, and vice versa [...]. No third image is optically possible that could unify these two images: they are essentially disparate and cannot be superposed within the axiomatic of two-dimensionality. To bring about a coherence that incorporates them, it is necessary that they become the foundation of a world perceived within an axiomatic in which disparation [...] becomes, precisely, the index of a new dimension.[5]

We will see that this process of disparation forms the basis for Simondon's conception of signification and individuation.

Berns and Rouvroy grasp algorithmic governmentality from this Simondonian perspective, but also with Deleuze. Hence they subject Simondonian and Deleuzo-Guattarian concepts to the test of facts, through which it seems that these ideas are brought to their limit and put *back* into question, re-*mobilized* through a quantum leap that overturns their interpretation – in this intermittence that is the doubly epokhal redoubling formed by digital tertiary retention, which is the operator of 24/7 capitalism and algorithmic governmentality.

This getting thinking *going* again [*re-mise en* fonctionnement *de la pensée*], as the putting in *question* of thinking and of what gets us thinking (stupidity), would suggest [*donnerait à penser*] a dysfunctioning – precisely that referred to by Deleuze and Guattari in *Anti-Oedipus*, and in terms of a necessary default.[6]

To think algorithmic governmentality *within* algorithmic governmentality as an age of immanence and as a *possible new regime of truth* would be to get Deleuze and Guattari's thought of *dysfunction* functioning again – also called *shifting phase* (which is the condition of all disparation) by Simondon, *delinquere* by Esposito, *pathology* (and infidelity) by Canguilhem, *supplement* (or différance) by Derrida, and so on – and to do so by mobilizing the concepts and thoughts of these authors *in inventive modalities, productive of differences*, and not just through 'bad repetitions' of these concepts.[7]

In the Simondonian conception of disparation, the difference between two points of view of a single world in two dimensions engenders, through disparation, a third dimension. Conceived in this way, disparation is a specific case of the more general question of individuation as the *changing of order of magnitude*. Commenting on Kurt Lewin and his use of the concept of *field* stemming from the theory of form, Simondon shows that, contrary to the pragmatic perspective used by Lewin to interpret this notion, the relationship between the noetic individual and his or her milieu must be thought not as *adaptation* but as *individuation*.

Individuation is possible only because, between the milieu and the individual, 'there exists a condition of disparation in the mutual relationship of these elements; if the elements were as heterogeneous as Kurt Lewin assumes, opposed like a barrier that repels them and a goal that attracts them, the disparation would be too great for a common signification to be found'.[8] In other words, between these two poles a transductive relation forms, such that it constitutes the differentiation of these two poles (and as their différance), which is also to say, their co-individuation, in the course of which 'it is necessary for a principle to be discovered, and for the former configuration to be incorporated into this system'.[9] It is *thus* that disparation produces *signification*, and that, to put it in Aristotelian language, potential passes into actuality.

But here the potency [*puissance*] lies in preindividual funds loaded with potentials [*potentiels*], and the act is what combines these potentials by differentiating the polarities of a transductive relation that can itself occur only through being supplied by what Simondon called a seed, making an analogy with crystallography.

62.   Orders and disorders of magnitude

The difficulty of thinking in these terms with regard to what concerns *us* is that, through functional integration, in the epoch or absence of epoch of digital tertiary retention, the *milieu merges with* and in some way *blends into* the global digital network constitutive of algorithmic governmentality and 24/7 capitalism, where, as Berns and Rouvroy say, automatic government no longer has any need for disparation, for individuals or for signification.

In and through the network, and the network effect, the condition of disparation is *shunted*, that is, both *diverted* (which is the original meaning of the verb *to shunt*) and *short-circuited* (which is the meaning of this same verb when it is extended to electronics) by algorithms that substitute for it, so as to engender a functional integration of psychic and collective individuals – which is to literally disintegrate them. Hence is created *a new order of magnitude* wherein meaning and signification *are lost*, thereby creating a disorder: this new order is a *disorder of magnitude*, so to speak, typical of nihilism on the way to fulfilment.[10]

Algorithmic governmentality has no need for meanings or significations. It needs only those psychic and collective individuals through which and by the individuation of which this algorithmic governmentality constitutes itself while *dividuating them*. In this sense automatic 'transindividuation' no longer produces the transindividual but only the 'trans*dividual*', through a '*dividuation*' that would be the specific feature that emerges in control societies and imposes itself as the a-normativity of societies of hyper-control.

Are such societies still societies? The automatic and computational liquidation of disparation dissolves processes of transindividuation, *which are always in some way idiomatic and localized*, that is, characterized by natively disparate psychic and collective individuals, originally put into default by an originary default of origin, and producing, through their disparations, many new dimensions, that is, new meanings and significations – forming what we call worlds.

By diluting, dissolving and ultimately disintegrating these processes of psychic and collective individuation that are always idiomatic and improbable, that is, incalculable, algorithmic governmentality and 24/7 capitalism eliminate anything incalculable – and do so on a planetary scale. A toxic anthropization is thereby produced,[11] in relation to which we will try, in the second volume of *Automatic Society*, to think the theoretical and practical conditions of effecting a *neganthropology* in algorithmic governmentality and a passage from fact to law.

Established by the new technical individual formed by this reticular system, the disorder of magnitude *incommensurable* to psychic individuals who become its servants is an electronic Leviathan that promises only generalized dysfunctionality. For this automaton cannot maintain its 'autonomy' in this form for very long: it *needs* the psychic individuals whom it disintegrates, just as the latter need the social systems that they themselves disintegrate in serving the decadent – that is, self-destructive – electronic Leviathan.

63.   Information and knowledge

Meaning, significance [*signification*], is the result not of an adaptation, but of an individuation generative of meanings (what we call an adoption[12]) – through a *transductive amplification*[13] whereby information leads to an individuation that is a trans-formation *beyond* in-formation. Simondon's theory of information allows us to think this need to go beyond information. But it also contributes to the *concealment* of this necessity, owing to the absence of a pharmacological critique of 'mechanology', that is, the absence of an organology that does not apprehend information independently of its supports.

Simondon's mechanology is indeed based on the contention that the independence of information in relation to its supports, its medium, is not only possible but necessary. Simondon shares this perfectly metaphysical assumption with cybernetics and cognitivism. The illusion is engendered by the fact that information can circulate from support to support while maintaining its structure. But this circulation alters both this maintaining (this 'maintenance') and information itself (intensifying or depleting its potential), which is trans-*formed* by its supports.

Information that circulates from support to support is maintained in a metastable way. It varies at the limit of instability according to its supports, which can support it only so long as they do not completely destroy it. It is through these alterations at the limit that information becomes significance and meaning [*signification*]: it metastabilizes itself by forming the transindividual, which is no longer information. *The transindividual is a metastable relation between its supports, of which the nervous systems of psychic individuals are instances:*[14] the supports of the transindividual (as the relation between these supports) are distributed between psychic individuals as psychic retentions and protentions, and between collective individuals as collective secondary retentions metastabilized by tertiary retentions. In this way transindividuation constitutes knowledge, which is not simply information.

Meaning, significance, *constitutes* the transindividual: it establishes the *trans*-individual by signi-fying it. The transindividual can be trans-*individual* only by producing for individuals a common dimension of significance. The formation of this common dimension is effected through a disparation that is a *process* of transindividuation. In the course of this process, *circuits* of transindividuation form. It is these circuits, the organs they presuppose (psychosomatic, technical and social) and the arrangements formed by these organs that constitute what Foucault called a 'regime of truth'.[15]

These circuits *pass* through the psychic *individuation* of those they traverse by trans-*forming* them in the sense that, through this, these individuals reflexively trans-*form themselves*. This does not mean that they do so deliberately: *trans*-forming oneself can occur (and, even, can *only* occur) in complete unconsciousness, in assuming the unconsciousness (the improbability) necessitated by this trance [*transe*], so to speak.[16]

This unconsciousness can today take on a *machinic* dimension only because it has always and in general been primordially orga-nological: *noesis is a technesis*[17] formed through the interiorization of artefactual automatisms. This becomes noesis in actuality only intermittently, and does so by dis-automatizing the automatisms on which it is based. The passage to the noetic act is not a becoming-conscious of what was previously unconscious, but an *adoption* of this unconsciousness, as the individuation of the preindividual funds of which it consists.

64. Everybody is Nobody: flatness and verticality in the electronic Leviathan

The three-dimensionality produced by the disparation in which the process of transindividuation always consists is reduced to two dimensions by algorithmic governmentality. In this way it flattens both psychic and collective individuation, (de-)forming people who see themselves only as a profile, so to speak – like Cyclops calling everyone Nobody [*Personne*]. The two dimensions of this anthropic milieu are:

- the *technical individual* that is the fully computational technical system, made to serve the oligarchic organization that *controls* the implementation of algorithms, and that constitutes a new (dis-) order;
- those who *serve* this oligarchy, that is, *us* – which is who we are, whether we know it or not – which disintegrates us, so that we in some way form an automatic One or They [*On*].[18]

This psychosocial disintegration eventually and inevitably leads, however, to the disintegration of the oligarchic level itself: the 'we' includes the oligarchs – and such a system, being *thoroughly* entropic, is bound to disintegrate *in totality*. In the current state of things, this fully computational milieu is one-eyed and monocular. This flattening engenders the desertification of the web.

Since the appearance of the web in 1993, it has undergone a process of levelling, through which it has been completely subjected to the imperative of calculability, itself exclusively configured by business models mostly invented in California. This has led to the logic of platforms[19] – just as the culture industries levelled the world starting in the 1980s (with the conservative revolution), a steamroller subjecting all opinions to the law of audience ratings and subjecting all media to a competition for access to the advertising market, thereby achieving the functional integration of marketing and ideology.

In *La Démocratie Internet*, Dominique Cardon shows how in the 1990s the web was initially and visibly horizontalized and 'networked' by the technology of hypertext links from peer to peer made possible by HTML writing and URL addresses. Starting from the 2000s, however, and founded on the participatory technology of Web 2.0, the combination of the collaborative production of metadata, the page ranking of the Google search engine and the network effect of social networking have together engendered a kind of *vertical flatness* constituting an invisible digital wall, installed from top to bottom:

> Google's PageRank [...] becomes increasingly plebiscitary [...]. The structure of links between sites leads to an extremely hierarchical landscape: some nodes (hubs) exercise a great deal of authority over the network [...]. If we pay attention only to the top of the hierarchy of information, the agenda of the internet shows only minor differences from traditional media. The participatory internet only reproduces the criteria of legitimacy of the gatekeepers [...]. This metric requires no actual participation from users. It simply records their behaviour.[20]

The social web[21] may sometimes seem to be forming itself[22] contra to such an algorithmic massification, with Web 2.0 inventing 'metrics' of 'communitary recommendation', but 'these are very fragile. They can be "distorted" under pressure from the commercial interests of platforms.'[23]

This is so because all these processes produce 'data' that the systems of algorithmic governmentality recover and functionally integrate into a computational system that is itself integrated. Its always hidden face, cloud computing, is located not in the clouds, as minds that have themselves been rendered cloudy and vaporous believe, but in data centres, which are increasingly often located in high-security areas and sometimes in underground bunkers.[24]

We must stress here the specific problems posed by the *infrastructures* of the web and the internet,[25] as they were described by Andrew Blum in an interview with Mediapart:

> My biggest concern is the speed and scale with which data centres are being granted access to so many parts of our lives, without fully understanding what they are. The greatest risk would be to find that a small number of very large companies have been allowed to dominate everything. Google, for example, is less like a company than a true, separate network, parallel to the internet. It is a rupture. A city changes depending on whether the houses it contains are owned by small proprietors or if they are all owned by a single person. This is a little like what Google has become: a city unto itself.[26]

It is a question of *reconstituting depth on the web, creating a relief* – by forming not neighbourhoods of small proprietors but what we will call *knowledge cooperatives*.[27]

Until now there have been two main epochs in the history of the web: the first was characterized by hypertext links and websites. The second was that of blogs, evaluated by search engines, wherein 'recommendations' and 'reputation' are based on the network effect – enabling platforms to channel and functionally integrate the 'expressions' generated by this 'expressivism'.[28]

A third epoch must arise, founded on a new organology, derived from supplementary invention conceived as political technology, and with the goal of *repotentializing disparation*, that is, with the goal of diachronizing the web and providing interpretative instruments for this disparity. Hence a neganthropology could and should be reconfigured capable of projecting a negentropic future into entropic becoming.

65.   The macropolitics of relief

The reduction of three-dimensionality and the flattening of relief are the outcome of a *sterilization* of participatory and collaborative technologies. We (Ars Industrialis, pharmakon.fr and the IRI) understand these technologies as representing a pharmacology of unprecedented dangerousness, but also as elements bearing the potential for another organology and for a contributory society. Similarly, Dominique Cardon sees in these technologies the condition of a rebirth of democratic and political life in an epoch where, according to Lawrence Lessig, 'code is law'.[29] Cardon has commented on this idea as follows: 'On the internet, the choice of software infrastructure constrains users more than do legal prohibitions.'[30]

Such an account of how the situation stands in the twenty-first century, shaped from its origin and in a way from its very birth by the technologies of Web 2.0,[31] confirms and seems even to extend Foucault's twentieth-century discourse on technologies of power, as we have already seen. As Cardon states: 'The choice of software infrastructure [...] profoundly structures the way users "see" information and represent the digital world.'[32] The participatory technology constituting the social web seemed to promise a new relief (and hence seemed to provide hope of an escape from the mediatized flattening caused by the culture industries that Deleuze described as control society), and it is the reduction of this depth that has had as its consequence the domination of algorithmic governmentality.

This governmentality now appears even more alienating and addictive, and even less open to critique, than analogue media – because it is much less visible and ultimately much more dangerous: it merges with the world that it absorbs, flattens and annihilates by engulfing it and dissimulating it. This dissimulation is all the more profound inasmuch as algorithmic governmentality seems in a way to be secreted by those whom it governs, hence coinciding with this same world through those who are functionally integrated '*like everyone else*', that is, as tending to no longer form their sole and unique horizon. This would be a horizon without depth or key-points,[33] a desert horizon that anticipates and precedes every behaviour, like a two-dimensional sky in which everything has been written and calculated in advance, 'as if the universe was already *independent of any interpretation* – saturated with meaning, as if it were no longer necessary, therefore, for each of us to be connected to one another through language'.[34]

Berns and Rouvroy here quote Maurizio Lazzarato, who refers to the Guattarian concept of a-signifying semiotics: 'A-signifying semiotics [...] [are a function of] "machinic enslavement" [...] causing the affects, perceptions, emotions, etc., to function like component parts, like the elements in a machine.'[35] That is, they constitute a functional integration in the Simondonian sense, and do so as a kind of human associated milieu: 'We can all function like the input/output elements in semiotic machines, like simple relays of television or the Internet.'[36] To deepen Guattari's observations, and the commentaries by Lazzarato, and the commentaries by Berns and Rouvroy on these commentaries – all of which constitute *interpretations* – requires a pharmacological approach to associated milieus and to contribution, that is, an organological approach.

In such an approach, the main question is that of arrangements [*agencements*]. But here it is not possible to remain on the micropolitical plane: a three-dimensional perspective, understood as creating relief (the depth of multiple disparities producing lines of flight), and as the disparation of 'key-points', is necessarily also and from the outset macropolitical.[37] It is a question not of moving to the macropolitical, that is, to the One as the dream of a unity and process of unification, but of enacting a pharmacological critique of its always organological realization, and of positing as a starting point that any *realization* of a dream is pharmacological, that is, it *is no longer* a dream – unless it becomes a nightmare.

Such a shared, three-dimensional perspective must project a politics that is always macropolitical. It must feed 'molecular' lines of flight, which it must 'three-dimensionalize' by problematizing the stakes of the *transformation of becoming into future* that is always the question of any noesis qua passage from facts to laws, that is: qua projection of existences onto the plane of consistences – consistence trans-forming entropy into neganthropy through the individuation of the potentials and tensions that constitute organologically supported preindividual becoming.

66.   De-proletarianization as dis-automatization

The 'dividuation' that obstructs any consistence is the result of proletarianization in all its forms: the stakes of the neganthropic question are de-proletarianization. Proletarianization and de-proletarianization constitute the two poles of an experience and a test of being *put into question* – in our case, by the technological shock that would be the invention of the web, installing the first moment of an doubly epokhal redoubling, which it is now a matter of *politicizing*.

In algorithmic governmentality, 'the production of subjectivity has become an obsession for many people, their very reason for living'. Berns and Rouvroy conclude that it would be 'hasty to simply conclude that these ongoing transformations produce nothing but de-subjectivation'.[38] And on this basis they envisage the possibility that 'intelligent environments that save us from having to constantly make choices in completely trivial areas [could] also free the mind and make us available for more interesting or more altruistic tasks, etc.'.[39]

We must go further still. Automatisms should be put at the service of dis-automatization qua neganthropic imperative and 'value of values'[40] – including and firstly in the service of their own dis-automatization: as the functional integration of everyone into an algorithmic governmentality concretized by algorithmic technical systems founded on a broad culture of digital tertiary retention and founding a new age of parity.

We shall see why this requires both a supplementary organological invention *and* a categorial organological invention – that is, *a new regime of transindividuation*, capable of constituting the regime of truth that will emerge from this supplementary invention. If it is true that a regime of truth can form only by making a difference between fact and law, this new regime of truth would be a new jurisdiction formed by a new *epistēmē* giving rise to new epistemological legalities.

Rouvroy has developed these ideas further in an article published by Mediapart, where she asks:

> [H]ow then to use the systems of digital society for the purpose of re-enchanting the commons? By making this vocation a priority, pro-tecting it by law, and by making these uses effective. To 'put man in the machine', as Félix Guattari invited us to do, would perhaps be, today: to get on with producing interstices, play, within which the commons can occur, that is, the interruption of flow, the gap, the opportunity for a recomposition of what, for human beings, can 'create consistency', even temporarily – even if these interstices and this play, allowing the emergence of consistent arrangements, 'seizing' the 'machine', effec-tively puts algorithmic rationality into crisis.[41]

Indeed: 'Far from being a pathological consequence, disequilibrium is functional and fundamental [...]: it is *in order to function* that a social machine must *not function well*.'[42] Only a malfunction allows an organology not only to function but also to individuate – and to do so by dis-automatizing.

There is subjectivation in the automatic milieu, according to Berns and Rouvroy, but it is not reflexive: 'What is first noticed is the dif-ficulty in producing an algorithmic subject who is self-reflexive or who thinks as such.'[43] This 'subjectivation' is *unreflective* because what this algorithmic arrangement produces breaks with processes of transindividuation, cutting the servants off from the process they serve at the very moment they believe it is serving them:

> Our problem [...] is not that we are dispossessed of what we con-sider to be our own [...]. It would more fundamentally lie in the fact

that *our statistical double is too detached from us*, that we have no 'relationship' with it, even though contemporary normative actions are enough for this statistical double to be effective.[44]

To take possession of our double, to reach the point of analysing the dividuation of the self in which it consists, would be to be capable of dis-automatizing, and to create a reflective and specular interface. One can imagine how *social engineering* could be developed in this direction.

67. Hermeneutics of the Leviathan

Let us recapitulate, on the basis of this proposal, what we have observed since the beginning of this book. With social networking based on the self-production of traces, the network effect and high-performance computing applied to 'big data', and with the formation of artificial crowds that is the basis of 'crowdsourcing' (that is, of the data economy), the digital stage of grammatization is leading psychic individuals throughout the world to grammatize their own behaviour by interacting with computer systems operating in real time.

These systems produce an automatic performativity that channels, diverts and short-circuits individual and collective protentions by outstripping and overtaking the noetic capacities of individuals precisely insofar as they are protentional capacities – that is, *oneiric* capacities – and at the same time by short-circuiting the collective production of circuits of transindividuation.

Every form of noesis is thereby overtaken through this incitement of protentions operating by remote control. These protentions are continuously being redefined and are always already being erased by new protentions that are even more dis-integrated, that is, dividual. This is an obstacle to dreaming, wanting, reflecting and deciding, that is, the collective realization of dreams, and it forms the basis of algorithmic governmentality inasmuch as it is the power of fully computational 24/7 capitalism. On this point, Berns and Rouvroy converge with Crary.

These analyses of the computational development of behaviour generated by digital doubles derived from user profiling should clearly be brought together with Greenspan's observations about the economic effects of the automation of financial transactions, enabling the formation of a system that is also called the 'financial industry', encompassing subprime mortgages and speculative technologies such as credit default swaps and high-frequency trading, all 'founded' on speed.[45]

If 'our statistical double is too detached from us', it is because the data industry, as the automatized production and exploitation of traces, dispossesses us of the possibility of *interpreting* our retentions and protentions – both psychic and collective. To change this state of fact and open up the possibility of a new state of law, we must invent an organology based on the potentials contained in the digital technical system. And we must do so even though currently this system does indeed give every appearance of being a gigantic technical individual, a digital Leviathan exerting its power over the entire earth *through its ability to continually outstrip and overtake*, and to do so on behalf of a decadent, uncultivated and self-destructive oligarchy – an oligarchy that is *absolutely* venal, that is, *perfectly* nihilistic.

This contemporary Leviathan is global, and it is the result of the reticular and interactive traceability of 24/7 capitalism, which has now become a part of common awareness. Hence it is not that this traceability operates 'behind the back of consciousness', as Hegel said about the phenomenology of spirit (of its epiphany as exteriorization), but rather that it operates by outstripping and overtaking the protentions that produce this consciousness, that is, by proposing and substituting prefabricated protentions – even if they are also 'individualized' or 'personalized'. All this represents a radical and unprecedented rupture with Husserl's description of the temporal activity of any noetic consciousness.

The latter is constituted by primary retentions that consciousness selects (without being conscious of doing so) at the time the experience occurs, selections made on the basis of the secondary retentions this consciousness contains – and that thereby constitute the criteria for these selections. The primary retentions resulting from this selection encode individually lived experience, and are formed through the accumulation of past experience – becoming in their turn secondary retentions.

The play between primary and secondary retentions generates protentions that are themselves primary and secondary (though Husserl did not himself employ this distinction). Primary protentions are tied to the object of lived experience, so that, through habit, reasoning, physiological automatisms, or through the knowledge that the perceiving subject accumulates about the object of perception, such 'primarily retained' traits result in 'primarily protended' traits, that is, expected and anticipated traits – whether consciously or otherwise.

These primary and secondary retentions and protentions are composed of mnesic traces, which, like the 'neurones' in Freud's 'Project for a Scientific Psychology', are 'charged' with and 'tend' towards protentions,[46] through circuits and facilitations formed between these mnesic traces that Freud called 'contact-barriers', as potentials for action and as *expectations that constitute the lived experience of these potentials*.[47] This play of retentional and protentional mnesic traces is conditioned and overdetermined by the play of those hypomnesic traces that tertiary retentions form.

In the case of *digital and reticulated* tertiary retention, that is, arrangements of psychic retentions and protentions via automatisms operating at near-light speed, the retentional selections through which experience occurs as the production of primary retentions and protentions are outstripped and overtaken by prefabricated tertiary retentions and protentions that are 'made to measure' through user profiling and auto-completion technologies, and through all the possibilities afforded by real-time processing and associated network effects – and augmented by this performativity.

It should be noted here that, if the average speed of a nervous impulse circulating between the brain and the hand is around 50 metres per second, reticulated digital tertiary retentions can circulate at 200 million metres per second on fibre-optic networks – four million times faster. Such considerations call for an organology and a pharmacology of speed and will.

It is indeed *will in all its most elementary forms* that *is emptied of all content, outstripped and overtaken by traceability*. When noetic individuals live the time of an experience in which they select traits as primary retentions on the basis of secondary retentions, they at the same time and in return[48] interpret these secondary retentions insofar as they form ensembles.

These ensembles are charged with protentions derived from previous experiences. Some of these protentions are transindividuated and transformed into a common rule, that is, into habits and conventions of all kinds, metastabilized between the psychic individuals and the collective individuals associated with these experiences (a con-vention being what con-venes a plurality of individuals: it is what *gathers* their *coming* together). Others, however, continue to await transindividuation, that is, expressions and inscriptions that continue the development of already-existing circuits of transindividuation. For a psychic individual to interpret, during a present experience, the ensembles of secondary retentions that constitute his or her past experience is to make actual the protentions that these ensembles contain as potential.[49]

By short-circuiting the protentional projections of psychic and collective noetic individuals, by phagocytically absorbing the milieus associated with them, and by sterilizing the circuits of transindividuation woven between them through their individual and collective experiences, algorithmic governmentality annihilates those traumatypical potentials in which consist protentions that bear the possibility of neganthropological upheavals.

When noetic experience is fulfilled in actuality and 'fully' (in the plenitude of actuality that constitutes what Aristotle called entelechy), it constitutes a support for the expression of traumatypes that participate in the inscription of noetic singularity into circuits of transindividuation. It is these circuits through which knowledge is woven as the accumulation of previous experiences insofar as they are original and yet recognized and identified, thereby forming factors conducive of neganthropic bifurcations.

If it is a question of re-establishing a genuine process of transindividuation with reticulated digital tertiary retentions, and of establishing a digital age of psychic and collective individuation, then the challenge is to generate tertiary retentions with all the polysemic and plurivocal thickness of which the hypomnesic trace is capable, reflecting the hermeneutic play of the improbable and of singularity that pertains to the protentions woven between psychic and collective retentions.

To do this, *systems must be built and implemented that are dedicated to the individual and collective interpretation of traces* – including by using automated systems that enable analytical transformations to be optimized, and by supplying new materials for synthetic activity.

68. Organology of jurisprudence

A supplementary invention, necessary in order to complete the system that produces reticulated digital tertiary retentions, must enable transindividual, rather than transdividuated, reticulation. That is, it must enable noetic and not just algorithmic reticulation, synthetically formative and not analytically deforming: synthetic in the Kantian sense, as the life of reason, and not just analytical, as automated understanding.

This supplementary invention must make possible a categorial invention that generates a new process of transindividuation through the implementation of a graphic language of visual digital traces created for the individual and collective annotation of traces, for their sharing and for their disparation – via the mediation of a new kind of social network, allowing both for data to be individually dis-automatized and for the treatment of data provided by automatons, as well as enabling the projection of this hermeneutic dis-automatization onto the collective plane.

This new digital organology must re-establish the process of disparation through which circuits of transindividuation are formed, by facilitating the confrontation of individual interpretations, by supporting processes of collective interpretation (that is, of collective individuation) and by projecting the third constitutive dimension of the transindividual.

As Harry Halpin and Yuk Hui have shown, this requires the implementation of a social networking technology based on the Simondonian model of individuation rather than on Moreno's sociogram[50] – so that the network effect will enable the constitution of interpretative communities producing contributory, alternative and idiomatized categorizations, and the *traceability of disputes* engendered by hermeneutic and idiomatic differences.

Such contributory categorizations are the sources of the projection and realization – by the authors of self-produced traces of all kinds, that is, by the so-called 'bottom up' – of 'top-down' systems without which no 'bottom-up' activity (nor any dream) can function. To pass from the individual dream to its collective realization is to open up the possibility of an individuation. The question of law can thus be posed anew by and with the technology of power that digital tertiary retention makes possible as a *governmentality that is more than algorithmic*.

Law must take account here of both its organological conditions and its pharmacological necessity. Marx dismissed the question of law as ultimately contingent on the ideological field, but he did so only after having himself failed to ground a new conception of law: this is what has been shown by the research of Mikhaïl Xifaras. The 'very young Marx' studied both law and philosophy, and his

> rejection of transcendental metaphysics borrowed not just from the work of Hegel but also from the historical school, particularly that of Savigny, who also claimed to depart from a metaphysical approach to law, by giving new force and meaning to the expression *jurisprudentia vera philosophia est.*[51]

For the very young Marx, this attempt, which will pass through the interpretation of the law on thefts of wood adopted in 1842 by the Rhine Diet,[52] called for

> the constitution of a science of law that, confronting the failures of the speculative science and historical science of law, can honour the critical claim of philosophy by producing a truly universal juridical language [...], a truly universal science of law, a science of law for the populace of all countries.

But Marx did not succeed in this attempt:

> The search for a science of law that is authentically *vera philosophia* resulted [...] in failure, not, as is often read in Marxist writings, because of the mystificatory character of law itself, but because of the absence of a modern juridical language in which could be recognized the rights of humanity that are embodied in those of poverty.

The fundamental question here, for us, is that of 'mystification': the 'mystificatory character of law' *would not be the motive of the critique of law* for Marx. For, indeed, juridical 'mystification' would not be and could not be the *first* issue because human beings, by 'producing their means of existence', which Marx and Engels posit as the starting point for their critique of idealism in *The German Ideology*, 'artificialize' their organism as well as the relations between these organologically amplified organisms, and do so as social organization.

This question is fundamental given that, as we shall see, a social group cannot be formed without 'fictioning' (that is, dreaming) its past and future unity, and given that the passage from fact to law is indeed that from existence to consistence. It is in and from this primordial artefactuality and *from the resulting fact* of the inherently organological (and not just organic) character of human organizations – a *fatum* that constitutes the tragic ground of Presocratic Greece – that, politically and in law, a justice must be affirmed in the name of the criterion of truth, and affirmed as the differentiation of law from fact that is historically formed in the apodictic experience of geometry.[53]

Hence Xifaras can conclude:

> It has become a commonplace among commentators on Marx to highlight how his theory of justice is aporetic, torn between an unambiguous condemnation of capitalism and the impossibility of finding a non-ideological (in the Marxist sense of this term) foundation for this

condemnation. This aporia has its origin in the failure of his attempt to constitute a historical science of law that would be at the same time a political and philosophical critique.

It is on this complex foundation of the Marxist discourse on law that Foucault could oppose to juridical questions his thinking of power conceived on the basis of its technologies – which are factual and artefactual before being juridical, that is, the fact of which precedes the law.

A consideration that fully took account of the fact that the question of power includes its technological conditions would lead to an organological question that itself calls for a pharmacological critique *in the name of the law* – which we can understand in our time as the right and the duty to constitute a neganthropic future in the face of the entropic becoming imposed by the oligarchy via algorithmic governmentality. We shall see that this is also the profound but unthought stakes of Durkheim's research on the social and 'moral' meaning of the division of labour.[54]

Pharmacological critique can be conducted only on the basis of a principle of differentiation between fact and law. *It then becomes a question of an organology of law that critiques itself pharmacologically*, thereby constituting a *political* process of psychic and collective individuation.

In the *current* stage of grammatization, the question of law engendered by automatization is posed primarily as that of the law of work [*droit du travail*] and the right to work [*droit au travail*]. Alain Supiot has shown how work became the heart of social law with the 1944 Declaration of Philadelphia, and how social law itself became the heart of international law. Labour law and social law are conceived here not from the perspective of economic law, but from the perspective of social justice, that is, from a political right.[55]

From the moment automation triggers a massive process destroying employment, a pharmacological critique of the law of work and the right to work can and must be conducted on wholly other bases – inasmuch as law and work are understood as dimensions of organology. Such a pharmacology cannot, indeed, locate its criteria in the relations of production and the economy – unless the latter is conceived as a general economy in the sense of Georges Bataille, that is, such that it cannot be reduced to calculation, and such that it leads to a neganthropology.[56]

As a new epoch of psychic and collective individuation, the *political* individuation that arose in the seventh century BCE implemented the subjective principle of differentiation between fact and law as the criterion of the process of transindividuation that constituted *psychic* citizens by constituting them *politically*, in that this criterion is shared by all citizens who internalize it by frequenting the *skholē* – the *skholeion* being instituted precisely for this purpose. It is their *practical* and *active* frequentation of *theorein* that constitutes them as citizens.

This is why political individuation is founded on the collective critique of its sources, that is, on the critique of circuits of transindividuation that it inherits in the form of various forms of knowledge, themselves organologically constituted, concretized, *judged* and as such *realized* through institutions that are always retentional systems.[57] These institutional sources, which metastabilize the transindividual, reconvert them for any psychic individual into the preindividual funds that its social milieu forms, charged with potentials for individuation.

69.   Collective individuations, social systems and hermeneutic jurisprudence

This is so because the psychic individual, who individuates only through a co-individuation with other individuals, who with him or her form – by disparation – collective individuals, engenders the transindividual, which metastabilizes itself *beyond this diversity of psychic and collective individuals*, and does so as social systems of every kind. This is what was at stake in the measures taken by Solon to break the tribal organization of archaic Greek society, after which Cleisthenes imposed isonomy through those institutions lying at the foundation of democratic Athens.

Social systems are themselves more or less adjusted and disadjusted to the technical system, of which they are the concretized and realized pharmacology – and this is what is at stake in what Durkheim already described as the *anomic disadjustments* provoked by the industrial division of labour (but he could not himself see that the issue is the relationship between the technical system and the social systems).[58]

Social systems take the indefinite diversity of collective individuals who form 'civil society' and organologically localize and transindividuate them as a political *unity*. They thus constitute a social milieu that, through a feedback loop,[59] for each psychic individual becomes the preindividual funds (or ground) of its psychic and collective individuation. In this way the transindividual becomes, for the psychosocial individual, a preindividual charged with potential, that is, destined for interpretation qua the funds of collective retentions and protentions transindividuated according to rules that are also the associated milieu of the psychosocial individual – on the *frame* of which he or she inscribes *motives to exist* that constitute his or her own psychic retentions and protentions.

Political individuation is regulated by a legislation founded on the right and duty to *interpret* the law, such that it forms the preindividual fund charged with potential that is, fundamentally, jurisprudence, insofar as it consists in *hermeneutic jurisprudence*.[60] Thus political law opens up ever new possibilities of interpretation that, because the law is written, and because citizens are taught to read and interpret, directly or indirectly, constitute this new form of psychic and collective individuation *founded on that literal tertiary retention* which is the text.

The text, inasmuch as it is accessible *à la lettre*, is interpretable in terms of its spirit beyond its letters – as *jurisprudentia* and as *vera philosophia*. It is *polemical* interpretation that makes the law here – not just in the juridical field but *in all epistemic fields*. This is why Heraclitus could write that *polemos* is the father of all things.

Polemical interpretation stems from psychic and collective individuals co-individuating with other psychic individuals by forming with them, in the *public* political space made possible by written *publication*, groups of interpretations, confronting each other through rules of controversy, disputation (emerging from *disputatio*, itself linked to *lectio*) and *public* debate – that is, before opinion that itself testifies to a *res publica* which knows how to read and is not reducible to an audience.

In a republic in good health, interpretations lead to disparation, organized publicly, legally and legitimately on the basis of a process of certified decision in accordance with peer-based criticism. In this way, political individuation is founded on a conception of truth that throughout the whole course of Western history has generated various regimes of truth. These are themselves founded on political technologies constituting what we here call an organology, which has continuously generated those disputes that constitute the dynamic principle of these individuations, inasmuch as they always presuppose a phase shift.

As we have seen by referring to Alan Greenspan's self-defence, any organology of any kind – for example, that of algorithmic governmentality that delegates processes of decision-making to automatons, which can only indefinitely unfurl the analytical consequences of the power of automated understanding in which this governmentality consists – must always be able to be dis-automatized.

This dis-automatization can occur in trance, by consuming peyote, in 'the Dreaming', and so on. In political society, including in its capitalist stage, this dis-automatization occurs primarily through *critique*.[61] This requires frequenting *skholē*, that is, a stop, a break, a pause: the leisure of intermittence within which alone it is possible to access consistences.

70. From the semantic web to the hermeneutic web

Tim Berners-Lee, who conceived and invented the world wide web (which was a supplementary invention of a whole new kind, since it was based from the outset on a partially automated categorization technology, and founded on HTML language), has declared that he dreams of a new age of the web that he names the 'semantic web':

> I have a dream for the Web [in which computers] become capable of analysing all the data on the Web – the content, links, and transactions between people and computers. A 'Semantic Web', which should make this possible, has yet to emerge, but when it does, the day-to-day mechanisms of trade, bureaucracy and our daily lives will be handled by machines talking to machines [...]. The intelligent 'agents' people have touted for ages will finally materialize.[62]

Berners-Lee inscribes this project within the broader perspective of what he calls 'philosophical engineering', which is similar to what is also called 'web science'. The goal of the semantic web is to automate the processing of information by computational models, but to do so in the service of the noetic individuals that we are.

But as noetic individuals we are, in the first place, *knowing* beings, and there is no form of knowledge that is reducible to the processing of information. We are formed and trained – that is, *individuated* – by our knowledge (of how to live, do and conceptualize) insofar as it is constituted by processes of collective individuation, and insofar as these processes of collective individuation are subject to public rules and form circuits of trans-individuation through *bifurcations* (which in the conceptual field lead to 'paradigm shifts' and 'epistemological breaks') that *dis-automatize* the implementation of existing rules.[63]

The semantic web, inasmuch as it enables the *automated pre-treatment of the informational hyper-material* that digital tertiary retentions constitute, cannot *in any case* produce knowledge. Knowledge is always *bifurcating* knowledge, that is, an experience of non-knowledge capable of engendering, through a new cycle of images[64] (which is to say, on the basis of new dreams), a new circuit in the process of transindividuation in which all knowledge consists. And as such, all knowledge contains the possibility of being dis-automatized through the act of knowing, where this knowing *interiorizes* the automatisms in which this knowledge *also* consists, but which through being automatized becomes anti-knowledge, that is, a dogma that can be dogmatic only by concealing from itself its dogmatic character, in other words, its automatic character.[65]

What Berners-Lee describes with the project of the semantic web is on the contrary a complete exteriorization of automatisms, where the artefacts that constitute the web are utilized to deprive those conforming to the semantic web of the possibility of dis-automatizing. This is why such an *automated semantic web* must be designed in direct connection with a *dis-automatizable hermeneutic web* (with the aid of the semantic automatons made possible by the semantic web). This dis-automatizable hermeneutic web will be founded on:

- a *new conception of social networks*;
- a *standardized annotation language*;
- *hermeneutic communities* emerging from the various domains of knowledge that have been established since the beginning of anthropization, and as the varying modalities of neganthropization.

Such an *organological upheaval* must be implemented by Europe – where the web was invented – and it should become the foundation of a continental development strategy. Europe should plan this strategy as a conflict of interpretations on the global scale of algorithmic governmentality, in order to *shape a dis-automatizable automatic society*, one that would be critiquable, that would take advantage of the automated semantic web, and that would be desirable – because it will generate neganthropic disparations.

This upheaval, founded on a supplementary invention, must be socialized – that is, must generate new circuits of transindividuation – through being implemented in public research and education. Education must itself become the point of entry into a production space for new practical and social value 'throughout life'. *Conceiving education in this new way should become the propaedeutic to a new intermittent status that opens rights to resource allocations according to these intermittent activities.* (This will be developed in the following chapters.)

Such an organization of automatic society, founded on a contributory income for intermittence, should receive preliminary testing in willing regions – and where the younger generations, catastrophically afflicted by the unemployment inherited from an obsolete age, should be encouraged to seize the unprecedented opportunities presented by an *automatic society*, not of fact *but of law*.

71. Simondonian thought undone by its algorithmic concretization – where time is outstripped

Describing their own work, Berns and Rouvroy say they have transposed their 'dual investigation [...] into the Simondonian and Deleuzian/Guattarian registers'.[66] And they highlight that the tele-objectivity constituted by algorithmic governmentality, instead of and in place of the statistical governmentality of what Foucault called biopower, seems to somehow unfurl and concretize what had been described by Simondon, and at the same time to empty it in advance of its content – and, as it were, to fold back on itself like a glove:

> While it seems *a priori* [...] to allow what Simondon referred to as the process of transindividual individuation – which [...] designates a process of the co-individuation of the *I* and the *we* [...] in associated milieus [...] – [algorithmic governmentality] on the contrary forecloses the possibility of such transindividual individuations by folding processes of individuation back into the subjective monad.[67]

This means that psychic individuation no longer participates in collective individuation and, as such, if we have read Simondon well, goes nowhere [*tourne à vide*].

What we referred to earlier as *trans-dividuation* is this *false* trans-individuation that short-circuits psychic individuals. The process of transindividuation and the transindividual are replaced by the transdividual and transdividuation, *automatized and concealed by the speed of their production*, and founded on this high speed. This outstripping [*prise de vitesse*] of psychic and collective individuals is a *taking-apart* [*déprise*] *of the form of the noetic* by the computational formlessness [*informe*] in which this speed consists – where taking-form, which is the basis on which Simondon thinks the elementary conditions of individuation,[68] always arrives too late.

This outstripping, this overtaking speed, leads to the disintegration of all taking of noetic form[69] by annihilating the *plastic potential* borne by those who serve it, who are instrumentalized through the dispossession, flattening and annihilation of their singularities, subjected to the loss of three-dimensionality in which algorithmic transindividuation consists. Collective individuals are diluted by the hypertrophy of the economic sub-system as it becomes increasingly autonomous from the social systems and deterritorializes itself by parasitizing and completely engulfing the technical system – and psychic individuals, who are diluted in return.

This phagocytic engulfing leads to 'the abandoning of every form of "scale", "standard" and hierarchy'.[70] This means that 'bottom-up' logic, artificially and automatically horizontalized, comes at the cost of a hidden verticalization, engendering disenchantment and disappointment

> in favour of an immanent and eminently plastic normativity (Deleuze and Guattari, *A Thousand Plateaus*) [that] is not necessarily favourable to the emergence of new forms of life in the sense of an emancipation of the kind described by Deleuze and Guattari in the form of an overcoming of the organizational plane by the plane of immanence.[71]

It is therefore not only the Simondonian analysis that seems to be emptied of its content by its algorithmic realization: it is also Deleuze and Guattari's analysis – which is connected to Simondon's.

The issue here is the thought of *organization* and its *organs*[72] – that is, the thought of the organology of the 'body without organs', which is also, in other words, the machine or the machinic. The 'desiring machine' of the 'body without organs' seems in this way to present itself as Turing's abstract machine: a machine that does not exist (a mathematical dream).

This is, however, not the case for the a-signifying semiotics of the machinic unconscious analysed by Guattari: machinic refers to concrete machines, such as the automobile. How to think the machinic unconscious starting from the body without organs? And why not also think this automaticity of the body enslaved to this machinic organ in terms of the processes of dis-automatization that it also produces?

A machine is *primordially concrete*, and this is what affects an existence – generally by collapsing existence onto the plane of subsistences while dividuating the individuation in which this existence consists. Sometimes – and this is exceptional, extraordinary and intermittent – a concrete machine can also project the relief of consistences onto the flatness of existences (which should here be thought also as *existances*).[73]

At stake here is the relationship between the 'bottom up' and the 'top down', which is also to say, between the *micro* and the *macro*, between the *dia*-chronic and the *syn*-chronic. More precisely, what must be reconsidered is the question of the *pathological* conditions (in Canguilhem's sense) of the emergence of a *normative* process – and as *hermēneia* in the pharmacological sense, that is, in the tragic sense,[74] as well as *categorization*.

Algorithmic governmentality *concretizes*[75] but, at the same time, *de-realizes* Simondonian thought, inasmuch as it amounts to a *governmentality of relations*, whereas the Simondonian programme is precisely to 'shift [...] from an ontology [...] of substance [...] to an ontology of relations'.[76] The Simondonian relation, however, is generated and metastabilized psychosocially via transindividuation, which transductively arranges the diachronic and the synchronic, that is, the micro and the macro, or again, the 'bottom up' and the 'top down'. This is precisely what is at stake in *L'Individu à la lumière des notions de forme et d'information*, where, as we have seen, disparation is dimensionality as temporality, that is, individuation as diachronization linking the psychic to the collective and vice versa: 'Time itself, according to this ontogenetic perspective, is considered to be the expression of the *dimensionality of being individuating itself*.'[77]

In algorithmic governmentality it is no longer a question of the *noetic time* of psychic and collective individuation but of *analytical speed*, which outstrips and overtakes this noetic time of beings that temporalize by noetizing, by *taking the time of synthesis*, that is, by realizing their dreams, the sources of their protentions, and as neganthropic time, inasmuch as it projects itself as a future beyond becoming. This becoming and its future are themselves opened up by individuation that is at once psychic, collective and technical: hence we return to the question of the doubly epokhal redoubling as the arrangement of supplementary inventions and categorial inventions.

That noetic time can be outstripped and overtaken means that it is preceded by the automatic spatialization of retentions and protentions operating at two-thirds of the speed of light (on fibre-optic networks), whereas between the cerebral organ and the receptor organs, along the network of nerves, it has long been known that a nerve impulse travels at a mere few tens of metres per second.

72. The disparations of the improbable and their rhizomatic dissolution

The notion of the rhizome is a matter of 'breaking with the vertical movement that leads us from the general to the particular irrespective of direction'.[78] Again, it seems that this rhizomatic reticularity is a perfect description of what occurs with algorithmic governmentality

– but contrary to any 'possibility of emancipation', as Berns and Rouvroy emphasize, or rather, as I would put it, against any possible quasi-causality on the part of the enslaved. And this is so because 'algorithmic governmentality tends [...] to prevent both processes of transindividual individuation and the openness to new significations borne by the relations between "disparate" entities'.[79] But on this point there seems to be some confusion.

There is no 'process of transindividual individuation'. There are processes of collective individuation that produce the transindividual in the course of a process of transindividuation (which Simondon does not theorize as such). The process of transindividuation does not coincide with collective individuation: collective individuation is what results from circuits of transindividuation that are synthesized in one or more processes of collective individuation, and *which can and must traverse these collective individuals*.

This is so because the psychic individual is related to and individuates with collective individuals that may be in contradiction with each other. This is why it must project itself onto the plane of a transindividuation of reference[80] in order to overcome these contradictions – and the superego is one such plane, which can be embodied in artificial crowds like the Church or the Army, but also in other forms, like the Fatherland, the Party, and so on.

There are, then, psychic individuals, collective individuals *and* processes of transindividuation that produce the transindividual – which is more or less common to all these layers. There is no collective individuation without transindividuation, but the transindividual does not remain enclosed within collective individuation.

In dissolving collective individuals, the process of automatized and fully computational trans*dividuation* erases the potential for 'disparation'.[81] In trans*individuation*, disparation is accomplished as a diversified and as such diachronic process of metastabilization, through which *idiomatic reliefs* emerge, so to speak, constituting local attractive convergences, but also, and contradictorily, 'deterritorialized' attractive convergences. The tension between the local and the deterritorialized constitutes consistences, that is, the plane of three-dimensionality wherein the local can overcome itself, project itself beyond its automatisms and dis-automatize itself on the basis of itself as an other (and in an other).

That there is adoption rather than adaptation amounts to the question of disparation inasmuch as it requires a trans-formation, that is, a quantum leap – and, as we saw in chapter 3, this possibility must be handled by the constitution of a *time of intermittence*. This *noetic* quantum leap, which constitutes psychic individuals as well as collective individuals, is the intermittent expression of the improbable qua prospect of any noesis.

Societies that have disappeared can come to haunt current societies and continue to remain there as the spirit (that is, as the spirits) of an epoch only because, coming back through the reactivations effected by the circuits of transindividuation constituted by the epoch,[82] these revenances are *potentials for the dis-automatization of the future*, which I call traumatypes, and which *are, again, the potential for an interruption to come, and that may come long after.*[83]

Knowledge is always composed of such circuits, that is, of circuits haunted by such revenances, and this is why any living knowledge is also an anamnesis provoked by an interruption (an *epokhē*), of which Socrates' *daimōn* is the improbable witness. This is what ties *psychic* individuation and *collective* individuation to their *common preindividual funds*, projecting a transindividual horizon beyond them. These hauntings constitute the 'multitudes' of spirits, that is, of traumatypes, animated by singularities – and through which the neganthropic process is constituted.

Now, if *'in algorithmic governmentality*, each subject is itself a multitude', and if this is so *as always*, but *here* it is treated *as such* by its *automated dividualization*, and *realizes* its 'multiplicity' only *by de-realizing it* – and where what is true of 'subjects' is equally true of the groups that collective individuals form, disintegrated by their trans-dividuation – being *'multiple without alterity'* (my italics), then what alterity can there be in an algorithmic governmentality: '[W]here can the emancipatory aspect of a transindividual or rhizomatic perspective be found when the desires that move us precede us?'[84]

To address this question we must begin by showing why the automatic protentions generated from the digital doubles of profiling are not exactly desires.[85]

In addition, the 'transindividual perspective' is not first and foremost emancipatory (and in any case emancipation is not the issue for Deleuze and Guattari).[86] The transindividual is not a dream *to come*: it is on the contrary what *results* from the process by which protentions (desires, and also dreams) *are realized and sometimes de-realized*, or even turn into nightmares, through regimes of truth that then become, via various kinds of automatism, dogmas. Algorithmic automatization, however, constitutes a type of dogmatization (and of the 'dogmatic' in the sense of Legendre and Supiot) of a completely new kind.

73.   The common, work and knowledge

Having questioned the possibility of an 'emancipatory aspect of a transindividual or rhizomatic perspective' in the context of an algorithmic governmentality that seems precisely to concretize such a perspective, Berns and Rouvroy posit that 'the challenge is the common'.[87]

The question of the common is that of *droit*, law and right. But this requires an organology of the common that *constitutes* this right.[88] The *organological community* that constitutes the right to the common has long been constituted in Western history by the supplementary invention of writing, that is, of literal tertiary retention, which has given rise to categorial invention for 2,700 years – and so to a succession of 'regimes of truth'.

Digital [*numérique*] tertiary retention is a new form of writing. The whole aim of Clarisse Herrenschmidt's work is to show this, basing her argument on the history of money as an apparatus of calculation distributed in and literally borne by society – and more specifically in the pockets and purses of those who hold it. Hence was constituted what we might be tempted to describe as *numeric or numismatic governmentality*, which precedes and prepares algorithmic governmentality through this protentional technology that is money.[89]

It is then a question of configuring the new *pharmakon* that is digital tertiary retention, not just through therapeutic prescriptions but in terms of its organological 'parameters', so to speak. The reticular writing in which the web consists is defined by protocols, norms and standards that are derived from recommendations. The reticulation of digital tertiary retentions, which is the principle on which the web is founded, must, in the future, be made to serve a categorial invention assisted by automatons. Such an invention must therefore be hermeneutic, neganthropic and founded on a collective dis-automatization that reconstitutes processes of disparation.

When Berns and Rouvroy write that 'the common needs and presupposes non-coincidence, for it is from the latter that processes of individuation occur, since this is what obliges us to address one another', they inscribe disparation into the heart of the symbolic, which itself constitutes the transindividual. Conversely, they show that it is the symbolic as such that is *disintegrated* by purely computational algorithmic governmentality.

The transformation of this state of fact by a state of law that will invent the sense and meaning of this fact requires the development of a network architecture founded on processes of contributory categorization.[90] Such processes will reconfigure the reticulation of digital tertiary retentions and thereby reconstitute a transindividuation capable of projecting the third dimension without which the common cannot be constituted. And in these processes, doubles – that is, the elements derived from analytical dividuation and transdividuation – become materials for transindividual syntheses, in other words, the reasons and motives of this governmentality thereby constituted in law, and not just in fact.

It turns out, from the work of Berns and Rouvroy, that we must pose the question of law and right on a new basis. From this perspective, it is not only Simondon, Deleuze and Guattari who are *both concretized and put in question* by this algorithmic 'plane of immanence', and, along with them, we who read them: it is also Foucault, inasmuch as he downplays the juridical question. We must, on the contrary, re-pose the question of law – and we must do so with Foucault – not only from the perspective of technologies of power, but also from the pharmacological perspective required by the organological constitution of noetic individuation, and inasmuch as it originally raises the question of the *ergon*, that is, of work as trans-*formation*.

For this, we must rethink work as what, with the end of employment, the latter having over-determined the understanding of the former by submitting it to the 'dogmas' of twentieth-century capitalism, again becomes the primary question. *Employment has disintegrated work*, just as fully computational governmentality is now disintegrating collective individuation. Work is not employment. It is possible to confound them only if work is understood in terms of the constraints of subsisting – if we think it only on the plane of subsistence. Work, however, is constitutive, both on the plane of existence and on the plane of consistence.

The Greeks initially conceived the positive law of the *politeia* on the basis of a separation between those who work, in the sense of those who are subject to subsistence, that is, slaves, who must renew subsistences through their work, and nobles, who are thereby discharged from this need, to the benefit of their existences as open to consistences – as *skholē* and as *otium*. Solon and Cleisthenes complicate these divisions by breaking up the tribes and clans, but law and right nevertheless remained, at that time and up until the end of the Ancien Régime, structurally separate from the economic sphere, thereby constituting the political sphere, and doing so as this very separating out of *otium* and the *vita activa*.

This conception was put into question even before the classical age, especially with the Reformation and more generally with the rise of the bourgeoisie. But it was the industrial revolution that forever turned this upside down, by integrating knowledge into the functions of production – which was a radical transformation of knowledge, and a radical transformation of law itself. What Alain Supiot calls the spirit of Philadelphia is inscribed in this becoming.

The critique of social struggles in the context of the 'Fordist compromise', then the conservative revolution – which Bruno Trentin has characterized through the assertion that 'if it ever became fully conscious of its long cultural subordination to Taylorism and Fordism, the left would courageously start grieving'[91] – must now be reconsidered with respect to the end of employment. Far from being equivalent to an end of work, the latter is what should instead be rediscovered and redefined – for an essence of work is as non-existent as a Heaven of Ideas.

Alain Supiot, who reminds us that work alone creates wealth, analyses the conditions in which, starting from the 'neo-liberal counter-revolution' of the 1980s, capital has constantly undermined it, showing how the key notion of a social right arose from the Declaration of Philadelphia, and how this social right then itself became a political 'regime of law' incorporating the economic sphere.[92]

Rethinking work in the epoch of automatons, which will eliminate a vast number of jobs in the next twenty years, is a key element of a new arrangement between politics, economics *and knowledge*.

6

On Available Time for the Coming Generation

[T]o the degree that large industry develops, the creation of real wealth comes to depend less on labour time and on the amount of labour employed than on the power of the agencies set in motion during labour time, whose 'powerful effectiveness' is itself in turn out of all proportion to the direct labour time spent on their production, but depends rather on the general state of science and on the progress of technology, or the application of this science to production. [...] As soon as labour in the direct form has ceased to be the great well-spring of wealth, labour time ceases and must cease to be its measure, and hence exchange value [must cease to be the measure] of use value. The *surplus labour of the mass* has ceased to be the condition for the development of general wealth, just as the *non-labour of the few*, for the development of the general powers of the human head.

Karl Marx[1]

74. Law, work, wages

Mikhaïl Xifaras has taught or reminded us[2] that the 'very young Marx',[3] who began by studying law and legal history with Friedrich Carl von Savigny, wanted to turn jurisprudence into true philosophy. But Marx's critique of what he understood as the juridical fictions produced by what he then called the bourgeoisie – that is, by this 'revolutionary'[4] class who wanted to remove the legal right to collect dead wood, a right to the *commons* of *feudal* origin, which, as Xifaras shows, was for Marx a very uncomfortable reality[5] – ultimately led him to denounce the formal and fictional character of law in general.

In so doing, Marx inscribed *work* at the heart of what, as the 'effective reality' of the human condition, constitutes the relations of production through which human beings produce their 'means of existence' – and thus *transform* the world rather than merely interpreting it. *They realize it, that is, artificialize it,* by *realizing* the organological fictions occurring in the course of what we ourselves understand as processes of psychic, technical and social individuation.

Marx, however, will never problematize the question of *artifice as such,* beyond the perhaps too celebrated 'commodity fetishism', nor will he problematize the question of the relations and differences between fictions and artifices – so that we could, for example, argue that an artifice is *fictive* if it *is not realizable,* even though a fiction, as an unrealizable artifice, may be *necessary.*

Continuing the great discourse of Hegel on the exteriorization of spirit, while reversing its conditions, Marx described the fate of work, revolutionized as it was by the bourgeoisie – itself seizing upon a technical revolution and completing it, as a dialectical, ineluctable and general process of proletarianization through the development of wage labour. This is what led him in 1857 to the question of the *general intellect* – which is also to say, to the question of knowledge objectified by what we call tertiary retention.

Machinic retention therefore amounts to knowledge materialized *for* production, but no longer *by* it: conception is separated from production. The materialization of knowledge thus conceived and concretized (and this term must be understood also in the Simon-donian sense[6]) then constitutes the heart of the economic dynamic, and ultimately leads Marx to the question of automatization as such.

Work is above all, in all its forms ('manual' or 'intellectual'), a producer of retention: to produce is always in one way or another *to organize the inorganic,* or to contribute to its organization.[7] It is thus to form tertiary retentions that support the collective secondary retentions forming the circuits of transindividuation through which the transindividual is metastabilized.

The *operation* of work trans-forms the materials into which the elements of a *system of traces* have been inscribed and distributed. These elements are formed, on the one hand, from the organized inorganic matter[8] that constitutes utensils, tools, instruments, machines and devices, and, on the other hand, from *organological synaptic circuits*[9] that are *correspondingly* inscribed in the noetic brains of 'manual' or 'intellectual' workers,[10] and finally from rules implemented through social organizations (institutional or entrepreneurial, public or private), which, building upon the hypomnesic tertiary retentions derived from grammatization,[11] coordinate, prescribe, regulate, programme, standardize and certify this or that aspect of this vast traceology.

We can call hypomnesic those tertiary retentions whose primary functions are symbolization and the recording of memory – from the fetish to the algorithm – constituting the archives of principles (*arkhai*). In principle – that is, in law, and, in the Western societies that emerge from Greece and Judea, as *positive* law, law that is enunciated and formalized – the social systems founded on retentional systems that metastabilize collective individuations are transcendent in relation to both psychic and technical individuals.

In other words, *in principle*, hypomnesic tertiary retentions control the common tertiary retentions derived from production and work. *In fact*, in our epoch, digital tertiary retention invalidates this 'hierarchy of norms' while penetrating the ensemble of common objects – which will be even more true once IPv6 concretizes the general spread of the internet of things. This state of fact systematizes, and will increasingly systematize, the situation described by Laurent Thévenot.[12]

In a very general way, and since the beginning of hominization, the practice of tools and instruments has *disorganized* and *reorganized* the brains, minds and spirits of workers and instrumentalists of all kinds, which are formed during these practices. This reorganization of the organic is an 'organologization' and as such an artificialization of the cerebral organ – this is true for musical instruments, for the alphabet and for any instrumental practice. This is why Walter Ong is right to refer to Plato's 'literate mind'.[13]

Social organizations constitute the frameworks for cooperation between brains[14] as the transformation of the world, that is, as the realization of artifices, and through the imposition of law. But since Plato, and in legal thought in general, the hypomnesic and therefore organological foundations supporting the differentiation of fact and law, as Ong highlights, have been denied and repressed – both by philosophers and by jurists. Given the contemporary state of fact, this is no longer sustainable.

The operation of work opens the world as a system of traces, both inorganic and cerebral (these traces being themselves both organic and organological), forming and sedimenting the most elementary layers of the processes of transindividuation. And this sedimentation begins with the earliest forms of learning that constitute the premises and conditions of work: playing, walking, speaking and knowing how to live in society.

Processes of psychic, technical and collective individuation are organologically integrated through the operation of work as it 'per-laborates' – if we can take up this neologism derived from psycho-analysis (in order to translate *Durcharbeitung*, 'working through')

– the system of traces in which consist primary, secondary and tertiary retentions and the retentional systems through which processes of transindividuation (that is, of symbolization) are negotiated.

Technical individuation can be accomplished only to the extent that it generates psychic individuations themselves formative of collective individuations. This integration becomes a disintegration when technical integration occurs at the expense of psychic and collective individuations. Today we see this occurring, and we see it spreading. At this moment in which we are witnessing the collapse of wage labour, this state of fact demands reflection, critique and a politics of the functions and stakes of tertiary retention in the three organological layers that constitute a redefined 'total social fact'.[15]

75. The organology of proletarianization

Hominization is immediately engaged with and as the technicization of life, inasmuch as the biological organs of the technical living being are not sufficient to guarantee its survival, and inasmuch as, in order to survive, this new form of life must *invent artificial organs that in return 'organologize' its cerebral organ*. Hence arises the epiphylogenetic, technical and artificial memory in which consist the first forms of tertiary retention, some three million years ago.[16]

Much later, but still at least forty thousand years ago and probably longer, starting in the Upper Palaeolithic, mnemotechnical tertiary retentions in the strict sense appear. After the Neolithic, *hypomnēmata* arise in the form of systems of numeration, abacuses, ephemerides, calendars, various forms of ideographic writing, and so on.

The proletarianization of manual work begins at the end of the eighteenth century, when machinic tertiary retentions appear, derived in part from the automated formalizations of movement inaugurated by Vaucanson, and in part from the possibility, realized by Watt, of turning heat into usable motor power.[17] The trans-*formation* of the inorganic, organic and organological materials in which psychic, technical and collective individuations consist *are then functionally disintegrated*. 'Functionally' means that industrial capitalism is *based* on the dis-integration of the proletariat, who are thus *expelled* from the process of individuation.

It is through this proletarianization that wage labour is established, that is, employment, as the organization of this disintegrating functionality. Employment is characterized by the fact that the retentions produced by work no longer pass through the brains of the producers, who are themselves no longer individuated by work, and who are therefore no longer the bearers and producers of work-knowledge: de-singularized, they become a pure labour force and a commodity that can be replaced by a similar commodity in the job market.

It is from this traceological perspective,[18] from which employment is constituted as a *function of dis-apprenticeship*, that we must interpret Wiener's statement, cited by Friedmann, highlighting that generalized cybernetics continues to accentuate this state of fact: 'The modern industrial revolution is similarly bound to devalue the human brain [...]. [T]he average human being of mediocre attainments or less has nothing to sell that is worth anyone's money to buy.'[19]

Almost seventy years after this 'prophecy' by the 'founder of cybernetics', we note that systemic stupidity, which now afflicts each and every one of us in 24/7 capitalism (and it seems that the further up the hierarchy it 'rises', the more it is an affliction – from Greenspan to a large proportion of the 'decision-makers' and 'officials' ['*responsables*'], who thus become both unconscious and impotent), means that 'average human beings' no longer seem to exist – and this is so *at the very moment* when new oligarchies claim to have exempted themselves from the ordinary through purely techno-logical pathways.[20]

Wiener demonstrates that this figure of the average human being,[21] whose brain is devalued because it is disembrained, that is, short-circuited, represents a huge problem:[22] this means that the average human being and his or her brain are 'obsolete' – just as are theory and scientific method, according to Anderson – that is, useless and costly for society, and no doubt a danger to themselves and others, for a noetic soul cannot bear to remain in a state of pointlessness without any larger or more sublime alternative.

This 'average human being' first appears with the employee subject to protocols supported and defined by machines, apparatus, manuals, procedures, reporting systems and management control – even though this employee now finds himself or herself without employment, short-circuited by algorithms that outstrip psychic individuals and collective individuals, functioning *without a controller and without reason.*[23]

Beginning at the end of the eighteenth century and eventually generalized with cybernetics, the disorganization of the cerebral apparatus of producers and other proletarianized employees is no longer tied to any reorganization of their noetic brain via the interiorization of new circuits of transindividuation, that is, via the acquisition and enriching of knowledge. Instead, their reflex systems are subjected to objectified knowledge that has itself been turned into self-propelled automatisms (in relation to which proletarianized nervous systems are auxiliaries only to the extent that they remain absolutely necessary).

Until the advent of Taylorization at the beginning of the twentieth century, a turning point that proved very awkward for Lenin,[24] workers in the 'trades', such as fitters and turners, still managed to escape this desertification of the labouring brain: 'The turner was a partner, having usually benefited from an apprenticeship of at least three years. [...] Almost as much as his tools, he was attached to his machine by personal links.'[25] But the so-called 'scientific organization' of work brought an end to the specialization of tasks founded on automatisms: 'Today [in 1950] [...] most turners in large-scale industry are, in fact, specialized but unskilled manual workers, using their machines to execute fragmented and repetitive work, where the assemblies are all prepared, the tools set, the details strictly fixed in advance by the time and motion study department.'[26] Extending his analysis to the tasks of moulders and core setters, Friedmann quotes Henry Ford: '95 per cent are unskilled, or to put it more accurately, [they] must be skilled in exactly one operation which the most stupid man can learn within two days.'[27]

This functional 'stupidity' – specifically of those so-called 'specialized' but unskilled workers, and today this functional stupidity is also at work in algorithmic governmentality as much as in the 'trades' and in other, supposedly 'intellectual' 'professions' – now characterizes *all employees* insofar as they cannot and must not produce collective secondary retentions:[28] the employee sets the machines that utilize collective secondary retentions conceived, standardized and implemented by departments studying time and motion within automated organs. Collective secondary retentions are turned into machinic tertiary retentions or technologies of all kinds, and become invisible, that is, unthinkable – without controllers and without reason.

This is why, when Hegel describes work in the master/slave dialectic, he is *not* describing the job of the proletarianized employee. And it is also why Marxists misunderstand the dialectic of the master and 'slave':[29] what Hegel describes through the dialectical inversion of the situation of the servant, *Knecht* (and not the slave, *Sklave*), is the conquering power of the bourgeoisie, which generates new knowledge in the sphere of work and in society[30] – new forms of knowledge that form around retentional processes that the *work of the bourgeois* creates and deploys.

This power is in no way that of the proletarian. The power of the servant-become-bourgeois, dialectically inverting the condition given to him by his master, derives from the process of the work of 'perlaboration'[31] that he generates in the labour emerging from bourgs and their craftsmen and traders, enriching himself with a knowledge that the master never possessed. This cannot be the case for the proletarian, who is characterized precisely by the fact that he *can no longer* access knowledge – the impediment here being *organological*.[32]

Nowadays, with full and generalized automatization, and even more so in the future, there is and will continue to be a decreasing need for employees to serve and set machines that are increasingly becoming completely automatic. These machines are increasingly *externalities*[33] that produce the traces generated by 'connected' psychic individuals who set the parameters of the systems of production and distribution characteristic of algorithmic governmentality. They are increasingly integrated, increasingly autonomous and no longer served by producers but by consumers – despite which we remain within the generalized insolvency of what this system inherently installs.

The question of law, as posed by Antoinette Rouvroy,[34] requires that the liberation of the time saved by automatization be used not for production or consumption, nor even for finalized design,[35] but instead to open *new juridical possibilities*. The challenge is to know in what conditions a *new traceology*, as a *deliberate organological arrangement of psychic, technical and collective individuals*, this deliberation constituting these collective individuals as such, could move on from the 24/7, hyper-consumerist capitalism described by Crary, the structural insolvency of which can only increase as a result of the collapse of purchasing power brought about by the decline in wage labour. What are the constitutive conditions – that is, the *constitutional* conditions[36] – of such an organological deliberation qua deliberate traceological arrangement?

It is now increasingly the unpaid 'work' of consumers – which *is not* work but dividuation[37] as the *employment of unpaid time* – that, by *harnessing this employment of the time* of the individuals whom we try to remain, feeds, reinforces and sets the parameters of the automated and performative collective retentions produced by *totally* computational capitalism. This 24/7 traceology allows this new form of capitalism to automatically generate and control the collective protentions[38] that outstrip and overtake individuals, both psychic and collective. And it is for *this* reason that it can and should be called *totally* computational.

This state of fact became possible only because, during the twentieth century, and with the rise of the analogue culture industries, it was consumers who, in their turn, found themselves caught in a process of mass disindividuation: the proletarianization of life-knowledge then being tied to that of work-knowledge.[39] The collective secondary retentions that characterize ways of life were then produced by marketing firms, carrying out what was demanded by research and development departments, via systems for controlling collective retentions and protentions, short-circuiting the collective individuals who had hitherto metastabilized and transindividuated dialogical relations of co-individuation via social systems (which were subsequently and consequently completely discredited).[40]

In the twenty-first century, the analogue culture industries are replaced by the digital reticularity of 24/7 capitalism that Crary describes. Proletarianized consumers, functionally integrated into the computational technical system through their reticulation, and psychically and socially disintegrated by the resulting dividuation,[41] can then replace proletarianized producers or service providers, and themselves become the auxiliary agents of artificial organs of information, decision and production, now completely automatized.

The decerebration that Alfred Jarry saw was at work not long after Nietzsche had announced the growth of the desert seems to be realized as complete cerebral desertification – and as a global nightmare.

76.   The reinvention of work

The computerization of society began in the 1960s. It is thought as such at the end of the 1970s in the report by Simon Nora and Alain Minc to Valéry Giscard d'Estaing entitled *The Computerization of Society*,[42] and it amounts to a new age of automation, as Georges Elgozy showed in 1968 (ten years before *The Computerization of Society*):

> Until the middle of the twentieth century, a non-aggression pact stabilized a more or less peaceful coexistence between humans and machines. Like all pacts, it was transitional. [...] Infinitely more powerful and autonomous, the automations of the second half of the twentieth century will quickly break this equilibrium. Item by item, they will replace their less-evolved ancestors. And at the same time many workers, in offices and in factories.[43]

In 1993, the opening to the global public of the internet network, via the protocols of the world wide web, set in place an infrastructure that would profoundly transform telecommunications technology and lead to the total reticulation of every territory – *all of which* then become, along highly diverse paths, 'digital territories', including in the desert.

Territories that have become digital then 'equip' their inhabitants with mobile or fixed devices compatible with networks conforming to the internet protocol. Humans and machines find themselves connected twenty-four hours a day, seven days a week with the entire planet, that is, with the economic players of the entire world – and frequently also, if not always, with secret services.

During the 1990s, more than forty years after the work and warnings of Georges Friedmann, and with the productivity gains that have resulted from these immense transformations, the question of work and of its future has imposed itself on public opinion and become a major debate within European industrial countries – notably at the instigation of German sociology and social democracy, but also due to a bestseller by Jeremy Rifkin, *The End of Work*, to which Michel Rocard contributed the preface of the French edition, and on which André Gorz provided a commentary in 1995.[44]

After Friedmann foreshadowed the destruction of work during the 1950s, Gorz reintroduced this thesis in France in the 1980s. He did so on a new basis and by breaking with the traditional Marxist discourse on the historical destiny of the proletariat. Departing to a greater or lesser extent from the dominant discourse forged in the framework of the 'Fordist compromise' (which was already the case for Friedmann[45]), this debate was deepened in 1995 by Dominique Méda in *Le Travail. Une valeur en voie de disparition*,[46] and popularized in North America by Rifkin in the same year, and then reflected in French planning policies, and policies on the sharing of work-time.

Lionel Jospin and Martine Aubry, too, initiated a vote on the law limiting the working week to thirty-five hours. Prior to that, and by reviving a discourse of the French Popular Front, François Mitterrand had reduced the length of the working week from forty to thirty-nine hours, and extended annual leave, while at the same time grabbing attention by creating a Ministry of Free Time. Over these years, and through these changes of labour law founded on various studies, a question arose that has today arisen again, and in a more pressing way than ever, about the *principles by which to redistribute productivity gains* in forms other than wage increases and purchasing power.

This question must now be urgently raised once again, but on the basis of other principles than those advanced in the framework of the debate over what would eventually be called the 'reduction of work time'. For what was feared by Friedmann and also by Elgozy has now materialized – to a degree that probably neither of them could have imagined, and where the issue is no longer the reduction of the 'time of work', which in reality referred to the *reduction of the time of employment*, but rather *the end of employment* and, as the title of Dominique Méda and Patricia Vendramin's most recent book seems to indicate, *the reinvention of work.*[47]

Friedmann wondered in 1950 if '*only* [my italics] the scholar and the *manager* are assured [...] of surviving the technical substitutions proliferated by the development of automation in the current phase of industrial revolutions'.[48] But if we are to believe Anderson and Greenspan, in fact *neither* the scholar *nor* the manager will be spared from proletarianization, that is, ultimately, from the obsolescence of their functions, or some of their functions – and in any case their principal one, namely, to make *decisions*. Hence a blind becoming is established, a becoming that is without future and thoroughly entropic.

We must re-establish a *difference* between fact and law that will give control of decision-making back to psychic and collective individuals insofar as they are noetic. This concerns not only the work of the scholar or the manager but indeed that of all noetic individuals insofar as they have a right and a duty to *access not employment*, which is clearly in decline and the function of which has become obsolete, *but work*, as what develops outside employment, and as the *power of dis-automatization*, that is, as constituting the neganthropic future of a new industrial age of life on earth.

We must ground an algorithmic governmentality *in law* on a *new law of work* as well as on a new conception of work. This new conception of work must itself be based on a *new status* of knowledge and of its elaboration, transmission and the way it is implemented in economic life. This new law of and right to work must *constitute* (in the juridical as well as the philosophical sense) a new epoch of work, and we shall see that this notion is thoroughly historical, rather than containing any ontological dimension: it can be thought only in, after and as a field of possibilities within an organological situation, which is obviously also and immediately an economic and political situation – and it must be thought as constituting the various modalities of knowledge (of how to live, do and conceptualize).

77.   Hands, works, brains

In his preface to the third edition of *Où va le travail humain?*, Friedmann writes that, in its euphoric period between 1950 and 1955, the literature about automation was mostly fuelled by a remarkable faith in the ability of machines to lead to new skilled employment, in the rapid reabsorption of 'displaced' personnel and in the highly cultural use of (increased) leisure time by the beneficiaries of a reduced working week. Today, these hopes have been placed into serious doubt, if not dashed.[49]

Such hopes persist in France, and attempts are made to revive them by specialists in automation like Michel Volle and Marc Giget, however different their perspectives may be, and to do so while emphasizing the gravity and the urgency of the situation, thereby introducing new considerations that amount to fundamental shifts.

Marc Giget extols in classical fashion an innovation policy founded on what he calls a creative synthesis of technologies derived from the 'creative destruction' in which full and generalized automatization still consists.[50] He stresses, however, that in the United States, a country that in Friedmann's eyes was already 'ahead' on these questions in the 1950s, destruction has become more destructive than creative, with countless analysts focusing above all on the completely unprecedented character of the employment situation resulting from digital technologies.

Having shown the collapse in the number of jobs created by start-ups in Silicon Valley between 2006 and 2011, Giget quotes and comments on Chris Zook, who in June 2012 published an article in the *Harvard Business Review*, 'When "Creative Destruction" Destroys More Than It Creates', in which he reports that 'of the 70,000 companies with market data available, more than 42,000 [...] failed to create any value for investors. [...] Only 9% of companies achieved even a modest level of sustained and profitable growth.'[51]

In March 2013, A. M. Gittlitz published 'Your iPhone Kills Jobs'.[52] In May 2013, an article by Bernice Napach in Yahoo's *Daily Ticker* took up and analysed a statement by Jaron Lanier in *Who Owns the Future?*: 'The Internet is killing more jobs than it creates.'[53] In June 2013, David Rotman published 'How Technology Is Destroying Jobs' in the *MIT Technology Review*, pointing to the analyses of Erik Brynjolfsson:

Brynjolfsson, a professor at the MIT Sloan School of Management, and his collaborator and coauthor Andrew McAfee have been arguing [...] that impressive advances in computer technology – from improved industrial robotics to automated translation services – are largely behind the sluggish employment growth of the last 10 to 15 years.

Even more ominous for workers, the MIT academics foresee dismal prospects for many types of jobs as these powerful new technologies are increasingly adopted not only in manufacturing, clerical, and retail work but in professions such as law, financial services, education, and medicine.[54]

Fifty years earlier, in 1963, that is, at the peak of the famous Trente Glorieuses,[55] Friedmann had pointed out that in the United States

where the 'technological revolution' is more advanced than elsewhere, [...] the displacement [of jobs], of which it is the origin, is such that these losses are not absorbed, far from it, by new jobs in the expanding sectors. [...] This evolution is still in its infancy. The utilization of electronic machines has much further to go.[56]

This is what Michel Volle analyses in the current context by showing that the apparatus of what is no longer just the 'means of production' cannot now be understood in the terms of classical analyses, such that the labour force should be referred to in terms not of *handwork or manpower* [*main-d'œuvre*] but of *brainwork or brainpower* [*cerveau-d'oeuvre*].[57]

The 'absolute automaton' that is the computer – Derrida spoke, with respect to nuclear weapons, of the absolute *pharmakon*[58] – which Volle calls the 'ubiquitous programmable automaton' (UPA),[59] gives rise to a shift from a work-world centred on manpower to one centred on brainpower. Just as the coupling of hand and machine lay at the origin of the industrial revolution, the UPA and the brain form a revolutionary couple at the origin of a new society and a new economy – which Volle calls the iconomy.

To conceptualize this coupling, he relies on Simondon's theory of amplification (which I will myself discuss in the second volume of *Automatic Society*). This means that the passage from manpower to brainpower involves a transductive relation. Such a conception of the dynamic between the noetic living being and the microelectronic inorganic matter organized by algorithms that is the UPA is very close to an organological perspective.

In the iconomy, production is no longer based on working hours, which is a 'challenge for the education system', whose aim is no longer to form producers but ... but *who*? *for what*? What kind of human being, and for what kind of *work* [*oeuvre*] – if it is indeed a question of craft [*ouvrer*], of opening [*ouvrir*] and of working [*oeuvrer*] – should the education system *form rather than deform*? We will see in the next chapter that the question here is that of the *ergon* and *erga*: work and works. *It is a question of* Bildung *in the epoch of digital tertiary retention.*

The word 'oeuvre' in the phrase *main-d'oeuvre* is in truth *misleading* with respect to the coupling of human and machine, since this machine contributes to proletarianization such as it was described by, for example, Friedmann and Ford. In the relationship between the hand and the machine, it is the latter that 'works' – and it does so blindly, that is, automatically, in a way that cannot, however, easily be described as craft or work, *ouvrage* or *oeuvre*, given that this word always indicates an opening: this form of production, 'serial production', means on the contrary that the system is closed. We refer to serial production to the extent that the products are not works but rather *ready-made commodities*.

If it is indeed a question, as Volle stresses, of thinking the transductive relation between the brain and the absolute automaton that is the UPA – that is, between, on the one hand, this living organ that is the central nervous system, insofar as it has the capacity to interiorize social circuits of transindividuation supported and conditioned by tertiary retentions through which this organ disorganizes and reorganizes itself, and, on the other hand, the apparatus of production and the processing of digital tertiary retentions that is the UPA, which, in the current and factual state of social disorganization tends to short-circuit this interiorization, and thereby tends to de-socialize and de-noeticize this cerebral organ – then it is the whole of social organization that is at stake in this question, and, with it, law and right.

The traceology embedded in the ubiquitous (that is, reticular) programmable automaton is not limited to secondary collective retentions characteristic of a firm or an occupation. It encodes, over-codes and recovers worlds, 'representations of the world', 'conceptions of the world', 'understandings that being-there has of its being', which it 'materializes' and 'tertiarizes' while short-circuiting them: it integrates and disintegrates conception, production, distribution, consumption, recommendation, and so on, leading to the emergence of many new kinds of milieus around economic actors, so-called 'business ecosystems'.

Behind the question of right that imposes itself as that of a new right to work that can no longer be conceived as a right to wage labour, but must be seen as a *new age of noesis*, it is the solvency of the entirety of Fordist-Keynesian economics, and Schumpeterian economics, that is at stake – employment is no longer the issue. The question becomes, then, that of a *formation* conceived as *Bildung*, that is, as an in-advance struggle for psychic individuals, forming them and immunizing them as much as possible against the *deformation* that is the potentially absolute automaton, which is also and irreducibly an absolute *pharmakon* – that is, an absolutely entropic poison – and of doing so by producing a new kind of value.

When formation – both in general and as professional training – was no longer conceived within the framework of the specialization derived from Taylorism's extreme industrial division of labour, it still developed *fundamentally* as a function of *wage labour* production, extended to services and ultimately to all repetitive tasks, as Giget, Volle and many others have shown. Yet both general and professional training can no longer be envisaged or conceived from the perspective of the division of labour. Formation must be based on the new conditions created by the digital within the general intellect as introduced in the *Grundrisse*.

In these new conditions, where for the first time the question arises of the survival of humankind within a few generations, *wealth will in the future be evaluated and produced by and as the totality of society's new neganthropic capabilities.*

78. The fundamental contradiction of the left with respect to work, its status, its division and its time

In reading or rereading Gorz, and before him Friedmann, and today Giget, Volle and their many sources, the question that is raised, and that Dominique Méda and Patricia Vendramin raise in *Réinventer le travail*, is that of knowing whether productivity, which will escalate in spectacular fashion in the next few years thanks to full and generalized automatization, should *liberate time* or *liberate work*. It is a question of knowing the precise meaning (in terms of social reorganization) of 'free time' and 'liberated work'.

If it is a question of *liberating time*, in what conditions can it be said that time is *free* or *available*, as Gorz said,[60] and *for what* is it available – if not for advertisers on TF1, supplying them with what Patrick Le Lay called 'available brain time', or now for those on Netflix or Google?[61]

If full and generalized automatization must *liberate time in general*, how are we to avoid this 'liberated' and hence 'available' time becoming a new 'available brain time', no longer televisual but Googlian, Amazonian, Facebookian, or some other, as the time of the *contributory capture of attention* by algorithmic governmentality that Alain Giffard describes as a reading industry[62] and Frédéric Kaplan as an entropic economy of expression[63] – intensifying and complexifying the proletarianization of the consumer 'liberated' from the time of employment, that is, the proletarianization of the producer?

That time is liberated essentially for consumption, even if it is 'cultural' consumption, is what Jeremy Rifkin himself observes concerning the reduction of working time in France, but without perceiving either the stakes or the tragedy: 'More free time has also had an effect on consumption: cafés, cinemas, theatres and shops are doing well.'[64]

As for the *liberation of work*, how would it be possible for this to constitute anything other than the advent of Gary Becker's *entrepreneur of himself*,[65] or a generalization of work into 'projects', according, for example, to the Hollywood model described by Boltanski and Chiapello,[66] and by Rifkin,[67] or again, how could it lead to a figure other than that of Pierre-Michel Menger's *artist as worker*?[68]

In *Réinventer le travail*,[69] Dominique Méda and Patricia Vendramin show that these debates have developed mainly on the left and at the initiative of social democracy, on the basis of a profound contradiction and historical misunderstanding: whereas Marx, who inspired and founded leftist discourse on work, advocated the overcoming of wage labour and the advent of liberated work, trade unions, labour parties and social democratic parties have always defended employment, that is, wage labour. And during the current downturn they are defending it (when they are not in power) or claiming to defend it (when they are) more than ever. Gorz, who contributed greatly to the critique and overcoming of this state of fact, engaged in a dialogue with, and was inspired by, Bruno Trentin, who himself analysed this situation.[70]

Wage labour, work that has become employment, loses its *inherent interest*, that is, as *intrinsically producing knowledge* for those who work – insofar as it weaves processes of transindividuation and therein constitutes a circuit of recognition, or of what Alexandre Kojève described as the 'desire of desire'.[71] If we could argue that *consumerist* capitalism is condemned to disappear – even if it gives way to chaos – because it destroys the desire of the consumer, we see here that it also destroys the desire of the producer. From a knowing worker, forming knowledge [*savoirs*] and hence acceding to savours [*saveurs*], the producer-become-employee is confronted with the *insipidity* of a world that he or she no longer opens up, and that no longer opens to him or her in return.

No longer having knowledge, this employee, who embodies the de-brained average human being whom we have all more or less become, can no longer give to the world its savours or its tastes [*goûter*]: in relation to this 'world', of which he or she is neither the worker nor the opening that Hegel saw in the servant and his service, this employee is literally disgusted [*dégouté*].

We have already seen – as Méda and Vendramin say, but in different terms – that with Taylorization, then with the organization of consumption and the constitution of mass markets by the culture industries, proletarianization transforms work *in its totality* via jobs emptied of all knowledge and by defining skills only in terms of 'employability', that is, 'adaptability'. With work-knowledge and life-knowledge having been shifted into machines and into communications and information systems that transform them into automatisms without a subject, the proletarianization of all forms of knowledge finally reaches (in our time) the functions of planning and decision-making – Greenspan included.

Crafts and skills, métiers, give way to jobs that empty them of their content and no longer provide satisfaction to employees, and the *compensation* granted in order to negotiate the submission of the producer to the constraints of production is no longer founded on any knowledge or pleasure provided by the job (as individuation) but on purchasing power – with what Jean-Claude Milner called the 'wages of the ideal' being an attempt to escape from this condition.[72]

The 'defence of purchasing power' therefore becomes, in fact, a common concern for both 'capital' and 'labour', even though it obviously takes very different forms in each case. 'Capital' needs purchasing power in order to sell commodities, and the representatives of the 'workers' negotiate in order to maximize the compensation in which this purchasing power consists.

The result is what Trentin described and Linhardt anticipated,[73] namely, a *generalized conceptual disarming of the left*, a left who claim to be inspired by Marxist thinking and, more generally, by nineteenth-century socialist critiques of labour – which for Marx, as Méda and Vendramin recall, meant that *wage labour must necessarily be abolished*:

> For Marx, work was in itself a pure power of expression, creative freedom, but in order to actualize this potential it must first be liberated. As a good Hegelian, he believed in the need to liberate work – and therefore to abolish wage labour.[74]

For the twentieth-century left, however, 'far from being abolished, the bond to wage labour instead becomes anchored to different rights:

the right to work, the right to social protection, but also the right to consume':

> Wages become central and, as Robert Castel has shown, the very core of what must be preserved and what makes work desirable. Instead of abolishing the wage relation, social democratic discourse and practice will make wage labour the channel by which wealth will be spread and the means by which a more just social order (founded on work and capabilities) will be progressively put in place.[75]

Today, such a standpoint has become absolutely impossible. It is impossible because it has become increasingly clear that this point of view is based on a profound confusion of work and employment, on a misunderstanding of the nature of proletarianization as a loss of knowledge, and on a systematic denial of the fate of work when the general intellect turns into the computerization of society, eventually leading to the generalization of reticular writing.

This fate is the end of employment, the structural uselessness of the employee and therefore the *inevitable withering of wage labour*. The end of employment, which has become obvious, is the primary question that today confronts the left, and other political forces – whether they like it or not – just as it confronts capital and the representatives of the 'working world'.

79.   Alienated labour and liberated work

The conceptually impoverished and miserable state of the contemporary left, particularly in France, stems firstly from the contradictions and denials previously identified by Trentin and today by Méda and Vendramin. Proclamations in 'defence of employment' are issued in perfect harmony across both sides of industrial relations: 'The contradiction in relation to Marx's thought is complete, since social democratic discourse argues that work will become fulfilling even if it is today primarily wage increases and consumption that make work desirable.'[76] But for Marx, on the other hand, work can be fulfilling only if it ceases to be wage labour and becomes free.

Those who spout this 'social democratic discourse' are talking not about work but about employment. Referring to Jürgen Habermas, Méda and Vendramin add:

> [S]ocial democracy is founded on a profound contradiction to the extent that it thinks work [...] as the essential modality of human fulfilment, both individually and collectively [...], while no longer

> providing the means for creating *a* work (since work remains hetero-
> nomous, exercised with another goal in mind) and especially not a
> collective work for which work would be the site of some genuine
> cooperation.[77]

Social democracy that talks no longer about work but about employment thereby renounces the question of knowledge, and of work as
knowledge – 'knowledge' having become for it an issue for a highly
specific electoral clientele: the teaching body, 'from kindergarten to
the Collège de France'.

In the next few years, automation will make these contradictions
not only obvious but intolerable and unsustainable. To face up to
them, the left must eliminate this 'major confusion between the two
conceptions of work that socialist thought has always carefully distinguished: real, alienated work, of which the political struggle must
be to reduce its time, and liberated work, which will one day become
the premier vital need'.[78] That day on which 'liberated work' will
become 'the premier vital need' is now rapidly approaching.

Failing to take the measure of this situation, political, economic,
intellectual and media powers have allowed chaos to develop – ranging
from civil wars to international conflicts. Automation will have less
and less need for 'alienated labour', that is, for the proletarianized
employment that, in the 'growth' model that has dominated since
Keynes, has always been presented as the condition of everyone's
happiness, and which is also called the 'Fordist compromise'.

This 'compromise' is not, however, simply Fordist: its solvency
depended also on the Keynesian macroeconomic policies set up by
Franklin D. Roosevelt. Cracks in these policies began to show in the
1970s: the solvency of this model depended heavily on the massive
exploitation of resources captured by the colonial empires of Western
Europe, and this was challenged by decolonization. In addition, as
the rate of profit reached historical lows,[79] financial capitalism took
advantage of the 'oil crisis' to enact a post-Keynesian transformation that worked against any regulation by public powers: this is the
moment of the conservative revolution.

It is this that forms the geopolitical context of what in 1979
Lyotard called 'the end of grand narratives', characteristic of what
would become known as postmodernity, the analysis of which is contested by Gorz in *Critique of Economic Reason* (1988), who suggests
that modernity is on the contrary yet to be accomplished:

> What we are experiencing is not the crisis of modernity: we are
> experiencing the need to modernize the presuppositions upon which

modernity is based. The current crisis is not the crisis of Reason but that of the irrational motives, now apparent, of rationalization as it has been pursued thus far. [...] What 'postmodernists' take to be the end of modernity and the crisis of Reason is in reality a crisis of [...] irrational contents.[80]

Hence Gorz revives the questions posed by Adorno and the early Habermas. These irrational *contents* impose themselves as *motives* through a *fabrication of motivations*. It is all the more necessary for us to investigate this, at a moment when this fabrication of artificial motivations is being combined with algorithmic governmentality to create a new, even more irrational stage. But these 'irrational contents', which are 'reasons' in the sense of motivations, are the result, according to Gorz, of a 'selective and partial rationalization' characteristic of what he calls 'industrialism'.

For Gorz, it is a 'crisis of the quasi-religious irrational contents upon which is built the selective and partial rationalization we call industrialism, as bearer of a conception of the universe and a vision of the future that are now unsustainable'.[81] Rationalization thus becomes the *pharmakon* of reason, as was already demonstrated by Horkheimer and Adorno, and this is so because 'rationalization has ontological and existential limits, and [because] these limits can be crossed only by means of pseudo-rationalizations, themselves irrational, in which rationalization becomes its opposite'.[82]

What makes this pharmacology *possible*, however, is the *organological, retentional and grammatized embedding of reason in machines*, which is in turn possible only because *knowledge has always been organologically constituted and supported*. What makes machines themselves possible, as well as knowledge in general – as knowledge of how to do, live and conceive – is the fact that non-inhuman being, that is, noetic being, is *natively* organological, which is also to say that a worker exteriorizes himself or herself only by individuating, which occurs only via a passage through the outside, as Gorz highlights by paraphrasing Oskar Negt, for whom ' "work" must [...] be understood, as in Hegel, as the activity by which the human being externalizes his being'.[83]

If work lies at the heart of rationality and more generally of noetic life, as Negt argues, this is precisely because *reason*, irrespective of whether it is apodictic, as in the case of Greek *logos*, or derives from other, older attentional forms, or has yet other origins, *is the consistent motive of all existent motives* of any social form whatsoever. And as such, it constitutes the *therapeutics* that such an exteriorization always requires, because this exteriorization continually provokes disturbances in the individuation of the noetic being, that is, the non-inhuman being – which continuously tends, in these situations, to become inhuman and irrational.[84]

Hence arises the question of the *infidelity* specific to the organological milieu, referring here to Canguilhem's thesis in *The Normal and the Pathological*,[85] which results, fundamentally, from the *phase shift* typical of psychic and collective individuation. This infidelity of the organological milieu is also what Gille describes, following Durkheim, as a *structural and intermittent disadjustment*.[86] This becomes systematically organized and explicit starting from the industrial revolution, and even more so with creative destruction (that is, with consumerism). But with 24/7 capitalism and its algorithmic governmentality, this disadjustment *is no longer intermittent but continuous and total* – putting an end to intermittence as such.

All this proceeds above all from what Gorz describes, although without himself seeing how it contains an organological dimension, when he writes that what postmodernists present as a crisis of reason is in reality a 'crisis of that particular form of rationality we call economic'.[87] This is so because the industrial division of labour entails an *industrial division of rationality*, that is, a *rationalization*. It is an intellectual division of labour, but also of the collective individuals who form it, who are thereby placed into competition by it, at the service of the financial sub-system (the entrepreneurial economic system having been subordinated to the financial sub-system), and at the expense of the other social systems, which then find themselves destroyed. This last stage corresponds to what was described by Giget and Zook as the moment when destruction becomes more destructive than creative (of employment, but also of negentropy).

This emancipation of 'economic rationality' with respect to the other social systems imposes itself because *economic rationality* essentially becomes an *efficient causality*: this is how it is justified, recognized by everyone in terms of the 'Fordist compromise'. It imposes its domination through the mediation of a hegemonic appropriation of the technical system and, through the latter, of what Gramsci called 'culture'. At the same time, it destroys *final causality*, this final causality that the 'death of God', that is, of onto-theology,[88] leads us to rethink in terms of the *quasi-causality* required by the organological and pharmacological situation of the *'neganthropos'* that we always are when, intermittently, we are non-inhuman in actuality.

Gorz's reflections on the irrationality of economic rationalism connect to Polanyi's thesis. Gille shows, however, following *The*

Great Transformation,[89] that the rise of the modern state occurs in order to regulate disadjustments. It is not firstly and not only the market that establishes a new relationship between the technical system and the social systems, but the new dynamic of the technical system itself: it incorporates and materializes knowledge, captures the potential for investment and thereby enables a new economic dynamic that tends to deterritorialize and autonomize itself with respect to the other social systems, which remain local. It does so initially by transforming these other systems via the state, then by destroying them, discrediting them and destroying public power itself in all its forms, and not only the state.

It is in this rationality, and *as* this rationality, that the question of work arises in new terms. This also constitutes the foundation and the context of what Méda and Vendramin show with respect to the contradictions of social democracy. Over the course of his works, however, Gorz more and more frequently refers to *free time*, that is, available time, and has less and less to say about *liberated work*. And he eventually posits in principle that the question is no longer work but 'free time'. To exit from wage labour and employment is here to exit from the question of work as what lies at the heart of exteriorization, and in relation to which Negt proposed distinguishing '*true*' work from *false* work.

If, then, the 'end of grand narratives of emancipation' is inadmissible for Gorz, nevertheless the *end of the discourse on liberated work and therefore on the liberation of work* does indeed remain viable for him. I tend to think (and to regret) that this ultimately leads him back to the position of Lyotard: to the position of 'resistance', that is, to the *renunciation of invention*.[90]

80. Available time and free work

In 1988, in the introduction to *Critique of Economic Reason*, Gorz commented on 'Le chômage de prospérité', an article published in *Le Monde* on 31 October 1986, in which Lionel Stoléru asserted that 'new areas of activity' are made possible by technological progress and *productivity gains*, that is, *gains in time*, and that these new activities will mean the potential for '*jobs*, even if they are not strictly speaking "work"'.[91] Gorz comments that Stoléru wants to 'economicize' leisure: 'that is, to include within the economic field what was previously excluded, [which] means that economic rationalization will produce gains in time and gains in momentum, releasing increasing quantities of available time'.[92]

This is something that will also be made possible by the 'roboti-zation of household tasks'. All this will supposedly lead to savings in time, 'even in activities which were previously not counted as work. "Technological progress" inevitably raises the question of the meaning and content of available time [...], of the nature of a civi-lization and a society in which there is far more available time than working time.'[93] The intention of these technological innovations is not to provide work but to economize the need for work, says Gorz. Here this means: to save on paid work, that is, to reduce the propor-tion of paid (alienated) work in the economy.

And yet, the dominant social forces, as represented, for example, by Stoléru, deny this tendency. They want to 'economicize' – that is, to monetize at any cost – precisely that which escapes the com-mercial sector:

> We are thus faced with *a social system which is unable to distribute, manage or employ this new-found free time*; a system fearful of the expansion of this time, yet which does its utmost to increase it, and which, in the end, can find no purpose for it other than seeking all pos-sible means of turning it into money: that is, monetarizing, transform-ing into jobs and economicizing, in the form of increasingly specialized services for exchange on the market, even those previously free and autonomous activities capable of giving meaning to it.[94]

In 'Pourquoi la société salariale a besoin de nouveaux valets' (translated as 'The New Servants'), a lecture given on 6 March 1990 and published in *Le Monde diplomatique*, Gorz took up this theme of the inability to think the new question of time: 'We are leaving the work-based society behind, but we are exiting backwards [...] incapable of *civilizing* liberated time, or of founding a culture of available time.'[95] It is time that is liberated: it is no longer work. This *available time* is not that of *available work*, and it must be *civilized*. This question is posed in a context where 'the typical income of an American family in which the husband is under twenty-five is 43 per cent lower today than it was in 1973',[96] which means that it is from within a perspective foreshadowing the collapse of the Fordist-Keynesian model that Gorz reflects on the future of industrial society, which he calls 'post-industrial'[97] – in my view, incorrectly.

Available *time* is firstly that of the available *brain* – available for the capture and commodification of 'available brain time'.[98] In the absence of a genuine *politics of time*, which, in a manner contrary to that of time and motion study departments, integrates and covers the *totality of social functions* in all their dimensions, this capture of available brain time by organs that proletarianize life-knowledge (organs that are at least as toxic as those proletarianizing work-knowledge and conceptual knowledge) is inevitable. This is, however, underestimated by all the critiques of work and the measures proposed to remedy its crisis, and the crisis of its 'idea', as Gorz says.

Liberated time that does not free work becomes brain time available for the fabrication of mass consumer markets. As we have seen, Rifkin himself highlights this in 2006, in the preface to the second edition of the French translation of *The End of Work*. For Rifkin, the time liberated by the 'end of work' calls for the development of a third sector, beyond public and private. Michel Rocard took up this thesis in 2005, positing in principle the *inevitability* of increasing unemployment: 'How to distribute decent incomes, and not just a poverty-level income, to an unoccupied population that, including those working intermittently or with "odd jobs", is beginning to approach a quarter of the total active population, and within a few decades will represent half the population?'[99] If we are to believe what was written in *Le Soir* on 19 July 2014, this is the very situation that could transpire in Belgium and in most other industrial countries within ten years.

81. Free time, the third sector and the social economy

Faced with this situation, Rocard, with Rifkin, advocates public support for a third sector that would include, in addition to the social and solidarity economy, a 'vast network of regional authorities and businesses, including public utilities, which depend on it'.[100] Rocard regrets that Rifkin is content to mention ('too quickly and too unsystematically for my taste') the possibility of what Milton Friedmann described as a negative tax, which is referred to today as a guaranteed minimum income, in relation to which Rocard argues that the minimum integration income introduced by his own government would be, in France, one version. Then, following Gorz, he raises the question of liberated time in 'a society in which the market sector will be greatly reduced'. But what must be shown is why and how, especially now, with the algorithmic governmentality of 24/7 capitalism, this sector, far from being reduced, is continuously increasing. Rocard then argues that 'the creative and solidary use of free time needs transitions. The only possibility [...] will be a proper sharing of productive working time offered to all those who need it, ignoring the fact that we are creating the means of doing without it.' Today everything suggests that *the means of doing without it are coming very quickly*: they are already being set up, and will probably become a general reality within a generation – in this case, *the coming generation*.

In 1995, Gorz published a review of Rifkin's book, strongly criticizing the idea of this 'third sector', which he predicted would be recuperated and colonized by states, or even by 'the World Bank, all ready to offload the responsibilities that come with public authority. Has the Brazilian government, for example, not just reduced the education budget by 34.5% and the health budget by 50%, by relying on NGOs and solidarity networks to take over?'[101] And, indeed, David Cameron's highly libertarian 'big society' had the goal of eliminating the public power of the United Kingdom through the 'contribution' of associations of citizens as bearers and precursors of privatization.

The question becomes that of the constitution of a *contributory public power*, the contours of which remain to be outlined. We will see in the second volume of *Automatic Society* why a contributory public power presupposes a specific organology and requires a profound rethinking of the relations between the diachronic and the synchronic, microeconomies and macroeconomies, 'bottom-up' and 'top-down' models, all within a new publication space founded on digital tertiary retention.

In such a publication space, serving a new *res publica*, the essential aspect of the organological invention required for the constitution of a new *law* of algorithmic governmentality beyond its *fact* consists in functionally reconnecting the 'bottom up' and the 'top down', in making them explicit and in dis-automatizing the relations between them through an organology that techno-logically constitutes the juridical possibility of dis-automatizing automatons.

Like Gorz, we think that it is not a matter of creating a third sector out of the social and solidary economy. And we do not think that creating a negative tax, that is, a guaranteed minimum income, meets the challenges we face. Of course, we are not against the social and solidary economy – quite the contrary. Nor are we against a guaranteed minimum income, which we have always supported. But we argue that in addition, we must *now* invent another society founded on a *contributory income*, in an economy totally rethought in contributory terms on a macroeconomic scale – and not just in the non-market sector described by Rocard as an extended third sector.

This social invention must be produced *now*, and it is through it that we must commit to a transition conducted with and for the coming generation. This must be done firstly through regional experiments within a framework of action research protocols and supported by contributory technologies developed from this perspective – action research itself becoming *contributory research*.[102]

This implies the need to totally rethink, through these regional and experimental transitional practices, national policies and the way they are integrated: research policies, industrial policies, higher education and national education policies, cultural policies, that is, editorial policies, financial policies, and obviously regional policies and in the first place social policies – reinvented work policies constituting the cornerstone of a *general politics of recapacitation*.[103]

The redefinition of the theoretical question of work and its practical reinvention must be put at the heart of the reconstitution of a state of law that is not just a State of law, but the invention of a contributory public power. Work [*oeuvre*] – which is the condition of manpower [*main-d'oeuvre*] and brainpower [*cerveau-d'oeuvre*], but the concept of which disintegrates when manpower and brainpower are 'de-occupied' [*désoeuvres*], that is, disintegrated, first by the machine and then by the apparatus – is what the Greeks called *ergon*. The science of work is called ergonomics. The *ergon* is what occurs at the moment of *energeia* as the passage into action, that is, as the effecting of an action contained in potential in *dunamis*.

To reason in this way means revisiting the whole history of philosophy and onto-theology, starting from the question of work as transformation, and doing so beyond Marx, who never posed the question of de-proletarianization as such.[104]

7

Energies and Potentials in the Twenty-First Century

Economics are the method; the object is to change the heart and soul.

Margaret Thatcher[1]

So my life has been shit, and just for once I want to feel powerful and free.

Richard Durn[2]

82. Energy and power after the 'death of God'

Liberated *time* must be liberated *work*. This presupposes *reinventing* (and rethinking) not just *work* but *energy* – by reactivating its former meaning, *energeia*, as well as the meaning of *dunamis*, from which it is inseparable, and which is sometimes called potential, but also virtue, or in Latin *virtus*, which is also to say, force, strength, what the Greeks called *aretē*, also translated as excellence.

People constantly discuss, often by referring to Rifkin, how the 'energy transition' will produce new employment. But they rarely reflect on the intimate and original relationships that constitute and connect the work [*oeuvre*], the hand, the brain and energy.

Energeia, which as *en-ergeia* is bound up with the *ergon*, the work, activity, refers in Aristotle to the passage to the act of *dunamis*. It is in relation to the history of these concepts that we must think the inextricably conceptual and social evolution that leads to the unified concept of work founded on the existence of 'abstract labour' – in the sense suggested by Vernant: 'This unification of the psychological function of work goes hand in hand with the emergence of what Karl Marx calls abstract labor.'[3] It is by returning to the metaphysical considerations of onto-theology, founded in the age of Aristotle on the ancient Greek coupling of *dunamis* and *energeia*, that we must revisit in our time this *relation* that is always at work in any work.

Lazzarato draws attention to the fact that Tarde tried to think economics beyond dialectics, and also beyond Durkheim's theory of the division of labour, because he confronted the time of the death of God – and did so as a liberation of forces.[4] The death of God, however, has everything to do with the *dunamis/energeia* couple.

From a metaphysical perspective, the 'death of God' means the end of onto-theology, that is, of an ontology that begins by positing *energeia*, translated into Latin as *actus*, and *dunamis*, translated into Latin as *potentia*, on the basis of a *theos* that becomes, in the course of the Christianization of Aristotelianism, the 'supreme being'. This is what is inaugurated by the Aristotelian theory of the prime unmoved mover expounded in *Metaphysics* and *On the Soul*.

The force and the necessity of Simondon's philosophy – which is constantly attentive to the question of work, itself posed in relation to the 'technical individual' – are each rooted in a new interpretation of this energy/potential polarity that must be revisited as the milieu/individual couple and, more precisely, as a *transductive relation*: a transductive relation between a milieu that Simondon called preindividual and an individual that is thinkable only as individuation, that is, as a *process* that can accomplish itself only through leaps – through *intermittences*.

In extending Simondon beyond his own positions, we must understand the preindividual as a milieu composed of tertiary retentions themselves engendered by a form of life that is not just organic, but organological. This form of life, which is ours, is for us never just a given: we *must make* it our own. This is the sense in which we should understand Richard Sennett's assertion that making is thinking.[5]

We *make* this form of life *effectively* our own only by inscribing into it new circuits of transindividuation, via *bifurcations* – through which we become the quasi-causes of this necessity. It is this *making ours* that Oskar Negt calls 'true' work.

83.   Against the omerta

In Rifkin's 2006 preface to the French edition of *The End of Work* (which follows after Rocard's), he deftly manages to promote the theme of his more recent book, *The Hydrogen Economy*[6] – which I have discussed elsewhere.[7] The advent of this 'hydrogen economy', he informs us, brings with it the possibility of creating many new jobs.

Rifkin here adopts one of those arguments the vanity of which was shown by Georges Friedmann in the 1950s. In this way he avoids the true question, which is that of the outright disappearance of employment, that is, of that function vital for the consumerist economy. Rifkin never offers any warning of a looming end of employment, despite the words of Robert L. Heilbroner in his foreword to the book:

> [T]he number of 'service' employees [was] by 1870 [...] perhaps 3 million [...] and by the 1990s nearly 90 million. Service employment thus saved [...] modern economies [...] from absolutely devastating unemployment. [...] But it was the computer, of course, that brings the drama to a close, threatening [to let] the automata go to work.[8]

As for Rifkin, he himself predicts, on the first page of the introduction to his book, 'an economy of near automated production by the mid-decades of the twenty-first century'.[9] On this, Alain Caillé comments as follows:

> We will witness an anthropological and sociological transformation more colossal than any humanity has ever known. Only the Neolithic revolution is of comparable importance. And we are reluctant to imagine the consequences of such a mindboggling upheaval. Unfortunately, it is possible that they will prove to be apocalyptic.[10]

The first among those reluctant to draw these consequences, however, is Rifkin himself.

It is hard to see why, in fact, a 'hydrogen economy', however new its organization may be, would itself escape this fate. Rifkin says everything and its opposite. He argues that this hydrogen economy breaks with the 'centralized' Fordist-Keynesian model, founded on proletarianization as the functional separation and opposition between design, production and consumption, and with this we are in complete agreement. But he also says that this will create new jobs, which we profoundly doubt – and this is the point that has been taken up in varying ways by right and left, in terms of an 'energy transition' and a 'green economy'.

Rifkin (and behind him Rocard, social democrats and the left, including environmentalists) is profoundly wrong about this transition – that is, about how to define *the issue that must fundamentally guide the period of transition*, a transition that involves assisting in the disappearance of the obsolete world and the emergence of another world. Such a transition can be peacefully accomplished only on the condition of very clearly formulating and negotiating the expected costs and benefits.

There is a genuine omerta with respect to the end of employment. Because *nothing is said* about what is coming, but while the whole world feels it (even if nobody knows it for sure), in France in particular, and especially in the last two years, the far right continues to make great strides.[11] As long as this transformation is not *projected collectively*, the far right (and its fundamentalist defenders) will continue to advance throughout the world, to the degree that it concretizes the unthought and rapid effects of this 'anthropological and sociological transformation more colossal than any humanity has ever known'.

84.   Employment, knowledge, wealth

Only a resolute approach to public debate, transitional proposals and collective projections is capable of inspiring confidence. Contrary to this, Rifkin provides an ambiguous discourse that constantly tries to have it both ways, to have radical change so that ultimately nothing changes, since the energetic abundance supposedly created by this hydrogen economy means we would not have to abandon the consumerist economy of disposability – which we have called 'misgrowth'[12] – the basis of which Rifkin has never made the subject of critique.[13]

Furthermore, while emphasizing that the 'agriculture, manufacturing, and service' sectors are constantly and drastically reducing their workforce, and showing that this situation will continue until there is total automation (which is his first thesis, and his fundamental thesis, however much it contradicts his statements about 'hydrogen jobs'), Rifkin argues that the 'only new sector emerging is the knowledge sector'.[14] And he adds the following statement, with which we are in utter disagreement: 'While this sector is growing, it is not expected to absorb more than a fraction of the hundreds of millions who will be eliminated in the next several decades in the wake of revolutionary advances in the information and communication sciences.'[15] We, on the contrary, believe that *it is in, with and through knowledge that all this must be played out*, and that we must draw the economic and political consequences of the concretization, currently underway, of Marx's analysis in the *Grundrisse*, where he posits that alienated labour is bound to decline, and that the value of knowledge calls into question the distinction between use value and exchange value.[16]

As the sympathetic and seductive but incoherent storytelling of a brilliant international consultant, the entirety of Rifkin's construction is based on this sophism that consists in continuing to reason in terms of the jobs created by a new employment sector, that of energy, while at the same time maintaining that employment is what contemporary technology destroys.[17] He thereby avoids describing in any detail how an economy (in this case, the energy economy) could function *outside the framework of wage labour*.

It is indeed clear that even if knowledge is the 'only new sector emerging', it is not going to 'create jobs'. But this is the wrong question. It is instead a question of knowing if knowledge – including work-knowledge and life-knowledge, which a hydrogen economy, for example, might reconstitute *outside of activity founded on employment* – will recreate *wealth*, and sustainable wealth, by replacing wage labour, alienated through the knowledge materialized in machines (producing hyper-matter of a highly specific kind[18]), and by profoundly transforming knowledge in its totality, as time liberated by the work of dis-automatization, thereby transforming the 'value of value' itself.[19]

85.   *Otium*, value and negentropy

The question is then the following – and this is an alternative that is divided into two questions: will this *materialization* of knowledge, that is, this *automatization*, and the reticulated publication on which it is founded:

- enable the *production of negentropy*, that is, of *wealth*; or, rather,
- accelerate the global, massive and systemic entropic process in which the Anthropocene consists, leading to *ruin*?

The question of the 'value of value' must change so that this unevaluable and highly improbable *benchmark-value* of all values becomes negentropy and is concretized in terms of a *practical value* as *neganthropy*, that is, as the *valorization of those dis-automatization practices made possible by automatons*, as time liberated in favour of *practices of intermittence* that together form a neganthropology.[20]

Liberated and de-alienated labour, that is, freed from the conditions of wage labour and from this kind of employment of time, must be a time *free for transindividuation*. It must consist in the generalization of practices of leisure *in the ancient sense of the word*, which was *otium* in Latin and *skholē* in Greek,[21] that is, it must consist in the generalization of techniques of the self and others,[22] which are obviously to work for oneself and through others.

In a *contributory economy* founded on a *contributory income*, *otium* and *skholē* must be *cultivated* at all stages of life, and such a culture is clearly a form of *work* – given that any activity, *energeia*, is a trans-formation of oneself. And because the psychic individuation in which such a transformation consists is effective only if it participates in collective transindividuation, it is necessarily also a trans-formation of others.

What we call work *today* is what these circuits and their products designate after they have been made *utterly comparable by a market* – as Vernant said, quoted by Méda and Vendramin, and to which I will return. This equalization leads, moreover, to proletarianization, that is, to this work of transformation being replaced by a job from which the trans-formativity has been removed, replaced by *methods, procedures and behavioural models*, prescribed no longer by social systems of any kind but by departments of time and motion study[23] and by marketing firms.

Loisir in French, *skholē* in Greek and *otium* in Latin mean freedom as *Bildung*,[24] and not the absence of work, that is, of necessity. This is what Kant recalls at the end of his life (confronting those he calls mystagogues, priding themselves on being inhabited by genius, itself constituting a clairvoyant gift): '[T]he discursive understanding must employ much labor on resolving and again compounding its concepts according to principles, and toil up many steps to make advances in knowledge.'[25]

An '*otium* of the people', and of 'people who are missing',[26] an *otium* as experience of the (de)fault of *otium*, that is, of its intermittent condition, is the condition of any neganthropological knowledge, and it is made *possible* by reticulated digital tertiary retention.

Such would be an 'art of hyper-control', for which it would be a matter not of 'addressing a people, which is presupposed already there, but of contributing to the invention of a people'.[27] But this presupposes both:

- a genuine organological revolution, based on the deliberate and theorized supplementary invention of new instruments of knowledge and publication; and
- an epistemic and epistemological revolution that radically transforms the status, practices and axioms of knowledge in general (of living, doing, conceiving).

Both these issues will be developed in detail in the second volume of *Automatic Society*, but their outlines will be sketched in the conclusion of the present work.

The dual imperative that these two issues form means that the resolution of the crisis of the idea of work, and more generally the way out of the impasse in which what is now called the Anthropocene consists, cannot be reduced to an 'energy transition' as some purveyor of new jobs, or to the development of a third sector, or, again, to the adoption of a guaranteed minimum income – and not even to a combination of these three measures.

This dual imperative implies the need to concretize the second moment of a doubly epokhal redoubling through the constitution of a contributory economy, itself founded on contributory research, and taking account, at all levels of public action and the economy, of the consequences that follow when digital grammatization reaches the stage of full and generalized automatization.

Before coming to our conclusion from this perspective, and from the perspective of the reinvention of work conceived above all as intermittence, and before arguing, accordingly, for a contributory income dedicated to *contributory projects* founded on *contributory investments* and on *contributory credit*, we must deepen the question of whether – and how (irrespective of whether the answer is yes or no) – we can or cannot continue to talk about work while associating it with this freedom that we otherwise call leisure: for example, when Leibniz argued that writing allowed a statement to be 'examined at leisure', which means 'by having enough time'.

86.   The time of wealth

For the issue is indeed time – and the time of an individuation that is, in the case referred to by Leibniz, *the individuation of a knowing psychic individual*, which is at the same time *the individuation of knowledge itself*, and *as* collective individuation, which we can clearly see here involves both a *trans-formation of the noetic individual* through his or her very noesis, and a *trans-formation of the circuits* of transindividuation produced by this noesis.

A debate has thus been ongoing for almost twenty years based on Gorz's proposals on the question of knowing how to *gain* a *truly* free time, a debate that has defined this in terms of an opposition to work, even though Gorz himself, with Oskar Negt, raised the question of *'true' work*, as opposed to false work. This war of words about the meaning of the word 'work', which continually resurfaces, will have been in vain if it does not reach down to the sedimentary layers that precede this question. This includes the fact that for us the issue of work has been over-determined by the market, as was shown by Vernant: 'Through the market, all forms of work done throughout society are related to one another, confronted with one another, made comparable.'[28] But it also includes the fact that this question is put back into play with each organological transformation induced by the shock of a doubly epokhal redoubling that is each time original, and on the basis of which we must always rethink *everything*.

The market is itself constituted by a fiduciary space founded on a specific form of hypomnesic tertiary retention that we call money – and Clarisse Herrenschmidt has shown how the latter establishes a banal and generalized computational relation between individuals and through things:

> In the European mentality [...] figures and calculations are the rational key to the reading of the world.[29]

> The articulation between skilful calculation, scientific research, mathematization and the mechanization of the world and society took place through coins, the writing of numbers and the value they carry. Economics and mathematics are in fact anchored together through the existence of systems of measurement.[30]

In this monetarized world, Locke posits in principle that it is through work that things are constituted as things, as *my* things, as my own – as my *property*.[31]

The current notion of work results from layers of organological arrangements and there is no longer an *essence* of work rather than non-work (of what defines this or that activity as non-work): there are *social relations*, framed by a moving organological reality, at the core of which retentions and protentions (which is also to say, desires) are produced, metastabilized by attentional forms.[32]

In 'Bâtir la civilisation du temps libéré', published in *Le Monde diplomatique* in March 1993, Gorz mentions a saying by an anonymous disciple of David Ricardo that Marx was fond of quoting: 'Wealth [...] is disposable time, and nothing more.'[33] The question is wealth, and wealth is time. To have time, for example, to 'examine at leisure': such is wealth. This time is *available to intermittence*, and this intermittence is the quantum leap of an individuation, that is, more precisely: the time of a noetic individuation whereby a singularity trans-forms *itself*, takes form, and transindividuates, that is, trans-forms a milieu that is itself noetic, because it is organological.

We have seen with Crary that the time of intermittence is what organizes and sets the rhythm of all societies, and that it is what fully computational capitalism, operating twenty-four hours a day, seven days a week, tends to eliminate: the time of sleep, of dreams and of free time. We also know that intermittence is the very condition of thinking for Socrates[34] and for Aristotle[35] – both of whom quote the same line from Simonides. And we know, finally, that a scheme exists in France whereby those occasional workers in the entertainments industry known as '*intermittents du spectacle*' are indemnified against unemployment.

This scheme should become a model for a *law of work* in an economy of contribution, just as we believe that free software, *inasmuch as it is a challenge to the industrial division of labour*, should constitute a model for the *organization of work*. The widespread generalization of this organization of work requires a *contributory organology* that remains entirely to be developed[36] – in the first place with the free software communities that have been around now for thirty years.

The scheme covering the intermittents is even older: it was established in 1936 and has since been much transformed. It was threatened for the first time in 2003, and became the object of a struggle, in relation to which Antonella Corsani and Maurizio Lazzarato wrote in 2008: '[I]t is in reality a struggle whose stakes are the employment of time. To the injunction to increase the time of employment, that is, the proportion of life occupied by employment, the experience of intermittence opposes the multiplicity of the times of employment.'[37]

87.   The decline of the division of labour

The French intermittence scheme completely rearranges employment and time, precisely by considering the work of the 'intermittent' as time outside employment – as formation[38] and individuation, and hence as much more than just earnings and production. Corsani and Lazzarato therefore conclude that we must 'interrogate the very category of "work"':

> If there is activity during periods of unemployment, but also during the time of so-called living, during the time called free, during the time of training, until it flows over into the time for rest, what then does work encompass, given that it contains a multiplicity of activities and heterogeneous temporalities?[39]

In 2004, Lazzarato proposes a reconsideration of the question of time, employment and work from the perspective of *practices of intermittence*. In 2014, however, in the conclusion of *Governing by Debt*, he instead advocates the 'refusal of work':

> We need 'time', but a time of rupture, [...] an 'idle time'. [...] I call 'laziness' political action that at once refuses and eludes the roles, functions, and significations of the social division of labour and, in so doing, creates new possibilities. [Laziness] allows us to think and to practice the 'refusal of work'.[40]

I do not believe that the question, today, is either to oppose or to submit to the division of labour. The question posed by automatization is precisely the *decline* of the division of labour, replaced by the technological and organological differentiation of automatons, and where this necessarily raises the neganthropological question of dis-automatization. This last question was posed neither by Durkheim nor by Tarde, because they did not understand the history of the division of labour in terms of an economic, organological evolution, an evolution experienced in terms of alienated labour – so long as automatic organs do not make it superfluous.

Nowhere does Durkheim relate the causes of the division of labour, which he analyses at length, to technical and organological evolution, which a student of Mauss (who was himself a nephew of Durkheim and a thinker of the technics of the body) would later highlight. In *L'Homme et la Matière*, André Leroi-Gourhan showed that technological evolution is traversed by systemic and functional dynamics that we must understand as technical tendencies concealed behind what he calls technical facts.[41]

Tarde had no objections to Durkheim from this perspective. He may understand the economic fact as above all a question of cooperation between brains, but he neglects the question this immediately raises: in what conditions can these brains enter into a relation with each other? Missing in Tarde is the question of what we ourselves call tertiary retention, and the question of the organology it presupposes, given that the brain can cooperate with other brains only by interiorizing them along with the circuits of transindividuation formed by the individuation of psychic individuals – of which these brains are the cerebral organs (this individuation itself occurring through exteriorizations, which are also called expressions).

The question is not simply that of the status of work or of its 'refusal': it is that of the historical conditions of what Lazzarato himself takes from Tarde in his critique of Durkheim, namely, the thesis that 'we must start [...] from what political economy and its critique presuppose without explaining: the creative power of human beings and the inter-cerebral cooperation that makes it possible'.[42] Unless the organology and therefore the evolution of the cooperation between brains is analysed from the perspective of the question of retentions and protentions,[43] and in terms of grammatization, this issue will remain locked (by inverting it) within the reasoning it opposes. Hence Durkheim, who fundamentally ignored the organological dimension of any division of labour, at the same time ignored the advent of an *organological division* – but *without work* – of production, that is, without alienated and wage labour: without employment.

The question is what works, that is, trans-forms, and does so by producing attentional forms: behind the question of work, and beyond the word 'work', which has such an easy payoff, there is the question of *erga*, *ergon* and *energeia*. And, over the course of the two and a half millennia that separate us from Aristotle, when the categories of *dunamis* and *energeia* were placed at the very heart of his thinking, very large semantic and epistemic (that is, attentional) trans-formations have occurred, emerging from a process of transindividuation that has today become sedimented. But these concepts have always formed the background of any thinking of work, and do so now more than ever – they are concepts whose social and semantic evolutions have made the debate on 'work' itself either almost incomprehensible or precious, if not specious.

88.   Ergology and *energeia*: work as noetic activity and the dual economy of energy

We say of the works of Maurizio Lazzarato, Gabriel Tarde or Émile Durkheim that they are the 'fruits of their labour'. More accurately, we could say that such works are derived from processes through which their individuation, which is temporal, becomes spatial. And we could add that to do so is to transindividuate by 'tertiarizing' ourselves.

The question of works, that is, of *erga*, is that of individuation – and of the conditions required, during a particular epoch and in a particular part of the ecumene, for traces of differences to be produced on the basis of repetition[44] rather than indifference, that is, entropy. Such a production of differences or of indifference is always a *materialization* – including as the modification of any synaptic circuit that interiorizes or exteriorizes (by trans-forming or by auto-matically repeating) a circuit of transindividuation.[45]

Perhaps we can call 'work' everything that, in the technical form of life, which is also its noetic form, *differs from and defers [diffère]* entropy by intensifying 'neganthropy' – which is the work of dif-férance. But the technical form of life can also increase entropy. When in *The German Ideology* Marx and Engels conceived the idea of a new philosophical anthropology, which will become through that a critique of political economy, they put what they call work at the heart of anthropogenesis. Through this critique, they engaged in a historical, economic and philosophical study of work that is without precedent and without equal, but within which contradic-tions remain.

Work, as we conceive it after the sedimentation of layers of meaning described by Ignace Meyerson and taken up by Dominique Méda and Patricia Vendramin,[46] through whom we encountered it, is a specific case of what the Greeks regarded as *energeia*.

In the history of Western thought, which is also the history of the evolution of the vocabulary of this thought, the meaning of the word *energeia* has evolved a great deal: it has almost been reversed, given that in the ancient Greek language, and in particular in the work of Aristotle, *energeia* means the passage to the act, the accom-plishment of action, the leap towards *entelekheia*, that is, towards the end (*telos*) of that of which *energeia* is the passage to actuality. Nowadays, what we call energy – for example, fossil energy – refers to what for the Greeks and in particular for Aristotle constituted not *energeia* but its condition, which is precisely what is not and can never be *energeia* itself, namely, *dunamis*.

The semantic transformations of the words *energeia* and *dunamis* – having become, through successive transindividuations, as we shall see, energy, action, activity, dynamic, power and potential [*puissance*] – make the constitutive notions of the contemporary conception of work very confusing. Work is thought on the basis of energy, become *dunamis*, as the unit of *measurement of force*, which with Newton becomes a new notion in physics, while Watt, whose steam engine contributed to the theory that would come to be called thermody-namics and to its famous second law, would lend his name to this unit that measures what is called power [*puissance*], but such that it develops an 'energy' of *combustion*.

These semantic and scientific upheavals make it difficult to hear what, in the concept of *energeia*, remains of the *ergon* insofar as it designates work. It is insofar as it testifies to an *energeia* that we can refer to a work by the name *ergon*. *Energeia* is the passage to the actuality of the *ergon* stretched towards its *entelekheia*, which is its end, *enteles* meaning completion – and it is in this sense that we refer to a masterwork [*chef-d'oeuvre*] to designate the crowning work of a series of *erga*, works, labours. What is encountered on the market referred to by Vernant are the works produced by diverse forms of activity, which can be described in Greek as '*en-ergos*', in the sense of 'what is at work, in action, [...] proper to the activity, capable of acting [...], active, productive', as Bailly says.[47]

The word *energeia* always in some way involves a question of an activity of trans-formation, of a formation that is a *taking of form*, a passage to the act as *individuation* and accomplishment of a potential (*puissance, dunamis*) that Simondon called the *preindividual*.[48]

Simondon's gesture must itself be pursued further to the point of thinking *technical individuation* before the age of machinic proletarianization, and for which *what we call work is the energeia*. Simondon does not think this preindustrial stage in which psychic individuation, technical individuation and collective individuation are built upon the production of retentions and protentions via epiphylogenetic or hypomnesic tertiary retentions. He does show, however, how machinic individuation effects a break with technical individuation via work as *energeia* (in the Greek sense).

The *energeia* of work that is still a craft, a métier, a *ministerium* that always contains a *mysterium*, conditions and constitutes in return, as accumulation of traces, the preindividual funds of the psychic individual, who individuates this milieu only by interiorizing it – in the strict sense, that is, by inheriting collective secondary retentions and so generating psychic secondary retentions, which it sends back out by exteriorizing them: an elementary noetic loop on the basis of which all manner of 'exchanges' occur.

The technical individual concretizes work created from *psychic energy* then *socialized* as the work of *collective energy*, that is, a collective individuation (*energeia*) founded on a potential (*dunamis*) for transindividuation. With the appearance of mechanical tertiary retention and the grammatization of gesture, this individuation is captured and displaced by the technical individual at the expense of the psychic individual, who is thereby disindividuated.

Proletarianized, the labouring psychic individual then becomes a pure and simple *dunamis* of the technical organ-become-machine or apparatus. And these machines and apparatus have themselves become sites of an action that is no longer a 'passage to the act', that is, a leap into individuation, nor any *ergon*. Rather, they take the form of a proliferating series, served by caloric motive force (*dunamis*), as combustible energy or as the muscular force of a hand and body, or the nervous energy of a brain. We continue to describe this in terms of '*oeuvre*' only by the force of habit – even if, by conserving the memory of *energeia*, it remains today suggestive to thinking.

If there is work, that is, opening [*ouverture*], this no longer occurs at the level of this hand or this brain: it is, instead, at the level of the factory, which in its totality now forms an automaton – and does so as a 'technical ensemble':

> The worker's activity [is] reduced to [being] determined and regulated on all sides by the movement of the machinery, and not the opposite. The science [knowledge] [...] does not exist in the worker's consciousness, but rather acts upon him through the machine as an alien power, as the power of the machine itself.[49]

There is no longer any psychic re-interiorization; there is no longer the production of knowledge either by the hand or by the brain, but only its reproduction: it so happens that this is what was already described by Socrates, namely, the disindividuation of noetic beings by the *pharmakon* resulting from exteriorization.

Currently, as we have seen in the previous chapters, the pharmacological question raised by technical individuation as automation, leading to full and generalized automatization, is no longer damaging just to knowledge stripped of hands and brains and capacities for dis-automatization: it is a challenge to macroeconomic functioning in general, whereby 'the process of production has ceased to be a process of work',[50] becoming not only entropic, but *insolvent*.

89. The new value of work as open science

The commodities resulting from fully automatized production can find takers on the market only so long as there are *solvent* hands and brains capable of seizing them. They can do so only if 'objectified labour' in the form of automatons liberates alienated labour and constitutes a form of work free to dis-automatize automatons, with automatons and for automatons – instead of turning into unpaid work and into a process that blindly produces automatic traces and protentions.

This liberation that produces value, that is, neganthropy, can and must become the new source of any solvency, by reversing the entropic situation wherein 'the accumulation of knowledge and of skill, of the general productive forces of the social brain, is [...] absorbed into capital, which opposes itself to work: these hence appear as an attribute of capital, and more specifically of fixed capital'.[51] The functional integration of consumers through the algorithmic governmentality of 24/7 capitalism brings to completion the situation described by Marx. Yet Marx alone does not suffice to think this becoming: he could not have known of the reticulation of brains and their organs (hands and others) by automatons, as the automatic generation of protentions and the proletarianization of noesis by objectified knowledge.

If the question is indeed that of a neganthropology – that is, of a *dis-automatizing knowledge* through which it would be possible to struggle against the entropy inevitably entailed by automatization, which outstrips the reasoning of the understanding, in other words, subordinates the powers of interpretation to the correlationist and probabilistic computational systems that inherently deny the improbable without which no negentropy is conceivable – then it is a matter of thinking a new age of knowledge, of what Marx called science (*Wissenschaft*), and the conditions of its production, reproduction and trans-formation: of its opening. It is a question of thinking science, opened up as *open science*.

Such an open science is necessarily a work of science – a transformation, and in this sense an *energeia*. We conceive it as both *skholē* and *otium*, which are not the opposite of *negotium* but are distinguished from it in a fundamental way.

For many centuries, *otium*, that is, leisure and freedom, was opposed to *negotium* both as calculation and as labour, that is, submission to the necessity of providing subsistence to *otium* as to labourers themselves. This *division of labour* – which translates into an opposition between *manual work* and *intellectual work*, which combined with the oppositions stemming from Platonism and then Christianity between the soul and the body, the sensible and the intelligible, immortal life and mortality, spirit and matter, and so on – was, however, only an organological state of fact.

The Enlightenment opposed to this state of fact an inalienable right and duty of maturity, as Kant said, that nourished the inquiries of Hume on human understanding as the fruit of empiricism, the works of Diderot in the encyclopaedic field of the knowledge of all conditions, as well as those of Condorcet, lying between statistics, politics and education – the *otium* of the people – democratic voting, and so on.

If in ancient Greece the word *en-ergeia* in some way always passes through work and works (*ta erga*), the status of work in its relationship to noesis is over-determined by the absence of machines and automatons, so that the tasks of subsistence are deemed to be obstacles to noesis. Greece is fundamentally aristocratic, firstly in the sense that slavery is its condition, secondly in the fact that what the Greeks called *ponos* lies opposed to the *energeia* of the *noetic* soul, and by constituting rather *dunamis* as the subsistence provided to citizens – by those who cannot be citizens because they are their slaves.

This is why 'Greek has no term that corresponds to "work". A word such as *ponos* is applied to any activity involving painful, laborious effort.'[52] Work, as originally related to *ponos*, is conceived, in the history of Western mentality, as *excluding thinking*, that is, it excludes that which constitutes par excellence the *energeia* and *entelekheia* of the noetic soul.

In this world, noetic life – that is, the ability to access *skholē* – could only be to have freedom with respect to all the dependencies and constraints of subsistence, the latter being the accidental and contingent form of necessity. Rather than submission to *this* necessity, noetic life opens up access to the *universal* necessity of the essence and the end. Vernant adds, however, referring to Hesiod, that if work, which thus corresponds to no single word in Greek, can and must be thought through *ponos*, and as *ponos*, it is also *ergon*, a word by which it takes on another dimension: '[T]he *ergon* of each thing or being is the product of its own particular excellence, its *aretē*.'[53] In the Greece of Hesiod, that is, *two centuries before Plato, virtue,* the question of which would be the starting point for the whole Platonic construction, was thus thought starting from work as *ergon,* as works.

90.   The work of noesis and popular philosophy

Today, energy refers to potential, or, in other words, *dunamis*. The bipolarity *dunamis/energeia* has been *annulled*, as if it had imploded. With it has imploded what had individuated itself through this bipolarity as the trans-formation that Hegel thought in terms of exteriorization and the 'work of the concept' – in a sense of the word *work* that is not without relation to the maieutic, that is, childbirth. It is as if the world gave birth to itself by folding back on itself like a glove, 'de-worlding' itself, which Hegel does not think but which is the whole *negative* stake of Marx's materialist inversion of the dialectic.

There is no 'proletarianization' in Hegel: the real is rational in totality, everything is 'sublatable' and 'sublated', that is, redressable and redressed by the *Aufhebung*, soluble and dissolved in absolute knowledge as ab-*solution*. And if there is proletarianization in Marx – and not only that: if proletarianization is, in Marx, *still* work, *as the work of the negative* – this is because for Marx trans-formation remains dialectical, and therefore sublatable through a 'synthesis' that would be communism. Such a synthesis assumes, on the one hand, that the negative is a dynamic principle of trans-formation, and, on the other hand, that the *pharmakon* can be 'sublated', and therefore *no longer be a pharmakon*.

Contrary to what Marx would have us believe in *Capital*, it is not proletarianization that is the bearer of a transformation but, as he had envisaged in the *Grundrisse*, the end of employment, combined now with the organological mutation to which digital tertiary retention has given rise – and this transformation is a therapeutics, as care taken of a *pharmakon* that is always becoming more efficient because it is transindividuated by *objectified* knowledge, firstly as mechanical tertiary retention, then as analogical tertiary retention, and now as digital tertiary retention.

The end of employment can and must lead to the de-proletarianization of work, and in this sense its 'reinvention', inspired both by the organization of work in free software communities and by the intermittence scheme, in a society where employment is becoming a relic of an outmoded epoch, and where *neganthropic knowledge* becomes the *source of value* at once as life-knowledge, work-knowledge and conceptual-knowledge.

Before Marx, and before Hegel conceived the phenomenology of spirit as exteriorization, Kant, as we have already seen,[54] affirmed that laborious effort [*peine*] (*ponos*) is the condition of this *en-ergeia* that is the passage to the act of reason (an effort that would also be the lot of the experience of the sublime, but as affect): '[T]he discursive understanding must employ *much labor* on resolving and again compounding its concepts according to principles, and toil up many steps to make advances in knowledge.'[55] Again, Kant is here taking aim at those he describes as 'mystagogues' and who, because they '*have enough to live on*, whether in affluence or penury, consider themselves *superior* in comparison with those who must work in order to live'.[56] The *painful* [*pénible*] condition of noetic *energeia* is the lot of those who can be in actuality *only intermittently*, as Kant recalls here after Socrates and Aristotle. And this is also what renders *melancholic* the noetic soul considered as a practitioner of *pharmaka* of all kinds, including, for example, wine, so present in the Socratic dialogues, and hence it is that excess – paid for in hangovers, tomorrows cooked [*lendemains de cuite*] in black bile, *melas kholē* – must also be a form of intermittence.[57]

But unlike Socrates and Aristotle, for Kant this 'painful condition' is socially and historically translated into the philosophy of the Enlightenment, that is, into the rights and duties of knowledge. 'Dare to know!' is the injunction of the Enlightenment addressed to *every* citizen, Kant says,[58] and this is the very meaning of the *Aufklärung*. This is why it is a 'popular philosophy' concerning 'workers':

> I myself am a researcher by inclination. I feel the entire thirst for cognition [...]. There was a time when [...] I despised the rabble who knows nothing. *Rousseau* has set me right. [...] I would feel by far less useful than the common laborer if I did not believe that this consideration could impart a value to all others in order to establish the rights of humanity.[59]

The work of noesis as *faculty of thinking passing into actuality through work* – which becomes, with Hegel, exteriorization as history (history of reason and reason in history), and then becomes, with Marx, technical experience and the materialist dialectic – this noetic work has today been almost emptied of content. This ordeal – no longer just of kenosis and the death of God,[60] but of the *automatic fulfilment of nihilism* and of *generalized discredit* – is inherently tied to the fusion of *energeia* and *dunamis* in the machine, which has become the 'ubiquitous programmable automaton', and captures the *working knowledge* not only of the hand, but also of the brain.

91. Calculating power

It is now *computational power* [*puissance du calcul*],[61] determined by microprocessor speeds and data transfer speeds, which substitutes itself – as automaton – for *energeia*: taking form is replaced by correlation, which overtakes and outstrips. We will see that, with respect to this artificial intelligence, we should still not oppose it to an intuitive, original, *a priori* (that is, transcendental) intelligence. Intelligence is *always* artificial, that is, organological. It is therefore a question, as was said by Michel Volle, of the transductive coupling of living and inorganic organs.[62]

Contemporary science, having become, as 'technoscience', an *industrial power*, that is, an economic *dunamis*, understands the real as a mode of access to possibilities that it is then a matter of actual-izing: it is an organological mode of access (technologically assisted, via, for example, the scanning tunnelling microscope) to a *potential for trans-formations* in which it is a question of *actualizing possi-bilities without ends* within an interminable probabilistic becoming.

This science, which explores what could be and no longer describes what is, no longer passes from the real to the actuality of thinking, as the differentiation and distinction of law from fact, because it is no longer the 'science of being' – where being *is* thinking, and where the real is rational in this sense: the real is no longer a 'current state'.

This becoming without end, however, seems to be *without future*. What gives it this appearance is that the difference between facts and laws seems to have been erased – as if this difference was possible only in reference to an immutable being. We, on the contrary, think that it is by starting from another difference than that which opposes being and becoming – and, through this, what Ilya Prigogine and Isabelle Stengers call the new alliance[63] – that we must rethink law as the donation of the value of value in the epoch of the Anthropocene, which begins with thermodynamics as both technology and science, and hence as technoscience.

Such a thought must mobilize Whitehead's speculative cosmol-ogy.[64] This crucial and decisive difference is what distinguishes (but does not oppose) entropy and negentropy, and constitutes what we therefore call the neganthropological question. This question is orga-nologically and pharmacologically addressed to the non-inhuman being that it challenges – and that must become the quasi-cause of this challenge and this calling into question,[65] in order to trans-form becoming into future and as improbable singularity.

We have seen the advent of new forms of grammatization:

- the *mechanical* tertiary retention that every machine constitutes;
- *analogue* tertiary retention, which trans-forms consumer behaviour by channelling the attention of consumers and by short-circuiting trans-individuation (as the symbolic milieu of attentional forms); and
- *digital* tertiary retention, which enables all automatisms to be integrated.

These are the non-literal forms of grammatization that enabled the transformation of knowledge, which itself emerged from literal gram-matization, into an *industrial power and then into an industriousness without labour*, as an automatized force transforming the world. But this transformation of the world [*monde*] is increasingly experienced as its fouling [*immonde*] and *unworlding* [*immondialisation*], making the fortunes of fundamentalists and purifiers of all kinds, even while it threatens to send Europe along a dark path unless something happens to break once and for all with mass unemployment and to abandon the fable of a 'return to employment'.

Unemployment will remain so long as employment remains the standard of work. Employment, however, will soon become an outmoded epoch in the history of work.[66]

92. Two forms of energy

Alternatives to this impending catastrophe do exist. New forms of grammatization open *new opportunities for critical transindividuation* and a new field for the *ergon* – for action. Work, beyond the potential for the transformation of raw materials in which it indeed consists, and by which it is generally characterized, is also and more profoundly the invention of new possibilities of psychic and collective individuations. Work is also the trans-formation of potentials, hidden within preindividual funds, into *new forms of life* – in the sense of Ludwig Wittgenstein as of Georges Canguilhem and Marcel Duchamp.[67]

The *repression* of the role of work in the life of the spirit and of thought, that is, in the passage to the noetic act, and the opposition that was consequently formed between noesis and work,[68] based on disparaging technics in all its forms, has prevented work *in general* being thought as noetic *energeia*. The opposition between noesis and work is the result of a profound denial about the role of *tekhnē* in noetic *energeia*, and a denial of the *fact* that noesis is technesis (which was evidently excluded by Kant and Hegel, but not by Marx).[69]

The contemporary confusion of *energeia* with *dunamis* was made possible when, with the transfer of the automaton from Vaucanson to the mechanization of the workshops of royal manufacturing and with the advent of arithmetic machines, the process of grammatization began to move beyond the sphere of language. Consequently, as an analytical technology of the discretization and reproduction of gestures, then of perception, then of the analytical operations of the understanding, it was able to take hold of every field of existence, while the motive power of combustion took humanity into the thermodynamic era of the Anthropocene.

During the twentieth century, grammatization extended from cognitive functions to biological foundations (as the discretization and sequencing of the genome) and physico-chemical foundations (for example, as atomic nano-manipulation), passing through the standardization of everyday life (as marketing and the service industries), and now through the standardization of the processes of transindividuation themselves (as the algorithmic governmentality of 24/7 capitalism).

This sudden and vast extension occurs during the industrial revolution, as the grammatization of gestures and bodies and via the generalization of machinism. The *dynamic potential* that sets the machine in motion becomes confounded with this movement itself, which then reproduces and replaces the passage to the act of a noetic soul at work. In the twentieth century, with the extension of the process of grammatization to perception and understanding, proletarianization begins to affect all the functions of the noetic soul and to be extended not just to all forms of work but to *all forms of activity*, and therefore to 'leisure'. And the latter, having been turned into the capturing and deformation of attention, dis-integrates institutional *skholē* (that is, the scholarly institution, the school) as well as *otium*, which itself becomes industrial (as the 'leisure' industry).

Contemporary ill-being [*mal-être*] results from the fact that this generalized proletarianization has become massively entropic: everyone perceives this in a more or less confused way as the expression of the threat of disintegration, and it proceeds from the depletion of two forms of energy (and in this case I am using this word in both of the senses it has today): *combustion* energy and *libidinal* energy.

Combustion energy replaces the motility of the noetic body with industrial machinery that supplies power to motors, which in turn replace the subsistence work that in ancient Greece is called *ponos*, the nerve impulses of the proletariat supplying only some *extra motility* – insofar as automation, now capable of operating four million times faster than these nerve impulses, has not been *completely* accomplished.

Libidinal energy is what shapes and configures all the forms of noetic life, whether 'manual' or 'intellectual'. Noetic life is the psychosocial form of individuation, and everything that participates in a dialogical process of transindividuation is noetic – thereby constituting a form of sublimation passing through idealization and identification. Whether manual or intellectual, a worker is firstly and above all a noetic soul, that is, a noetic *body*.

Every gesture of a working body is charged with spirit – that is, inscribed on circuits of transindividuation. This body is not simply sensible, like the 'sensible soul' in Aristotle: it is sensational,[70] because it is capable of extra-ordinarily trans-forming the circuits of transin-dividuation on the basis of which, in which and with a view to which it always expresses itself technically – including through those ges-tures of the tongue in the mouth that constitute idioms.[71]

As the bearer and inventor of ex-pressions requiring the technical ex-teriorization of individuations that are concealed in preindividual funds and in-teriorized in the course of education, the noetic body inscribes itself and appears in and through this symbolic milieu, even via the smallest of gestures, gestures that are as such technical, as Mauss showed through his analysis of the 'techniques of the body'.[72] The body is organologically constituted through its mind and spirit, which is itself composed of collective retentions and protentions con-figuring libidinal energy by collecting the psychic retentions and pro-tentions through which the *psyche* is formed as psychic individuation.

'True' work is a process that is accomplished only in this libidinal economy, in all its more or less radicalized sublimatory forms – more or less sublime. Whether manual or intellectual, the worker trans-forms his or her milieu by dialogically exploring it as *technologos*. By revealing and bringing this milieu to light, dialogically and within a techno-logical *relation* of work (a relation that Durkheim tries to think without considering its organological and pharmacologi-cal dimensions), the manual or intellectual worker *trans-forms it by noetizing it*.

This noetic trans-formation involves desire – which Aristotle affirms for noesis in general by positing that it is *theos* as object of all desires that moves and stirs [*meut et émeut*] the soul. It is always in some way an idealizing form of a relationship of love. This is why every 'good professional' is *firstly* an amateur, and it is why all workers who have not been disintegrated into pure labour force and reduced to the forced employment of their time love their work. The refusal of work can make sense only when, having been reduced to merely an extra, backup force and as such an unworking, idle *dunamis*, the 'worker' no longer participates in the *energeia* in which any individuation consists.

93. Work and physics

Replaced by the machine he or she serves, the worker becomes its employee as pure labour force in the service of an *energeia* that the worker no longer embodies and in relation to which he or she has been disintegrated because hyper-materialized, his or her own *ener-geia* having been studied, formalized, discretized and standardized into some material form – template or algorithm – amounting to an industrially reproduced tertiary retention. What is now taking place, with algorithmic governmentality, extends this industrialization to transindividuation in all its forms, to the totality of social relations, which are thereby disintegrated in their turn, and it is this we refer to as the hyper-industrial epoch.

The ex-pression in which consisted the gesture with which the worker had hitherto expressed the world of his or her body, as one (ex)presses the juice from a fruit, has been replaced by a standard and a procedure defined by a time and motion study department. The proletarian, serving the machine that has replaced the worker, has become a pure *dunamis* deprived of his or her *energeia*, whereas the machine consumes engine power through which it is capable of going into action according to the programmes that emerge from grammatization, programmes that are set by the use of the labour force of the employee, who supplies that extra bit of force to which he or she amounts.

In this way 'energy' becomes power [*puissance*] – physics maintains a formal distinction between *power*, measured by the watt, and its effective consumption measured by the joule as *energy* developed in time (also measured in newton-metres). To this extent, which is a condition of 'rationalization', *work thereby becomes a concept of physics.*

In the past it was striking and encouraging to see workplaces in which wage labourers, having been deprived of their *energeia* through proletarianization, nevertheless developed 'amateur practices' outside wage labour, from the mining areas and mills of Nord-Pas-de-Calais, with their choirs, their bands, their poets and their painters, all 'amateurs', to the Rhodiaceta factories of Besançon and the Peugeot factories of Sochaux, where in 1967 the Medvedkin Groups were formed.[73]

The industrialization of culture has itself, however, *obstructed and prevented* the development of this amateurship, through which the proletarianized world could intermittently provide for itself and preserve times and spaces for thinking, and for the invention of friendship – and Crary's analyses of 24/7 capitalism describe this state of fact. Nevertheless, the only way of fighting against this state of fact is by elaborating and transindividuating a state of law founded on the neganthropic definition of the value of values required by the contemporary stage of organology and grammatization.

In 2008, the contemporary situation of generalized proletarianization revealed itself to be a global *economy of carelessness and negligence*, a *generalized dis-economy*. This installs an inherently irresponsible 'dis-society',[74] because it is systemically founded on the dilution of responsibility – that is, on a systemic, anti-noetic stupidity [*bêtise*], which is also a systemic infidelity and faithlessness of the consumer and the speculator, who jettison their objects. This generates a structural distrust in a manner destructive of its own conditions of possibility: it leads to the waste of energy and the depletion of all forms of energy, both the combustion energies of subsistence and the libidinal energies of existence.

These energies are sustainable, however, only insofar as they cultivate a relation of fidelity – of *attachment* (in John Bowlby's sense), of *investment* and *idealization* (in Freud's sense) – to *consistences*, that is, to idealities: to what does not exist, even though it consists more than anything that does exist. What consists is the object of desire – more or less sublimated. It does not exist since it is infinite, and because only what is finite exists (being thereby calculable). Furthermore, only desire can set in motion noetic individuations in all their forms, and through them *energeia* as individuation, *which is also to say, as care.*

Energies of subsistence and of existence can again become sustainable only insofar as noesis can be reconstituted in the contemporary pharmacological context, a context characterized by the most recent stages of grammatization. This is the thesis of Ars Industrialis: to rebuild a libidinal economy requires the installation of a new industrial model founded on the economy of contribution, that is, on a broad process of de-proletarianization.

The struggle for the economy of contribution is both micropolitical, in the sense in which Deleuze and Guattari used this term, and macropolitical, in the sense that it can never prevail without the implementation of regulatory measures by a reinvented public power – something of which Guattari himself was clearly not unaware.[75] This is so even if one of the infantile maladies of the legacy of Deleuze and Guattari has consisted in dismissing macropolitical struggle – and in dismissing public power, which is the only level on which this struggle can be conducted – thereby giving credence to libertarian ultra-liberalism.

94. Libidinal energy and care

For its part, since the early twentieth century ultra-liberalism has referred to the *creative economy*. What is 'creativity' if not *individuation par excellence* – that is, *energeia* in its original sense?

The creator is one who, through his or her psychic individuation, *coincides* without remainder with collective individuation, without any gap, perfectly, or even, we could say, *miraculously*. In this coincidence, to which we give the name of *creation*, the creator invents his or her epoch, making it his or her *dunamis*.

A 'creator' forms his or her epoch, makes it pass into actuality, and therein more or less trans-forms his or her time – in having always to struggle, certainly, against the *entropic forces of disindividuation*, which, most of the time, resist and reject the creator, and which is firstly the case for creators themselves, who are always and primarily involved in a struggle *with themselves*. Duchamp is an exemplary case of this austere self-reckoning, to the point that for him it is life itself that becomes a work of art.[76]

But is this actually what is at stake in the so-called 'creative economy', in particular in the sense given to it by John Howkins?[77] A true 'creative' economy would be an economy of contribution, and not the hyper-consumerist economy that is, obviously enough, the blocked horizon of the conception that Howkins shares with Richard Florida,[78] where a 'creative class', which is an oligarchy of 'creators', governs a hyper-proletarianized global mass.

An economy of contribution requires a complete change in industrial relations: this in turn requires an inversion of the logic of the *pharmakon*, which has become structurally poisonous through the process of fully automatized grammatization, in order to create a *new system of care* – a technique of the government of self and others founded in a new way on what must no longer be the biopolitics of a biopower, but the noopolitics of a psychopower.

Biopower is what, after the printing press, was made possible by the grammatization of the body, in terms both of the administrative writing machine[79] and of the machine-tool, which proletarianize workers by opposing capital and labour while disintegrating *energeia* into *dunamis* conceived as power. Today this is truer than ever, with the implementation of technologies of psychosocial individuation as *computational power* founded on traceability and social networks, and constituting the technology of trans*dividuation* called 'social engineering'. What is proletarianized and disintegrated is then the social relation itself, that is, collective individuation in totality and on a planetary scale – giving rise in return to fundamentalisms of every stripe.

Faced with this, and as Gorz invited us to do twenty years ago, we must observe the micropolitical struggles led by hackers and the thinkers of free software in general, whose amateur engineers and technicians work methodically towards the reinvention of work through the concretization of an industrial model *founded* on de-proletarianization.

Like the solar energy that so struck Bataille, libidinal energy seems inexhaustible and essentially renewable. And yet, libidinal energy is not a given: it is the fruit of the social work of the formation of attention, which the contemporary deformation of attention unbinds and releases in the form of *extremely* dangerous drive-based automatisms. Proletarianization is also what destroys attention, and makes inaccessible not only consistences but the enjoyment of existence, which is also to say, of recognition.

It was the death of Richard Durn on 28 March 2002, shortly before French voters chose Jean-Marie Le Pen ahead of Lionel Jospin to participate in the second round of the presidential election against Jacques Chirac, that led me to explore all these questions.[80] Durn killed eight local councillors, and then committed suicide by throwing himself from the window of the police station in Paris where he was being interrogated, three weeks after having written in his diary that he had *lost the feeling of existing.*

Those who volunteer for jihadist suicide undoubtedly suffer from a similar misery. De-proletarianization is the condition of the reconstitution of libidinal energy, which is renewable only on the condition of being treated for its many destructive tendencies – from the destructive destruction of contemporary capitalism to the fundamentalist 'martyrs'. *Inshallah.*

8

Above and Beyond the Market

Men assure their own subsistence or avoid suffering, not because these functions themselves lead to a sufficient result, but in order to accede to the insubordinate function of free expenditure.

Georges Bataille[1]

95. Organology of a positive right to interpretation

To pass from the algorithmic state of fact to its state of law is to make neganthropy the value of values – as the criterion of all valuation restoring long-term solvency. The algorithmic state of fact becomes an algorithmic state of law when the automatization of fact is made to serve, in law, the development of the ability to dis-automatize.

'In law' has, here, three main dimensions:

- an *epistemic* dimension, composed of circuits of transindividuation through which law is differentiated from fact from within the very core of facts, which means: 'not to go against the facts, but to go further than the facts', and by constituting the meaning, the prospect and the future with regard to this or that discipline or transdiscipline;
- an *ergological* dimension, which trans-forms this state of fact into a law of work and a right to *noetic* work in all its forms, inasmuch as there is noesis in all life-knowledge, work-knowledge and conceptual knowledge as the intermittence of dis-automatizing-knowledge;
- a *juridical* dimension, restoring the political right as such, that is, restoring it as the right to interpretation and the duty to interpret, so as to trans-form and thereby to work (this question

of right extending back to the *vera philosophia* of the 'very young Marx').

As Yann Moulier-Boutang recalls, the law is first and foremost that which requires interpretation (failing which it becomes a rule or a procedure): 'The judge interprets the law, and without this work of interpretation of the law, which may modify it or alter its meaning, there is no sustainable understanding of the norm.'[2] Collective normativity (borrowing the term *normativity* from Canguilhem) is interiorized to the extent that it is interpreted: it is respected only insofar as it is interiorized and it is interiorized only insofar as by right it can and must be interpreted, which also means individuated. Following Gadamer, we refer to *hermeneutic jurisprudence* in this sense.[3]

But such hermeneutics has positive conditions of possibility, which are organo-logical conditions. This is why *a right to interpretation presupposes a hermeneutic organology* – covering the levels of the psychic individual, the technical individual and collective individuals – and requires a *reorganization of public space* that would again make positive law possible: law can be *positive* only on the condition of being positively *published*.

The hermeneutic organology of ancient Greece, then, consists in *skholeion*. In algorithmic governmentality, the space of this publication is the world wide web, which makes the internet network accessible to everyone. For a state of law specific to algorithmic governmentality to be constituted, the web must become, through its publishing formats and languages, not just semantic but hermeneutic.

In the transductive relation that Volle describes between brainwork and a ubiquitous programmable automaton, a relationship between the 'memory [...] of the computer' and 'intellectual activity' is possible, writes Moulier-Boutang, only if it contains a 'margin for interpretation [...] [which] is a prime example of pollination'.[4] Moulier-Boutang thus introduces the key concepts of what, in *L'Abeille et l'Économiste*, he calls the pollen economy – which the economy of contribution would require if it is to go beyond a capitalism that has become 'cognitive'.

So-called 'cognitive capitalism' is what results from digital grammatization as an analytical organology that structures contemporary understanding and reshapes the synthetic (hermeneutic) vocation of reason (as kingdom of ends) by making a division between what is calculable (which Moulier-Boutang calls the codifiable digital) and what is not:

> From the moment we begin to operate within the framework of a digital cognitive capitalism, which takes over certain tasks performed by the brain by mechanizing them, and by making data objectifiable, infinitely repeatable, calculable by computer, we increasingly see things appear that had remained hidden until the computer separated the codifiable digital from the non-codifiable.[5]

We see things appear, in other words, that arise from interpretation, that is, from the dis-automatization accomplished by the synthesis of reason as a work, and insofar as it effects a *bifurcation* and practises an opening, however barely visible it may be, thereby suspending an automatism, however modest it may be. And it *always does so beyond the analysis of an understanding* that has become fully automatizable and analytically automatic because it is grammatized by the ubiquitous programmable automaton that is the reticulated computer.

Nevertheless, beyond the fact that the *border* separating the 'codifiable digital' from the 'non-codifiable' *is constantly shifting* – composed as it is of regimes of truth themselves conditioned by processes of exteriorization and interiorization, that is, processes of expression and impression, which are formed in the disorganized and reorganized brain through its 'prostheses' via the transductive relations between psychic individuals, collective individuals and the intellectual technologies that have failed to become technical individuals in Simondon's sense[6] (and insofar as they are ubiquitous programmable automatons) – beyond all this, *who actually* sees this separation between the codifiable digital and the non-codifiable digital come into appearance? *How* is this visible? And *through what procedures?*

96. Above and beyond the market – honey and the income of noetic pollination

As the trans*dividuated* individuals that we have become on the network of algorithmic governmentality, *dividuals* without future – that is, lacking protentions not always already captured and performatively diverted at the speed of light by computational becoming, thereby outstripped, overtaken and 'dividuated' in this sense – we *do not see* this differentiation between the codifiable digital and the non-codifiable digital come into appearance: we and they do not see this differentiation effected by coding itself. *It is precisely as such that we and they are dividuated.* And this means that:

- what is not codifiable is repressed;
- those who do see it divert it for their own benefit – we can, with McKenzie Wark and Yves Citton, call those who do so vectorialists – for whom hackers become appendages.[7]

Such is the automatic accomplishment of nihilism, which is not, however, absolutely automatic for everyone: those who possess the knowledge and can thus modify the algorithms and the conditions of their implementation could see it and should see it. But *they do not want to know*: they do not want to know that this anthropization of non-inhuman being leads to the entropy of the inhuman and to the unleashing of the inhumanity that is contained within any *anthropos* – especially when, for these dividuals without future that we have become, the only protention that remains is that of the worst, heralded by the Anthropocene.[8]

To *see*, to *make* and to *show* this difference, we must be able to practise the subjective principle of differentiation. The performative and automatic generation of protentions on the basis of 'big data', however, outstrips those who produce this data of the blind and undifferentiated – at the same time short-circuiting the *processes of transindividuation* that codify what supposedly *cannot be calculated* not just by computers but, as Moulier-Boutang says with respect to law, by right and by a judicial apparatus that implements justice hermeneutically: in a way that is neither calculable nor controllable by power.

The necessity that arises, then, consists in the *formation of attention* to what constitutes this differentiation between the calculable and the incalculable (which may nevertheless be codified) and in *protecting against its deformation*. The formation and protection of attention should, in a contributory economy, become a constant and free work based on an *otium* of the people, in turn based on a culture of positive externalities that are derived *not*, as libertarians of all persuasions from the left to the right would have us believe, from spontaneous generation, but rather from an institution: the institution of law, which forms part of any regime of truth constitutive of circuits of transindividuation for that epoch.

Such an institution of law, differentiating itself from facts (as juridical law, but also as scientific law, *jus* as well as *theoria*), has organological conditions, in relation to which it is, precisely, the therapeutics: these conditions are always pharmacological. In the epoch of what Moulier-Boutang calls cognitive capitalism, the stakes of these questions, for him as for us, are firstly and fundamentally economic (inscribed in an epoch where knowledge has become a primary 'production function'). This is why he emphasizes that 'the codifiable [in algorithmic form] has little value, since it is repeatable at marginal or zero cost. And since it is always identically repeatable, it loses value, just as in industry: what is mechanized loses value and eventually produces no value.'[9]

This is also why Marx posits that the general intellect, in the epoch of fully objectified knowledge (and we have now gone well beyond what Marx anticipated), must install *another* conception of value. Value has become work *that is not yet* objectified, or even *that cannot be* objectified, that is, not just codified but codified digitally, *encoded* in the sense of the crackers or writers of code who are the hackers.

But if wage labourers and employment cease to exist, in what conditions will it be possible to produce such value,[10] that is, to transform the value of value into values of all kinds, and by what associated circulations? This is the question of an economy founded on the macroeconomic valorization of positive externalities. Gorz, after reading *Vers un capitalisme cognitif*,[11] wrote in 2003 that the value produced in this new world is generated by positive externalities that, as in the case of free software, produce 'a collective outcome that transcends the sum of individual contributions'.[12] To facilitate understanding of what is at stake in these externalities and their valorization, Moulier-Boutang adopts the metaphor of pollination by bees in the plant world – and, by extension, the question of the viability of living things in totality. Interpretation, which is a fruit of intelligence qua 'understanding of the environment, [...] is akin to pollination by bees'.[13] We ourselves conceive contributory income as an *income for noetic pollination* – pollination practised as the *otium* of the people, and inasmuch as it is always 'missing'.[14]

This metaphor, which can be taken quite far, and which is thus something more than an allegory, makes it possible to think the conditions of a hermeneutic and noetic traceology, because it itself raises the question of an organology of traces: bees, like ants, secrete chemical traces called pheromones, while the algorithmic governmentality of 24/7 capitalism is itself a traceology in which it is the data industry that makes the honey.

It is precisely in this that this algorithmic governmentality *of fact* – based on a *structural legal vacuum* imposed by the *fact* that automatized analytical understanding outstrips the hermeneutic faculty that is reason – is intrinsically toxic, because it fundamentally destroys value: the 'value of value' that, on the contrary, treats pollination as *precisely not* honey.

Honey is 'monetized' in the form of exchange value by the bee-keeper, who, because of this fact, takes care to maintain the hive. But the value of value is produced by bees themselves *above and beyond the market* [*par-dessus le marché*], if we can put it like that – as a quasi-*sumptuary* surplus, and within this general economy that is the sumptuousness of life, and especially noetic life, as Bataille showed.[15]

The monetization of traces and of what automated management makes possible as the calculation of their protentions, that is, as the manipulation of these protentions, rapidly sterilizes protentional capacity itself by dividuating psychic individuals, that is, by depleting their libidinal energy, which we now know is noetic energy as such, that is, *energeia* as the work of trans-formation by which a noetic being can take care of itself – and of others into the bargain [*par-dessus le marché*].

The value of value is not monetizable, and this is what constitutes the new transcendence of the market, which is no longer here the god of *Beruf*[16] but the positive externality that makes any economy possible, and does so *above all as noetic economy* – and not just cognitive:[17] as an economy *cultivating intermittences* as the knowledge and power to dis-automatize in one way or another. This is also what is at stake in life and as that in it which is more than it [*en plus*], in a surplus value that is no longer a profit [*plus-value*] but the improbable side of life in its inventive generosity[18] – which, formulated in less lyrical terms, means its negentropic character.

It is necessary to refer to *neganthropology* with respect to what relates to us (us, potentially non-inhuman beings) because it is only by passing through the artefacts that are tertiary retentions in general that we produce the traces enabling a sumptuary economy, which is an economy of *otium*, that is, of spirit as that which is transmitted from generation to generation, and in letters, above and beyond the market, which here means: *as that which never loses its value*, thereby constituting the canon for any value.

To put it another way, through the traceology made possible by digital reticulation in the epoch of algorithmic governmentality and 24/7 capitalism, the *neganthropos* could and should produce great wealth, on the condition of not wanting to submit this wealth to the exchange value levied by shareholders (those McKenzie Wark calls vectorialists), whose infrastructure enables this noetic pollination to deplete individual and collective protentions – sterilizing and disorientating the *noetic hymenoptera* that we are, just as actual bees are today poisoned by pesticides and other *pharmaka* of 'rationalized' agriculture.[19]

97.   To subsist in order to exist through what consists

For Oskar Negt, it is through work that the relation to the adult world opens up, insofar as it is capable of providing for his or her needs: 'Employment and work essentially determine the horizon of my way of seeing the world.'[20] The child who does not yet speak, the *infans*, enters the world through the play of the transitional object: the *play of language* is pre-ceded by *play with the Thing* (*das Ding*), of which the cuddly toy or the blanket is the 'vicar'.[21] He or she then learns to speak, and so receives an education, firstly from his or her family, then from society, in order to become adult, that is, capable of providing for his or her own needs by contributing to those of society and of his or her eventual offspring.

Through these 'phases of life' the child traverses stages of individuation, in each case involving a trans-formational relation to *pharmaka*. A trans-formational relation to *pharmaka* is thus in play, and this play is that of an interpretation, a trans-forming noesis, an *en-ergeia*. It is this play that proletarianization and employment interrupt in an increasingly serious way[22] – parents today being themselves proletarianized, that is, dispossessed of the possibility of educating their own children.

Educating their children is what mothers or fathers or relatives do in order to make a happy life – for themselves and for their child. But in our epoch this is what they are less and less able to do: they are prevented by the control that has been taken of protentions, and from the earliest phases of life, through systems that capture the attention of both young and old alike, installing proletarianization, ruining attention and generating immense misery and poverty – affective, symbolic, sexual, intellectual, economic, political and spiritual.

The *enjoyment* of educating one's children can occur only in a sumptuary and intermittent way. It 'holds' for its own sake: this is what Donald Winnicott observed in relation to what he called transitional space.[23] All noesis occurs in such space, which lasts well beyond infancy (failing which, it is a sham). When the representatives of Christianity advocate the introduction of a family allowance, that is, of a contributory income remunerating this positive externality that is filial education, they understand on the basis of the sacraments that what is essential, which has no price, is always something that lies above and beyond the market.

Proletarianization reduces everything to a price on the labour market or to commodities and services, including the electronic babysitting of un-education. With the generalized liquidation of noetic *energeia* in all its forms – of which the transitional form that takes care of the *infans* is the matrix of all the others – the negan-thropology concretized in the organological history of non-inhuman being becomes an entropology brought about by proletarianized employment, which is inhuman, as Friedmann says, and which is 'false' work, as Negt adds.

'True' work is a *poiēsis* that responds to 'the need the individual feels to appropriate the surrounding world, to impress his or her stamp upon it and, by the objective transformations he or she effects upon it, to acquire a sense of him- or herself as an autonomous subject possessing practical freedom'.[24] To realize objective trans-formations is to project into the world – through some process of transindividuation – a diurnal dream whose matrix is the transitional object. Whether nocturnal or diurnal, *a dream is a primordial noetic intermittence*, itself transitional.

Negt's definition of work is very close to that of the noetic soul. Today, 'real, existing "work" [...] is predetermined in its procedures and aims, specialized and de-materialized [and] is not "true" but "false" work'.[25] In 1991, Gorz concluded that it is now a matter of undertaking the economico-political struggle to reverse this state of fact:[26] 'Now, there is no social space in which "true work" – which, depending upon the circumstances, I prefer to call "work-for-oneself" or "autonomous activity" – can deploy itself in such a way as to *produce society* and set its stamp upon it. *It is this space we have to create.*'[27]

This space for the *production of society* (a production that is also for Godelier[28] what characterizes the human) is transitional space, that is, opened by consistences, and it is the space of the *otium* of the people. Installing and instituting this as a new state of law requires:

- on the one hand, completing digital organology;
- on the other hand, developing practices of the right to interpreta-tion as the right to intermittence and the duty to participate in collective individuation through a new apparatus of the culture of the self and others – and this must be done *above and beyond the market*.

What we call work – which, before becoming a pure force of labour, was par excellence this participation in collective individuation (which Durkheim tried to describe), long divided between manual and intellectual, and distributed into activities of all kinds and then unified by the market – is what arranges, according to modalities that are constantly being recomposed, the irreducible dimensions of subsistence, existence and consistence.

'True' work always, in some way or another, contributes to these three dimensions. And these are the three dimensions explicitly arranged in the work of those hackers who are adherents of free software, dimensions that Linus Torvalds, in his preface to Pekka Himanen's *The Hacker Ethic*, called ' "survival", "social life", and "entertainment" '.[29] We must distinguish between these three dimensions that combine in any 'true' work as:

- subsistence, which is what Marx called the reproduction of the labour force;
- existence, which engenders recognition and what Durkheim called organic solidarity, which he linked directly to the division of labour, and which we understand as a signature case of participation in collective individuation;
- consistence, which inscribes subsistence and existence within a process of transindividual idealization wherein they participate in a collective dream – what indigenous Australians call 'the Dreaming', and which we Westerners call reason.[30]

There are varying degrees of mixing between these different layers: until the great rise of proletarianization, there were but few situations limited only to the work of subsistence. And there were no situations concerned *only* with the work of consistence: such would be the work of God alone. This is what both Socrates and Aristotle are telling us through their quotation of Simonides – and this, in turn, is connected to Kant's discussion of work with respect to a popular philosophy.[31]

It is through the intermittent work of consistences – which do not exist, which are idealized and as such dreamed because they are intrinsically improbable – that neganthropy is possible as the realization of dreams, that is, as the realization of possibilities arising from intermittence qua noetic *energeia* that cultivates the value of value by taking care of it.

98.   Organology of the Anthropocene and 'opium of the people'

Today, humanity is confronted with the toxicity of its own development – to the point that we now have a term, the 'Anthropocene', to designate an age of the biosphere in which 'human activities have become the dominant strain above all other geological and natural forces that have hitherto prevailed: the action of the human species has become a true geophysical force acting on the planet'.[32]

It is as a figure or motif silhouetted against this horizon that we must defend the model of intermittence, where it is no longer a matter of 'making one's life into a work of art' but of *making organological life into a neganthropic work* – through the reinvention of work, restoring a global solvency differing from and deferring cosmic entropy.[33]

Work, as *energeia*, is the moment par excellence wherein psychic, technical and social individuations are arranged as the play of traces and the agent of transindividuation. This play operates through the adjustment and disadjustment of the technical system and social systems, the psychic apparatus of the worker being the operator of these adjustments and disadjustments, and the agent of a generalized phase shift through which a preindividual potential is individuated.

The Anthropocene is indeed the epoch of the globalization of the technical system and of the destruction of social systems through a deterritorialization of uncaring, negligent financial capital, producing a vast irrationality, totally devoid of care, as evidenced by countless negative externalities. To this transduction between the *technical system and the social systems*, however, we must add the cosmological dimensions that are the *geophysical system* and the *biological systems*, which have been co-implicated in this transductivity to such an extent that 'human activities have become the dominant strain above all other geological and natural forces that have hitherto prevailed'.

With industrialization, the relationship between the technical system and the social systems has had a massive and uniform retroactive impact, on a global scale, on biological systems in all their forms and on the geographical system in its totality.

> Succeeding the Holocene, a period of 11,500 years marked by a rare climatic stability [...] a period of blossoming agricultures, cities and civilizations, the swing into the Anthropocene represents a new age of the Earth. As Paul Crutzen and Will Steffen have emphasized, under the sway of human action, 'Earth is currently operating in a *no-analogue state.*'[34]

This new geological reality is political: 'Besides being a geological event, the Anthropocene is at the same time a political event [...], the entire functioning of the Earth becomes a matter of human political choices.'[35]

As neganthropology, taking responsibility for the question of the Anthropocene must constitute a new age of care that will also be a new age of economics, where economizing will mean taking care and where the economy will again become economical. To think and act in such an epoch necessitates a reading of Whitehead that:

- interprets his speculative cosmology from the perspective of general organology and pharmacology – which he himself calls for when he writes that 'the major advances in civilization are processes which all but wreck the societies in which they occur';[36] and
- analyses the stakes of a historical fact that still awaits its law precisely as a theory of the Anthropocene: the advent of *thermodynamic science* arose in some way from the socialization of the *thermodynamic machine* with which anthropic activities have become the dominant strain imposed on geological forces and on the negentropic forces that constitute life.[37]

It is as the specific challenge of the Anthropocene that we must conceive and install the *otium* of the people, where the *value of value is, as neganthropy, that which is cultivated and remunerated through leisure* – the leisure that Friedmann himself tried to think as an *otium* of the people, which risks, as he said at the time (that is, in the 1960s), becoming an opium of the people. After observing 'the multiplication of courses taken outside work' as a result of the reduction of working time, he then asks: 'These courses, are they "leisure"?'[38] And at this point he develops, with an impressive prescience, the terms with which to frame an alternative to the situation we find ourselves urgently confronting some fifty years later:

> If leisure continues to follow the direction it is heading in today, is the risk not [...] of it becoming a new 'opium of the people'? Is this risk not intensified by the plethora of information provided by the mass media, which develops in the masses the taste for superficial conversation about all kinds of subjects, that is, a substitute for action in all domains?[39]

Everything we have described of the 'symbolic misery' engendered by the culture industries of consumerism serves to confirm Friedmann's fears. But what Crary, Berns and Rouvroy describe as 24/7 capitalism and algorithmic governmentality goes even further than Friedmann feared: 24/7 capitalism channels and deforms an age much more alienated than that of wage labour and of the 'leisures' shaped by the culture industries. This is why it cannot simply be a question of providing 'free time'.

99. Contributory income for intermittence

Without a *political economy of noetic intermittence*, the end of wage labour becomes *the automatized employment of 'free' time*. Without an *otium* of the people[40] founded on a generalization of intermittence and on a reconfiguration of knowledge, and of the conditions of its production and transmission, 'liberated time' is bound to become a time of consumption and unpaid work – through a functional integration of 'free time' into the market in the form of psychosocial disintegration.

Gorz quotes the 1987 declaration by Peter Glotz that German social democracy must 'create a situation in which the time each person may dispose of for their own *search for meaning* is greater than the time they need for their work, their recreation and their rest. You say the left no longer has a goal? Then here is a goal for it.'[41] But *meaning* is what is *felt* during the process of *trans*individuation when *we feel the passing*, occurring, happening and trans-forming of meanings in force – generating new, temporarily metastabilized significations, such that former meanings are no longer felt: they lose their meaning. Meaning, understood in this way, inhabits all 'true' work, however minor it may be, and does so as the play of traces.

In March 1993 Gorz proposed the establishment of a dual income:

> Since the economic apparatus produces more and better with less and less work, income levels can no longer depend on the evolution of the amount of work provided by each. [...] The redistribution of productivity gains [...] requires a comprehensive politics, appropriate for the time. This necessarily involves the introduction of a binomial income: income from work, on the one hand, which may decrease with the duration of work; and social income, on the other hand.[42]

This 'binomial income' presupposes a 'comprehensive politics'.

We ourselves take up this proposal, but it must be reversed, and Gorz's recommendation of a comprehensive politics requires new determinations that it lacked at the time. For since this was written, one month before the opening of the web, great transformations have taken place, which in 2003 were partially integrated by Gorz himself into *The Immaterial*,[43] in terms of the valorization of positive externalities. But this integration must now be completed in his absence, in order to specify the critical elements of such a politics in the context of reticular writing, generalized automatization and the disintegration that occurs as a result, via the industry of traces controlled by a capitalism that has become totally computational and purely nihilistic.

Today, 'big changes are coming to the labor market that people and governments aren't prepared for', as Bill Gates put it in a speech given in Washington on 13 March 2014.[44] If the founder of Microsoft is now raising this topic, along with many other 'observers',[45] it is firstly because this issue has become highly relevant, and because it heavily involves his own company. But it is also because he himself intends to prescribe the use of this *pharmakon* that is software automation, enabling software substitution, the result of which should be, according to Gates himself, competition between automatons and employees.

Obviously he does not present it in these terms, but rather as a recommendation, at the American Enterprise Institute, addressed to governments 'around the world' by an unparalleled expert who embodies the 'leading fortune' of this world to whom he addresses himself and dispenses counsel, which a journalist from *Business Insider*, Julie Bort, summarized as follows:

> Gates believes that the tax codes are going to need to change to encourage companies to hire employees, including, perhaps, eliminating income and payroll taxes altogether. He's also not a fan of raising the minimum wage, fearing that it will discourage employers from hiring workers in the very categories of jobs that are most threatened by automation.
>
> He explained: 'When people say we should raise the minimum wage, I worry about what that does to job creation...potentially damping demand in the part of the labor spectrum that I'm most worried about.'[46]

Such 'solutions' amount to the macroeconomic absurdity that consists in impoverishing employees still further, that is, in further reducing social solvency in favour of an even greater siphoning off of the new capital gains made possible by the algorithmic automaton. These solutions consist not only in failing to redistribute the immense new productivity gains made possible by software substitution, but in further diminishing the redistribution processes derived from the old model.

Downwards pressure on wages inevitably leads to a fall in demand. And we know that the way this issue was resolved by the conservative revolution was through the introduction of subprime mortgages and credit default swaps, enabling the formation of an ultra-speculative and automatized financial market, which was then bound to leave both banks and states fundamentally insolvent. It seems that the lesson drawn by Greenspan in October 2008 has not been learned by Gates: the latter's proposal could lead only to a repetition of this madness – or worse.

Financialization, which was the disastrous response of the conservative revolution to the limits of Fordist-Keynesianism, still feeds into the derelict reasoning of Bill Gates, who fails to see that if it fails to value work, *including outside wage labour*, capital will be incapable of prospering.[47] On this point, we radically disagree with the analyses of Yann Moulier-Boutang.[48]

100. Organology of speculation

Moulier-Boutang rejects the opposition between the real and the virtual, and with reason:[49] the opposition between a 'good' economy, which would stick to 'real' production, and a 'bad' economy, which would speculate on the future by deviating from the real present, is superficial. Since the Neolithic, the economy has always been what 'speculates' on a surplus of production to come, and the economy is in this sense speculative in a way that is very elementary and necessary. Thinking in general is itself speculative, and in the twentieth century Whitehead conceived a speculative (processual) cosmology.[50] In general, to speculate is to conjecture about the possible on the basis of observation.

In Kantian philosophy, speculative (that is, theoretical) pure reason is nevertheless constrained by experience and understanding: only by building upon these can it take flight (that is, speculate). This philosophy is called critical in the sense that speculative reason finds itself limited by itself insofar as it is self-observing, and speculative primarily in this sense: self-observing critical reason fundamentally distinguishes the spheres of speculation and experience without opposing them. Pure theoretical (that is, speculative) reason can do nothing without experience, nor without the understanding. The understanding *should have no power* without reason, nor reason without the understanding, with which it constitutes the faculty of knowledge, which is a speculative faculty.

In fact, however, what we find is that the automatized understanding can do many things without reason. But we also see that such a power devoid of knowledge, that is, devoid of law, having become purely automatic, is entropic, that is, self-destructive. Kant did not himself foresee this possibility of a pure automatization of the understanding because he believed he could identify a transcendental schematism that precedes any empiricity.

It is the transcendental imagination that governs the relationships between the data of experience and the concepts of the understanding. I argued in the third volume of *Technics and Time*[51] that the three syntheses of the transcendental imagination, from which are deduced the pure (*a priori*) concepts of the understanding, presuppose a fourth, which is the condition of what Kant called the schematism and also of what he called the synthesis of recognition. This fourth synthesis is that carried out via tertiary retention,[52] and therefore it cannot, strictly speaking, be called transcendental.[53]

That tertiary retention conditions the three syntheses of the imagination and the schematism of the understanding means that there is an organology and a pharmacology of the speculation in which the faculty of knowing always consists (which already for Augustine was a 'critique' as *libido sciendi*), which is a faculty of looking (*specto*), of observer and conjecturer (*speculor*) on the basis of an artefact that is always a *speculum*.

The *speculator* who is the philosopher cannot take flight without the organological discretization in which grammatization consists, which supports the analytical categorization of the understanding that encounters intuition, and that enables apodictic reasoning that can 'examine at leisure' – that is, observe and speculate – as Leibniz understands:

> This is the principal aim of this great science that I have become accustomed to calling Characteristics, of which what we call algebra, or analysis, is only one small branch; for it is this science that gives words to languages, letters to speech, numbers to arithmetic, notes to music, and that teaches us the secret of fixing reasoning, and compelling it to leave a small volume of visible traces on paper to be examined at leisure; and it makes us reason at little cost, by putting written characters in place of things in order to disencumber the imagination.[54]

This fragment by Leibniz received extensive commentary and analysis by Derrida in *Of Grammatology*, introduced into his grammatological project through the interpretation of a correspondence between Descartes and Mersenne.[55] But it seems to me that the organological and pharmacological consequences for grammatology were never drawn, in particular where Leibniz considers the possibility 'of fixing reasoning, and compelling it to leave a small volume of visible traces on paper to be examined at leisure'.

That Derrida contested Husserl's opposition between primary retention and secondary retention in fact led him to simply ignore tertiary retention,[56] that is, the artefact as organological condition of universal Characteristics as envisaged here by Leibniz.

The stakes of these questions were shown by Canguilhem in *Knowledge of Life*, where the faculty of knowledge as *knowledge of life by life* is both conditioned by and required by the organological and pharmacological being that we are: knowledge of life is *vital* for this *form of life that constantly trans-forms life* because it belongs to the *technical* form of life, where 'knowledge [...] is one of the ways by which humanity seeks to assume its destiny and to transform its being into a duty'.[57] It is because noetic life is this technical form of life that in biology 'knowledge and technique are indissolubly linked'.[58]

I will again take up these considerations on the basis of Leibniz and Canguilhem in the second volume of *Automatic Society*. For now, they allow us to introduce the question of *economic knowledge* as *critique of economic technology* and finally as critique of political economy understood as an organology, a pharmacology and a therapeutics of the fiduciary question. In this political economy, economics and law are tied together by the question of belief and trust inasmuch as it assumes an organological investment in the monetary artefact, while law always implies, and as a preliminary condition, the fiduciary question in the broadest sense.[59]

Money is a tertiary retention with the power to control protentional possibilities and to make calculations about them that we also call speculations. Such possibilities must be made the object of a pharmacological critique inasmuch as they can provoke impossibilities, that is, *discredit*. Jean-Michel Rey's analysis of the bankruptcy of John Law in *Le Temps du crédit* is of key importance here.[60] What is obvious is that monetary regimes, regimes of money qua numismatic tertiary retention and protentional support, modify the risks and toxicity of speculation insofar as these *pharmaka* acquire specific characteristics in the computational age of reason.

101. Therapeutics as neganthropology

Speculation in general can become beneficial, do good, and be a common good, only if it is cultivated by the disciplines, which constitute technics of the self and others as *otium* – and which thereby sometimes constitute what we call knowledge, the sciences, but also and more generally work-knowledge and life-knowledge, the knowledge of how to do and live. Such forms of knowledge have a vocation for pharmacologically discerning their own limits, that is, the organological limits that they set up and put to work – this discernment can operate without explicit awareness of its organological and pharmacological character.

The project of digital studies is to develop knowledge that possesses an explicit awareness of its organological and pharmacological status in this Anthropocene era that is wholly shaped by computational power (into the distorted form of an absence of epoch), which today unavoidably raises the speculative question from a therapeutic perspective – digital tertiary retention having set up a state of crisis from which a new *krinein* must arise as the epoch of a *new critique* bearing a new organology.

It is in this register that we must situate the lessons to be learned from Alan Greenspan. What Greenspan teaches us is not only the fact that a hyper-entropic automatization of finance that lacks the power to dis-automatize is a global public danger. This fact, *factum*, is also a *fatum*, a law, *jus*: what we learn from Greenspan is also that we need science, that is, *otium*, inasmuch as it is not soluble into *negotium*.

Otium is this power of the self-limitation of speculation through the dis-automatization of the drive in which it fundamentally consists (and this is why the *libido sciendi* of Augustine can be reinterpreted through Freud's libidinal economy). It must be widely distributed between the knowledge of how to live, how to do and how to formally conceptualize.

These observations today involve research policies, and in particular the problem of financial incentives for innovation-driven research. The latter proceeds from *fundamental research*, which is always conceived in intermittences dedicated to the 'pure life of the mind'. This purity is obviously an ideality, since the life of the mind and spirit is conditioned by organological and pharmacological impurity. It is, however, by being projected onto the plane of consistences to which the organological can grant access – for example, in the way Leibniz sees in leisure the possibility of examining and speculating – that spirit noetizes in its *effects*.

So-called 'breakthrough' innovations are possible only on the condition of allowing such improbable occurrences to occur, and by letting them occur after these non-programmable intermittences – even if the most favourable conditions for such an emergence, without which they would remain the hidden face of the improbable, can and should be maintained and cultivated. In industrial capitalism, which has from the beginning rearranged *otium* and *negotium*, scientific research that generates innovation, thereby installing 'technoscience', has always involved organological transformations that themselves generate positive but also negative pharmacological consequences.

A reorganization of science from a neganthropological perspective is indispensable today, in this current stage of the new speculative organology in which digital tertiary retention consists – and which enables the best and the worst *speculative pharmacologies*. To investigate this question, by way of a conclusion that in turn prepares the way for the second volume of *Automatic Society*, we are obliged to return to Yann Moulier-Boutang's allegory.

Conclusion
Noetic Pollination and the Neganthropocene

Rather than anthropology, we should change the spelling to 'entropology', as the name of the discipline concerned with the study of the highest manifestations of this process of disintegration.
Claude Lévi-Strauss[1]

It is not necessity but its contrary, 'luxury', that presents living matter and humankind with their fundamental problems.
Georges Bataille[2]

102. Summary traceology of the architect

Firstly, let us recall Marx's well-known passage on the bee and the architect:

> We presuppose labour in a form in which it is an exclusively human characteristic. [...] But what distinguishes the worst architect from the best of bees is that the architect builds the cell in his head before he constructs it in wax. At the end of every labour process, a result emerges that had already been conceived by the worker in the beginning, hence already existed as an idea.[3]

This famous text by Marx is also highly problematic, and profoundly regressive in relation to *The German Ideology*, which appeared twenty-two years earlier, and even more so in relation to the *Grundrisse*, which was written ten years earlier – as if Marx had abandoned something from which he had turned away, confronted with a question too awkward and troubling, that is, aporetic in the Socratic sense.

Prior to this passage, Marx writes:

Labour is, first of all, a process between man and nature, [...] through [the mediation of] his own actions. [...] He confronts the materials of nature as a force of nature. He sets in motion the natural forces which belong to his own body, his arms, legs, head and hands, in order to appropriate the materials of nature in a form adapted to his own needs.[4]

Here, Marx says nothing of what precedes such a relation as its condition of possibility, which is the organological condition (which is also a 'condition of impossibility', since the artificial *organon* is always also a *pharmakon*). He certainly indicates that:

Through this movement [man] acts upon external nature and changes it, and in this way he simultaneously changes his own nature. He develops the potentialities slumbering within nature, and subjects the play of its forces to his own sovereign power.[5]

Such a statement evinces a disarming classicism. Marx skips over the aporetic fact that the possibility of such a development of the potentialities of humankind is constituted by exteriorization itself, that is, by a 'logic of the supplement' that escapes us – and it is this that troubles him. For what occurs here involves a transductive relation that could hardly be sublated by a dialectic: humankind is not the cause of technics, nor is the reverse the case.

The transductive relation human/technics, that is, interior/exterior, is a *transitional* (fictional and speculative) space in which quasi-causality exceeds any simple causality (material, formal, efficient or final). This is why Marx says not one word about what it is that allows 'man and nature' to enter into contact, the answer being that it is not simply culture, but technics. On this point already, he has completely regressed from his position in *The German Ideology*, which challenged the notion that humans and animals can be distinguished 'by consciousness, by religion or anything else you like. They themselves begin to distinguish themselves from animals as soon as they begin to *produce* their means of subsistence, a step that is conditioned by their corporeal organization.'[6] Marx argues for a completely different perspective when he posits in *Capital* that the architect has something 'in his head', neglecting the primary fact that there is nothing in the head of this architect that was not put there through a process of transindividuation that begins before his birth – as the Inuit know in their way.[7] And this negligence sends him back to the idea that what is in the head of the architect is an idea – which *The German Ideology* described as the thesis of idealism.

One can become an architect only if there is in one's head, if not lead,[8] at least something like a specular *analogon* of a plumb line, as well as a set square and a flat surface. These artefacts do not arrive in this head by the grace of God, or as an innate idea, but as that of which the body of this head and through it this head itself, that is, this brain, have had experience, during an apprenticeship that is made possible and necessary by the 'corporeal organization' of human beings.

What constitutes the head of the architect is neither its 'consciousness' nor its 'idea', but the tertiary retention that enables the heritage of circuits of transindividuation to which it is connected and which precede it as its preindividual milieu, supersaturated with potentials – which endows it with the power to dream and to realize its dreams.

Marx seems to be telling us that the architect speculates, that is, firstly, observes without acting, contemplates his activity in suspense, and at-tends to it, that is, tends towards ...: *specto* meaning also *attendre*, to have in view, aim at, tend to, project. Before acting, the speculator, like the architect, makes hypotheses that he or she models or simulates as imagined *possibilities*.

But, according to us, such a construction is an arrangement of traces and, more precisely, it is a *montage* of retentions and protentions: noesis proceeds from an arche-cinema conditioned by tertiary retentions that are trans-formed in the course of the process of grammatization. The architect, *like* capitalism, can speculate only through this process of exteriorization – which is also the origin of proletarianization. Without something like a map [*un plan*], that is, a projection on a flat surface, made in advance of what it will realize, a map or a plane that can be examined at leisure and polished or corrected, but also calculated, and so on, and that is not a 'master plan', there is no architect in the sense referred to by Marx. Whether the map begins in the epoch of the inscriptions, such as the Bedolina map found in the Camonica valley caves,[9] or before, or after, does not change the fact that architecture, as Marx understood it, and as that which is destined to remain unknown to the bee, is founded on this tertiarization of its 'representation' – through a process of grammatization that is also the origin of currency, that is, of the tertiary retention enabling protentional potentials to be accumulated through a highly specific type of trace.

Source: Miguel Beltrán Lloris, 'Los grabados rupestres de Bedolini (Val-camonica)', *Bolletino del Centro Cammuno di Studi Preistorici* 8 (1972), pp. 121–57, via Wikimedia Commons.

103. Therapeutics as neganthropology

Bees, too, secrete traces outside themselves, as do ants, in the form of those chemical emissions we call pheromones. It is at this precise point that what Moulier-Boutang presents as a metaphor becomes an allegory. The bee, he writes, 'creates a network, finds places to pollinate [and] through chemical signals [...] is able to indicate to its fellow bees the variety of plants and the different kinds of pollen and sap that are found'.[10] This reticulation is created collectively and 'it is exactly what occurs when human beings solve a problem by adding their cognitive forces together in a network':[11]

> All this occurs as if the human brain or body, which has only one thirty-sixth of the sense of smell of a dog, one fiftieth of the eyesight of an owl, one one-hundredth of the sense of touch of a bee or a dragonfly, compensates for these handicaps by combining all these elements.[12]

Here, like Marx, Durkheim, Tarde and Lazzarato, Moulier-Boutang leaves unexplored the role of technical traces in which consist, for example, the words that he himself writes on paper,[13] or that he writes using a computer and that a publisher, a printer and a distributor cause to be circulated, nowadays mostly by way of Amazon, a social network that largely relies on profiling based on the traces of reading, and that is on the way to destroying both bookstore chains and major publishers themselves, destabilizing Hachette just as Google destabilizes Springer.

If it is true that 'the metaphor of pollination is only one specific illustration of a general phenomenon that we call the contributory economy of the production of knowledge and life in general',[14] then the passage from this metaphor, which is a kind of dream, to the realization of this dream, which we call an allegory, ultimately leads us to a question of contributory organology – which has been made possible by the traces of our epoch as digital tertiary retentions, beyond literal, mechanical and analogical tertiary retentions.

Let us propose that a contributory economy is a noetic form of pollination, and that this noesis is supported by traces that we call tertiary retentions. If we recall that these traces are *pharmaka*, then this allegory must be interpreted from a pharmacological perspective. And to do so, we must examine the ant and its pheromones – including the way they have been modelled in a particular field of cognitive science, so-called 'artificial life', and more particularly as an example of a multi-agent system.

I myself made this connection in *Symbolic Misery*, in formulating an 'allegory of the digital anthill' as a way of identifying the stakes of the digital stage of grammatization. And, in trying to think what at that time were yet to be called social networks, I speculated about the potential toxicity of the expanded automatization to which this stage logically leads. Within this 'digital anthill', I suggested, readers and writers connected by reticulated writing would produce digital traces allowing them to be integrated into an artificial anthill, and which would in turn lead to their social and psychic disintegration.[15] This has since occurred. And it is what Thomas Berns and Antoinette Rouvroy describe as algorithmic governmentality.

An ant emits pheromones through which it communicates information to the rest of this biological network controlled by the DNA of the ants that form the anthill. This information allows the constitution of a homeostatic metastability so that, for example, if the nurse ants are removed from the nest, and if they therefore no longer emit the message informing the rest of the anthill that they are taking care of the larvae, all the other ants will tend to become nurses – until the proportion of nurse ants required by the anthill is reached, as defined by the genetic envelope of the species.

In the same way, and especially through 'big data', the powers that control the platforms collecting personal data, by exploiting the performativity of the real-time treatment of massive data, provoke a functional integration through which these platforms disintegrate the social. Such platforms thereby become automatized artificial crowds, related to what we could call artificial anthills. This is especially striking in the case of members of the Twitter network, who emit messages informing their followers of something or other that they have done. But this is equally true of social networks in general, insofar as they are based on capturing data, which is processed and fed back into the entire network in real time (at a speed up to four million times faster than organic nerve impulses) – in this case, however, the envelope is no longer genetic, but algorithmic.

These technologies calculate correlations, then, in order to automatically anticipate individual and collective behaviour, which they also provoke and 'auto-realize' by short-circuiting and bypassing any deliberation. If so, and if the social is that which can influence the causal factors involved in making decisions, then the result of such technologies amounts to the destruction of social and deliberative – that is, noetic – causality. What is thereby destroyed is both social temporality and rational temporality, as Berns and Rouvroy show.

If society is what deliberates,[16] and if algorithmic automatisms outstrip the possibility of such deliberation, then in what conditions is an automatic society still possible? Our answer is simple: *it is possible only above and beyond the market* – the latter constituting what Augustinian Rome called *negotium*. It is only *above and beyond* the market (which is not to say *against* it) that it is possible to place automatisms in the service of reason, that is, of decision, and therefore of individual time in its participation in the formation of a time that would be historical and political – that is, awaited expectantly, projected collectively and neganthropic. It is starting from this imperative to embed *negotium* within *otium*, to constitute this *imperium* as the value of values, that we must conceive a contributory economy founded on noetic pollination.

104. The noetic hive

Positive externalities are to human societies what pollination is to the plant kingdom – the latter being the condition of the animal kingdom, which itself, in return, performs a vital function for the plant kingdom via the hymenoptera. Pollination fertilizes a potential for diversifying – that is, negentropic – reproduction. By in general constituting organizations of care, noetic positive externalities fertilize potential individuations from their preindividual funds.

As pollinators, noetic societies produce entropy and negentropy. Negentropy becomes neganthropy when the mutual fertilization of noetic souls, which Socrates described as the primordial dialogism of noesis – and as such a *dianoia* – becomes the therapeutic quasi-cause whereby the *pharmakon* remediates entropy and improbably defers its progress.

Here we should return to the question of the *Leviathan*, and to the ways Hobbes justifies monarchical sovereignty, on the basis of his observation of ants and bees, social insects that interested him just as they did Aristotle,[17] the latter ranking them among the 'political creatures':

> It is true, that certain living creatures, as bees, and ants, live sociably one with another, (which are therefore by Aristotle numbered amongst political creatures;) and yet have no other direction, than their particular judgments and appetites; nor speech, whereby one of them can signify to another, what he thinks expedient for the common benefit: and therefore some man may perhaps desire to know, why mankind cannot do the same.[18]

Arguing against the thesis he has just put, Hobbes then asks why it would not be possible to obtain social unity and cohesion in humans as in insects, that is, 'without [the] coercive power'[19] of this Leviathan that is the sovereign state under an absolute monarch.[20]

In order to show that this is impossible, Hobbes analyses six traits by which humans are distinguished from insects, and that together explain the necessity for human beings to submit to a monarch who ensures their unity – in particular when faced with an enemy, whether internal or external.[21]

Unlike insects, he writes, people are inhabited by competition, envy and hatred, which lead to war, and they furthermore distinguish the public from the private. Animals possess no reason (they are described as *aloga* in the passage of *Protagoras* that narrates the myth of Prometheus and Epimetheus), whereas human beings argue by reasoning and consequently fall into dispute (as is also related in *Protagoras*: this is why Zeus sends Hermes to create within them the feelings of shame, *aidōs*, and justice, *dikē*). Animals, devoid of language, are unable to lie or deceive, and they naturally understand and get along with one another, unlike people, who, compelled to live together, must seek common accord conventionally and artificially.

Therefore, mutually and reciprocally, and unlike animals, human beings who want to live in society must surrender their rights to a sovereign and confer upon him or her the power of constituting what, to introduce an anachronism, we will call the 'top-down' function: 'I authorize and give up my right of governing myself, to this man, or to this assembly of men, on this condition, that thou give up thy right to him, and authorize all his actions in like manner.'[22] Algorithmic governmentality is an electronic Leviathan to the strict degree that it fundamentally proceeds from such a *reciprocal surrender of noeticity*, but in a completely involuntary fashion induced by the network effect.

If noeticity is indeed constituted through the process of mutual pollination, this primordial noetic mutuality constituting the dia-logical character of any noesis, then surrendering 'my right of governing myself' to a purely computational automatic government can lead only to the sterilization of that transindividual fertility that had hitherto been the agent of negentropy and producer of neganthropological facts and rights – that is, the producer of cultures, cults, cures and cares. To abandon one's diachronic and singular ability to contribute by oneself to collective individuation is *very precisely* that to which algorithmic governmentality leads, in particular in social networks, and more particularly still on Facebook.

Therefore, since algorithmic governmentality is based on a computational traceability that is massive, systemic and permanent, and that operates in real time and across the planet, it is growing harder to discern what distinguishes human beings from ants. Digital pheromones delegate to the electronic Leviathan the automated 'management' of *every* event and behaviour that they induce, just as the pheromones of ants trigger behavioural sequences controlled by the genetic sequences encoded in their *soma* and reproduced by their *germen*, which evolve only under the influence of the combined effects of environmental variations and the pressure of selection.

In the electronic Leviathan, however, algorithms – which calculate behavioural gradients via digital doubles and according to the traces produced, playing the role of the genetic envelope of the species in the anthill, by dividualizing and 'personalizing' it (as distinct from genetic 'coding') – are themselves transformed (and with them 'behavioural sequences') much more rapidly than the genetic envelope or the behaviour of arthropods: the goal is precisely to induce a constant adoption of new behaviours in response to new 'offers' made on the market and supplied by innovation.

It is possible, however, for this entire apparatus founded on digital organology to be pharmacologically inverted. Digital and reticulated tertiary retention is inherently toxic only because the 'top-down' algorithmic process has been monopolized by the 'vectorialist' power of the industry of traces, which disintegrates psychic and collective individuation by instrumentalizing hackers and unleashing the drives – in order to capture them for the benefit of an unlimited consumption that has, however, become structurally insolvent and entropic.

The prospect of an end of employment, however, means that we must transform digital reticulation so that it instead fosters a vast process of noetic pollination, that is, an *otium* of the people reconstituting a long-term solvency and based on neganthropy as value of values.

105. Before the immense. The digital *res publica* and the editorial question

In the second volume of *Automatic Society*, we will propose a programme of practical organology, that is, of supplementary conception and invention, founded on a theoretical organology, that is, on a digital epistemology that involves a reconsideration of all forms of knowledge – of living, doing and conceptualizing – on the basis of a history of tertiary retention. We will try to show that a supplementary invention always generates a categorial invention that amounts to the second moment of the doubly epokhal redoubling. We will try to describe the specific features of this second moment in the context of digital tertiary retention, which creates possibilities for contributory categorization and a new organization of related research.

The history of tertiary retention is not limited to that of grammatization, the latter beginning only in the Upper Palaeolithic: such a history tries to take account of the constitution of epiphylogenesis as a whole. It corresponds to what Derrida called a *history of the supplement*, but understood from the Bachelardian perspective of *phenomenotechnics*.[23] And it is conceived with the goal of formulating the project – at once scientific, political, juridical and economic – of a neganthropology. General organology and pharmacology therein constitute a new critique of anthropology in the Anthropocene era.

Knowledge is always a *making-known* [*faire savoir*], that is, an exposition within a being-together. It is only starting from the moment when literal tertiary retention appears, and inasmuch as it becomes accessible to all those who form the *politeia*, that a truth regime in terms of communities of peers is constituted, for which the apodictic reasoning emerging from geometry becomes the canon of any *alētheia*.

The consequence of such a perspective – which is a highly abbreviated reformulation of Husserl's perspective in 'The Origin of Geometry' – is that *the organology of publication conditions and underwrites any truth regime*, and that every science policy, every research policy and every industrial policy is based on a politics of publication insofar as it is constitutive of politics conceived as care taken of the public thing in general.

In France, every student who enrols in the final year of school is expected to know that the Republic of Letters was conditioned by the publishing revolution from which sprang gazettes and then newspapers, and that the philosophy of the Enlightenment that inspired the French Revolution itself emerged from this Republic of Letters.

Reticulated, digital tertiary retention constitutes a publishing and editing revolution in the same register. But it is occurring on an immeasurable scale and at an unprecedented speed that affects the heart of economic life, which thereby itself enters into a process of change. Faced with this *im-mense transformation*,[24] which we describe also as a meta-morphosis, national and European public powers seem completely blind, impotent, negligent and stunned – which is also to say stupid, and totally discredited.

It is all the more striking and concerning for France and Europe that universities and academic institutions in general – inasmuch as they produce a public intelligence that cultivates a reason capable of dis-automatizing noxious states of fact in order to inscribe into them bifurcations of law – must, in the coming years, either become publishing and editing powers that take action capable of responding to this noetic metamorphosis, or else disappear, that is, transform themselves into nurseries for jobless young people, which to a large extent they are already.

We will study this question in depth in the second volume of *Automatic Society*. But for now we must introduce it as a major industrial and economic question concerning the future of work, to the extent that, with the rise of 3D printing, additive manufacturing and the maker movement, it is the publishing industry, too, that is seeing its field extended to the *grammatization of volumes*. The very notion of publishing is being radically reshaped within a stratified complex of automatisms affecting the noetic process, from its faculty of dreaming, whether nocturnally or diurnally, intermittently but primarily, to the material and social realization of these dreams.

The liberation of work is not a question of 'reducing work-time' in order to share it out and thereby reduce the rate of unemployment: it is a matter of eliminating unemployment by eliminating employment as the key status and function of a macroeconomic system that was conceived and implemented by Keynes and Roosevelt but whose effects have been reversed. Maintaining the same discourse on wage labour and purchasing power allows those who extract profit to constantly exert downward pressure on the cost of labour in the employment market, in order to increase their profits still further. Unions have become complicit in this situation by perpetuating themselves in the ways that Trentin and Gorz have described.

We are not arguing that proletarianization is disappearing – quite the contrary. We are saying that it is ceasing to take the form of wage labour: digital working,[25] the digital manufacturing environment and digital labour are the names of this new condition of real labour, alienated and usually devoid of salary in the sense presented below, if it is not entirely unpaid.[26] Digital working is related to the 'Hollywood' model of organizing work by projects (Boltanski, Rifkin). It is a perfect fit with the ideology of Gary Becker on the basis of which Bill Gates foreshadowed a decline in employment in order to encourage labour cost reductions. In *Pour une écologie de l'attention*, Yves Citton has identified the major analyses of digital labour that have been proposed in the last few years of this evolution of the 'division of labour', which is increasingly a matter of algorithmic automatons assisted by humans – as is the case for the CAPTCHA system, for example – rather than of humans assisted by automatons.[27]

106.   The new system of objects

For some three million years, existing possibilities of exteriorization, of editorialization and of publication have left impressions on, stimulated and modified, but also short-circuited, the synaptic 'circuitry' of the noetic cerebral organs that appeared in the biosphere along with epiphylogenetic tertiary retentions.[28]

Some tens of thousands of years ago, that is, in the Upper Palaeolithic, these possibilities intensified with the appearance of *hypomnesic* tertiary retentions, which initiated the process of grammatization – from the Chauvet cave to the Bedolina petroglyph.

A few thousand years ago, ideographic noetic forms appeared, along with the great empires, after which, around 2,700 years ago, literal tertiary retention constituted the *apodictic* noetic form described by Husserl in 'The Origin of Geometry'.

With the Renaissance there began the circulation of printed works, which left impressions on noetic minds and transformed everyday life, through calculation and with the widespread dissemination of coins, banknotes and printed scripture – and which amounted to the advent of capitalism.

With the industrial revolution, grammatization discretized the gestures of the labouring body, capturing and fixing their work-knowledge, their knowledge of how to make and do. Analogue grammatization then channelled, discretized and quantified perceptual and attentional processes.

In the epoch of reticulated, digital tertiary retention, it is possible to reach, almost simultaneously, the connected brains of more than two billion earthlings: the editorial question is thereby raised in absolutely unprecedented [*inédits*] terms – and here we must take this expression literally. What is absolutely unprecedented is not only the ability to perform immense calculations at lightning speed,[29] installing, as we have seen, a new age of performativity and calling for a new hermeneutics: the absolutely unprecedented character of the organological and pharmacological situation established by reticulated, digital tertiary retention lies in the fact that it installs *a new age of the printed impression*, an age opened up by 3D printing.

With *digital printing*, we can now print three-dimensional objects, and this profoundly changes the question of that artefact which, since the advent of hominization, has consisted of epiphylogenetic tertiary retention. As a *printed object*, the most everyday forms of epiphylogenetic tertiary retention become *at once* hypomnesic, transitional and industrial – especially as RFID tags and other chips are increasingly embedded into these objects. So-called 'communicating' objects,[30] integrating internet modules and with their own internet address (and in relation to which the IPv6 protocol will allow their widespread generalization), constitute the internet of things as a stage of *hyper-reticulation* in which it is the world that is doubled, and not just its inhabitants: it is *grammatized through and through* – 'smart cities' being the concretization of this fact.

Beyond the fact that digital and reticulated tertiary retention has weakened for ever the oppositional and functional partition between production and consumption, the functions by which *industrial designs and concepts are rendered in material form* have shifted towards those robotic terminals that are 3D printers. This seemingly amounts to a complete industrial metamorphosis, unremittingly condemning to obsolescence the centralized reticulation that had hitherto been propagated in the United States, then in Europe, and that had taken the form of a network of factories connected by roads, highways and the electromagnetic networks of radio and television broadcast.

3D printers use the G-code programming language that was developed in the 1960s for CNC (computerized numerical control) machines. This extends and completes grammatization qua the writing of volumes and the hyper-materialization of industrial objects. Bruce Sterling has coined the term *spime* (a contraction of space and time)[31] in order to conceptualize this 'new system of objects'.[32] In a lecture for Ars Industrialis, Olivier Landau formed the hypothesis that in the new industrial model borne by digital printing, the 3D printer may constitute 'a major new link in the digital economy. After the de-materialization of supports, then the virtualization of exchanges and transactions offered by the Web 2.0, could 3D printing mean the completion of a genuine ecosystem for a digital society?'[33] Such a digital society, which we are here calling automatic society, could, however, *form a society*, and overcome the *immeasurably worsened stage of dis-society* in which algorithmic governmentality and 24/7 capitalism consists, only on the condition of major economic and political change.

Through the reticulated printing of concepts developed and materialized in a contributory way as objects printed in three dimensions – which are also able to become 'internet objects' inscribed within a 'smart' urbanity, and which constitute the supports of an automatized hypomnesic region[34] – a new territoriality indeed becomes possible, and with it another social form and another process of collective individuation, constituted through a re-capacitation[35] of noetic bodies, and of the local social bodies [*faire-corps*] in which regions and territories consist.

Such a perspective presupposes, however, an organological and pharmacological critique of 'solutionist' discourses (in the sense in which Evgeny Morozov refers to 'technological solutionism'[36]) and of the states of fact that they legitimate while short-circuiting in advance any opportunities to constitute states of law.

If we are to believe Chris Anderson,[37] for example, then after the 'digital utopia', the utopia of 'fab labs' and 'makers' will be next in line to take over this alternating series of dynamics by which technology keeps reshuffling the cards in its quest to constantly project better horizons. Yet nobody ever reaches these horizons: the utopias of technological solutionism, a solutionism that never undertakes any pharmacological critique, allow societies to be anaesthetized to these highly toxic, disintegrating *pharmaka*.

Faced with these *structurally immature* projections – immature because they never do the work of transindividuation required for any real socialization, and held in this immature state by incessant, extremely imaginative storytelling, and by the copious use of the arts and letters to produce smoke and mirrors that deceive both 'technophiles' and 'technophobes' – it is time to constitute a deliberative understanding of what amounts to a new organological and pharmacological age of the noetic forms of so-called 'human life'.

Anderson is, of course, not to be outdone in terms of better proposals concerning the new hyper-materiological context established by automatized generalization – his drones and 3DR (3D Robotics) are themselves consequences of reticular decentralization – and so he replays his analysis of the 'long tail'.[38] He shows how the Arduino module has opened the era of free hardware – which 'fab labs' combine together with free software, wikis and 3D printers.[39] He supports a position seemingly comparable to that of Landau,[40] except that he effaces every neganthropological question of the kind we have been posing here: for this peerless storyteller, the pharmacological approach is always occluded.

Unlike Anderson, Landau highlights that through a 'slide from functions and tasks to clients, [...] evolutions [that] cause deep social ruptures both for employment and for the daily life of citizens',[41] a massive concretization of 3D printing will likely lead to offsetting the functions of material production onto the consumer, who will access robotized spaces, either domestic or shared. This will be done not in order to increase the knowledge of 'makers', but to transfer to consumers the burden of investment, the management of stocks of materials for printing, and so on.

In addition, Landau shows that, at the core of businesses themselves, 3D printers modify the modes of production – for example, in aeronautics – by shifting them towards new types of workers carrying out the functions of realization, doing so on site and in ways more adaptable to the contexts involved in the production of objects that have been pre-conceived by design offices.

In an article published in 2013 that made reference to the work of the American historian David Noble,[42] Johan Söderberg, too, grasps the stakes of 3D printing from the perspective of the history within which additive manufacturing is inscribed, which he presents as follows:

> They are all based on the same principle, using software to help guide the movements of a machine tool, and the one that has attracted the

most media attention is a printer that prints three-dimensional objects, with a nozzle that lays down a plastic material layer by layer. Designs for the printer of such objects as doorknobs or bicycles can be downloaded from the net.[43]

Söderberg recalls that 3D printing was developed after a long history of automation that led to numerically controlled machines. Throughout the course of this history, the stakes were the privatization of the knowledge produced by workers:

> Catherine Fisk, a lawyer, has gone through old trials in the US in which employers and employees confronted each other over the ownership of ideas. In the early 19th century, courts tended to uphold the customary right of works to freely make use of knowledge gained at the workplace, and attempts by employers to claim the mental faculties of trained white workers were rejected by courts because this resembled slavery too closely. As the knowhow of workers became codified and the balance of power shifted, courts began to vindicate the property claims of employers.[44]

Fisk has shown that the logic of the free and open (free software and hardware, open source, open science, open data, and so on), while initially conceived in order to struggle against the privatization of knowledge and the plundering of those who possessed it, was able to be turned against the latter into the logic of what we earlier described as new algorithmically governed crowds in the service of hyper-proletarianization. Söderberg continues:

> Some researchers have warned that these might end with workers exploiting themselves. There is a crowdsourcing platform owned by Amazon, where net users are invited to solve simple tasks, such as identifying people in photographs. The average income of an 'employee' is \$1.25 an hour.[45]

Here we see very clearly that the industrial future constitutes a new, highly pharmacological question. It requires the definition of a new therapeutics, itself founded on a new criterion of value – and we claim that this new criterion is noetic negentropy concretized by knowledge in the service of the Neganthropocene.

107. Of what work consists in the Neganthropocene

Contrary to the 'hyper-proletarianizing' scenario that can be anticipated on the basis of the analyses of Landau, a scenario that would be insolvent for the reasons previously argued, we can and must imagine how offsetting production functions to reticulated and decentralized 3D printing terminals could instead reconstitute a more tightly conjoined territoriality, beyond 'globalization' – how it could give rise to an economy of short circuits rather than short-circuits. This would require, however, the constitution of local capacities for conception, *that is, for dis-automatization* – failing which, it would be bound to concretize only the tendencies described by Landau.

Such a re-capacitation would require a profound redefinition of national and European regional policies, but also of the policies undertaken by the regions and territories themselves. And this necessitates allowing and encouraging regional experimentation and contributory learning between reticulated territories, no longer by Amazon and other *algorithmic governors*, but by *associated local intelligences, forming what we have called an 'internation'*, in the sense proposed by Marcel Mauss in 1920, that is, at the very moment of formation of the League of Nations (this will be discussed in the second volume of *Automatic Society*).[46]

In digital territories – and *all* territories have become more or less digital, given that the spread of smartphones is now global – and in particular in the 'smart cities' that are implementing the digital (both tactile and numerical) hyper-materialization of urban objects and public things, algorithmic governmentality could either completely short-circuit and bypass populations and their representatives, or generate a new age of the *res publica*. The latter depends on localities becoming pollinators, that is, sources of neganthropy, by cultivating fields of positive externalities – failing which they will become digital anthills.

When Hobbes wrote about those insects that had previously interested Aristotle, he was not aware and could not have known that arthropods and hymenoptera produce traces (as do all animals, and some plants).[47] Therefore, he failed to comprehend the scope and singularity of the traces that he himself produced in the seventeenth century. Nor could he understand how the impressions to which his own traces led are of another kind than those of which he remained unaware, the latter being, for example, the chemical pheromones emitted by arthropods: his own traces are of another kind, and yet they are linked to them within a 'history of the supplement'. What Hobbes did not see is that the question is the *changing nature of traces* – which become tertiary retentions, that is, *pharmaka*.

Leibniz, on the other hand, *was* interested in these traces in terms of conditions of possibility of his own speculative work, leading to the *characteristica universalis*. Kant reproached him for this unlimited speculativity, without seeing that it is made possible by the fourth synthesis that is the schematism supported by tertiary retentions. These tertiary retentions thereby constitute the *pharmaka* through which the critique of reason – which exists only by default, that is, as natively impure, but as the quasi-cause of an originary default of origin – imposes itself as a *pharmacology of speculation* (and as a 'kingdom of ends' that is, consequently, organological and pharmacological).

Digital tertiary retention is a form of digital pheromone that is also a *pharmakon*. This means that this organo-logical, computational, reticulated pheromone, which is also highly automatizable via processes of statistical and probabilistic rewriting, must nevertheless always be *interpreted* – unlike chemical pheromones. Through this interpretation, it is the pharmacological condition itself that *must* be interpreted – as is suggested by the fact that in *Protagoras* Hermes is sent *after* Prometheus and Epimetheus – in the absence of which, in our epoch, digital tertiary retention tends to function as a regime of quasi-chemical pheromones: a regime that is *absolutely* computational and algorithmic, that is, *nihilistic*.

To transvaluate the reversal of all values by calculation: it is in this that work and its value in the Neganthropocene consists. Therein lies its future as a neganthropic economy of noetic pollination founded on the valorization of intermittences, that is, on the processes of capacitation and de-proletarianization made possible by positive externalities, and in relation to which it is accordingly a matter of redistributing the huge gains in time resulting from full and generalized automatization.

In the conclusion of *Tristes Tropiques*, Claude Lévi-Strauss writes:

> The world began without man and will end without him. [...] [Man is working] towards the disintegration of the original order of things and precipitates a powerful organization of matter towards ever greater inertia, an inertia that one day will be final. From the time when he first began to breathe and eat, up to the invention of atomic and thermonuclear devices, by way of the discovery of fire – and except when he has been engaged in self-reproduction – man has *done nothing other* than blithely break down billions of structures and reduce them to a state in which they are no longer capable of integration.[48]

Lévi-Strauss poses with rare radicality the question of *becoming without being*, that is, of the *inevitably ephemeral character* of the cosmos in its totality, as well as of the localities that form therein through negentropic processes that are themselves always agents of entropic accelerations.

If we were to take this *profoundly nihilistic* statement by Lévi-Strauss literally (when, for example, he writes that 'man has *done nothing other* than blithely break down billions of structures and reduce them to a state in which they are no longer capable of integration'), we would be forced to assume that very little time separates us from the 'end times'. We would be forced to reduce this time to nothing, to *annihilate* it, and to discount negentropy on the grounds of its ephemerality: we would have to dissolve the future into becoming, to assess it as null and void, as never coming, that is, *as having ultimately never happened, the outcome of having no future – as becoming without future.*[49]

This is, to the letter, what the anthropologist says. As neganthropologists we must object, firstly, that the question of quasi-causal reason is always of being 'worthy of what happens to us', and, secondly, that this bitter and disillusioned sophistry neglects two points:

- on the one hand, life in general, as 'negative entropy', as negentropy, is itself produced from entropy, and leads back there: it is a detour – as Freud said in *Beyond the Pleasure Principle* and as Blanchot claimed in *The Infinite Conversation*;
- on the other hand, technical life is an amplified and hyperbolic form of negentropy, that is, of an organization that is not just organic but organological, but which produces an entropy that is equally hyperbolic, and which, like living things, returns to it, but does so *by accelerating the speed of the differentiations and indifferentiations* in which this detour consists.

This *detour* in which technical life consists is *desire as the power to infinitize*. It is misleading to give the impression, as Lévi-Strauss does here, that humanity has an *entropic essence* and that it destroys some 'creation', some 'nature' that would on the contrary have a *negentropic essence* – alive, profuse and fecund, animal and vegetable. Plants and animals are indeed organic orderings of highly improbable (as is all negentropy) inert matter, yet all life unfurls and prospers only by itself intensifying entropic processes: plants and animals are themselves only an all too temporary and in the end futile detour in becoming.

Unlike purely organic beings, those beings called human are *negentropic on two levels*: both as living beings, that is, organic beings, which through reproduction bring about those 'minor differences' that lie at the origin of evolution, and hence at the origin of what Schrödinger called negative entropy;[50] and as artificial beings, that is, organological beings. These artifices are other detours, themselves more or less ephemeral, like those insects called ephemera, which are neither more nor less 'without why' than roses, themselves largely artificial.[51]

There is no doubt that the question of speed in relation to thermodynamic physics, as well as biology and zoology, is a crucial issue. But the question here is of a *politics* of speed in which there are opposing possibilities, and where it is a matter of *knowing in what way, where, on what plane and for how long* the 'urge to conquer time and space'[52] increases or reduces entropy. The grim [*triste*] statement of the anthropologist effaces this question and somehow erases the *indeterminacy* of the future under the *probabilistic* weight of becoming.

If the hyperbolic negentropy in which the organological becoming of the organic consists installs a neganthropology that accelerates (entropic and anthropic) becoming, it nevertheless also transforms this acceleration into a future that differs and defers this becoming, according to the two senses of the verb *différer* mobilized by Derrida in his term différance. Hence a (negentropic and neganthropic) future *could* be established from this infinitizing form of protention that is the object of desire as an agent of (psychic, social and technical) individuation and integration – failing which, différance will remain merely formal. It is in the light of these questions that Spinoza must today be reinterpreted.

108.   Noetic intermittence and cosmic potlatch

The vanity and futility of 'human' works, announced so sententiously by Lévi-Strauss while annihilating the time of desire, in the first place affects his own enterprise: 'As for the creations of the human mind [*esprit*], their significance exists only in relation to it, and they will merge into disorder once it has disappeared.'[53] What is missing from these statements is the dimension opened when organic life becomes organological, so that it remains to come [*à venir*] and therein forms its future [*avenir*], that is, its inherently incomplete character. Obviously, the time that remains to come is ultimately that of consumption: it is the time of the combustion of a desire that clearly always leads back to disorder, but which, in its sumptuary brilliance, constitutes the events of a quasi-causality projected onto a plane of consistence in immanence, whatever these events may be, and that Lévi-Strauss here wrongly, blindly and poorly reduces to entropic *nothingness*.

Organological beings are capable of purposefully organizing the negentropic and organo-logical works that we are referring to here as neganthropic. Depending on how they undertake this psychic and social organization, depending on the way they do or do not take care of the anthropic and neganthropic power in which their behaviour consists, they can either indifferently precipitate a release of entropy, or, on the contrary, differ and defer it – thereby constituting a *dif-férance* that Simondon called individuation and that he thinks as a process, as does Whitehead.

We ourselves are in favour of a neganthropological project conceived as care and in this sense as an economy. This economy of care is not simply the power with which we anthropologically transform the world (as 'masters and possessors of nature').[54] It is a neganthropological knowledge constituting a neganthropology in the service of the Neganthropocene, in the way that Canguilhem conceives the function of biology as the knowledge of life in technical life,[55] and in the way that Whitehead thinks the function of reason within a speculative cosmology.[56]

Neganthropology constitutes, within the cosmos, a regime of individuation, and we can clearly see that this is what Lévi-Strauss is unable to conceive, as, for instance, when he writes: 'Every verbal exchange, every line printed, establishes communication between two interlocutors, evening out a level where before there was an information gap and consequently a greater degree of organization.'[57] It is completely wrong to posit *a priori* that any interlocution, whether spoken or written, is reducible to an exchange of information that increases entropy. There is nothing here about the processes of psychic and collective individuation in which symbolic exchanges in all their forms consist, and where they are in fact symbolic only insofar as they are 'pollinators', that is, producers of meaning. The neglect of this neganthropy in which alone the symbolic *consists* is striking in an anthropologist who would make the symbolic, conceived on the basis of the 'floating signifier', the very motif of his work.[58]

Of course, we must identify and describe the 'negative externalities' that the 'neganthropy' generated by anthropization propagates in 'anthropized' milieus. But this is not a question of nullifying neganthropy. It is rather, on the contrary, a matter of passing from anthropization to neganthropization by cultivating a positive pharmacology no more nor less ephemeral than life that is carried along in becoming, just as is everything that 'is' in the universe. This care is the very thing in which this neganthropology *consists*, and it is what

Lévi-Strauss always ignored, by ignoring and deliberately censoring the thought of Leroi-Gourhan.[59]

We will see in the second volume of *Automatic Society* that this situation stems from the fact that Lévi-Straussian anthropology is *founded* on the repression of organology (to which Leroi-Gourhan drew attention), and on ignoring the *neganthropological* question that prevails *beyond* any anthropology. This repression of the organological can be related to the notion of *dépense*, of expenditure as conceived by Georges Bataille:

> Every time the meaning of a discussion depends on the fundamental value of the word *useful* – in other words, every time the essential question touching on the life of human societies is raised, [...] it is possible to affirm that the debate is necessarily warped and that the fundamental question is eluded. In fact [...], there is nothing that permits one to define what is useful to man.[60]

At stake here are those 'so-called unproductive expenditures'[61] that are always related to sacrifice, that is, to 'the production of sacred things [...] constituted by an operation of loss'.[62]

Let us say for the moment that *every loss sacrifices, sacralizes and sanctifies a default of being older than any being* (and this is how I read Levinas). In this *tenor of primordial default*, noetic intermittence is constituted, and it can project itself speculatively, only in and as a cosmic totality conceived neganthropo-logically – that is, as the knowledge and power to create bifurcations within entropy. And it is here that the thought of Deleuze is of prime importance (but it, too, is flawed, since he ignores the organo-logical tenor of quasi-causality).

All noetic bifurcation, that is, all quasi-causal bifurcation, derives from a *cosmic potlatch* that indeed destroys very large quantities of differences and orders, but it does so by projecting a very great difference on another plane, constituting another 'order of magnitude' against the disorder of a *kosmos* in becoming, a *kosmos* that, without this projection of a yet-to-come from the unknown, would be reduced to a universe without singularity.[63] A neganthropological singularity (which does not submit to any 'anthropology') is a negentropic bifurcation in entropic becoming, of which it becomes the quasi-cause, and therein a point of origin – through this improbable singularity that establishes it and from which, intermittently and incrementally, it propagates a process of individuation.

Intermittence is the 'work of the concept' itself conceived anew as the projection of the organological beyond the organic and the inert, and for a neganthropization that will mean the world again becomes a world. Lévi-Strauss, on the other hand, is a symptom of the anthropological nihilism that follows after the death of God – for example, again, here: '[C]ivilization, taken as a whole, can be described as an extraordinarily complex mechanism, which we might be tempted to see as offering an opportunity of survival for the human world, if its function were not to produce what physicists call entropy, that is inertia.'[64] To this we must respond, with Bataille, by undertaking an organological interpretation of sacrifice in 'the community of those who are without community', which would also be a critique of the Fordist-Keynesian 'compromise':

> Thus expenditure, even though it might be a social function, immediately leads to an agonistic and apparently antisocial act of separation. The rich man consumes the poor man's losses, creating for him a category of degradation and abjection that leads to slavery. Now it is evident that, from the endlessly transmitted heritage of the sumptuary world, the modern world has received slavery, and has reserved it for the proletariat.[65]

In this proletarianized world, the expenditure of the 'rich man' nevertheless becomes sterile:

> The expenditures taken on by the capitalists in order to aid the proletarians and give them a chance to pull themselves up on the social ladder only bear witness to their inability (due to exhaustion) to carry out thoroughly a sumptuary process. Once the loss of the poor man is accomplished, little by little the pleasure of the rich man is emptied and neutralized; it gives way to a kind of apathetic indifference.[66]

At a time when the becoming-automatic of knowledge forms the heart of the economy, and does so at the risk of denying itself by taking the form of *a-theoretical computation*, we will take up this project once again, from an epistemic and epistemological perspective, in the second volume of *Automatic Society*. There we will show:

- that the question of the future of knowledge is *inseparable* from that of the future of work; and
- that this question must be translated into an *alternative industrial politics* that assigns to France and to Europe their place in becoming – and does so as trans-formations of this becoming into futures.

Notes

1 Gaston Bachelard, *L'Activité rationaliste de la physique contemporaine* (Paris: PUF, 1951), p. 10.
2 Maurice Blanchot, *The Infinite Conversation* (Minneapolis and London: University of Minnesota Press, 1993), p. 33.
3 Adolfo Bioy Casares, *The Invention of Morel* (New York: New York Review of Books, 2003), p. 91.

Introduction: Functional Stupidity, Entropy and Negentropy in the Anthropocene

1 Christophe Bonneuil and Jean-Baptiste Fressoz, *L'Événement Anthropocène. La Terre, l'histoire et nous* (Paris: Le Seuil, 2013), p. 89.
2 Frédéric Kaplan, 'Vers le capitalisme linguistique. Quand les mots valent de l'or', *Le Monde diplomatique* (November 2011), available at: http://www.monde-diplomatique.fr/2011/11/KAPLAN/46925. See also Kaplan, 'Linguistic Capitalism and Algorithmic Mediation', *Representations* 27 (2014), pp. 57–63.
3 Chris Anderson, 'The End of Theory: The Data Deluge Makes the Scientific Method Obsolete', *Wired* (23 June 2008), available at: http://archive.wired.com/science/discoveries/magazine/16-07/pb_theory.
4 This being what is referred to with the expression 'data deluge'.
5 Alan Greenspan, 'Greenspan Testimony on Sources of Financial Crisis', *The Wall Street Journal* (23 October 2008), available at: http://blogs.wsj.com/economics/2008/10/23/greenspan-testimony-on-sources-of-financial-crisis/.
6 'A Nobel Prize was awarded for the discovery of the pricing model that underpins much of the advance in derivatives markets', he explained (ibid.).
7 Ibid.

8   Kevin Kelly, 'On Chris Anderson's The End of Theory', *Edge: The Reality Club* (30 June 2008), available at: http://edge.org/discourse/ the_end_of_theory.html#kelly.

9   Nassim Nicholas Taleb, *The Black Swan: The Impact of the Highly Improbable* (New York: Random House, 2007).

10 *Translator's note*: This is a French proverb: 'Avec des *si*, on mettrait Paris en bouteille.'

11 'Tax havens, offshore companies, corruption, trafficking.... While politicians may want to reform it and make it more ethical, the globalized economic and financial system continues to adapt itself even more to "mafia" behaviour. Why do relations and forms of porousness develop between "healthy" economies and mafia economies? .How is it that the mafia intersects every kind of institution? Is it not, ultimately, inherent to capitalism?' Nathalie Brafman, 'Mafia, stade avancé du capitalisme?', *Le Monde* (15 May 2010), available at: http://www.lemonde.fr/idees/article/2010/05/15/mafia-stade-avance-du-capitalisme_1352155_3232.html.

12 This Fordist–Keynesian 'compromise' was itself based on looting the countries of the South (something generally forgotten by the defenders of this 'compromise'), which led to those limits uncovered by the Meadows report – *The Limits to Growth* having been submitted in 1972 by four MIT researchers, Donella Meadows, Dennis Meadows, Jørgen Randers and William W. Behrens III (New York: Signet, 1972) – (the looting of the South leading to the depletion of resources), and by René Passet in France (who described the growth of negative externalities, which today we relate to the hyper-exponential effects of the Anthropocene), all the while destroying the libidinal economy, a point to which we shall return in the first chapter of this work (see pp. 20ff.).

13 Max Weber, *The Protestant Ethic and the Spirit of Capitalism* (London and New York: Routledge, 1992).

14 On these questions, see Bernard Stiegler, *The Decadence of Industrial Democracies: Disbelief and Discredit, Volume 1* (Cambridge: Polity, 2011).

15 Paolo Vignola, *L'attenzione altrove. Sintomatologie di quell che ci accade* (Naples: Orthoes Editrice, 2013). And see the lecture 'Symptomatologies du désir entre XX° et XXI° siècles', 2013 summer academy at pharmakon.fr, available at: http://pharmakon.fr/wordpress/ academie-dete-de-lecole-de-philosophie-depineuil-le-fleuriel/academie-2013/.

16 See France Stratégie, *Quelle France dans dix ans? Les chantiers de la décennies* (Rapport au Président de la République, June 2014), p. 36: '[T]he problem with setting goals in absolute terms lies in not taking into account the global and European economic situation. Reasoning in relative terms avoids this pitfall. In this spirit, we can aspire to return sustainably to the top third of European countries in terms of employment. Given our knowledge that we are currently placed in the middle

third and have, a few years ago, found ourselves in the bottom third, this would represent a very substantial improvement.'

17   Ibid., p. 35.

18   Ibid.

19   Carl Benedikt Frey and Michael A. Osborne, 'The Future of Employ- ment: How Susceptible Are Jobs to Computerisation?', 17 Septem- ber 2013, available at: http://www.oxfordmartin.ox.ac.uk/downloads/ academic/The_Future_of_Employment.pdf.

20   'Vous serez peut-être remplacé par un robot en 2025', BFMTV (10 October 2014), available at: http://hightech.bfmtv.com/logiciel/vous- serez-peut-etre-remplace-par-un-robot-en-2025-839432.html.

21   'Les robots vont-ils tuer la classe moyennes?', *Le Journal du diman- che* (26 October 2014), available at: http://www.lejdd.fr/Economie/ Les-robots-vont-ils-tuer-la-classe-moyenne-696622.

22   BFM Business stresses that 'the productivity gain generated by the mech- anization of these tasks will save 30 billion euros in tax revenue and budget savings, and generate the same amount of private investment, according to the study. Companies would also pay out 60 million euros to equip employees and machines. Thirteen billion euros of purchasing power would then be liberated, in the form of dividends or lower prices. But in the long term, the population would be at risk of forced inactiv- ity.' 'Trois millions d'emplois détruits par les robots?', BFM Business (27 October 2014), available at: http://bfmbusiness.bfmtv.com/emploi/ trois-millions-d-emplois-detru-842702.html.

23   For a historical reconstruction and a critical analysis of the concept of the Anthropocene, we can refer to Christophe Bonneuil and Jean- Baptiste Fressoz, *The Shock of the Anthropocene: The Earth, History and Us* (London: Verso, 2016).

24   We refer here to the title of the book by Dominique Méda and Patricia Vendramin, *Réinventer le travail* (Paris: PUF, 2013). We shall take up a dialogue with this work on pp. 170–3.

25   See Stiegler, *The Decadence of Industrial Democracies*, pp. 81–5 and 116–19.

26   Bonneuil and Fressoz, *The Shock of the Anthropocene*, p. 17. *Transla- tor's note*: Please note that the quotation from Crutzen and Steffen has been amended to match the English original. See Paul J. Crutzen and Will Steffen, 'How Long Have We Been in the Anthropocene Era?', *Climate Change* 61 (2003), p. 253, available at: http://stephenschneider. stanford.edu/Publications/PDF_Papers/CrutzenSteffen2003.pdf.

27   Bonneuil and Fressoz, *The Shock of the Anthropocene*, pp. 72–9, and we shall see why in Bernard Stiegler, *Automatic Society, Volume 2: The Future of Knowledge* (forthcoming). In summary they show that, from the beginning of the Anthropocene, the consequences of industrial anthropization are the issue. But this has been censored by economic and political actors using everything in their power – including lob- bying, control of the media, and so on – to thwart the growth of this

consciousness. Bonneuil and Fressoz show that today many scientists and philosophers are complicit in this dissimulation of the *primordially political* dimension of the Anthropocene.

28 Bonneuil and Fressoz, who refer to the 'grand narrative' of the history of industrialization, then critique ideological simplification. We will return to this critique in *Automatic Society, Volume 2.*

29 Jimmy Carter, speech delivered 15 July 1979, cited in Bonneuil and Fressoz, *The Shock of the Anthropocene*, p. 148, transcript available at: http://www.pbs.org/wgbh/americanexperience/features/primary-resources/carter-crisis/.

30 Bonneuil and Fressoz, *The Shock of the Anthropocene*, p. 148.

31 See Bernard Stiegler, *What Makes Life Worth Living: On Pharmacology* (Cambridge: Polity, 2013).

32 See 'Organologie', in 'Vocabulaire d'Ars Industrialis', in Bernard Stiegler, *Pharmacologie du Front national*, followed by Victor Petit, *Vocabulaire d'Ars Industrialis* (Paris: Flammarion, 2013). On the IRI, see: http://www.iri.centrepompidou.fr/?lang=en_us.

33 Bonneuil and Fressoz, *The Shock of the Anthropocene*, p. 51. 'Anthropocenologists' divide the Anthropocene into three stages: the industrial revolution; post-Second World War, called the 'great acceleration'; and the period in which the Anthropocene is thematized as such. Bonneuil and Fressoz discuss these analyses, frequently challenging them in order to politicize them, treating the Anthropocene as a properly historical, that is, political, event. And they propose a different approach, in terms of the Thermocene, Thanatocene, Phagocene, Phronocene and Polemocene. We shall return to this remarkable and fertile work in Stiegler, *Automatic Society, Volume 2.*

34 Confronted with what Bonneuil and Fressoz call the Thanatocene. See *The Shock of the Anthropocene*, p. 124.

35 *Translator's note*: On Stiegler's term *mal-être*, see Bernard Stiegler, *Technics and Time, 3: Cinematic Time and the Question of Malaise* (Stanford: Stanford University Press, 2011).

36 Furthermore, Leroi-Gourhan already drew the conclusion highlighted by Bonneuil and Fressoz, namely, that there is no unity of the human species. See p. 1 and *The Shock of the Anthropocene*, pp. 40 and 65–72.

37 Erwin Schrödinger, 'What is Life? The Physical Aspect of the Living Cell' (1944), in *What is Life, with Mind and Matter and Autobiographical Sketches* (Cambridge: Cambridge University Press, 1992).

38 Francis Bailly and Giuseppe Longo, 'Biological Organization and Anti-Entropy', *Journal of Biological Systems* 17 (2009), pp. 63–96.

39 But this makes sense only if accompanied by the grammatization of *savoir-faire* as what leads to what Marx in the *Grundrisse* called automation.

40 This is the reality of what Heidegger called the *Ereignis* of 'modern technics', that is, of the industrial revolution, of the 'calculation of

the calculable' and of its *Gestell*, its enframing. See Martin Heidegger, *Identity and Difference* (New York: Harper & Row, 1969), p. 40. Yet this is precisely what Heidegger fails to think.

41 This is how Heidegger describes Dasein, that is, 'the being that we ourselves are': Dasein is the being that has an understanding of itself, but this understanding changes with time (it is *geschichtlich*, 'historical'), and, constantly changing as it does, puts Dasein itself into question – this being-in-question governing all its ways of being, even and including when it refuses to 'ask itself questions'.

42 Kant's rational cosmology (see Immanuel Kant, *Critique of Pure Reason* [Cambridge: Cambridge University Press, 1998]) is precisely what cannot take into account the organological question of the artefact, which lies at the heart of the Anthropocene, and as a factor that is both entropic and negentropic. We will see in *Automatic Society, Volume 2* that taking account of the organological question, which is also the pharmacological question, presupposes a critique of the Kantian schematism.

43 On this subject, see the courses of pharmakon.fr of 10 November 2012, available at: http://pharmakon.fr/wordpress/2012-2013-cours -n°-1-10-novembre-2012/, and 17 November 2012, available at: http:// pharmakon.fr/wordpress/cours-20122013-seance-n°2-17-novembre- 2012/.

44 This would be the true *Ereignis* of what Heidegger called *Gestell* – but this is not Heidegger's own point of view. In 'Heidegger II', *Ereignis* designates the advent of what he also calls a 'turn' (*Kehre*) in the 'history of being', and that he characterizes by the installation of what he calls *Gestell* (literally, 'installation'), which is the 'situation' arising from 'modern technics', which he understands fundamentally in terms of the domination of cybernetics.

45 The notion of *epokhē* is set out repeatedly in the three published volumes of my *Technics and Time*: *Technics and Time, 1: The Fault of Epimetheus* (Stanford: Stanford University Press, 1998), *Technics and Time, 2: Disorientation* (Stanford: Stanford University Press, 2009), and *Technics and Time, 3*. It is also discussed in various other of my works, in particular *What Makes Life Worth Living*. I will come back to this in the following section and on pp. 29–30, 34 and 71.

46 On this subject, see Georges Canguilhem, *The Normal and the Pathological* (New York: Zone Books, 1991), p. 198, and my commentary in *What Makes Life Worth Living*, p. 29.

47 On transindividuation and the transindividual, see Gilbert Simondon, *L'Individuation psychique et collective* (Paris: Aubier, 2007), and Bernard Stiegler, *La Télécratie contre la démocratie* (Paris: Flammarion, 2007), pp. 120ff.

48 This cannot but radically affect ecological science, and not just ecological politics, but it does so by inscribing the political event at the very heart of the science of the living in its negotiation with the organized non-living and with the resultant organizations.

49 This is the point of view I defend in *Technics and Time, 1*, p. 135.

50 Karl Marx, *Grundrisse: Foundations of the Critique of Political Economy (Rough Draft)* (London: Pelican, 1973), p. 705.

51 Jacques Généreux, *La Dissociété* (Paris: Le Seuil, 2006).

52 Michael Price, 'I'm Terrified of My New TV: Why I'm Scared to Turn This Thing On – and You'd Be Too', *Salon* (31 October 2014), available at: http://www.salon.com/2014/10/30/im_terrified_of_my_new_tv_why_im_scared_to_turn_this_thing_on_and_youd_be_too/.

53 See Christophe Alix, 'Des tee-shirts connectés franco-japonais à la fibre sportive', *Libération* (7 December 2014), available at: http://www.liberation.fr/economie/2014/12/07/des-tee-shirts-connectes-franco-japonais-a-la-fibre-sportive_1158732.

54 Jérémie Zimmermann, 'La surveillance est massive et généralisée', interview in *Philosophie magazine* (19 September 2013).

55 Stephen Hawking, Stuart Russell, Max Tegmark and Frank Wilczek, '*Transcendence* Looks at the Implications of Artificial Intelligence – But Are We Taking AI Seriously Enough?', *Independent* (1 May 2014), available at: http://www.independent.co.uk/news/science/stephen-hawking-transcendence-looks-at-the-implications-of-artificial-intelligence–but-are-we-taking-ai-seriously-enough-9313474.html.

56 Evgeny Morozov, 'The Rise of Data and the Death of Politics', *Guardian* (20 July 2014), available at: http://www.theguardian.com/technology/2014/jul/20/rise-of-data-death-of-politics-evgeny-morozov-algorithmic-regulation.

57 See the courses of pharmakon.fr from 2012–13 and 2013–14.

58 Tim O'Reilly, quoted in Morozov, 'The Rise of Data and the Death of Politics'.

59 On the concept of digital tertiary retention, see pp. 32–3.

60 See Jean-Christophe Féraud and Lucile Morin, 'Transhumanisme: un corps pièces et main-d'oeuvre', *Libération* (7 December 2014).

61 'The company 23andme […], a subsidiary of Google, run by the wife of Sergey Brin, filed for a patent for a method that would enable the creation of a "bébé à la carte", thanks to the selection of gametes from donor eggs and sperm, provoking outrage among bioethicists. Nevertheless, the start-up continues to offer its customers a genetic analysis service for families for $99, based on a saliva sample.' Féraud and Morin, 'Transhumanisme'.

62 Morozov, 'The Rise of Data and the Death of Politics'.

63 Ibid.

Chapter 1 The Industry of Traces and Automatized Artificial Crowds

1 Robert Musil, 'On Stupidity', in *Precision and Soul: Essays and Addresses* (Chicago and London: University of Chicago Press, 1990), p. 280, translation modified.

2   Thomas Berns and Antoinette Rouvroy, 'Gouvernementalité algo-rithmique et perspectives d'émancipation', *Réseaux* 1 (177) (2013), pp. 163–96.

3   Also called data-intensive scalable computation, grid dataform archi-tecture and petascale data-intensive computing. See Kevin Kelly, 'The Google Way of Science', available at: http://kk.org/thetechnium/2008/06/the-google-way/.

4   *Translator's note*: The author uses the term 'discretize' to refer to every process that makes the continuous discrete, by taking something tem-poral and making it spatial, that is, material, such as, for example, the discretization of spoken language in the form of alphabetic writing, or the discretization of the gestures of the human hand made possible by the invention of the mechanical loom.

5   On hypomnesic tertiary retentions, see p. 35, and Bernard Stiegler, *Pharmacologie du Front national*, followed by Victor Petit, *Vocabulaire d'Ars Industrialis* (Paris: Flammarion, 2013), p. 380.

6   Gilles Deleuze, 'Postscript on Control Societies', in *Negotiations* (New York: Columbia University Press, 1995).

7   On algorithmic governmentality, see pp. 58 and 98.

8   Henri Lefebvre, *Critique of Everyday Life, Volume 1: Introduction* (London: Verso, 2008), *Critique of Everyday Life, Volume 2: Foun-dations for a Sociology of the Everyday* (London: Verso, 2008), and *Critique of Everyday Life, Volume 3: From Modernity to Modernism (Towards a Metaphilosophy of Daily Life)* (London: Verso, 2008).

9   Bernard Stiegler, *Symbolic Misery, Volume 1: The Hyper-Industrial Epoch* (Cambridge: Polity, 2014).

10 Bernard Stiegler, *Symbolic Misery, Volume 2: The Catastrophe of the Sensible* (Cambridge: Polity, 2015).

11 The issue of what may be called the 'industrial revolution of music' is at once economic, political, aesthetic and organological. The artistic questions that result are unthinkable without a critique of this politi-cal economy of the numbification [*insensibilisation*] and desensitiza-tion [*désensibilisation*] in which consumerism consists, a consumerism that is also cultural. In a forthcoming work, I attempt to show that proletarianization is a key issue in the 'an-artistic' work of Marcel Duchamp.

12 Symbolic misery and the ruining of desire have causes both economic and organological (Stiegler, *Symbolic Misery*, Vol. 2, p. 115; on the concept of organology, see Petit, *Vocabulaire d'Ars Industrialis*, in Stiegler, *Pharmacologie du Front national*, p. 419): the instruments for capturing attention utilized by the culture industries are themselves in the service of a consumerist model. From the beginning of the twentieth century, and under the control of marketing, these instruments short-circuit the *savoir-vivre* of consumers, proletarianizing them, just as the short-circuits of *savoir-faire* proletarianized producers in the nineteenth century.

   This industrial capturing of attention is also a *deformation* of attention: (1) attention is formed in the course of *education* through the *processes of (primary and secondary) identification* that are the intergenerational relations in which *savoir-vivre* [knowledge of how to live, manners, mores, and so on] is elaborated; (2) to raise a child is to transmit in a singular way a *savoir-vivre* that the child will in turn transmit *singularly* – to his or her comrades, friends, family, peers and descendants, near and far; (3) this, which is thus *formed* on all the pathways of education (including formal teaching), is what the industrial capture of attention systematically *deforms*.

13 Sigmund Freud, *Beyond the Pleasure Principle*, in Volume 18 of James Strachey (ed.), *The Standard Edition of the Complete Psychological Works of Sigmund Freud* (London: Hogarth, 1953–74).

14 On the concept of attentional form, see Bernard Stiegler, *States of Shock: Stupidity and Knowledge in the Twenty-First Century* (Cambridge: Polity, 2014), p. 152.

15 During the second half of the twentieth century, the industrial capture of attention occurred increasingly early, *juvenile* available brain time constituting the prime target of the audiovisual mass media in the 1960s – in France, through radio (for example, the 'Salut les copains' programme on Europe1) – and which continues today with the French radio station and social networking site Skyrock, but, at the end of the century, *infantile* available brain time became the target, diverted from its affective and social environment by all manner of dedicated programmes and channels (for example, Canal J and Baby First). I have analysed these questions in greater detail in Bernard Stiegler, *Taking Care of Youth and the Generations* (Stanford: Stanford University Press, 2010), ch. 1.

16 See Sigmund Freud, 'The Ego and the Id', in Volume 19 of Strachey (ed.), *The Standard Edition of the Complete Psychological Works of Sigmund Freud*.

17 On this point, see Bernard Stiegler, *The Decadence of Industrial Democracies: Disbelief and Discredit, Volume 1* (Cambridge: Polity, 2011), pp. 89–90.

18 The object of desire arouses a spontaneous belief in life that presents itself as its *extra-ordinary* power. All love is phantasmal in the sense that it *gives life to what is not* – to that which is not ordinary. But because the fantasy of loving, and of what Abdelkebir Khatibi calls 'aimance', beyond that which separates love and friendship (Abdelkebir Khatibi, *Aimance* [Paris: Al Manar, 2008]), is what gives civilizations their most durable forms, the literally *fantastic* feeling in which love *consists* is the embodiment of a knowledge of the *extra-ordinariness of life* that constantly *exceeds* life – through which life is *invented* (*Toujours la vie invente* being the title of a work by Gilles Clément [Paris: Éditions de l'Aube, 2008]) by going *beyond* life, and as the pursuit of life by means other than life: *through the constant and ever-increasing profusion and evolution of artifices*.

19 'What is substituted for the sexual object is some part of the body [...] or some inanimate object [...]. A certain degree of fetishism is thus habitually present in normal love.' Sigmund Freud, *Three Essays on the Theory of Sexuality*, in Volume 7 of Strachey (ed.), *The Standard Edition of the Complete Psychological Works of Sigmund Freud*, p. 154.

20 Jean-Jacques Rousseau, *Discourse on the Origin of Inequality*, in *The Social Contract and Discourses* (London: Everman's Library, 1973), pp. 44ff.

21 For a synthesis of these questions, see Paul-Laurent Assoun, *Le Fétischisme* (Paris: PUF, 2006).

22 Gilbert Simondon, *L'Individuation à la lumière des notions de forme et d'information* (Grenoble: Jérôme Millon, 2013), pp. 165ff.

23 On this question, see especially John Bowlby, *Attachment. Attachment and Loss, Volume 1* (London: Hogarth Press, 1969), *Separation: Anxiety and Anger. Attachment and Loss, Volume 2* (London: Hogarth Press, 1973), and *Loss: Sadness and Depression. Attachment and Loss, Volume 3* (London: Hogarth Press, 1980); and Arnold Gehlen, *Anthropologie et psychologie sociale* (Paris: PUF, 1980).

24 Jacques Généreux, *La Dissociété* (Paris: Le Seuil, 2006).

25 I coined this term at a public meeting of Ars Industrialis. On this subject, see my interview with Dominique Lacroix, 'Le blues du net' (29 September 2013), available at: http://reseaux.blog.lemonde.fr/2013/09/29/blues-net-bernard-stiegler/.

26 Jonathan Crary, *24/7: Late Capitalism and the Ends of Sleep* (London and New York: Verso, 2013).

27 Fred Turner, *From Counterculture to Cyberculture: Stewart Brand, the Whole Earth Network and the Rise of Digital Utopianism* (Chicago and London: University of Chicago Press, 2006).

28 See Deleuze, 'Postscript on Control Societies'.

29 This is how Clarisse Herrenschmidt describes the digital – reticular writing, which is also and firstly, however, a networked reading. The meaning of this remark will be explained in Automatic Society, Volume 2.

30 This point, which will be developed further throughout this work, continues the work begun in Bernard Stiegler, *What Makes Life Worth Living: On Pharmacology* (Cambridge: Polity, 2013), p. 22, and especially in Stiegler, *States of Shock*, pp. 15–59.

31 Crary, *24/7*, p. 40.

32 Mats Alvesson and André Spicer, 'A Stupidity-Based Theory of Organizations', *Journal of Management Studies* 49 (2012), pp. 1194–220.

33 Stupefaction, which is not just stupidity [*bêtise*], but which generally provokes it, is the modality – typical of our epoch – of what I earlier called 'disorientation'. See Bernard Stiegler, *Technics and Time, 2: Disorientation* (Stanford: Stanford University Press, 2009).

34 See p. 58.

35 Chris Anderson, 'The End of Theory: The Data Deluge Makes the Scientific Method Obsolete', *Wired* (23 June 2008), available at: http://archive.wired.com/science/discoveries/magazine/16-07/pb_theory.

36 Including that of the pre-Platonic Socrates.

37 I have opened this question of the question, as the challenging and putting in question of technical life by the *pharmakon*, in the last chapter of Stiegler, *What Makes Life Worth Living*, especially pp. 105ff.

38 See the pharmakon.fr course of 28 January 2012, available at: http://pharmakon.fr/wordpress/cours-20112012-28-janvier-2012-seance-n%c2%b0-7/.

39 Inasmuch as she intermittently causes the return of heroes, every nine years. See Plato, *Protagoras* 344c.

40 Jean-Pierre Vernant, 'At Man's Table: Hesiod's Foundation Myth of Sacrifice', in Marcel Detienne and Jean-Pierre Vernant, *The Cuisine of Sacrifice Among the Greeks* (Chicago and London: University of Chicago Press, 1989).

41 And it is necessary here to analyse in detail what differentiates all these fundamental words the Indo-European root of which, *(s)teu* – which designates what strikes, the blow, the shock, and refers to *stuprum*, the Latin word at the origin of 'stupre' [debauchery] – is also the etymon of 'stupéfiant' [narcotic], which is the 'expedient' par excellence: the *pharmakon*.

42 Crary, *24/7*, p. 81.

43 This question is in a certain way raised by the conclusions of Pietro Montani in *Bioesthétique. Sens commun, technique et art à l'âge de la globalisation* (Paris: Vrin, 2014), when he investigates the meaning of interactivity from the perspective of a biopolitics that would also be a bioaesthetics, having integrated the technical dimension of noetic living.

44 See G. W. F. Hegel, 'Preface', in *Phenomenology of Spirit* (Oxford and New York: Oxford University Press, 1977), and my commentary in *States of Shock*, ch. 5.

45 I have made this argument in several ways and in several texts and contexts, notably in Bernard Stiegler, *For a New Critique of Political Economy* (Cambridge: Polity, 2010), pp. 29ff.

46 As if *data* had taken the place of Coca-Cola in Andy Warhol's America. *Translator's note*: The reference here is to the following quotation by Andy Warhol: 'America started the tradition where the richest consumers buy essentially the same things as the poorest. You can be watching TV and see Coca-Cola, and you know that the President drinks Coca-Cola, Liz Taylor drinks Coca-Cola, and just think, you can drink Coca-Cola, too. A Coke is a Coke and no amount of money can get you a better Coke than the one the bum on the corner is drinking. All the Cokes are the same and all the Cokes are good. Liz Taylor knows it, the President knows it, the bum knows it, and you know it.' Andy Warhol, *The Philosophy of Andy Warhol (From A to B and Back Again)* (New York: Harcourt Brace Jovanovich, 1975), pp. 100–1. And see

the author's commentary on this quotation in Stiegler, *States of Shock*, pp. 215–16.

47 See, under the direction of Francis Jutand, *La Métamorphose numérique. Vers une société de la connaissance et de la coopération* (Paris: Éditions Alternatives, 2013), p. 9.

48 See Stiegler, *What Makes Life Worth Living*, pp. 127–8.

49 I return to this point on pp. 54–5 and 87.

50 On the question of amplification, see Bernard Stiegler, *Automatic Society, Volume 2: The Future of Knowledge* (forthcoming).

51 I have developed this point in Stiegler, *Pharmacologie du Front national*, pp. 159 and 181.

52 Stiegler, *For a New Critique of Political Economy*, pp. 96–129. *Translator's note*: In French, the section referred to here was in Bernard Stiegler, *Ce qui fait que la vie vaut la peine d'être vécue* (Paris: Flammarion, 2010), ch. 7.

53 See Stiegler, *Pharmacologie du Front national*, ch. 6.

54 The possibility of de-proletarianization, through a socialization of the factors that have led to proletarianization, is the hypothesis that underpins the new critique of political economy advocated by Ars Industrialis.

55 See pp. 213 and 231–2.

56 The social relation, as shown clearly by André Leroi-Gourhan in *Gesture and Speech* (Cambridge, MA and London: MIT Press, 1993), is based on affect. No social organization can survive if it does not mobilize the fundamental affects concealed in what Gilbert Simondon called pre-individual funds, which are made effective through the transindividual, and as such made affective (on these notions, see the remainder of this sub-section and *Vocabulaire d'Ars Industrialis*, in *Pharmacologie du Front national*: sensibility is not just psychic or psychosomatic; it is immediately and originally social because it is constituted through the symbolic, that is, through the transindividual itself derived from a process of transindividuation).

57 Edmund Husserl, *On the Phenomenology of the Consciousness of Internal Time* (Dordrecht: Kluwer, 1991).

58 These epochs are constituted by epiphylogenesis, which begins with hominization, then by graphic, literal, mechanical, analogical and digital hypomnesic retentions – a classification that we will clarify on pp. 200–1.

59 'In many scientific and socio-economic areas, the *volume* and *variety* of existing data, and hence the *requirements for computing time*, have created new challenges. In the highly varied fields of *fundamental science* (high-energy physics, fusion, earth science, cosmological physics, bioinformatics, neuroscience), as in the sectors of the *digital economy* (business intelligence, the web, e-commerce, social networks, e-government, health, pharmaceutical design, telecommunications and media, terrestrial and air transport, financial markets), of the *environment* (climate, natural risk, energy resources, smart cities, connected homes), of *security* (cyber-security, national security) or *industry* (smart

industry, customized production, the design/production chain of end-to-end integrated products), new scientific and technological methods are necessary.

'Massive data (or "big data") is traditionally described as having three characteristics:

- *Volume*: volumes will, according to IDC (International Data Corporation), exceed 4 zettabytes (10^{21}) in 2013. It is this axis that is best controlled today through the use of the PC farms of the Cloud, or by large servers, particularly those of the Web pioneers (Google, Facebook, eBay, Amazon) who have developed the infrastructure (often available as "open source") necessary to scale up.
- *Variety* (structured data, text, voice, image, video, social network data, the sensors of the internet of things and mobile devices) is the main source of *value*, by *crossing* these multiple data sources, but control of which still requires much scientific and technical work.
- *Velocity* (data flow operating so that it can be processed in "real time"), finally, also requires research in order to optimize computing time.

'Massive data offers many economic opportunities. France has missed the first step (infrastructure), but can still achieve strong economic expansion in the implementation of *applications that valorize this data*. Doing so requires setting up research activities in order to develop third-generation architectures. Integrating infrastructure, algorithms, mobile devices and applications serving billions of users, these applications will generate, according to the Afdel project on big data, more than 40 billion euros in revenue in 2016 and create a potential value of 200 billion euros in European public administrations.

'*High-performance computing* is today a real strategic challenge, not just for the production of new scientific knowledge, but also for economic competitiveness and risk prevention.' Rapport d'Allistène, *Contribution d'Allistène et des pôles de compétitivité à la Stratégie nationale de recherche Sciences et Technologies du Numérique* (July 2013), pp. 42–3, available at: https://www.allistene.fr/wp-content/uploads/Stratégie-Nationale-de-Recherche-Numérique-V1 1_Partie-231.pdf.

60 They are countless and infinitely varied: automatic teller machines, train system ticketing gates, mobile phones, radio-frequency identification (RFID) tags, supermarket checkouts, motorway tolls, remote-controlled navigation systems, messaging, dating sites, electronic toys, social networks, MOOCs (massive open online courses), the sensors of 'smart cities' and all kinds of tracing technologies that are now spreading into everyday life at a speed unequalled in the history of technics.

61 I develop this point below, pp. 53 and 106. This is possible only because the understanding has always passed through the exteriorization of tertiary retentions of which it was then the interiorization.

62 See Stiegler, *Pharmacologie du Front national*, pp. 125ff. Carr, too, has published a work on digital automation: Nicholas Carr, *The Glass Cage: Automation and Us* (New York: W. W. Norton & Co., 2014).

63 Which is also to say, of home: 'Desire [...] is hope', writes Maurice Blanchot in *The Infinite Conversation* (Minneapolis and London: University of Minnesota Press, 1993), p. 40.

64 On the relation between co-individuation and transindividuation, see the pharmakon.fr seminars of 2012 and 2013.

65 The social systems structured by collective individuals are formed on the basis of circuits of transindividuation, themselves founded on forms of knowledge and the disciplines.

66 It is indeed because the question of technological shock lies at the heart of the genesis of tertiary retention that Sylvain Auroux can title his book on the relations between writing and the sciences of language *La Révolution technologique de la grammatisation* (Liège: Mardaga, 1994).

67 See Horatia Harrod, 'Chris Anderson: The Do It Yourself Guru', *Telegraph* (12 October 2012), available at: http://www.telegraph.co.uk/technology/9586312/Chris-Anderson-the-do-it-yourself-guru.html: 'As it happens, Anderson's great-grandfather, Jo Labadie, was one of the founding members of the American Anarchist movement, and Anderson himself was a punk in his twenties. [...] There's certainly a libertarian flavour to his conversation, although he doesn't like to be pigeonholed.

'Anderson's vision is unsparing: it's a world of perfect competition and pure capitalism. "I think infinite competition has made us better," he says. [...] "I'm motivated primarily by social change, and my preferred tool is business."'

68 One might object that dreams constitute an experience that lies apart from the primary or secondary retentional field. But the dream is itself constituted from primary, secondary and tertiary remnants, which it rearranges according to oneiric possibilities, which are exceptional – in the sense that they *except themselves* from empirical possibilities. I will return in detail, in *Mystagogies* (forthcoming), to this subject, which was the object of courses, seminars and the 2013/14 summer academy at pharmakon.fr.

69 Perceived primary retentions are selected by previously memorialized secondary retentions.

70 On this point, see Stiegler, *Automatic Society, Volume 2*.

71 Jacob von Uexküll, *A Foray into the Worlds of Animals and Humans, with A Theory of Meaning* (Minneapolis: University of Minnesota Press, 2010).

72 Gilbert Simondon, *Imagination et invention* (Chatou: Transparence, 2008).

73 This merits a brief explanation. I argue here that the concept of différance formed by Jacques Derrida makes it possible to think the advent of *psychic and collective individuation as the artefactualization of life.*

But, for Derrida, life in general is *already* the process of such a dif-férance – which occurs, for example, through the replication of DNA, which is already a trace. I myself argue that the artefactual traces that are tertiary retentions create *new regimes of différance*, which are the principle of bifurcation on the basis of which vital individuation gives way to psychic and collective individuation, which is also a technical individuation.

74 See the preceding note.

75 Which he or she has received by having inherited collective secondary retentions that are constituted, in coming into the world (because these retentions constitute this world as words, utensils, objects, monuments, knowledge), by collective retentions made possible by tertiary retentions and instituted by social systems, and which it can reactivate, but also transgress and dismiss.

76 On this theme, see Stiegler, *What Makes Life Worth Living*, § 19.

77 The network effect is an economic mechanism of positive externality, as a result of which the value of goods or services depends on the number of other users. 'When a network effect is present, the value of a product or service is dependent on the number of others using it. The classic example is the telephone. The more people who own telephones, the more valuable the telephone is to each owner.' Wikipedia: 'Network Effect', accessed 27 June 2016.

78 Sigmund Freud, 'Group Psychology and the Analysis of the Ego', in Volume 18 of Strachey (ed.), *The Standard Edition of the Complete Psychological Works of Sigmund Freud*, p. 124, translation modified.

79 Gustave Le Bon, *Psychologie des foules* (1895), cited in ibid., pp. 72–3, translation modified.

80 The connectionist and multi-agent models of self-organization found in cognitive science would describe the phenomena analysed by Le Bon in terms of the emergence, at the collective level, of characteristics that do not exist at the individual level.

81 See Bernard Stiegler, *La Télécratie contre la démocratie* (Paris: Flammarion, 2007).

82 On the transformations generated by social networking and the crowd-sourcing that is one of its results, see Geert Lovink and Miriam Rasch (eds), *Unlike Us Reader: Social Media Monopolies and Their Alternatives* (Amsterdam: Institute of Network Cultures, 2013), especially the chapter by Ganaele Langlois, 'Social Media, or Towards a Political Economy of Psychic Life', pp. 50–60.

83 See Christopher Newfield, 'The Structure and Silence of the Cognitariat', *Eurozine* (2010), available at: http://www.eurozine.com/pdf/2010-02-05-newfield-en.pdf. And see my commentary in *Pharmacologie du Front national*, § 38. French Wikipédia presents 'crowdsourcing' in the following way (accessed 30 December 2013): 'Crowdsourcing (in French, *collaborat* or *externalisation ouverte*), one of the emerging areas of the management of knowledge, consists in the utilization of

the creativity, intelligence and *savoir-faire* of a large number of people, by enlisting them to carry out certain tasks traditionally performed by an employee or contractor. This is done by a targeted appeal (when a minimum level of expertise is required) or by an open appeal to other actors. The work may possibly be paid. It may simply be a matter of externalizing tasks not relevant to the core business of the company, or some more innovative approaches.

'There are many forms, tools, goals and strategies of crowdsourcing. The work can be collaborative or, on the contrary, carried out purely *in parallel*. In an economic approach, it may be a matter of completing a task at lower cost, but more collaborative, social or altruistic approaches exist, making appeals through specialized networks or the general public. Some approaches from participatory science and citizen science use it in order to acquire a greater amount of data, on geographical scales that would otherwise be inaccessible to researchers who are insufficiently numerous or cannot conduct tests everywhere at once (for example, in astronomy or environmental science).

'Crowdsourcing can be *active* (people collaborating to find a solution to a problem) or *passive* (one can, for example, deduce from the number of internet searches on a particular theme the *popularity of a subject* and create information of interest: Google has for example observed a close relationship between the number of people doing a search on the word "flu" and the number of people who have flu symptoms. The number of searches for "flu" increases during epidemics, and the number by those suffering the flu, and this could be of interest to epidemiologists or the WHO, while also taking account of the possible effects of "hype" prompted by media coverage of a subject.'

Wikipedia is itself the most exemplary and promising result of the curative aspects of the *pharmakon* that is crowdsourcing.

84 See Yves Citton, *Pour une écologie de l'attention* (Paris: Le Seuil, 2014).

85 On this performativity, see my commentary in chapter 3 on the arguments of Thomas Berns and Antoinette Rouvroy, pp. 103–4.

86 Noetic différance, which is the différance characteristic of psychic and collective individuation, encompassing everything that participates in transindividuation – and is not limited, in other words, to the intellectual and spiritual life that metaphysics opposes to sensible, working and social life.

87 And they also annihilate the projection of consistences that, not existing, mobilize them towards that which remains to come and as such 'moves' [*émeuvent*] all psychic individuals and all collective individuals. Hence a digital desublimation operates that is far more complex than that described by Herbert Marcuse.

88 'Mental matter become memory, or rather memory content, is the associated milieu present in me.' Gilbert Simondon, *L'Individuation psychique et collective* (Paris: Aubier, 2007), p. 164.

89 On the transformation of singularities into particularities, see *The Decadence of Industrial Democracies*, pp. 46–7.
90 This is the challenge undertaken by the Conseil national du numérique on the acquisition of basic algorithmic knowledge at school and university.
91 The latter are investigated at IRI through the Digital Studies Network (see: digital-studies.org). See also Bernard Stiegler et al., *Digital Studies: organologie des savoirs et technologies de la connaissance* (Limoge: FYP, 2014).

Chapter 2 States of Shock, States of Fact, States of Law

1 Immanuel Kant, *Critique of Pure Reason* (Cambridge: Cambridge University Press, 1998), p. 397.
2 Joseph A. Schumpeter, *The Theory of Economic Development: An Inquiry into Profits, Capital, Credit, Interest, and the Business Cycle* (New Brunswick, NJ: Transaction Publishers, 1983).
3 Joseph A. Schumpeter, *Capitalism, Socialism and Democracy* (London: Allen & Unwin, 1976).
4 The work of Thomas Berns and Antoinette Rouvroy is invaluable in this regard.
5 See Jean-Pierre Vernant, *Myth and Thought Among the Greeks* (New York: Zone Books, 2006), pp. 209 and 214.
6 Ibid., pp. 197f.
7 Gilbert Murray, *Greek Society* (Oxford: Clarendon Press, 1947), pp. 66–7, and E. R. Dodds, *The Greeks and the Irrational* (Berkeley and London: University of California Press, 1951).
8 Dodds, *The Greeks and the Irrational*, p. 180.
9 Vernant, *Myth and Thought Among the Greeks*, pp. 204–6.
10 See Bernard Stiegler, *Automatic Society, Volume 2: The Future of Knowledge* (forthcoming).
11 In Foucault's sense, and beyond this sense. See p. 98, and see the English summary of 'La "Verité" du numérique', Entretiens du nouveau monde industriel 2014, IRI/Centre-Pompidou, available at: http://enmi-conf.org/wp/enmi14/summary/.
12 'Phenomenotechnics replaces a purely descriptive phenomenology, since "it must rebuild its phenomena from scratch on the plane rediscovered by the spirit by removing parasites, disruptions, mixtures, impurities, which abound in raw and disordered phenomena".' 'Bachelard, ou l'écriture de la formule (2). L'écriture comme phénoménotechnique. D'une écriture à l'autre', available at: http://www.implications-philosophiques.org/actualite/une/bachelard-ou-lecriture-de-la-formule-2/#_ftn7. At the beginning of his study, Chomarat observes that 'Bachelard's dynamology, in which thinking is a force and not a substance, seems to have an essential relationship to the written sign. This is not a matter of a sign

that represents a being or a reality, but rather the sign of a realization, of an operation. The sign is not recapitulative, it initiates a creation of being [...]. We must pose here the possibility of a truly active writing of thinking, through which the thinker would be the contemporary of his own thinking and give birth to himself. Hence the cultural human being is defined, in Bachelard, through his *development* [*devenir*] of culture: he is this living book who "makes you want, not to start reading, but to start writing", in the words of Theosophist Franz von Baader that, surprisingly, conclude *L'Activité rationaliste de la physique contemporaine*. At this point where writing has the function of preparing a future, of effecting a psychic reform, it seems that the same schematization of rupture of the given is found in both the poem and the scientific text.' Available at: http://www.implications-philosophiques.org/actualite/une/bachelard-ou-lecriture-de-la-formule-1/.

13 Franck Cormerais and Jacques Gilbert, statement for the journal *Études digitales*, available at: http://amage.eu/digitales/: 'Why *Études digitales* rather than *numériques*? Because the term "digital" preserves in French the reference to the fingers with which one counts rather than the numerical reference to calculation by a machine.'

14 'It seems that, under the influence of Latin, *politus*, the adjectival past participle of *polire* [from which derives the adjective "poli"], gained the figurative sense of "chosen", in spoken language.' Entry for 'Polir', in Alain Rey (ed.), *Dictionnaire historique de la langue française* (Paris: Le Robert, 2012).

15 As well as bearing witness to the sublime infinitude that this judgement introduces as an analogue.

16 See Bernard Stiegler, *Symbolic Misery, Volume 2: The Catastrophe of the Sensible* (Cambridge: Polity, 2015), §§ 49 and 52, and 'Dans le cycle des images – cercle ou spirale? Imagination, invention et transindividuation', in *Le Théâtre de l'individuation* (forthcoming), or 'The Theatre of Individuation: Phase-Shift and Resolution in Simondon and Heidegger', in Arne de Boever, Alex Murray, Jon Roffe and Ashley Woodward (eds), *Gilbert Simondon: Being and Technology* (Edinburgh: Edinburgh University Press, 2012).

17 See Hesiod, *Theogony*, and Jean-Pierre Vernant, 'At Man's Table: Hesiod's Foundation Myth of Sacrifice', in Marcel Detienne and Jean-Pierre Vernant, *The Cuisine of Sacrifice Among the Greeks* (Chicago and London: University of Chicago Press, 1989).

18 Bernard Stiegler, *Uncontrollable Societies of Disaffected Individuals: Disbelief and Discredit, Volume 2* (Cambridge: Polity, 2013).

19 On inhuman being and non-inhuman being, see Bernard Stiegler, *Taking Care of Youth and the Generations* (Stanford: Stanford University Press, 2010), § 53.

20 And of the sublime beyond the beautiful, according to Lyotard ... but I leave this as an open question in anticipation of two other books: Bernard Stiegler, *Mystagogies 1 and 2* (forthcoming).

21 See Immanuel Kant, 'What is Orientation in Thinking?', in *Political Writings* (Cambridge: Cambridge University Press, 1991), on which I commented in Bernard Stiegler, *Technics and Time, 3: Cinematic Time and the Question of Malaise* (Stanford: Stanford University Press, 2011), p. 200: 'Kant's central question has to do with knowing how and through what agency can reason be guided and oriented "in thought" when it no longer has recourse to experience. This is, of course, the question of God and of a rational faith – a question asked in the immediate wake of Frederick the Great's death in the fear of a return to censorship, and in the context of a conflict between Mendelssohn and Jacobi amounting to nothing less than a crisis of the *Aufklärung*. We will return later to the questions of faith, fidelity, and belief in the Eternal Father, the "Father of all fathers", and to the idea that in any monotheism it is necessary to *adopt*, just as all fathers must adopt in order to be adopted (cf. Moses); what is of interest to us here is the question of rational thought devoid of any possible actual experience, and that thus finds itself obliged to fictionalize.

'This question, which in Kantian thought is that of the *need* for theoretical reason and a *duty* to practical reason, should engage us at the moment at which (science having become technoscience) it also claims to be a techno-science-fiction that is itself asking, in a completely new register, the question regarding the end, the end of all things. That is, it is immediately practical, not only theoretical.'

22 See p. 85, and the Digital Studies seminar led at IRI on the theme of academic categorial invention in digital associated milieus, available at: digital-studies.org.

23 I began to open up this question in Bernard Stiegler, *What Makes Life Worth Living: On Pharmacology* (Cambridge: Polity, 2013), in relation to *das Ding*, see p. 62.

24 It is this forgetting that constitutes the horizon of the *anamnesic response* of Socrates to the aporia of Meno – and it is also forgetting that is at stake in the Heideggerian thought of Dasein as capable of being affected by *a-letheia*. This problematic has been developed throughout the courses of pharmakon.fr since 2010.

25 Here, it may be useful to read or re-read these sentences of Kant, which follow those previously cited on p. 41: 'A constitution providing for the *greatest human freedom* according to laws that permit *the freedom of each to exist together with that of others* [...] is at least a necessary idea, which one must make the ground [...] of all the laws too; and in it we must initially abstract from the present obstacles, which may perhaps arise not so much from what is unavoidable in human nature as rather from neglect of the true ideas in the giving of law. For nothing is more harmful or less worthy of a philosopher than the vulgar appeal to allegedly contrary experience, which would not have existed at all if institutions had been established at the right time according to the ideas, instead of frustrating all good intentions by using crude concepts

in place of ideas, just because these concepts were drawn from experience.' Kant, *Critique of Pure Reason*, p. 397.

26　Notably in the sublime pp. 397–8 of ibid., a portion of which was cited in the previous note.

27　Grégoire Chamayou, *A Theory of the Drone* (New York: The New Press, 2015), pp. 34–5.

28　Ibid., p. 59. The citation is from Mary Ellen O'Connell, 'Unlawful Killing with Combat Drones: A Case Study of Pakistan, 2004–2009', abstract, Notre Dame Law School, Legal Studies Research Paper no. 09-43 (2009).

29　See Patrick Crogan, conference to the 2013 summer academy at pharmakon.fr, ' "We don't need another hero". Sur le "vecteur percevoir-agir" dans le discours des robotiques militaires', available at: http://pharmakon.fr/wordpress/academie-dete-de-lecole-de-philosophie-depineuil-le-fleuriel/academie-2013/.

30　G. W. F. Hegel, *Phenomenology of Spirit* (Oxford and New York: Oxford University Press, 1977), §§ 178–96.

31　Plato, *Meno*, §§ 81–2.

32　Edmund Husserl, 'The Origin of Geometry', in Jacques Derrida, *Edmund Husserl's Origin of Geometry: An Introduction* (Lincoln and London: University of Nebraska Press, 1978), p. 164.

33　And this is the issue in Alan Greenspan's response to the House of Representatives on 23 October 2008, see p. 2.

34　A petabyte is a billion megabytes.

35　Chris Anderson, 'The End of Theory: The Data Deluge Makes the Scientific Method Obsolete', *Wired* (23 June 2008), available at: http://archive.wired.com/science/discoveries/magazine/16-07/pb_theory.

36　Chris Anderson, *Makers: The New Industrial Revolution* (New York: Crown Business, 2012).

37　See p. 157.

38　See Stiegler, *What Makes Life Worth Living*, pp. 9ff.

39　Gilbert Simondon, *Du mode d'existence des objets techniques* (Paris: Aubier, 2012), p. 15.

40　Hence it is here that we must again take up the question posed by Crary in relation to the drive to possess, and the question of its overcoming.

41　See Marcel Mauss, 'La nation', in *Oeuvres, tome 3: Cohésion sociale et divisions de la sociologie* (Paris: Minuit, 1969), and my commentary during the 2013 summer academy, 'Pourquoi et comment philosopher dans l'internation', available at: http://pharmakon.fr/wordpress/academie-dete-de-lecole-de-philosophie-depineuil-le-fleuriel/academie-2013/.

42　Kevin Kelly, 'The Google Way of Science', available at: http://kk.org/thetechnium/2008/06/the-google-way/. On Kevin Kelly, see Fred Turner, *From Counterculture to Cyberculture: Stewart Brand, the Whole Earth Network, and the Rise of Digital Utopianism* (Chicago and London: University of Chicago Press, 2006).

43 Gilles Châtelet, *To Live and Think Like Pigs: The Incitement of Envy and Boredom in Market Democracies* (London: Urbanomic, 2014), p. 48.

44 Arthur Rimbaud, letter to Paul Demeny (15 May 1871), in *Rimbaud: Complete Works, Selected Letters. A Bilingual Edition* (Chicago and London: University of Chicago Press, 2005), pp. 378–9. *Translator's note*: After writing that 'the poet is truly the thief of fire' (ibid., p. 377), Rimbaud states that a language for this poet must be found, and he continues: 'This language will be of the soul for the soul, containing everything, smells, sounds, colors, thought holding on to thought and pulling. The poet would define the amount of the unknown awakening in his time in the universal soul: he would give more – than the formulation of his thought, than the expression *of his march toward Progress!* Enormity becoming normal, absorbed by all, he would really be a *multiplier of progress!*

'This future will be materialistic, as you see; – Always filled with *Number* and *Harmony*, these poems will be made to endure. – Fundamentally, it would be Greek poetry again in a way. Eternal art would have its functions; since poets are citizens. Poetry will not lend its rhythm to action, it *will be in advance.*'

45 We will frequently return to this theme in the following chapters: this tension is at the heart of digital reticulation, but remains deliberately hidden by what we will call the digital Leviathan.

46 Kelly, 'The Google Way of Science'.

47 See Victor Petit, *Vocabulaire d'Ars Industrialis*, in Bernard Stiegler, *Pharmacologie du Front national* (Paris: Flammarion, 2013), p. 414.

48 On this question, see Antoine Berman, *The Experience of the Foreign: Culture and Translation in Romantic Germany* (Albany: SUNY Press, 1992).

49 See my commentary in *Pharmacologie du Front national*.

50 Kelly, 'The Google Way of Science'.

51 See my commentaries on Kant in *Technics and Time, 3*, chs 2 and 6.

52 Kelly, 'The Google Way of Science'.

53 Alfred North Whitehead, *The Function of Reason* (Princeton: Princeton University Press, 1929).

54 Kelly, 'The Google Way of Science'.

55 Sean Carroll, 'What Good is a Theory?', *Discover* (1 July 2008), available at: http://blogs.discovermagazine.com/cosmicvariance/2008/07/01/what-good-is-a-theory/#.VWeQhmDDYyA.

56 In French, an 'aporia' is a question without an answer. But in ancient Greek it refers to an embarrassment, a problem, a lack, an uncertainty. See Plato, *Meno*.

57 Simondon, *Du mode d'existence des objets techniques*, p. 15.

58 Ibid., p. 9.

59 Here I call *metaphysical* a thought that does not see its limits and speculates by transgressing in a systematic way: cognitivism, which

constitutes an interpretation and an appropriation of the questions opened by cybernetics, thrived on such a metaphysics. On Simondon and cybernetics, see Jean-Hugues Barthélémy, *Simondon* (Paris: Les Belles Lettres, 2014), p. 144; Yuk Hui, 'La notion d'information de Shannon à Simondon', summer school of pharmakon.fr (2014), available at: https://drive.google.com/file/d/0B2ik-uN6bspBUlBVMkt6bnhkdEE/ edit; and Yuk Hui, *On the Existence of Digital Objects* (Minneapolis and London: University of Minnesota Press, 2016).

60 See Stiegler et al., *Digital Studies: organologie des savoirs et technologies de la connaissance* (Limoge: FYP, 2014). This work lies at the origin of the constitution of the Digital Studies Network, see: digital-studies. org.

61 I have developed this point especially in *States of Shock: Stupidity and Knowledge in the Twenty-First Century* (Cambridge: Polity, 2014), ch. 7.

62 Rhys Blakely, 'All at Sea? Billionaire PayPal Founder Puts His Money on Dream of a Floating Utopia', *The Times* (25 August 2011).

63 *Translator's note*: '*Formation*' in French also means the process of education and training, but this processual aspect, the relationship with a culture of *Bildung* and finally the distinction the author makes between formation and deformation are sometimes more clearly indicated by leaving the term untranslated.

64 In Stiegler, *Automatic Society, Volume 2*.

65 See pp. 72–3.

66 According to the remark by Paul Claudel that is included in the heart of the first manifesto of Ars Industrialis: 'There must be, in the poem, a number that prevents counting.'

67 'The construction and the constitution of Europe are intended [...] to *create a new process of individuation*, causing the convergence of *existing* processes of individuation. [...] Europe must *invent* a process of psychic and collective individuation essentially guided by the objective of *struggling against generalized disindividuation*.' Bernard Stiegler, *Constituer l'Europe, 1. Dans un monde sans vergogne* (Paris: Galilée, 2005), p. 11.

68 See chapter 3.

69 Among which are: the dis-integration of national taxation systems as a result of digital technology; the dis-integration of privacy and intimacy, privatized by the digital economy, and as such the very destruction of public space (private life is made possible by public space, by distinguishing itself from public space, and vice versa – the privatization of public space therefore inevitably entails the dis-integration of private life); the destruction of all labour law by human computing and digital labour (see Trebor Scholtz, *Digital Labor: The Internet as Playground and Factory* [London and New York: Routledge, 2013]), which is a case of crowdsourcing; the transformations of education by digital technologies and the need to totally rethink pedagogy, research and epistemology

in this context; remote guidance of all kinds, from GPS to the 'smart city' and the 'autonomous vehicle' inspired by the Google driverless car, which literally heralds the disintegration of the metallurgical car industry and its reintegration within a much larger industry of connected mobility; new regional and urban issues posed by 'digital territories' and 'smart cities'; the liquidation of the economy and institutions of publication (book stores, newspapers, publishers, cultural industries, educational institutions and universities, and juridical, administrative and political institutions); and a thousand other questions (medical confidentiality, insurance, security, espionage, and so on).

70 Dominique Berns, 'Les robots pourraient occuper la moitié de nos emplois', *Le Soir* (19 July 2014). I thank Pierre-Yves Defosse for alerting me to this article.

71 Julie Bort, 'People Don't Realize How Many Jobs Will Soon Be Replaced by Software Bots', *Business Insider* (13 March 2014), available at: http://www.businessinsider.com/bill-gates-bots-are-taking-away-jobs-2014-3.

72 Pavithra Rathinavel, 'Bill Gates: "Robot Apocalypse" on the Way! Is Software Automation Stealing the Pie from Humans?', *International Business Times* (18 March 2014), available at: http://www.ibtimes.com.au/bill-gates-robot-apocalypse-way-software-automation-stealing-pie-humans-1335211.

73 See p. 4 above.

74 The meeting between Barack Obama and those American data manufacturers who were implicated in the NSA affair, held at the end of 2013, has in this respect received too little attention from commentators.

75 'RFID-driven robots are highly suitable for manufacturing lines in industries ranging from electronic to vehicle production and furniture assembly'. John Edwards, 'RFID: The Next Stage', available at: https://www.rfidjournal.com/purchase-access?type=Article&id=8113&r=%2Farticles%2Fview%3F8113%2F4. 'A cell production system using a robot and automatic machines having special functions is developed. The robot transfers parts and tools for the automatic machines. A RFID is attached to each part, and the quick change in the functions of the automatic machines is executed as the kinds of products change.' Makoto Matsuoka and Tohru Watanabe, 'Flexible Manufacturing by Application of RFID and Sensors in Robot Cell Manufacturing Systems', *Proceedings of the 17th World Congress, The International Federation of Automatic Control* (2008), available at: http://www.nt.ntnu.no/users/skoge/prost/proceedings/ifac2008/data/papers/4154.pdf.

76 See the 'Entretiens du nouveau monde industriel', IRI (2009), available at: http://amateur.iri.centrepompidou.fr/nouveaumonde/enmi/conf/program/2009_2.

77 Hence I describe this state of fact by citing Alain Supiot, who talks of the 'total market', himself referring to 'total mobilization' in the sense of Ernst Jünger.

78 Gilles Deleuze, 'Letter to Serge Daney: Optimism, Pessimism, and Travel', in *Negotiations* (New York: Columbia University Press, 1995), p. 75.
79 Ibid., my emphasis, translation modified.
80 Which is also to say, then, a reference to the trace in the sense of *Of Grammatology*, which I argue calls for reflection on the process of grammatization – and a reference, obviously, to the *pharmakon*. See Serge Daney, *La Rampe* (Paris: Cahiers du cinéma, 2014).
81 I addressed the theme of quasi-causality as the condition of de-proletarianization in *Pharmacologie du Front national*, p. 318.
82 Stiegler, *States of Shock*, § 27.
83 Glenn Greenwald (2013), transcript available at: https://github.com/poppingtonic/greenwald-30c3-keynote/blob/master/transcript/transcript.md.
84 See Bernard Stiegler, *The Decadence of Industrial Democracies: Disbelief and Discredit, Volume 1* (Cambridge: Polity, 2011), pp. 74–80, and *Pharmacologie du Front national*, § 44.
85 Jean Renoir, *My Life and My Films* (New York: Atheneum, 1974), p. 62, translation modified.
86 On these questions, see the 2014 summer academy at pharmakon.fr.
87 I refer to this in *Technics and Time, 3*.
88 See the 2012–13 and 2013–14 courses of pharmakon.fr.
89 André Bazin, cited in Jean-Louis Comolli, 'Technique et idéologie', in *Cinéma contre spectacle* (Lagrasse: Verdier, 2009), p. 139. The citation is from André Bazin, *What is Cinema? Volume 1* (Berkeley and London: University of California Press, 1967), p. 17, translation modified.
90 Comolli, 'Technique et idéologie', p. 139.
91 Daney, *La Rampe*.
92 Godard wrote in 1978: '[A] novelist [...] needs a library to see what is being done, to receive books by other people, so as not to have to read only his own books. And, at the same time, a library that would also be a print shop [*imprimerie*], to know what it is to print [*imprimer*]. For me an atelier, a film studio is both a library and a print shop for a novelist.' Jean-Luc Godard, *Introduction to a True History of Cinema and Television* (Montreal: Caboose, 2014), p. 25.

Chapter 3   The Destruction of the Faculty of Dreaming

1 Gustave Flaubert, *Oeuvres Complètes. XV, Correspondance. 1871–1877* (Paris: Club de l'Honnête Homme, 1975), p. 448.
2 *Translator's note*: In French, '*doubler*' can also mean 'to overtake'.
3 Jonathan Crary, *24/7: Late Capitalism and the Ends of Sleep* (London and New York: Verso, 2013), p. 3.
4 Ibid., pp. 3–4.
5 Ibid., p. 40. I have described the same processes in relation to the practices of neuromarketing: see Bernard Stiegler, *Pharmacologie du*

Front national, followed by Victor Petit, *Vocabulaire d'Ars Industrialis* (Paris: Flammarion, 2013), ch. 6.

6 In the sense of Henri Lefebvre. See Lefebvre, *Critique of Everyday Life, Volume 1: Introduction* (London: Verso, 2008), and *Vers le cybernanthrope. Contre les technocrats* (Paris: Denoël/Gonthier, 1971).

7 Crary, 24/7, pp. 30–1.

8 I wrote on this subject in 2012, starting from the establishment of strategic marketing as conceived and practised by financialization: '[T]he ultra-liberal "ideas" and "concepts" that emerged from the conservative revolution, which form the ideology of the end of the twentieth century, and which lead to the intellectual defeat of the left as well as to the collapse of Europe, are *products of marketing and advertising* that, in this ideological war, have, for those conducting this war, the advantage of *no longer being subjects of discussion*: they are *perfect lures* – in the same way that we refer to the perfect crime. For, in this organization of ideological domination via psychopower, it is no longer a question of choosing the side of capital against that of labour – what matters according to this ideological domination is to not be a "square", to be "plugged in", and so on.' Stiegler, *Pharmacologie du Front national*, p. 56.

9 Crary, 24/7, p. 43.

10 Ibid., p. 48.

11 Ibid., p. 44.

12 This should generate a discussion between Jonathan Crary and Pietro Montani, author of *Bioesthétique. Sens commun, technique et art à l'âge de la globalisation* (Paris: Vrin, 2014), on the question of interactivity and its pharmacological character.

13 Crary, 24/7, p. 58: 'Because of the permeability, even indistinction, between the times of work and of leisure, the skills and gestures that once would have been restricted to the workplace are now a universal part of the 24/7 texture of one's electronic life.'

14 Ibid., p. 59.

15 Ibid.

16 Ibid., p. 60.

17 Ibid., p. 68.

18 Fredric Jameson, 'The End of Temporality', *Critical Inquiry* 29 (2003), p. 699, cited in ibid., p. 66.

19 Crary, 24/7, p. 67.

20 Ibid., p. 70.

21 This is an expression that I prefer not to use myself: it assumes that the worldwide movements of 1968 would have been revolutionary, which I do not believe – except as bringing about a revolution of capitalism through this 'protest'. I explained this in Bernard Stiegler, *The Lost Spirit of Capitalism: Disbelief and Discredit, Volume 3* (Cambridge: Polity, 2014), via my commentary on the book by Luc Boltanski and Ève Chiapello, *The New Spirit of Capitalism* (London and New York: Verso, 2005).

22   Crary, *24/7*, p. 71.

23   Ibid., p. 80.

24   Ibid., pp. 83–4.

25   Ibid., p. 71. Deleuze's analysis of control societies 'effectively operating 24/7' in a way inaugurates the analysis of 24/7 capitalism. But it does not seem that Crary understands Deleuze when he objects that the use of 'confinement is greater today than at any time previously' (ibid., p. 72). Control, for Deleuze, is clearly a panopticon, and now more than ever. But in control societies, unlike disciplinary societies, this is no longer based on coercion, according to Deleuze, and this is why, when Crary writes that as 'disciplinary norms in the workplace and in schools lost their effectiveness, television was crafted into a machinery of regulation' (ibid., p. 81), he is almost literally paraphrasing the Deleuzian analysis.

26   I have analysed these evolutions in Bernard Stiegler, *Technics and Time, 3: Cinematic Time and the Question of Malaise* (Stanford: Stanford University Press, 2011), p. 125.

27   Crary, *24/7*, p. 84.

28   See pp. 38–9.

29   I have developed this idea, in particular in Bernard Stiegler, *For a New Critique of Political Economy* (Cambridge: Polity, 2010), p. 99.

30   Gilbert Simondon, *L'individuation psychique et collective* (Paris: Aubier, 1989), p. 13.

31   On this point, see Bernard Stiegler, *The Decadence of Industrial Democracies: Disbelief and Discredit, Volume 1* (Cambridge: Polity, 2011), pp. 48–9.

32   We will return to this question in Bernard Stiegler, *Automatic Society, Volume 2: The Future of Knowledge* (forthcoming).

33   See Gilbert Simondon, *Communication et information. Cours et conférences* (Chatou: Éditions de la Transparence, 2010), p. 161.

34   Crary, *24/7*, p. 88.

35   See Simone Weil, 'Factory Time', in Barry Castro (ed.), *Business and Society: A Reader in the History, Sociology, and Ethics of Business* (New York and Oxford: Oxford University Press, 1996).

36   Marc Azéma, *La Préhistoire du cinéma. Origines paléolithiques de la narration graphique et du cinématographe* (Paris: Errance, 2011), p. 21.

37   This point will be argued in detail in Stiegler, *Automatic Society, Volume 2*.

38   See Yves Hersant, 'Peindre le rêve?', catalogue of the exhibition *La Renaissance et le Rêve. Bosch, Véronèse, Greco*, RMN-Grand Palais (2013).

39   Yves Bonnefoy, *L'Improbable et autres essais* (Paris: Mercure de France, 1992), and Maurice Blanchot, *The Infinite Conversation* (Minneapolis and London: University of Minnesota Press, 1993), p. 41.

40 The drives, as Freud shows in *Beyond the Pleasure Principle* (Volume 18 of James Strachey [ed.], *The Standard Edition of the Complete Psychological Works of Sigmund Freud* [London: Hogarth, 1953–74]), always lead back to the 'fatal moment' (Raymond Queneau, *L'Instant fatal* [Paris: Gallimard, 1989]) and are formed in and through its anticipation and its attraction/repulsion, so that they are constituted by the *irreducible* play of the death drive and the life drive.

41 Crary, *24/7*, p. 88.

42 Ibid., p. 89.

43 In this respect, his book, published in 2013, completely belongs to the age of 'net blues'. It is politically dangerous, when analysing the digital situation, to efface the potential alternative that it harbours and concretizes in various forms, which are obviously inchoate and embryonic yet in a strict sense fundamental. Highlighting the toxicity of the digital *pharmakon* may be salutary, but forgetting how it can be beneficial, and how it is pharmacological, is dangerous – and is what is sought by the ideologization of shock: this enables this ideology to claim that 'there is no alternative'. The same problem is found in the perspective, otherwise so rich, outlined by Evgeny Morozov in 'The Rise of Data and the Death of Politics', *Guardian* (20 July 2014), available at: http://www.theguardian.com/technology/2014/jul/20/rise-of-data-death-of-politics-evgeny-morozov-algorithmic-regulation.

44 Crary, *24/7*, p. 49.

45 Ibid., p. 50.

46 This is why I talk about a return to the tragic sources of the West. The pharmacological and technical dimension of life can no longer be concealed for a thousand reasons, some of which I analyse in *What Makes Life Worth Living*, to which I now add some new motives, including the massive effects of automation analysed here, and especially with big data, which generalizes the questions posed by the 'absolute *pharmakon*' that for Derrida was the nuclear weapon, of which Paul Virilio showed the geopolitical consequences in the 1970s – shortly before the advent of the conservative revolution (on this subject, see Bernard Stiegler, *What Makes Life Worth Living: On Pharmacology* [Cambridge: Polity, 2013], p. 37).

47 Thomas Golsenne and Patricia Ribault, 'Essais de bricologie. Ethnologie de l'art et du design contemporain', *Techniques & culture*, available at: http://tc.revues.org/6839.

48 See Antoinette Rouvroy, 'The End(s) of Critique: Data-Behaviourism vs Due Process', in Mireille Hildebrandt and Katja de Vries (eds), *Privacy, Due Process and the Computational Turn: The Philosophy of Law Meets the Philosophy of Technology* (Abingdon, Oxon: Routledge, 2013), pp. 143–68.

49 That is, for example, promenades, in Jean-Jacques Rousseau's sense in *The Reveries of the Solitary Walker* (Indianapolis: Hackett, 1992).

50 See Bernard Stiegler, *Taking Care of Youth and the Generations* (Stanford: Stanford University Press, 2010), pp. 154–5.

51 In this sense, to critique 24/7 capitalism must also be to put forward a new critique of political economy that must equally be a critique of biopolitics and of the thinking of biopower itself, not just in that it becomes a psychopower and neuropower that is *explicitly and functionally anti-political* (such is the specificity and radicality of the libertarianism of Peter Thiel), but in the sense indicated by Pietro Montani's demonstration of why it is no longer possible to maintain the question of 'bare life': biopolitics is always the organological amplification of *bios*, and 'that biopolitics has a decisive relationship to technics, and especially to biotechnology, is obviously insufficiently thematized in specialist works'. Montani, *Bioesthétique*, p. 7.

52 Rationality and rationalization are purported to be contradictory, but here it is precisely a matter of turning this contradiction into an individuating dynamic that makes 'neganthropy' through what I call a *composition*. See Stiegler, *The Decadence of Industrial Democracies*, p. 58.

53 William Shakespeare, *The Tempest*, Act IV, Scene 1.

54 Aristotle, *On the Soul* and *Metaphysics*, and see my commentary in *The Decadence of Industrial Democracies*, pp. 133–5.

55 Plato, *Protagoras*, 344c.

56 See pp. 18 and 190.

57 '[O]ur little life is rounded with a sleep.'

58 See Marcel Mauss, 'Techniques of the Body', in Jonathan Crary and Sanford Kwinter (eds), *Incorporations* (New York: Zone Books, 1992), p. 467.

59 In Bernard Stiegler, *Technics and Time, 2: Disorientation* (Stanford: Stanford University Press, 2009), this is how I refer to arrangements of 'programmes', that is, rhythmologies, as Pierre Sauvanet might say (see *Le Rythme et la Raison, tome 2, Rythmanalyses* [Paris: Kime, 2000]), formed by cosmic cycles, genotypes and biological rhythms, socio-technical programmes in Leroi-Gourhan's sense and hypomnesic processes of grammatization in all their forms, that is, technical programmes and automatisms in general.

60 Which we should think with Alfred North Whitehead. I have outlined a path in this direction in 'General Ecology, Economy and Organology', in Erich Hörl and James Burton (eds), *On General Ecology: The New Ecological Paradigm in the Neocybernetic Age* (New York: Bloomsbury, forthcoming).

61 As rituals and cults, and as religious then secular, if not consumerist, festivals and holidays – for this is precisely the structure that consumerism destroys. See Jean Lefort, Jacques Le Goff and Perrine Mane, *Les Calendiers. Leurs enjeux dans l'espace et dans le temps* (Paris: Somogy, 2002), and Paul Ricoeur, *Time and Narrative, Volume 1* (Chicago: University of Chicago Press, 1984).

62 Such a therapeutic, and any therapeutic in general, can always itself become toxic: it is and remains thoroughly pharmacological.

63 I discussed this subject in *The Decadence of Industrial Democracies*, and I return to it on pp. 155 and 186–8.

64 Raymond Queneau, *The Sunday of Life* (New York: New Directions, 1977), and, with respect to *dreaming* and *thinking*, they are both very close to and very far from the parable of Zhuangzi that gives form and substance to another Queneau novel, *The Blue Flowers*: 'Zhuang Zhou dreamt he was a butterfly. But is it not the butterfly who dreams he is Zhuang Zhou?' Raymond Queneau, *The Blue Flowers* (New York: New Directions, 1985), p. 228, translation modified.

65 See Roberto Esposito, *Communitas: The Origin and Destiny of Community* (Stanford: Stanford University Press, 2010). I will return to this book in a forthcoming work on friendship.

66 See Barbara Glowczewski, *Desert Dreamers* (Minneapolis: Univocal, 2016), and her article 'Guattari et l'anthropologie: aborigènes et territoires existentiels', *Multitudes* 34 (2008), pp. 84–94, available at: http://www.multitudes.net/guattari-et-lanthropologie-aborigenes-et-territoires-existentiels/.

67 The cinema being itself an industry of dreams and a factory conceived by Horkheimer and Adorno in 1944 as a kind of nightmare of the transcendental imagination (Max Horkheimer and Theodor W. Adorno, *Dialectic of Enlightenment: Philosophical Fragments* [Stanford: Stanford University Press, 2002]); and it is here important to note that *La Jetée* is a photomontage and contains only still images.

68 Crary, 24/7, p. 92.

69 Ibid., p. 94.

70 We should also situate surrealism in the wake of the Dadaism of Marcel Duchamp inasmuch as it seems to confront the dual shock of scientific war (which struck both Valéry and Husserl) and generalized proletarianization (which affects the artist becoming thus an an-artist). I will return to these questions in Bernard Stiegler, *Mystagogies 1. De l'art et de la littérature* (forthcoming).

71 I have developed this thesis in Bernard Stiegler, 'The Proletarianization of Sensibility', *Boundary 2* 44(1) (2017) (an earlier version appeared in *Lana Turner* 8 [2015]). It is also a question to which I will return in Stiegler, *Mystagogies 1*.

72 Crary, 24/7, pp. 93–4.

73 Ibid., p. 97.

74 T. Horikawa, M. Tamaki, Y. Miyawaki and Y. Kamitami, 'Neural Decoding of Visual Imagery During Sleep', *Science* (April 2013). The article begins thus: 'Visual imagery during sleep has long been a topic of persistent speculation, but its private nature has hampered objective analysis. Here we present a neural decoding approach in which machine learning models predict the contents of visual imagery during the sleep onset period given measured brain activity, by discovering

links between human fMRI patterns and verbal reports with the assistance of lexical and image databases. Decoding models trained on stimulus-induced brain activity in visual cortical areas showed accurate classification, detection, and identification of contents. Our findings demonstrate that specific visual experience during sleep is represented by brain activity patterns shared by stimulus perception, providing a means to uncover subjective contents of dreaming using objective neural measurement.' Thanks to Robert Jaffard, who drew my attention to this article.

75 This is the 'stuff' to which Prospero refers ('We are such stuff as dreams are made on; and our little life is rounded with a sleep'), but such that it is woven with *improbable motifs* – motifs (or figures) to which I will return in *Mystagogies 1*, through a reading of the Henry James short story 'The Figure in the Carpet'.

76 According to the thematic statement of the collection by Paul-Laurent Assoun and Markos Zafiropoulos (eds), *Psychanalyse et pratiques sociales* (Paris: Anthropos, 1994).

77 See Crary, *24/7*, pp. 105–11, where he highlights the devaluation of dreams that began in the nineteenth century, and which, he argues, very strangely, culminates with Freud's *An Interpretation of Dreams*, a work that is 'the most consequential moment in the devaluation of dream' (ibid., p. 107), to which he opposes André Breton, who, however, relied precisely on Freud. I understand the reproach made by Crary – like Breton – to Freud, namely, of underestimating if not totally denying the social dimension of the dream. I myself argue for the absolute necessity of profoundly rethinking psychoanalysis within a socio-therapeutic and not just psychotherapeutic perspective (see Bernard Stiegler, *Uncontrollable Societies of Disaffected Individuals: Disbelief and Discredit, Volume 2* [Cambridge: Polity, 2013]). And I affirm that, to do so (as I develop it here), we must inscribe the *pharmakon* at the heart of the constitution of desire. But it is only on the basis of Freud's work on the dream, which is not a 'devaluation of dream' but, on the contrary, the recognition of its *founding* dimension for the life of the mind and spirit, that such a social conception of care is conceivable and possible.

78 Crary, *24/7*, p. 98. Here we should dwell on David Cronenberg's *Videodrome*.

79 Ibid., p. 108.

80 I am responding here to a question from Tania Espinoza.

81 Ibid., pp. 35–6.

82 Ibid., p. 36.

83 Which are also contributory technologies: I will return to this point on pp. 113 and 142.

84 Ibid.

85 Ibid., p. 37.

86 See pp. 38–40.

87 See Christian Salmon, *Storytelling: Bewitching the Modern Mind* (London and New York: Verso, 2010), and especially, in relation to the state of permanent transition, 'The Destructuring Effects of the Apologia for Permanent Change'.

88 Joseph A. Schumpeter, *Capitalism, Socialism and Democracy* (London: Allen & Unwin, 1976), pp. 81–6.

89 Alain Supiot, *The Spirit of Philadelphia: Social Justice vs the Total Market* (London and New York: Verso, 2012).

90 I have developed this point in Stiegler, *For a New Critique of Political Economy*, pp. 73–96.

91 Patrice Flichy, *Les industries de l'imaginaire* (Paris: Presses Universitaires de Grenoble, 1991); see also Flichy, *The Internet Imaginaire* (Cambridge, MA and London: MIT Press, 2007).

92 See Dominique Cardon, *La Démocratie Internet. Promesses et limites* (Paris: Le Seuil, 2010), and Fred Turner, *From Counterculture to Cyberculture: Stewart Brand, the Whole Earth Network, and the Rise of Digital Utopianism* (Chicago and London: University of Chicago Press, 2006).

93 Michel Volle, *Iconomie* (Paris: Economica, 2014).

94 See Marc Giget, 'L'automatisation en cours des compétences intellectuelles', Entretiens du nouveau monde industriel 2013, available at: http://fr.slideshare.net/iri-research/marc-giget. And see 'Les robots vont-ils tuer la classe moyennes?', *Le Journal du dimanche* (26 October 2014), available at: http://www.lejdd.fr/Economie/Les-robots-vont-ils-tuer-la-classe-moyenne-696622.

95 Crary, *24/7*, p. 37.

96 I have tried to show that this is what Freud describes in *Civilization and Its Discontents*. See Stiegler, *What Makes Life Worth Living*, p. 14.

97 Simondon, *Communication et information*, p. 161.

98 Bertrand Gille, *The History of Techniques*, 2 vols (New York: Gordon and Breach, 1986).

99 These themes will be the subject of Stiegler, *Automatic Society, Volume 2*.

100 See chapter 2, note 41.

101 Denis Diderot, *D'Alembert's Dream*, in *Rameau's Nephew/D'Alembert's Dream* (London: Penguin, 1966). Diderot is one of the great thinkers of the relationship between automatisms and dis-automatization – in particular in the famous 'The Paradox of Acting'.

102 See p. 133.

103 The dissolution of everyday life is not caused by its technicization: the latter is the condition of all everydayness. Nor is it due to its formalization or its abstraction: all synchronization imposes formalisms. This dissolution results from the channelling of everyday life by industrial means in the service of computational models, whether relative (those that calculate, for example, television audience ratings) or totalized,

if not absolute, through the functional integration made possible by digital traceability twenty-four hours a day, seven days a week.

104 I argue in Stiegler, *The Decadence of Industrial Democracies*, ch. 4 (and I will come back to it here) that noesis is what only occurs intermittently and is even, as such, the experience of an irreducible intermittence.

105 I borrow Bataille's term without adhering to the opposition he makes between *Homo faber* and *Homo ludens* in *Prehistoric Painting: Lascaux, or The Birth of Art* (Geneva: Skira, 1955). On the critique of a parallel opposition that Hannah Arendt makes in *The Human Condition* (Chicago and London: University of Chicago Press, 1958) between *animal laborans* and *vita activa*, see Richard Sennett, *The Craftsman* (New Haven and London: Yale University Press, 2008).

106 For, in America too, the autonomization of large groups in relation to the political power of the federal government harms American citizens as never before – and the American Dream has for many become a nightmare, even if America still dreams, *and even if this is its main strength*.

107 See p. 133 on the birth of the web.

108 Turner, *From Counterculture to Cyberculture*.

109 Cited by Pierre Collin and Nicolas Colin, *Mission d'expertise sur la fiscalité de l'économie numérique* (Paris: Ministère de l'Économie et des Finances, 2013), p. 17, available at: http://www.economie.gouv.fr/files/rapport-fiscalite-du-numerique_2013.pdf. *Translator's note*: In fact, Collin and Colin misquote Doerr, who referred to the 'four great horsemen of the Internet', as can be seen from the article they themselves refer to by Andrew Nusca, 'Kleiner Perkins' Doerr: Google, Facebook, Amazon, Apple the "Four Great Horsemen of the Internet"', *ZDNet* (24 May 2010), available at: http://www.zdnet.com/article/kleiner-perkins-doerr-google-facebook-amazon-apple-the-four-great-horsemen-of-the-internet/.

110 See Boltanski and Chiapello, *The New Spirit of Capitalism*, pp. 437–8.

111 Ibid., p. 88.

Chapter 4   Overtaken: The Automatic Generation of Protentions

1 Georges Canguilhem, *Knowledge of Life* (New York: Fordham University Press, 2008), p. 22.

2 On this notion see Christian Fauré, 'Dataware et infrastructure du cloud computing', in Bernard Stiegler, Alain Giffard and Christian Fauré, *Pour en finir avec la mécroissance* (Paris: Flammarion, 2009).

3 *Translator's note*: IPv6 is the most recent version of the internet protocol, intended to deal with the problem of address exhaustion, that is, with the fact that the currently dominant protocol, IPv4, contains an insufficient number of possible address combinations (around 4.3

billion) to cope with the increasing proliferation of IP addresses, and in particular with the vast growth in addresses that is projected to be demanded by the rise of the so-called 'internet of things'.

4 This open prospect, however, has not been concretized due to incompatibilities with the current system.

5 Béatrice Sutter, 'Plus de robots employés chez Amazon', *Le Monde* (26 May 2014). *Translator's note*: The quotation from Adam Littler is cited in 'Amazon Workers Face "Increased Risk of Mental Illness"', *BBC* (25 November 2013), available at: http://www.bbc.com/news/business-25034598.

6 Gilbert Simondon, *Du mode d'existence des objets techniques* (Paris: Aubier, 2012).

7 Émile Durkheim, *The Division of Labour in Society* (Houndmills and London: Macmillan, 1984), pp. 2–3.

8 Ibid., p. 85.

9 Hartmut Rosa, *Social Acceleration: A New Theory of Modernity* (New York: Columbia University Press, 2013), p. 300.

10 Ibid., p. 315.

11 Ibid.

12 This is already the theme of Bernard Stiegler, *Taking Care of Youth and the Generations* (Stanford: Stanford University Press, 2010).

13 Alain Supiot, analysing the 'horrors of this period of unparalleled atrocities, from Verdun to Hiroshima via Auschwitz and the gulag', and the reification that succeeded it, where populations are 'treated as things', and where 'the industrial management of human beings [...] became a general principle of government', denounces 'two variants of scientism. One adopted biological and anthropological laws, the other economic and historical ones.' *The Spirit of Philadelphia: Social Justice vs the Total Market* (London and New York: Verso, 2012), pp. 2–3. There is no doubt that the new behaviouralist cognitivism that is being unfurled with purely computational capitalism is in the course of effecting a synthesis of these two variants, as, for example, in neuroeconomics, and more generally what might be called 'datascientism'.

14 Thomas Berns and Antoinette Rouvroy, 'Gouvernementalité algorithmique et perspectives d'émancipation', *Réseaux* 1 (177) (2013), p. 165. See also Antoinette Rouvroy, 'The End(s) of Critique: Data-Behaviourism vs Due-Process', in Mireille Hildebrandt and Katja de Vries (eds), *Privacy, Due Process and the Computational Turn: The Philosophy of Law Meets the Philosophy of Technology* (Abingdon and New York: Routledge, 2013), pp. 143–68.

15 *Translator's note*: 'Alethurgy' is a neologism that forms a key concept in Foucault's lectures on the 'government of the living'. See Michel Foucault, *On the Government of the Living: Lectures at the Collège de France 1979–1980* (Houndsmills and New York: Palgrave Macmillan, 2014), pp. 6–7: 'I shall say that the exercise of power is almost

always accompanied by a manifestation of truth understood in this very broad sense. And, looking for a word that corresponds, not to the knowledge useful for those who govern, but to that manifestation of truth correlative to the exercise of power, I found one that is not well-established or recognized, since it has hardly been used but once, and then in a different form, by a Greek grammarian of the third or fourth centuries – well, the experts will correct me – a grammarian called Heraclitus who employs the adjective *alēthourgēs* for someone who speaks the truth. *Alēthourgēs* is the truthful. Consequently, forging the fictional word *alēthourgia*, alethurgy, from *alēthourgēs*, we could call "alethurgy" the manifestation of truth as the set of possible verbal or non-verbal procedures by which one brings to light what is laid down as true as opposed to false, hidden, inexpressible, unforesee-able, or forgotten, and say that there is no exercise of power without something like an alethurgy. [...] This is to say, in a barbarous and rough way, that what we call knowledge (*connaissance*), that is to say the production of truth in the consciousness of individuals by logico-experimental procedures, is only one of the possible forms of alethurgy. Science, objective knowledge, is only one of the possible cases of all these forms by which truth may be manifested.'

16 Bernard Stiegler, *Technics and Time, 1: The Fault of Epimetheus* (Stanford: Stanford University Press, 1998), p. 1.
17 Bernard Stiegler, *Symbolic Misery, Volume 1: The Hyper-Industrial Epoch* (Cambridge: Polity, 2014), p. 45.
18 On this concept, see p. 103.
19 Laurent Thévenot, 'Autorités et pouvoirs à l'épreuve de la critique', p. 13, available at: http://sociologia.uahurtado.cl/wp-content/uploads/2012/01/Laurent-Thevenot-Autorites-et-pouvoirs-a-l-epreuve-de-la-critique.pdf.
20 Ibid., pp. 13–14. This short-circuiting of the critical function 'is accompanied [...] by a shift in authority towards things constituting the options in the engagements of opting individuals. The authority of these things is more difficult to subject to critique. It is therefore necessary to renew the theory of power and domination in order to distinguish how the treatment of reality affects the capacities of people.' The things referred to here by Thévenot have, like the algorithms to which Berns and Rouvroy refer, a 'claim to certainty in the assurance that the thing has properties that make it able to withstand any eventuality, "any test", as one says of a bulletproof vest. It may well be that the latest configuration of power and of its government that is based on the objective, under cover of putting political measures to the test like never before, succeeds in dispensing with deep questioning only by making the object the test of critique.' Ibid., pp. 16–17.
21 See Fred Turner, *From Counterculture to Cyberculture: Stewart Brand, the Whole Earth Network, and the Rise of Digital Utopianism* (Chicago and London: University of Chicago Press, 2006).

22 'To breed an animal who can *make promises* – is that not the para-doxical task that nature has set herself with regard to humankind? Is that not the true problem of humankind?' Friedrich Nietzsche, *On the Genealogy of Morality* (Cambridge and New York: Cambridge University Press, 2006), p. 35, translation modified.

23 That is, the absence of epoch in the 'change of epoch'. See Maurice Blanchot and what he called, commenting on Nietzsche, the 'exigency of return': Maurice Blanchot, 'On a Change of Epoch: The Exigency of Return', in *The Infinite Conversation* (Minneapolis and London: University of Minnesota Press, 1993), p. 264.

24 I have developed this in Bernard Stiegler, *Symbolic Misery, Volume 2: The Catastrophe of the Sensible* (Cambridge: Polity, 2015). Rouvroy herself utilizes this reference to the *Arabian Nights*.

25 See Marcel Mauss, 'La nation et l'internationalisme', in *Oeuvres, tome 3, Cohésion sociale et divisions de la sociologie* (Paris: Minuit, 1969), p. 630. See also Bernard Stiegler, *States of Shock: Stupidity and Knowledge in the Twenty-First Century* (Cambridge: Polity, 2014), § 82.

26 See Mikhaïl Xifaras, 'Marx, justice et jurisprudence. Une lecture des "vols de bois"', available at: http://www.philodroit.be/IMG/pdf/Xifaras_voldeboisMarx.pdf. Xifaras concludes thus: 'The search for a science of law that is authentically the *vera philosophia* therefore ended in failure, which lies not, as can often be read in Marxist writings, in the mystifying character of law considered in itself, but in the absence of a modern juridical language in which could be recognized the rights of humanity that are embodied in the poor. Someone other than Marx, similarly ambitious but less implacably opposed to his law professors, might have sought to constitute *ex nihilo* this undiscoverable science. Marx chose to turn to the description of social relations, soon to be associated with the formation and historical development of capital. This choice could lead only to abandoning any support for the normative question of justice as immanent critique of law, and cor-relatively the intention to make of this new science the true philosophy, one that says not only what things are, but what they should be for the common good of all.'

27 See pp. 30–1.

28 Berns and Rouvroy, 'Gouvernementalité algorithmique et perspectives d'émancipation', p. 165.

29 Mark Weiser, 'The Computer for the 21st Century', *Scientific American* (September 1991), cited in Bernard Benhamou, 'L'Internet des objets', *Revue Esprit* (March–April 2009), available at: http://www.netgouvernance.org/INTERNETdesOBJETS-RevueESPRIT.pdf.

30 Saskia Sassen, 'Talking Back to Your Intelligent City', available at: http://voices.mckinseyonsociety.com/talking-back-to-your-intelligent-city/.

31 Ibid.

32 Berns and Rouvroy, 'Gouvernementalité algorithmique et perspectives d'émancipation', p. 173.

33   Right up to the toothbrush. See Evgeny Morozov, 'De l'utopie numérique au choc social', *Le Monde diplomatique* (August 2014), available at: http://www.monde-diplomatique.fr/2014/08/MOROZOV/50714.

34   On these questions see Alain Desrosières, *The Politics of Large Numbers: A History of Statistical Reason* (Cambridge, MA and London: Harvard University Press, 1998) and Christian Fauré, 'La question des catégories à la lumière du schème probabiliste bayesien', 2013 summer academy of pharmakon.fr, available at: http://pharmakon.fr/wordpress/academie-dete-de-lecole-de-philosophie-depineuil-le-fleuriel/academie-2013/.

35   Berns and Rouvroy, 'Gouvernementalité algorithmique et perspectives d'émancipation', p. 173.

36   I have developed this theme in 'Literate Natives, Analogue Natives and Digital Natives: Between Hermes and Hestia', in Divya Dwivedi and Sanil V (eds), *The Public Sphere from Outside the West* (London: Bloomsbury Academic, 2015). I will also pursue this question in *Aimer, s'aimer, nous aimer, tome 2* (forthcoming).

37   And, in the same movement, we must also take up the question of the division of labour, of the evolution of tasks and specialization as studied by Durkheim, though he never did so from the perspective of organological evolution – that is, the co-differentiation of artificial organs, psycho-somatic organs and social organizations.

38   Berns and Rouvroy, 'Gouvernementalité algorithmique et perspectives d'émancipation', p. 166.

39   I will return to this question of interiorization in detail in Bernard Stiegler, *Automatic Society, Volume 2: The Future of Knowledge* (forthcoming).

40   Berns and Rouvroy, 'Gouvernementalité algorithmique et perspectives d'émancipation', p. 166.

41   From an *ana-lysis*, a word that literally means 'de-composition'.

42   See Desrosières, *The Politics of Large Numbers*, p. 103.

43   Berns and Rouvroy, 'Gouvernementalité algorithmique et perspectives d'émancipation', p. 167.

44   Ibid.

45   We will see in the next chapter, remaining with Berns and Rouvroy, how statistical data and therefore government has been privatized by large corporations at the expense of states and other public powers.

46   See p. 104.

47   Berns and Rouvroy, 'Gouvernementalité algorithmique et perspectives d'émancipation', p. 172.

48   See Michel Foucault, 'The Meshes of Power', in Jeremy W. Crampton and Stuart Elden (eds), *Space, Knowledge and Power: Foucault and Geography* (Aldershot: Ashgate Press, 2007), a text that should be compared to Gilles Deleuze's 'Postscript on Control Societies', in *Negotiations* (New York: Columbia University Press, 1995). On the

question of modulation, see Yuk Hui, 'Modulation After Control', *New Formations* 84–5 (2014/15), pp. 74–91.

49   Deleuze, 'Postscript on Control Societies', pp. 178–9, translation modified.

50   Foucault, 'The Meshes of Power', p. 158.

51   Ibid., p. 159.

52   Ibid., pp. 160–1.

53   See Desrosières, *The Politics of Large Numbers*, pp. 8–9.

54   Foucault, 'The Meshes of Power', p. 161.

55   Berns and Rouvroy, 'Gouvernementalité algorithmique et perspectives d'émancipation', p. 167.

56   Desrosières, *The Politics of Large Numbers*, pp. 114–15.

57   Ibid., pp. 125–6.

58   Berns and Rouvroy, 'Gouvernementalité algorithmique et perspectives d'émancipation', p. 173.

59   Laurence Allard and Olivier Blondeau, 'L'activisme contemporain: défection, expressivisme, expérimentation', *Rue Descartes* 55 (2007), pp. 47–58. I have placed the word 'users' in quotes because I believe that a social network such as Facebook produces no use value for consumers (it does produce, but for those who organize the consumption). Rather, it produces *misuse*, that is, the automated destruction of values. Digital social networks as currently designed are ultra-nihilistic.

60   Berns and Rouvroy, 'Gouvernementalité algorithmique et perspectives d'émancipation', p. 173.

61   Ibid., p. 174.

62   Ibid., p. 181.

63   Ibid., p. 184.

64   Ibid., p. 168.

65   Ibid.

66   Algorithmic governmentality thus accomplishes Zygmunt Bauman's 'liquid society'.

67   Berns and Rouvroy could have added Derrida and his critique of Austin to Simondon and Deleuze and Guattari when they show that the latter are thinkers of these objects but that these objects reverse and invert those who have thought them. Derrida posited in fact that the performative and the constative can never be opposed, and I agree that he was right to do so. But this indifference of the performative and the constative is what an institution must *differentiate* through a normativity and a work of categorization and formation of retentional systems and certifications that constitute what Foucault called a regime of truth. I will return to these questions in Stiegler, *Automatic Society, Volume 2*. Such fictional activity amounts to the realization of a dream through which society practises transindividuation as *dreaming*, that is, as the inheritance of transgenerational potentials for individuation.

68   Berns and Rouvroy, 'Gouvernementalité algorithmique et perspectives d'émancipation', p. 170.

69 Ibid., p. 171.

70 Ibid.

71 This is, for instance, what happened to Servier. *Translator's note*: Servier is a French pharmaceutical company that sold the very popular drug benfluorex (under the brand name of Mediator) as a weight-loss treatment for diabetics (and eventually for non-diabetics), from 1978 until 2009, until it was found that the harmful side-effects of the medication were greater than the benefits, including the likelihood of many hundreds if not thousands of fatalities. Accusations that the company knew of the dangerous side-effects led to lengthy legal battles and political repercussions.

72 Viktor Mayer-Schönberger and Kenneth Cukier, *Big Data: A Revolution That Will Transform How We Live, Work, and Think* (Boston: Houghton Mifflin Harcourt, 2013).

73 Berns and Rouvroy, 'Gouvernementalité algorithmique et perspectives d'émancipation', pp. 182–3.

74 Ibid.

75 Ibid., p. 182.

76 Ibid., p. 183.

77 I am not treating the category 'politics' as a reality inherent in any human society. Politics appears with the *polis*, and is then spread more widely via Christianity. But for me there is no 'political' power in Indian chiefdoms, for example, contrary to what Pierre Clastres assumes in *Society Against the State: Essays in Political Anthropology* (New York: Zone Books, 1989).

78 Desrosières, *The Politics of Large Numbers*, p. 8.

79 Ibid., p. 9.

80 In the sense that individuation is always a matter of taking form [*prise de forme*], as Simondon thinks it in *L'Individuation à la lumière des notions de forme et d'information* (Grenoble: Jérôme Millon, 2005).

81 Berns and Rouvroy, 'Gouvernementalité algorithmique et perspectives d'émancipation', p. 183.

82 '*Ce qu'il faut*', that which is necessary: this *falloir*, this necessity, which is also a *faille*, a fault, does not establish a duty to be but a *duty to make happen, to create the future* [*devoir faire advenir*].

83 Berns and Rouvroy, 'Gouvernementalité algorithmique et perspectives d'émancipation', p. 174.

84 See p. 69 and Gilbert Simondon, *Communication et information. Cours et conférences* (Chatou: Éditions de la Transparence, 2010), p. 78.

85 Blanchot, *The Infinite Conversation*, p. 41.

86 And this is also the structure of being in the Heideggerian conception of what is thought on the basis of what Heidegger calls the ontological difference, and this is why Blanchot continues: 'It is infinitely more than the most probable: "that is to say, what is",' which is a quotation from Yves Bonnefoy ('I dedicate this book to the improbable, that is

to say, to what is') in *L'Improbable et autres essais* (Paris: Mercure de France, 1992), p. 7. Then Blanchot adds: 'And yet what is remains the improbable.' Yet: that is, even though it *is*.

87 Blanchot, *The Infinite Conversation*, p. 41.

88 On the incessant, see Maurice Blanchot, *The Space of Literature* (Lincoln and London: University of Nebraska Press, 1982).

89 I have developed this allegory of the flying fish in Bernard Stiegler, 'How I Became a Philosopher', in *Acting Out* (Stanford: Stanford University Press, 2009), which I have over time expanded into an allegory of the 'noetic salmon' in the courses of pharmakon.fr, especially that of 28 January 2012, available at: http://pharmakon.fr/wordpress/cours-20112012-28-janvier-2012-seance-n°-7/.

90 On this subject, see the lecture given by Pierre-Yves Defosse during the 2014 summer academy of pharmakon.fr, 'Le Titanic de James Cameron et un discours de Steve Jobs: prétextes pour une contribution à l'anthropotechnique' (available at: http://pharmakon.fr/wordpress/academie-dete-de-lecole-de-philosophie-depineuil-le-fleuriel/academie-dete-2014/), to which I will return in Stiegler, *Automatic Society, Volume 2*.

91 Simondon, *Du mode d'existence des objets techniques*, p. 164.

92 We will draw the consequences with respect to the theory of value in economics on pp. 136–7 and 186.

93 Berns and Rouvroy, 'Gouvernementalité algorithmique et perspectives d'émancipation', p. 182.

94 Ibid.

95 See Francis Bailly and Giuseppe Longo, *Mathematics and the Natural Sciences: The Physical Singularity of Life* (London: Imperial College Press, 2011).

96 Berns and Rouvroy, 'Gouvernementalité algorithmique et perspectives d'émancipation', pp. 187–8. I have myself commented on the difference between the interindividual and the transindividual in Stiegler, *States of Shock*, pp. 59–60.

97 *Translator's note*: There is also here the sense of a missed encounter in the relation, as in a deviation.

98 He did, however, say clearly why the transindividual is not the interindividual.

99 Blanchot, *The Infinite Conversation*, p. 46.

100 Berns and Rouvroy, 'Gouvernementalité algorithmique et perspectives d'émancipation', p. 189.

101 *Translator's note*: The meaning of '*coupe l'herbe sous le pied*' lies between 'pulling the rug out from under their feet' and 'beating them to the punch'.

102 Berns and Rouvroy, 'Gouvernementalité algorithmique et perspectives d'émancipation', p. 190. *Translator's note*: The quotation is from Didier Debaise, 'What is Relational Thinking?', *Inflexions* 5 (2012), p. 6.

103 Berns and Rouvroy, 'Gouvernementalité algorithmique et perspectives d'émancipation', p. 190.

104 Blanchot, 'Interruption (as on a Riemann Surface)', in *The Infinite Conversation*, p. 75.

105 I am referring here to Roberto Esposito, *Communitas: The Origin and Destiny of Community* (Stanford: Stanford University Press, 2010), a text to which I will return in *Aimer, s'aimer, nous aimer 2* (forthcoming).

106 See Gerald Moore, *Politics of the Gift: Exchanges in Poststructuralism* (Edinburgh: Edinburgh University Press, 2011).

107 Berns and Rouvroy, 'Gouvernementalité algorithmique et perspectives d'émancipation', pp. 190–1.

108 See Stiegler, *States of Shock*, pp. 165–6.

109 Behaviours always have an energetic, psychic or mental cost (and mental fatigue always also consumes physical energy) that these automatisms allow us to save.

110 I respond here to a question posed to me by Maryanne Wolf during the symposium, 'General Organology: The Co-Individuation of Minds, Bodies, Social Organisations and Technè'. See: nootechnics.org.

111 This might seem, to the eyes of a distracted or hasty reader, to resemble the argument of Michel Serres in a bestseller that I will discuss in the next volume, where he narrates a kind of Christmas tale for the brutes we have become (and that he has perhaps himself become, in which case he's telling himself stories, as we say), pulling the wool over our eyes on a basis that is, exactly, *sophistical* – in the strict sense that Socrates gives to this in describing the sophist as a manipulator who takes advantage of the *pharmakon* by denying its toxicity, and thereby unleashes this toxicity. Contrary to Serres, the question raised here is to know what, confronted with the *automaton*, we should preserve as interiorized competences, and firstly at the level of motor skills [*motricité*]. This is the problem that Maryanne Wolf raises when, in *Proust and the Squid: The Story and Science of the Reading Brain* (New York: Harper, 2007), she analyses the effects of the digital automated environment on the brains of the younger generations (those forming the 'digital natives'), and asks what must be saved from oblivion and preserved as elementary and higher learning.

112 Berns and Rouvroy, 'Gouvernementalité algorithmique et perspectives d'émancipation', p. 175.

113 I have previously approached this question in *Uncontrollable Societies of Disaffected Individuals: Disbelief and Discredit, Volume 2* (Cambridge: Polity, 2013). The situation has since then considerably worsened.

114 Berns and Rouvroy, 'Gouvernementalité algorithmique et perspectives d'émancipation', p. 176.

115 Ibid.

116 See Bernard Stiegler, *Pharmacologie du Front national*, followed by Victor Petit, *Vocabulaire d'Ars Industrialis* (Paris: Flammarion, 2013), ch. 6.
117 Berns and Rouvroy, 'Gouvernementalité algorithmique et perspectives d'émancipation', p. 177.
118 Jacob von Uexküll, *A Foray into the Worlds of Animals and Humans, with A Theory of Meaning* (Minneapolis: University of Minnesota Press, 2010).
119 See p. 212.
120 Berns and Rouvroy, 'Gouvernementalité algorithmique et perspectives d'émancipation', p. 177.

Chapter 5   Within the Electronic Leviathan in Fact and in Law

1 Georges Canguilhem, *Knowledge of Life* (New York: Fordham University Press, 2008), p. 19.
2 'There is a molecular machinic unconscious, which relates to coding systems, automated systems, moulding systems, loan systems, etc., which does not involve semiotic chains, or the subjectivation of subject/object relations, or phenomena of consciousness; but which does involve what I call the phenomena of machinic enslavement, where functions and organs enter into direct interaction with machinic systems, semiotic systems. I always give the example of driving a car in a state of reverie. Everything functions outside of consciousness, all by reflex, we think about something else, and even, at the limit, we sleep; and then, there is a semiotic signal to wake up, and suddenly we regain consciousness, reinjected into signifying chains. There is, therefore, an unconscious machinic enslavement.' Félix Guattari, seminar of 9 December 1980, available at: http://www.revue-chimeres.fr/drupal_chimeres/files/801209.pdf.
3 Thomas Berns and Antoinette Rouvroy, 'Gouvernementalité algorithmique et perspectives d'émancipation', *Réseaux* 1 (177) (2013), p. 178.
4 I use the word 'system' here to refer to processes of individuation understood from the perspective of Gille, who speaks of social systems and the technical system. We will see in Bernard Stiegler, *Automatic Society, Volume 2: The Future of Knowledge* (forthcoming) that Simondon himself refers to quasi-systems.
5 Gilbert Simondon, *L'Individu et sa genèse physico-biologique* (Grenoble: Jérôme Millon, 1995), p. 206.
6 '[I]t is *in order to function* that a social machine must *not function well*.' Gilles Deleuze and Félix Guattari, *Anti-Oedipus: Capitalism and Schizophrenia* (Minneapolis: University of Minnesota Press, 1983), p. 151.
7 In Gilles Deleuze's sense in *Difference and Repetition* (New York: Columbia University Press, 1994).
8 Simondon, *L'Individu et sa genèse physico-biologique*, p. 178.

9   Ibid., p. 208.

10   It was around 1880 that Nietzsche said that this will last for two hundred years: 'What I relate is the history of the next two centuries. I describe what is coming, what can no longer come differently: *the advent of nihilism.*' Friedrich Nietzsche, *The Will to Power* (New York: Vintage, 1968), p. 3.

11   The notion of anthropization arose in geography with the concept of the anthropized milieu, that is, the environment dominated by the transformational forces mobilized by the *anthropos* – namely, its technics. It thus foreshadows the more recent notion of the Anthropocene.

12   See Victor Petit, *Vocabulaire d'Ars Industrialis*, in Bernard Stiegler, *Pharmacologie du Front national* (Paris: Flammarion, 2013), p. 371.

13   This will be explained in Stiegler, *Automatic Society, Volume 2*.

14   I will return to this question in ibid.

15   I will also return to this question in ibid.

16   We can refer to trance, here, to the extent that transindividuation can be produced only as a kind of possession, which is a kind of hallucination, that is, a collective dream. On this point, see the discussion of dreaming on p. 216. *Transe* means at the same time stupefaction, the passage from life to death, or beyond life, possession, and 'dream, ecstasy, in particular in the field of love'. Alain Rey (ed.), *Dictionnaire historique de la langue française* (Paris: Le Robert, 2012), p. 3893.

17   Bernard Stiegler, *Symbolic Misery, Volume 2: The Catastrophe of the Sensible* (Cambridge: Polity, 2015), p. 30.

18   On the *On*, see Bernard Stiegler, *Acting Out* (Stanford: Stanford University Press, 2009), pp. 60–2.

19   See the report of the Conseil national du numérique, *Avis sur la neutralité des plateformes: réunir les conditions d'un environnement numérique ouvert et soutenable* (13 June 2014), available at: http://www.cnnumerique.fr/plateformes/.

20   Dominique Cardon, *La Démocratie Internet. Promesses et limites* (Paris: Le Seuil, 2010), p. 96.

21   Clay Shirky, *Here Comes Everybody: The Power of Organizing Without Organizations* (New York: Penguin, 2008).

22   The *reflexivity* denoted by this turn of phrase, '*s'être formé*', is that of new forms of sociation and association that have appeared on the web and more generally the internet as an associated milieu of inter-locution and transindividuation, promising the possibility of a new form of collective individuation. This promise must give birth to a new state of law exceeding the current state of fact. This is possible only by overcoming the purely libertarian temptation of these new forms of community – a temptation that, when it demands the reduction of any vertical or diagonal (ascending or descending) dimension to two dimensions, one horizontal, instituting a seeming parity, and one vertical, always hidden, opens the way for ultra-liberal libertarianism, if not for the extreme right, which dividualizes society itself and in totality from a strictly

oligarchic perspective: on the one side, dividuating individuals; on the other side, the dividuated (that is, disindividuated: proletarianized). Such is the issue with the floating city without state or law that Peter Thiel hopes to build outside American territorial waters close to San Francisco (see p. 57).

23 Cardon, *La Démocratie Internet*, p. 97.

24 And, more specifically, under mountains. See 'La Suisse se lance dans le business des "cyberbunkers"', *Le Figaro* (12 May 2013): 'Switzerland has entered the cyberbunker business. The Swiss Confederation plans to transform its old fallout shelters inherited from the Cold War into centres for the storage of sensitive digital data.' Available at: http://www.lefigaro.fr/secteur/high-tech/2013/12/05/32001 -20131205ARTFIG00613-la-suisse-se-lance-dans-le-business-des-cyberbunkers.php.

25 On this subject, see Christian Fauré, 'Dataware et infrastructure du cloud computing', in Bernard Stiegler, Alain Giffard and Christian Fauré, *Pour en finir avec la mécroissance* (Paris: Flammarion, 2009).

26 Andrew Blum, 'L'envers des data centers (3/3): "Je rêve d'un fournisseur d'emails qui soit comme l'épicerie du coin"', *Mediapart* (10 August 2014). Blum is the author of *Tubes: A Journey to the Center of the Internet* (New York: HarperCollins, 2013).

27 In Stiegler, *Automatic Society, Volume 2*.

28 See p. 110.

29 Lawrence Lessig, 'Code is Law', *Harvard Magazine* (Jan.–Feb. 2000), available at: http://harvardmagazine.com/2000/01/code-is-law-html.

30 Cardon, *La Démocratie Internet*, p. 95.

31 Provided that a new age is 'born', which is obviously an illusion – but this kind of illusion has performative effects that are far from illusory.

32 Cardon, *La Démocratie Internet*, p. 95.

33 Gilbert Simondon, *Du mode d'existence des objets techniques* (Paris: Aubier, 2012).

34 Berns and Rouvroy, 'Gouvernementalité algorithmique et perspectives d'émancipation', p. 178, my italics.

35 Maurizio Lazzarato, '"Semiotic Pluralism" and the New Government of Signs: Homage to Félix Guattari', available at: http://eipcp.net/ transversal/0107/lazzarato/en.

36 Ibid.

37 Deleuze and Guattari wrote in this regard that 'every politics is simultaneously a *macropolitics* and a *micropolitics*'. Gilles Deleuze and Félix Guattari, *A Thousand Plateaus: Capitalism and Schizophrenia* (Minneapolis: University of Minnesota Press, 1987), p. 213. And they add that 'from the viewpoint of micropolitics, a society is defined by its lines of flight, which are molecular', whereas a society is defined by its contradictions 'only on the larger scale of things' (ibid., p. 216). For us, this means that a macropolitics must *arrange lines of flight and contradictions*, that is, *key-points and horizon* – and must do so through

a political technology capable of therapeutically arranging the *bottom up* ('teeming' with disparities) and the *top down* (through which the horizon is verticalized). This will be the central question in Stiegler, *Automatic Society, Volume 2.*

38 Berns and Rouvroy, 'Gouvernementalité algorithmique et perspectives d'émancipation', p. 179.

39 Ibid.

40 See p. 186.

41 Antoinette Rouvroy, 'Mise en (n)ombres de la vie même', *Mediapart*, available at: http://blogs.mediapart.fr/blog/antoinette-rouvroy/270812/mise-en-nombres-de-la-vie-meme-face-la-gouvernementalite-algorit.

42 Deleuze and Guattari, *Anti-Oedipus*, pp. 150–1, translation modified.

43 Berns and Rouvroy, 'Gouvernementalité algorithmique et perspectives d'émancipation', p. 180.

44 Ibid., p. 181, my italics.

45 See Amir Rezaee, 'Le Trading Haute Fréquence, une méthode de spéculation ultra rapide … et ultra dangereuse', *Le Nouvel Observateur* (18 April 2014): 'Thanks to recent advances in the domain of information and communication technology, it is now possible to make an exchange of stock (an offer of sale or security) in an infinitesimal fraction of a second. For example, currently on the New York Stock Exchange, members can place an order every 37 microseconds, while barely ten years ago this time was one second.' Available at: http://leplus.nouvelobs.com/contribution/1191975-le-trading-haute-frequence-une-methode-de-speculation-ultra-rapide-et-ultra-dangereuse.html.

46 Sigmund Freud, 'Project for a Scientific Psychology', in Volume 1 of James Strachey (ed.), *The Standard Edition of the Complete Psychological Works of Sigmund Freud* (London: Hogarth, 1953–74).

47 On these questions, see 'À propos du *Wunderblock* de Freud', the paper given by Hidetaka Ishida at the 2014 summer academy of pharmakon.fr, available at: http://pharmakon.fr/wordpress/academie-dete-de-lecole-de-philosophie-depineuil-le-fleuriel/academie-dete-2014/.

48 On this 'return shock', this 'counter-thrust', and its relation to the 'speculative proposition' in Hegel, see Bernard Stiegler, *States of Shock: Stupidity and Knowledge in the Twenty-First Century* (Cambridge: Polity, 2014), p. 120.

49 I will return in detail to these questions, passing through Bergson, in the sixth volume of *Technics and Time* (forthcoming).

50 I rely here on the work done by Yuk Hui and Harry Halpin at IRI during 2012. See 'Collective Individuation: The Future of the Social Web', available at: http://www.iri.centrepompidou.fr/wp-content/uploads/2011/02/Hui_Halpin_Collective-Individuation.pdf. For a profound extension of these questions, see Yuk Hui, *On the Existence of Digital Objects* (Minneapolis: University of Minnesota Press, 2016).

51 Mikhaïl Xifaras, 'Marx, justice et jurisprudence. Une lecture des "vols de bois"', available at: http://www.philodroit.be/IMG/pdf/Xifaras_voldeboisMarx.pdf.

52 Karl Marx, 'Debates on the Law on Thefts of Wood', available at: https://www.marxists.org/archive/marx/works/download/Marx_Rheinishe_Zeitung.pdf.

53 Obviously this does not mean that there would be no principle of differentiation before Greece. It means that starting from Greece this principle is given apodictically, and that this apodictic donation reconfigures all the criteria of transindividuation by constituting their canon.

54 In *The Division of Labour in Society*, Durkheim targets all these questions without conceiving them as such because, if he thinks the evolution of societies *on the basis of the division of labour*, that is, on the basis of organological evolutions, he never thinks these evolutions *as such*: he never investigates the *evolution of the division of labour* with respect to *technical evolution*.

55 Having noted that the Declaration of Philadelphia affirms that 'labour is not a commodity', Supiot shows that 'the link established between spiritual freedoms and material security implied that the economic must be organised according to the principle of *social justice*' (Alain Supiot, *The Spirit of Philadelphia: Social Justice vs. the Total Market* [London and New York: Verso, 2012], p. 13), and that law cannot and must not be subjected to the relations of production – whether they are conceived in an ultra-liberal way or in a Marxist way.

56 What we are here calling general economy and neganthropology constitute a perspective that infinitizes the term 'anthropization' as the power to realize dreams beyond any calculation.

57 On this concept, see Bernard Stiegler, *Technics and Time, 3: Cinematic Time and the Question of Malaise* (Stanford: Stanford University Press, 2011), ch. 5.

58 Hence Durkheim opens up the question that Bertrand Gille would put at the heart of the relations between the technical system and the social systems.

59 This will be analysed in more detail in the second volume of this work.

60 See Gustavo Just da Costa e Silva, *Interpréter les théories de l'interprétation* (Paris: L'Harmattan, 2005).

61 Luc Boltanski and Ève Chiapello, *The New Spirit of Capitalism* (London and New York: Verso, 2006), pp. 437ff.

62 Tim Berners-Lee, with Mark Fischetti, *Weaving the Web* (New York: HarperCollins, 2000), pp. 157–8.

63 These circuits of transindividuation are infinitely long, that is, they give access to consistences that are both idealized and infinite, because infinitely open to trans-formation in the course of processes of collective individuation themselves infinite: it is because geometry is structurally infinite that 'we geometers', as Husserl says, also are. And this infinitude of knowledge is the counterpart of Socratic anamnesis. For noetic

individuation to occur, psychic individuals must reconstitute within themselves the circuits of transindividuation on which it is inscribed.

64   In Simondon's sense, in Gilbert Simondon, *Imagination et invention* (Chatou: Transparence, 2008).

65   We should analyse from the perspective of Pierre Legendre the algorithmic automatization of what he himself calls the dogmatic. Pierre Legendre, *Law and the Unconscious: A Legendre Reader*, ed. Peter Goodrich (Houndmills and London: Palgrave Macmillan, 1997), chs 5 and 7.

66   Berns and Rouvroy, 'Gouvernementalité algorithmique et perspectives d'émancipation', p. 184.

67   Ibid., pp. 184–5.

68   Simondon, *L'Individu et sa genèse physico-biologique*, pp. 44ff.

69   Taking form is ontogenesis conceived as transductive relation, that is, as relation having the rank of being, and constituting in that its terms, in a relationship that is no longer hylemorphic, and that therefore is no longer based on the substantialization either of matter or of form. Such transduction is essentially quasi-causal and pharmacological, given that the 'resolving transduction *undertakes the inversion of the negative into the positive*' (Simondon, *L'Individu et sa genèse physico-biologique*, p. 32), an inversion that is not a synthesis, and which is therefore not dialectical, since it trans-forms the tension into a new potential for future resolutions. Despite this, however, Simondon did not conceive this transduction in pharmacological terms in the sense we understand it, that is, in the sense where organology is constitutive of psychic and collective individuation and yet proves at the same time to be necessarily 'destitutive', so to speak.

70   Berns and Rouvroy, 'Gouvernementalité algorithmique et perspectives d'émancipation', p. 185.

71   Ibid. It might be objected here that Deleuze and Guattari never, strictly speaking, projected an emancipation.

72   A question that is also at the heart of Durkheim's *The Division of Labour in Society*.

73   Bernard Stiegler, *For a New Critique of Political Economy* (Cambridge: Polity, 2010), pp. 117ff.

74   And not in the sense of hermeneutics of which Thomas Carlyle is a good representative, that is, understood as the process of the disclosure of a revelation. See Thomas Carlyle, *On Heroes, Hero-Worship and the Heroic in History* (New Haven and London: Yale University Press, 2013).

75   And here we must recall the meaning of the words 'concrete' and 'concretization' in Simondon, *Du mode d'existence des objets techniques*.

76   Berns and Rouvroy, 'Gouvernementalité algorithmique et perspectives d'émancipation', p. 185.

77   Simondon, *L'Individu et sa genèse physico-biologique*, p. 32. *L'Individu à la lumière des notions de forme et d'information* is the later edition in integrated form of two works that were published separately, *L'Individu*

et sa genèse physico-biologique and *L'Individuation psychique et col-lective*. I refer here to the two earlier editions, which are those I have annotated and studied.

78 Berns and Rouvroy, 'Gouvernementalité algorithmique et perspectives d'émancipation', p. 186.

79 Ibid., p. 187, n. 22.

80 On the transindividuation of reference, see Stiegler, *La Télécratie contre la démocratie* (Paris: Flammarion, 2007), p. 112.

81 After Gilles Deleuze, Anne Sauvagnargues ('Simondon, Deleuze, and the Construction of Transcendental Empiricism', *Pli. Special Volume: Deleuze and Simondon*, 2012, pp. 1–21.) gives great importance to this concept, of which Jean-Hughes Barthélémy highlights the 'occasional' use by Simondon (Barthélémy, *Simondon* [Paris: Les Belles Lettres, 2014], p. 208). The fact remains that the concept of disparation makes it pos-sible to think the arrangement of diversity and unification in a process of transindividuation that Simondon, in fact, never himself problematized.

82 I understand such a reactivation in the Husserlian sense, that is, as an anamnesis in the Socratic sense.

83 This is the issue in Pierre Judet de La Combe and Heinz Wismann, *L'Avenir des langues: Repenser les humanités* (Paris: Éditions du Cerf, 2004).

84 Berns and Rouvroy, 'Gouvernementalité algorithmique et perspectives d'émancipation', p. 192, my italics.

85 This is what remains unclear in Deleuze and Guattari.

86 And this is why Daniel Bensaïd could write: 'The 1980s were years of a strategy degree zero, not only for strategies of subversion, but also, contrary to appearances, for strategies of domination. For their logics are, as has often been brought to my attention, isomorphic. They mutually entered into a specular play. There is nothing surprising in this. Subversion is condemned by its very immanence (which it cannot escape) to remain subordinate to what it resists and opposes. This is not a trivial inconvenience for the rhetorics of resistance, despite their virtue, in the 1980s, of not yielding to the shameful and disgusting rhetoric of resignation to the order of things and the world. Deleuze, Guattari and Foucault, each in their own way, perceived and translated this emerging strategic crisis. They in some way revealed it. But, in so doing, they also nourished it, and this is probably the reason why their success was based on a misunderstanding. [...] Deleuze and Foucault were both symbolic markers heralding a triple crisis: a crisis of modern historicity, a crisis of emancipatory strategy and a crisis of critical theory, or, in other words, a combined crisis of a critique of weapons and of the weapons of critique. This was the epoch when, thanks to an unfortunate misinterpretation, '68 was taken as a great leap forward, only to be exposed, at the turn of the 1970s and through one of those ironic twists that are the key to history, as a phenomenal regression. A derisory dialectical reversal: "We have been sent", wrote Foucault in

1977, "back to 1830, that is to say, we have to begin all over again." '
Daniel Bensaïd, 'Grandeur et misère de Deleuze et Foucault', available
at: http://danielbensaid.org/Grandeurs-et-miseres-de-Deleuze-et.

87 Berns and Rouvroy, 'Gouvernementalité algorithmique et perspectives
d'émancipation', p. 193.

88 It is necessary here to profoundly investigate the thought of the
commons, from the perspective of *droit,* and open a dialogue with
Elinor Ostrom, Michel Bauwens, Philippe Aigrain and Valérie Peugeot.
I will return to this in Stiegler, *Automatic Society, Volume 2.*

89 See Stiegler, *For a New Critique of Political Economy,* pp. 66–70.

90 This will be described in detail in Stiegler, *Automatic Society, Volume 2.*

91 Bruno Trentin, *La città del lavoro. Sinistra e crisi del fordismo* (Milan:
Feltrinelli, 1997), pp. 107–8; the French edition (to which Alain Supiot
contributed an introduction) is Bruno Trentin, *La Cité du travail. La
gauche et la crise du fordisme* (Paris: Fayard, 2012), p. 211.

92 Supiot, *The Spirit of Philadelphia,* pp. 17–18.

Chapter 6   On Available Time for the Coming Generation

1   Karl Marx, *Grundrisse: Foundations of the Critique of Political
Economy (Rough Draft)* (London: Pelican, 1973), pp. 704–5.

2   See pp. 142–3.

3   The question of the *ages of Marx* deserves further treatment. Marx-
isms could be defined by the way in which they describe (or identify)
the ages of the great man.

4   As Marx and Engels will describe the bourgeoisie in *The Communist
Manifesto.*

5   Mikhaïl Xifaras, 'Marx, justice et jurisprudence. Une lecture des "vols
de bois" ', available at: http://www.philodroit.be/IMG/pdf/Xifaras_
voldeboisMarx.pdf: 'How could this law be criticized, which was
obviously created exclusively to serve the interests of the wealthy
forest owners, depriving the poor of a resource that for them was
essential, without appearing to be the defender of a feudal conception
of property?'

6   That is, as a *process of functional integration* characteristic of
machines.

7   It is also to disorganize and reorganize the organic by subjecting it to
the organized inorganic.

8   I have defined this concept in *Technics and Time, 1: The Fault of
Epimetheus* (Stanford: Stanford University Press, 1998), p. 49.

9   See Bernard Stiegler, *Pharmacologie du Front national,* followed by
Victor Petit, *Vocabulaire d'Ars Industrialis* (Paris: Flammarion, 2013),
pp. 133–48.

10 In the brains referred to by Saussure as preserving the 'treasure of
language' (Ferdinand de Saussure, *Course in General Linguistics* [New

York: Philosophical Library, 1959], pp. 13–14, translation modified), as in those of which Maryanne Wolf analyses the disorganizations and reorganizations, and which correspond in Deleuze and Guattari to 'synaptic microfissures' (Gilles Deleuze and Félix Guattari, *A Thousand Plateaus: Capitalism and Schizophrenia* [Minneapolis: University of Minnesota Press, 1987], p. 15). I will return to this point in *Automatic Society, Volume 2: The Future of Knowledge* (forthcoming).

11 I will also return to this point in *Automatic Society, Volume 2.*

12 See p. 101.

13 Walter J. Ong, *Orality and Literacy: The Technologizing of the Word* (London and New York: Routledge, 2002), pp. 77–8.

14 Including in the sense of Gabriel Tarde, analysed by Maurizio Lazzarato in *Puissances de l'invention. La psychologie économique de Gabriel Tarde contre l'économie politique* (Paris: Les Empêcheurs de penser en rond, 2002). Tarde, however, did not problematize the organological conditions of this cooperation. See pp. 191–2.

15 Which is also to say, redefining *taonga, hau, mana,* and so on (see Marcel Mauss, *The Gift: Expanded Edition* [Chicago: HAU, 2016]) as specific and fundamental aspects of the process of transindividuation.

16 See Stiegler, *Technics and Time, 1*, pp. 134–42.

17 If thermodynamic motorization is what the historians and analysts of industrialization usually emphasize, the reproducible formalization of gestures is what they usually neglect – with the exception of Marx. This is still the case in Georges Friedmann, *Où va le travail humain?* (Paris: Gallimard, 1967).

18 A traceological approach in theoretical computing has been developed in France, through the concept of the modelled trace, by Pierre-Antoine Champin, Alain Mille and Yannick Prié, in 'Les traces numériques comme objets de premier niveau: une approche par les traces modélisées', *Intellectica* 59 (2013), pp. 171–204.

19 Norbert Wiener, quoted by Friedmann in *Où va le travail humain?*, p. 14, originally from Wiener, *Cybernetics: or Control and Communication in the Animal and the Machine* (Cambridge, MA: MIT Press, 1961), pp. 27–8.

20 On the issue of ordinary and extraordinary men, see Maurice Godelier, *The Metamorphoses of Kinship* (New York: Verso, 2012), cited by Pierre-Yves Defosse, 'Le Titanic de James Cameron et un discours de Steve Jobs: prétextes pour une contribution à l'anthropotechnique', at the 2014 summer academy of pharmakon.fr, available at: http://pharmakon.fr/wordpress/academie-dete-de-lecole-de-philosophie-depineuil-le-fleuriel/academie-dete-2014/, to which we will return in Stiegler, *Automatic Society, Volume 2.*

21 Whose *inherent banality* is such that it is difficult to refer to an ideal type.

22 This is undoubtedly to a large extent the stakes of the complex tension between Simondon and Wiener (besides the question of the

convergence of technical individuals as Simondon raises it in *Du mode d'existence des objets techniques* [Paris: Aubier, 2012]). See Jean-Hugues Barthélémy, *Simondon* (Paris: Les Belles Lettres, 2014), p. 144.

23 Alain Supiot shows in some very beautiful pages how Kafka's work relates to his job, from which he learned of the condition of workplace accident victims. Supiot could also have drawn attention to the condition of this employee who was Kafka himself, subject to all manner of desertifying procedures and regulations. See Alain Supiot, 'The Grandeur and Misery of the Social State' (29 November 2012), available at: http://books.openedition.org/cdf/3093.

24 See Bernard Stiegler, *States of Shock: Stupidity and Knowledge in the Twenty-First Century* (Cambridge: Polity, 2014), p. 136.

25 Friedmann, *Où va le travail humain?*, p. 292.

26 Ibid.

27 Henry Ford, quoted in ibid., p. 293, from Henry Ford, with Samuel Crowther, *My Life and Work* (New York: Garden City, 1922), p. 87.

28 It is in this sense that we must interpret the statement of an applied psychologist responsible for the recruitment of factory workers in Belgium in 1948: 'Once a worker shows a quick understanding of the processes in the instructions they have been given to execute in the test, they are *awake*. [...] In the choice we have to make, we must be wary of those who are too successful in these tests: in the long run they cannot get used to just doing very basic tasks.' Cited by Friedmann, *Où va le travail humain?*, p. 317.

29 I have introduced this point in Stiegler, *States of Shock*, § 44, by reading Lyotard as a thinker of the general intellect in the epoch of what he called the 'postmodern condition', which he then analysed in direct relation to the 'computerization of society'.

30 Which is also to say, which generates new bourgeois life-knowledge, sometimes unfortunate but often admirable: in France, from Balzac to Baudelaire and from Tzara to Breton, passing through Stendhal, Flaubert, Mallarmé and Proust, this is a treasure that, today squandered by a mafia of illiterate climbers ('of the right' and 'of the left'), was the fruit of this grandeur.

31 See pp. 159–60.

32 And this is in addition to the fact that he has no inheritance, and so cannot be subject to debt seizure, as Mikhaïl Xifaras insists, after Foucault, and while criticizing him. See EHESS, 'Autour de Michel Foucault: *La Société punitive (1972–1973)*' (17 December 2013), available at: http://www.canal-u.tv/video/ehess/2eme_session_autour_de_michel_foucault_la_societe_punitive_1972_1973.13899.

33 I take up this term used in the discussion opened by André Gorz, building upon the analyses of Yann Moulier-Boutang – and more generally the journal *Multitudes* and Moulier-Boutang's work *Cognitive Capitalism* (Cambridge: Polity, 2011) – in Gorz, *The Immaterial:*

Knowledge, Value and Capital (New York: Seagull Books, 2010), p. 97. And I return to this on p. 212.

34 See p. 154.

35 This is the issue in the questions raised by Bernard Aspe and Muriel Combes. See Gorz, *The Immaterial*, pp. 11ff.

36 In October 2013 I spoke before the Conseil d'État, which was at the time engaged in its 'annual study', later published as *Le numérique et les droits fondamentaux: 50 propositions du Conseil d'État pour mettre le numérique au service des droits individuels et de l'intérêt général* (La Documentation française, September 2014). I argued that the question put to me by the Conseil d'État related not only to the Conseil constitutionnel, which makes judgments as to whether laws conform to the Constitution de la République, but also to a new constitution, that is, to an exceptional moment in collective individuation, *re-establishing the legal, fundamental and legitimate conditions* of its individuation, and thereby posing the question of a *reconstitution* of citizenship in the epoch of rights. This is, for example, what Antoinette Rouvroy claims for the psychic individuals we are ourselves, confronting the technical individuals that are digital technologies, but confronting especially the disindividuating networks of disintegration, controlled by corporations, resulting from the functional integration of our disembrained nervous systems – that is, incapable of interiorizing contemporary organology, not only because it is not possible in itself, but because *this is not in the interests of reticular corporations that have become tentacular corporations.*

37 This continues what Marie-Anne Dujarier has called the work of the consumer in *Le Travail du consommateur. De McDo à eBay* (Paris: La Découverte, 2014).

38 I have tried to show that capitalism is above all a protentional system in *For a New Critique of Political Economy* (Cambridge: Polity, 2010).

39 It was starting from a reading of Gorz in 2003 (*The Immaterial*) that I myself took up and continued his ideas and analyses, by mobilizing a conceptual apparatus that was not his, involving the concepts of retention, protention and trace.

40 With the proletarianization of consumers, the collective secondary retentions generated by the tertiary retentions emerging from production (as consumer goods), or by the services that exploit these tertiary retentions, cease to be the fruit of the psychic individuation processes of consumers. On the contrary, and as was the case for proletarianized production, they tend to short-circuit these psychic individuals, who adapt themselves to the behavioural models encapsulated in and prescribed by these goods and services, but without adopting them: psychic individuals who are no longer individual either collectively or psychically. In the twenty-first century, it is the 'intellectual workers', that is, designers, conceptualizers, decision-makers, who in turn find

themselves excluded from circuits of transindividuation that are structurally externalized.

41 That this begins with analogue retentions is shown in the exchanges
between Guattari, Deleuze and Daney. See p. 61.

42 Simon Nora and Alain Minc, *The Computerization of Society: A
Report to the President of France* (Cambridge, MA and London: MIT
Press, 1980). The report was originally published in French in 1978.

43 Georges Elgozy, *Automation et humanisme* (Paris: Calmann-Lévy,
1968), p. 11.

44 André Gorz, 'Un débat tronqué. Commentaire et choix de textes',
appendix to Jeremy Rifkin, *La Fin du travail*, second edition (Paris:
La Découverte, 2006).

45 See Friedmann, *Où va le travail humain?*, p. 17.

46 Dominique Méda, *Le Travail. Une valeur en voie de disparition* (Paris:
Aubier, 1995).

47 Dominique Méda and Patricia Vendramin, *Réinventer le travail* (Paris:
Presses Universitaires de France, 2013).

48 Friedmann, *Où va le travail humain?*, p. 14.

49 Ibid., p. 26.

50 See Marc Giget, 'L'automisation en cours des compétences intellectuelles', available at: http://fr.slideshare.net/iri-research/marc-giget.

51 Chris Zook, 'When "Creative Destruction" Destroys More Than It
Creates', *Harvard Business Review* (27 June 2012), available at: http://
blogs.hbr.org/2012/06/when-creative-destruction-dest/.

52 A. M. Gittlitz, 'Your iPhone Kills Jobs', *Salon* (28 March 2013), available at: http://www.salon.com/2013/03/28/your_iphone_kills_jobs/.

53 Jaron Lanier, quoted in Bernice Napach, 'The Internet Kills More
Jobs Than It Creates: Jaron Lanier', *Daily Ticker* (8 May 2013),
available at: http://finance.yahoo.com/blogs/daily-ticker/internet-kills-
more-jobs-creates-jaron-lanier-124549081.html. Cf. Jaron Lanier,
Who Owns the Future? (New York: Simon & Schuster, 2013).

54 David Rotman, 'How Technology Is Destroying Jobs', *MIT Technology
Review* (12 June 2013), available at: http://www.technologyreview.com/
featuredstory/515926/how-technology-is-destroying-jobs/. See also
the discussion with Erik Brynjolfsson et al., 'The Great Decoupling', *McKinsey Quarterly* (September 2014), available at: http://
www.mckinsey.com/industries/public-sector/our-insights/the-great-
decoupling; the interview with Laurent Alexandre (transhumanist uro-
logical surgeon) by Gabriel Siméon, 'Les gens voudront vivre 250 ans',
Libération (5 October 2014), available at: http://www.liberation.fr/
futurs/2014/10/05/les-gens-voudront-vivre-250-ans_1115337; and 'Les
robots vont-ils tuer la classe moyennes?', *Le Journal du dimanche* (26
October 2014), available at: http://www.lejdd.fr/Economie/Les-robots-
vont-ils-tuer-la-classe-moyenne-696622 – see p. 4.

55 *Translator's note*: The Trente Glorieuses refers to the postwar economic boom between 1945 and 1975.

56 Friedmann, *Où va le travail humain?*, pp. 26–7.
57 Michel Volle, *Iconomie* (Paris: Economica, 2014), p. 105, available at: http://www.volle.com/travaux/iconomie.pdf.
58 Jacques Derrida, 'No Apocalypse, Not Now: Full Speed Ahead, Seven Missiles, Seven Missives', in *Psyche: Inventions of the Other, Volume I* (Stanford: Stanford University Press, 2007).
59 Volle, *Iconomie*, p. 35. Cf. Michel Volle, 'The Effects of Informatization on the Economic and Financial Crisis' (4–5 October 2010), available at: http://www.aea-eu.com/2010Ankara/DOCUMENTS/Publication/Text/Volle_Michel.pdf.
60 André Gorz, 'Introduction', in *Critique of Economic Reason* (London and New York: Verso, 1989).
61 *Translator's note*: This is a phrase infamously used by Patrick Le Lay when he was president of the French television network TF1, to describe what it is that commercial television networks sell. As quoted in 'M. Le Lay: TF1 vend "du temps de cerveau disponible"', *Le Monde* (11–12 July 2004): 'Questioned, along with other chiefs, in a work entitled *Les Dirigeants face au changement* (éditions du Huitième Jour), the president of TF1, Patrick Le Lay, noted that "there are many ways of speaking about television. But from a 'business' perspective, being realistic, the base, the job of TF1, is to help Coca-Cola, for example, sell its product." And he went on: for "an advertisement to be perceived, it is necessary that the brain of the tele-spectator be available. Our programmes are there in order to make this available, that is, to divert it, and to relax it, to prepare it between two ads. What we sell to Coca-Cola is available brain time." "Nothing is more difficult," he continues, "than to obtain this availability."'
62 Alain Giffard, 'Des lectures industrielles', in Bernard Stiegler, Alain Giffard and Christian Fauré, *Pour en finir avec la mécroissance* (Paris: Flammarion, 2009).
63 Frédéric Kaplan, 'Quand les mots valent de l'or. Le capitalisme linguistique', *Le Monde diplomatique* (November 2011), available at: http://www.monde-diplomatique.fr/2011/11/KAPLAN/46925.
64 Jeremy Rifkin, 'Préface à la deuxième édition', in *La Fin du travail*, p. xlv.
65 *Translator's note*: This reference to the economist Gary Becker is undoubtedly drawn from a reading of Michel Foucault, *The Birth of Biopolitics: Lectures at the Collège de France, 1978–79* (Houndmills, Basingstoke and New York: Palgrave Macmillan, 2008), p. 226: 'In neo-liberalism – and it does not hide this; it proclaims it – there is also a theory of *homo oeconomicus*, but he is not at all a partner of exchange. *Homo oeconomicus* is an entrepreneur, an entrepreneur of himself. This is true to the extent that, in practice, the stake in all neo-liberal analyses is the replacement every time of *homo oeconomicus* as partner of exchange with a *homo oeconomicus* as entrepreneur of himself, being for himself his own capital, being for himself his own

producer, being for himself the source of [his] earnings. [I]n Gary Becker there is a very interesting theory of consumption, in which he says: We should not think at all that consumption simply consists in being someone in a process of exchange who buys and makes a monetary exchange in order to obtain some products. The man of consumption is not one of the terms of exchange. The man of consumption, insofar as he consumes, is a producer. What does he produce? Well, quite simply, he produces his own satisfaction. And we should think of consumption as an enterprise activity by which the individual, precisely on the basis of the capital he has at his disposal, will produce something that will be his own satisfaction.' And see Gary S. Becker, 'On the New Theory of Consumer Behavior' and 'A Theory of the Allocation of Time', in *The Economic Approach to Human Behavior* (Chicago and London: University of Chicago Press, 1976). Foucault draws on the reading of Becker by Henri Lepage, 'Les révolutions de Gary Becker: L'économie du temps et la nouvelle théorie du consommateur', in *Demain le capitalisme* (Paris: Livre de Poche, 1978), esp. p. 327: 'In this perspective, the consumer is not only a being who consumes; he is an economic agent who "produces". Who produces what? Who produces satisfactions of which he is the consumer?'

66 Luc Boltanski and Ève Chiapello, *The New Spirit of Capitalism* (London and New York: Verso, 2006), ch. 2.

67 Jeremy Rifkin, *The Age of Access: The New Culture of Hypercapitalism, Where All of Life is a Paid-for Experience* (New York: Tarcher/Putnam, 2000).

68 Pierre-Michel Menger, *Portrait de l'artiste en travailleur* (Paris: Le Seuil, 2003); Menger, 'Artists as Workers: Theoretical and Methodological Challenges', *Poetics* 28 (2001), pp. 241–54; and Joseph Confavreux, 'L'intermittence constitue le rêve fou d'un patron capitaliste', interview with Pierre-Michel Menger, *Mediapart* (5 July 2014), available at: http://www.mediapart.fr/journal/culture-idees/050714/lintermittence-constitue-le-reve-fou-dun-patron-capitaliste.

69 See also Dominique Méda, *L'Avenir du travail* (Paris: Institut Diderot, 2013), available at: http://www.institutdiderot.fr/wp-content/uploads/2015/03/Lavenir-du-travail.pdf.

70 See Stiegler, *Pharmacologie du Front national*, p. 303.

71 Alexandre Kojève, *Introduction to the Reading of Hegel: Lectures on the Phenomenology of Spirit* (New York: Basic Books, 1969).

72 Jean-Claude Milner, *Le Salaire de l'idéal. La théorie de classes et de la culture au XXe siècle* (Paris: Le Seuil, 1997): it mainly concerns the professorial function. But this is being 'devalued' at great speed, and with it the 'vocations' vanish, leading to a state of fact on the verge of widespread collapse.

73 See Stiegler, *Pharmacologie du Front national*, p. 304.

74 Méda and Vendramin, *Réinventer le travail*, p. 21.

75 Ibid., p. 22.

76 Ibid.
77 Ibid., p. 23.
78 Ibid.
79 I have expanded upon this point in Stiegler, *For a New Critique of Political Economy*, pp. 77ff.
80 Gorz, *Critique of Economic Reason*, p. 1, translation modified.
81 Ibid., translation modified.
82 Ibid., p. 2, translation modified.
83 André Gorz, *Capitalism, Socialism, Ecology* (London and New York: Verso, 1994), p. 55.
84 This is a question that Jacques Schote poses in the psychiatric field, to which I will return in Stiegler, *Automatic Society, Volume 2*. See also Alain Supiot's inaugural lecture to the Collège de France, 'The Grandeur and Misery of the Social State' (29 November 2012), available at: http://books.openedition.org/cdf/3093.
85 Georges Canguilhem, *The Normal and the Pathological* (New York: Zone, 1991). See Bernard Stiegler, *What Makes Life Worth Living: On Pharmacology* (Cambridge: Polity, 2013), ch. 2.
86 Bertrand Gille, 'Prolegomena to a History of Techniques', in *The History of Techniques, Volume 1: Techniques and Civilizations* (New York: Gordon and Breach, 1986).
87 Gorz, *Critique of Economic Reason*, p. 2.
88 See the commentary on Gabriel Tarde by Lazzarato in *Puissances de l'invention*; see also Simondon, *Imagination et invention*, and my commentary in Stiegler, *States of Shock*, p. 79; and Stiegler, *Le Théâtre de l'individuation* (forthcoming).
89 Karl Polanyi, *The Great Transformation: The Political and Economic Origins of Our Time*, 2nd edn (Boston: Beacon, 2001).
90 I have begun to open up this question in Stiegler, *States of Shock*, pp. 98ff.
91 Gorz's paraphrase of a statement by Lionel Stoléru, in Gorz, *Critique of Economic Reason*, p. 2. Stoléru declared in particular that 'savings in manufacturing costs and in working time will increase purchasing power and *create new areas of activity elsewhere in the economy (if only in leisure activities)*' (quoted in ibid.).
92 Gorz, *Critique of Economic Reason*, p. 3, translation modified.
93 Ibid., p. 4, translation modified.
94 Ibid., p. 7, my emphasis.
95 André Gorz, 'The New Servants', in *Capitalism, Socialism, Ecology*, p. 45, translation modified.
96 Ibid., p. 46.
97 Chapter 6 of *Capitalism, Socialism, Ecology* is 'The Crisis of "Work" and the Post-Industrial Left'. The French title is 'La crise de l'idée de travail et la gauche post-industrielle'.
98 In the manner of Patrick Le Lay, as we have said, that is, in the *economy of the culture industries* analysed in 1944 by Horkheimer

and Adorno in *Dialectic of Enlightenment*, or in the manner of Eric Schmidt, that is, as *privative* algorithmic governmentality disarming, discrediting and liquidating all public power, as analysed by Thomas Berns and Antoinette Rouvroy, 'Gouvernementalité algorithmique et perspectives d'émancipation', *Réseaux* 1 (177) (2013), pp. 163–96.

99 Michel Rocard, 'Préface', in Jeremy Rifkin, *La Fin du travail*, p. x.

100 Ibid., p. xii.

101 Gorz, 'Un débat tronqué. Commentaire et choix de textes', p. 445. Gorz adds to his critique that Rifkin's proposals concerning the financing of this third sector are not acceptable (tax cuts for solvent and taxable volunteers, a 'social wage' for the poor who lack the means to be volunteers, so to speak, and who are therefore forced to make use of volunteers – who will therefore do what is less interesting: whatever keeps them in employment) – the third sector perpetuating and legitimating an unjust situation.

102 I will return to this proposal in Stiegler, *Automatic Society, Volume 2*.

103 This has been outlined in Stiegler, *Pharmacologie du Front national*.

104 This is what I have tried to analyse in Stiegler, *States of Shock*, pp. 143ff.

Chapter 7   Energies and Potentials in the Twenty-First Century

1 Margaret Thatcher, interviewed in 'Mrs Thatcher: The First Two Years', *The Sunday Times* (3 May 1981), available at: http://www.margaretthatcher.org/document/104475.

2 *Translator's note*: On 27 March 2002, Richard Durn, a 33-year-old with a master's degree in political science, perpetrated a mass murder at a council meeting in Nanterre, killing eight and wounding nineteen. The quotation is from a letter he wrote prior to the massacre. Stiegler has previously discussed Durn in 'To Love, to Love Me, to Love Us: From September 11 to April 21', in *Acting Out* (Stanford: Stanford University Press, 2009).

3 Jean-Pierre Vernant, *Myth and Thought Among the Greeks* (New York: Zone Books, 2006), p. 293.

4 Maurizio Lazzarato, *Puissances de l'invention: La psychologie économique de Gabriel Tarde contre l'économie politique* (Paris: Les Empêcheurs de penser en rond, 2002).

5 Richard Sennett, *The Craftsman* (New Haven and London: Yale University Press, 2008).

6 Jeremy Rifkin, *The Hydrogen Economy: The Creation of the World-wide Energy Web and the Redistribution of Power on Earth* (New York: Tarcher/Penguin, 2002).

7 Bernard Stiegler, *What Makes Life Worth Living: On Pharmacology* (Cambridge: Polity, 2013), pp. 90ff.

8 Robert L. Heilbroner, 'Foreword' to Jeremy Rifkin, *The End of Work: The Decline of the Global Labor Force and the Dawn of the Post-Market Era* (New York: Tarcher/Putnam, 1995), pp. xii–xiii.

9 Rifkin, *The End of Work*, p. xv.

10 Alain Caillé, 'Postface' to Jeremy Rifkin, *La Fin du travail*, second edition (Paris: La Découverte, 2006), p. 433.

11 This point is developed in Bernard Stiegler, *Pharmacologie du Front national*, followed by Victor Petit, *Vocabulaire d'Ars Industrialis* (Paris: Flammarion, 2013), pp. 25ff.

12 Bernard Stiegler, Alain Giffard and Christian Fauré, *Pour en finir avec la mécroissance* (Paris: Flammarion, 2009).

13 It is equally striking that Rifkin has no space for the free software economy in *The Age of Access: The New Culture of Hypercapitalism, Where All of Life is a Paid-for Experience* (New York: Tarcher/Putnam, 2000).

14 Rifkin, *The End of Work*, p. xvi.

15 Ibid., p. xvii.

16 Karl Marx, *Grundrisse: Foundations of the Critique of Political Economy (Rough Draft)* (London: Pelican, 1973), p. 705.

17 Since nobody is ready to understand another discourse, Rifkin, who is first and foremost a businessman, takes care of his clientele – which is not always compatible with clarity.

18 See Vincent Bontems, Philippe Petit and Bernard Stiegler, *Économie de l'hypermatériel et psychopouvoir* (Paris: Mille et une nuits, 2008), p. 105.

19 Cf. Lazzarato: the *economic psychology* of Tarde 'is inscribed within a debate that [...] has as its stake [...] the definition of the "value of value"' (Lazzarato, *Puissances de l'invention*, p. 9). 'The death of God [...] requires [...] the reconsideration of the *origin* of the *constitution* of values' (ibid., p. 10).

20 Value is what supplies the selection criteria in the flows of retentions and protentions through which circuits of transindividuation are produced. With the current automation of data capture, characteristic of the algorithmic governmentality imposed by 24/7 capitalism, circuits of transindividuation have become circuits of transdividuation: they have been short-circuited by automatons. The materialization of knowledge and the automatization in which it consists must lead to a change in the definition of value, which is always a criteriology, involving in some way a 'transvaluation of all values' (on Marx, Nietzsche and value, see Barbara Stiegler, 'Éthique financière et violence du capitalisme', *Revue d'économie financière* 26 [1993], pp. 303–29): the value of value is what must evaluate any selective process on the basis of the meta-criterion of negentropy.

21 See Bernard Stiegler, *The Decadence of Industrial Democracies: Disbelief and Discredit, Volume 1* (Cambridge: Polity, 2011), pp. 121–2.

22 Ibid., pp. 74–80; and Bernard Stiegler, *Taking Care of Youth and the Generations* (Stanford: Stanford University Press, 2010), pp. 154–6.

23 These are the engineering teams responsible for Taylorist rationalization.

24 See also Barbara Stiegler, 'Nietzsche et la critique de la *Bildung*', *Noesis* 10 (2006), § 18, available at: https://noesis.revues.org/582: 'The lectures on *Bildung* explain that individuation, far from being unconditionally guaranteed or already given, passes through originary obedience to form or to law, which obliges the one who individuates to decide, with rigour, within the linguistic continuum from which he or she emerged. The principle of individuation, however, cannot be implemented by a solitary individual. Collective procedures of formation (model, education, culture) are indispensable to the formation of oneself and, above anything else, the assiduous practice of the ancient great classics, which, first, ensure the development of "the feeling of the difference between form and barbarism". It is this need for a formation of oneself through the recourse to "models" or "pre-images" (*Vorbilden*) already forged in the past that gives this indissolubly individual and collective meaning to *Bildung*. This proposition builds on the argument already made in *The Birth of Tragedy*: far from being solitary, individuation involves a composition between the carnal continuum (the carnal Dionysian archi-unity) and the relation to the law and model, whose value is by definition collective (the Apollonian measure).'

25 Immanuel Kant, 'On a Recently Prominent Tone of Superiority in Philosophy', in *Theoretical Philosophy After 1781* (Cambridge: Cambridge University Press, 2002), p. 431, where Kant begins by positing and recalling that the 'first meaning' of philosophy was 'scientific *wisdom of life*' [*savoir-vivre rationnel*].

26 Gilles Deleuze, *Cinema 2: The Time-Image* (Minneapolis: University of Minnesota Press, 1989), p. 217; and Deleuze, 'Literature and Life', in *Essays Critical and Clinical* (London and New York: Verso, 1998), p. 4. *Translator's note*: Here, Stiegler adds a Deleuzian inflection to the concept of '*otium* of the people' that he develops at length in *The Decadence of Industrial Democracies*, and more specifically to the notion of the 'people' it contains. If *otium* is that way of existing in time that is directed beyond the calculability of *negotium*, that is, towards the incalculable, here Stiegler draws attention to the way this implies that the people themselves exist only by default, and consist only as some kind of transformational, inventive and performative movement. In *Cinema 2*, Deleuze contrasts the classical political cinema of, for example, Eisenstein, in which the people are 'already there' (p. 216), with a new kind of political cinema in which the people are missing: 'This acknowledgement of a people who are missing is not a renunciation of political cinema, but on the contrary the new basis on which it is founded, in the third world and for minorities. Art, and especially cinematographic art, must take part in this task: not that of addressing

a people, which is presupposed already there, but of contributing to the invention of a people' (p. 217). Similarly, in 'Literature and Life', Deleuze undertakes a complex composition of health and disease, in which the 'ultimate aim of literature is to set free, in the delirium, this creation of a health or this invention of a people, that is, a possibility of life. To write for this people who are missing ... ("for" means less "in the place of" than "for the benefit of")' (p. 4).

27 Deleuze, *Cinema 2*, p. 217.
28 Vernant, *Myth and Thought Among the Greeks*, p. 294, translation modified.
29 Clarisse Herrenschmidt, *Les trois écritures. Langue, nombre, code* (Paris: Gallimard, 2007), p. 225.
30 Ibid., p. 226.
31 John Locke, 'The Second Treatise: An Essay Concerning the True Original, Extent, and End of Civil Government', in *Two Treatises of Government and A Letter Concerning Toleration* (New Haven and London: Yale University Press, 2003).
32 See Bernard Stiegler, *States of Shock: Stupidity and Knowledge in the Twenty-First Century* (Cambridge: Polity, 2014), and Yves Citton, *Pour une écologie de l'attention* (Paris: Le Seuil, 2014).
33 André Gorz, 'Bâtir la civilisation du temps libéré', *Le Monde diplomatique* (March 1993), p. 13, available at: https://www.monde-diplomatique.fr/1993/03/GORZ/45105. *Translator's note*: This quotation is from a pamphlet entitled 'The Source and Remedy of the National Difficulties, Deduced from Principles of Political Economy, in a Letter to Lord John Russell' (1821), available at: https://www.marxists.org/reference/subject/economics/dilke/1821/sourceandremedy.htm. Marx makes use of this quotation, for example, in the *Grundrisse*, p. 397. The authorship of the pamphlet has since been identified as belonging to Charles Wentworth Dilke, attributed by his grandson, Sir Charles Wentworth Dilke, 2nd Baronet.
34 'God alone has this privilege' of being constantly in actuality (*energeia, entelekheia*), and not *just intermittently*, says Socrates in *Protagoras*, 341e–344c.
35 Aristotle, *Metaphysics*, Book 1 (A), 30–1.
36 This will be the theme of the final chapter of Bernard Stiegler, *Automatic Society, Volume 2: The Future of Knowledge* (forthcoming).
37 Antonella Corsani and Maurizio Lazzarato, *Intermittents et précaires* (Paris: Amsterdam, 2008), p. 121.
38 *Translator's note*: On formation, see chapter 2, n. 63.
39 Corsani and Lazzarato, *Intermittents et précaires*, p. 121.
40 Maurizio Lazzarato, *Governing by Debt* (South Pasadena, CA: Semiotext(e), 2015), p. 246.
41 André Leroi-Gourhan, *L'Homme et la matière* (Paris: Albin Michel, 1943), p. 336.
42 Lazzarato, *Puissances de l'invention*, p. 18.

43 If algorithmic, 24/7 capitalism consists in the automatic production of protentions, the birth of capitalism in its primitive forms was based on the control of currency, as enumerated tertiary retention and as a technology for the control of protentions. On this subject, see Bernard Stiegler, *For a New Critique of Political Economy* (Cambridge: Polity, 2010), pp. 66–70 and 84–6.

44 Cf. Lazzarato, *Puissances de l'invention*, p. 8: Tarde 'revisits the categories of political economy in terms of difference and repetition'.

45 The study of such a materialization requires a materiology that is also a traceology and that understands these materials as metastable states of matter apprehended in a process of trans-formation, that is, of hyper-materials, beyond or beneath the opposition between form and matter.

46 Dominique Méda and Patricia Vendramin, *Réinventer le travail* (Paris: Presses Universitaires de France, 2013), p. 17.

47 Anatole Bailly, *Dictionnaire Grec–Français* (Paris: Hachette, 1935).

48 In Aristotle, *energeia* is primarily characteristic of an animated being, a soul, *psukhē*, whose power to act (*dunamis*) passes to the act. This couple *energeia/dunamis* structures the whole of Aristotelian ontology – a couple with which we have not yet finished, which passes in Simondon to the polarity individual/milieu (we also find the question of the milieu, as *mesotēs*, in Aristotle), and which thereby tends towards exceeding a mere ontology. This gesture constitutes the precise stakes of Simondon's onto-*genetic* thought.

49 Marx, *Grundrisse*, p. 693.

50 Ibid.

51 Ibid., p. 694, translation modified.

52 Vernant, *Myth and Thought Among the Greeks*, p. 275, translation modified.

53 Ibid.

54 See p. 187.

55 Kant, 'On a Recently Prominent Tone of Superiority in Philosophy', p. 431, my italics.

56 Ibid.

57 Aristotle, *Problems*, Book XXX.

58 Immanuel Kant, 'An Answer to the Question: "What is Enlightenment?"', in *Political Writings* (Cambridge: Cambridge University Press, 1991), p. 54.

59 Immanuel Kant, 'Remarks in the *Observations on the Feeling of the Beautiful and Sublime*', in *Observations on the Feeling of the Beautiful and Sublime and Other Writings* (Cambridge and New York: Cambridge University Press, 2011), p. 96.

60 On this theme, see Stiegler, *What Makes Life Worth Living*, ch. 4, especially p. 75.

61 In Stiegler, *Automatic Society, Volume 2* we will see, with Étienne Delacroix and Pierre-Yves Defosse, how *energeia* and potential once again underwent a shift when 'humanity changed its relation to the

material, through the discovery of the atom and the application that is the transistor. It was this combination of the atom, the "bit" and language that allowed calculation to become a power, and to create computational power' (Pierre-Yves Defosse, 'Les hommes extraordinaires', communication to the 2014 summer academy of pharmakon.fr).

62   Michel Volle, *Iconomie* (Paris: Economica, 2014), available at: http://www.volle.com/travaux/iconomie.pdf. It is in this that David Bates provides food for thought, in analysing the primordial automaticity and artefactuality of thinking by summoning a body of thinkers that runs from René Descartes to Alan Turing and Douglas Engelbart, as well as Maryanne Wolf, conceiving the brain as an organ of the adoption of artefactuality constitutive of a noetic milieu. See David Bates, 'Automaticity, Plasticity, and the Deviant Origins of Artificial Intelligence', in David Bates and Nima Bassiri (eds), *Plasticity and Pathology: On the Formation of the Neural Subject* (New York: Fordham University Press, 2015); and 'Unity, Plasticity, Catastrophe: Order and Pathology in the Cybernetic Era', in Andreas Killen and Nitzan Lebovic (eds), *Catastrophes: A History and Theory of an Operative Concept* (Berlin: De Gruyter, 2014). This will form the subject matter of Stiegler, *Automatic Society, Volume 2*.

63   Ilya Prigogine and Isabelle Stengers, 'The New Alliance, Part One – From Dynamics to Thermodynamics: Physics, the Gradual Opening Towards the World of Natural Processes', *Scientia* 112 (1977), pp. 287–318; and 'The New Alliance, Part Two – An Extended Dynamics: Towards a Human Science of Nature', *Scientia* 112 (1977), pp. 643–53.

64   These perspectives have been outlined in Bernard Stiegler, 'The Anthropocene and Neganthropology' (available at: https://www.academia.edu/12693668/Bernard_Stiegler_The_Anthropocene_and_Neganthropology_2014_), a lecture given at the symposium 'General Organology: The Co-Individuation of Minds, Bodies, Social Organisations and Techne', at the University of Kent, Canterbury, November 2014, organized by nootechnics.org.

65   On this point, see Stiegler, *What Makes Life Worth Living*, ch. 7.

66   'Les robots vont-ils tuer la classe moyennes?', *Le Journal du dimanche* (26 October 2014), available at: http://www.lejdd.fr/Economie/Les-robots-vont-ils-tuer-la-classe-moyenne-696622.

67   I am referring here to two texts by Lazzarato: the final chapter of Lazzarato, *Governing by Debt*, and Lazzarato, *Marcel Duchamp and the Refusal of Work* (Los Angeles: Semiotext(e), 2014).

68   This opposition between noesis and work is tied to a series of other oppositions, between soul and body, intelligible and sensible, mind and matter, science and technics, ends and means, and so on.

69   And this means that the question is what proceeds from a putting into question by the *pharmakon* – a fact of which thinking becomes the quasi-cause and as such the law. Only the technical process of the

grammatization of speech enabled the thematization of the passage to the noetic act as this stage of noetic history itself: as *logos* posing the question of its logic, that is, of its constitution. It did so, however, while remaining blind to the *hypomnesic and historical* conditions of this constitution, that is, of the fact that the soul is noetic only insofar as:

- as temporal, it can become historical;
- it is temporal *in this sense* only because it has a relation to its own time, which is pre-historically technical, then proto-historically, then, when it is trans-formed into lettered form, it engages a *new process of psychic and collective individuation* that initiates the *writing of history.*

In the course of this new process of individuation that is history, the soul of the psychic individual, who then understands himself or herself essentially as a citizen, exists only in and through his or her *literate* relation to the *polis* (in his or her relationship to *lettered* collective individuation). Through this, the psychic individual constantly diachronizes the metastable synchrony to which *nomos* tends.

This historical trans-formation of the noetic soul thematizing itself as such – but in ignorance and even in the *repression* of the hypomnesic conditions resulting from grammatization and from its historiality (*Geschichtlichkeit*) – is in effect the advent of a process of *critical transindividuation* that is the source of this *diachronic regime* (wherein history writes itself, including as the history of philosophy, the sciences, literature, law, and so on, and as the 'profusion of types') and of the synchronic (as the tendency towards theoretical unification of the One).

This event, which is therefore the *critical regime of the One and the Many*, is blind to itself in the context of the conflict of philosophy – which operates this noetic thematization – with sophistry and with its *tekhnē*, writing, which philosophical noesis understands then essentially as the *pharmakon* poisoning the city through logographic practice, and not as the condition of its own thematizing operation.

If it is true that noetic life is made possible – including as self-thematization and through that as affirmation of its autonomy – by this inaugural stage of grammatization that consists in the discretization of the flow of language, hence becoming a critical milieu open to critique, noetic autonomy is always dependent on technical heteronomy and on the work it imposes on the concept, which is not pure presence to itself, but the *praxis* of a poisonous *pharmakon* that then becomes the curative instrument of an originary and thoroughly pharmaco-logical situation.

70 On the difference between the sensible and the sensational, see Bernard Stiegler, *Symbolic Misery, Volume 2: The Catastrophe of the Sensible* (Cambridge: Polity, 2015), pp. 30ff.

71 Ibid., p. 102.

72 See Marcel Mauss, 'Techniques of the Body', in Jonathan Crary and Sanford Kwinter (eds), *Incorporations* (New York: Zone Books, 1992).

73 *Translator's note*: For an account of the formation and work of the Medvedkin Groups, a cinema production group set up by Chris Marker and the factory workers of Besançon and Sochaux, see Trevor Stark, '"Cinema in the Hands of the People": Chris Marker, the Medvedkin Group, and the Potential of Militant Film', *October* 139 (2012), pp. 117–50, available at: http://www.mitpressjournals.org/doi/pdf/10.1162/OCTO_a_00083. Stark writes: 'What was unique at Rhodiaceta was that one of the most prevalent demands of the striking workers was access to culture' (p. 120). Marker wrote in *Le Nouvel Observateur* in March 1967: 'The question for these men [...] is not to negotiate – in the American style – their integration into a "society of well-being", but to contest this society itself and the value of the "compensations" it offers' (Marker, quoted in ibid., p. 122). If this indicates something of the radical nature of the work of these groups, it should also be remembered that they were not simply some kind of very short-term intervention. As Stark says: '[T]his militant cinema would follow a collective and nonhierarchical model of production, seeking to abolish the separation between expert and amateur, between producer and consumer, a gambit that would last almost five years in Besançon before spreading to a Peugeot factory in Sochaux-Montbéliard' (ibid., p. 127). He ultimately concludes: 'Rather than deferring the utopian universalization of creativity into a potential postrevolutionary future, Marker and the worker-cinematographers at Rhodiaceta claimed that the operative entry into culture of a class of people previously denied access to it constituted not simply an intervention into the superstructure but the destabilization of a social order based upon the division of labor' (ibid., p. 150).

74 See Jacques Généreux, *La Dissociété* (Paris: Le Seuil, 2006).

75 See Félix Guattari, *The Three Ecologies* (London and New Brunswick, NJ: Athlone, 2000), pp. 66–7: 'In the future much more than the simple defence of nature will be required; we will have to launch an initiative if we are to repair the Amazonian "lung", for example, or bring vegetation back to the Sahara. The creation of new living species – animal and vegetable – looms inevitably on the horizon, and the adoption of an ecosophical ethics adapted to this terrifying and fascinating situation is equally as urgent as the invention of a politics focussed on the destiny of humanity.'

76 This is clearly what Lazzarato says. I have tried to show, in 'The Proletarianization of Sensibility', through Duchamp's experience of proletarianization and mechanical grammatization, that this affects not only the work of manual producers but the work of the artist, who thus becomes an an-artist (see *Boundary 2* 44(1) [2017]; an earlier version appeared in *Lana Turner* 8 [2015]).

77 John Howkins, *The Creative Economy: How People Make Money From Ideas* (New York: Penguin, 2001).

78 See Richard Florida, *The Rise of the Creative Class* (New York: Basic Books, 2002). On the 'creative class' and the 'vectorialist class', see McKenzie Wark, *A Hacker Manifesto* (Cambridge, MA and London: Harvard University Press, 2004), and Citton, *Pour une écologie de l'attention*, pp. 99–122.

79 Michel Foucault, *Discipline and Punish: The Birth of the Prison* (New York: Vintage, 1995).

80 Firstly in Stiegler, 'To Love, to Love Me, to Love Us: From September 11 to April 21', then in the three volumes of Stiegler, *Disbelief and Discredit: The Decadence of Industrial Democracies: Disbelief and Discredit, Volume 1* (Cambridge: Polity, 2011); *Uncontrollable Societies of Disaffected Individuals: Disbelief and Discredit, Volume 2* (Cambridge: Polity, 2013); and *The Lost Spirit of Capitalism: Disbelief and Discredit, Volume 3* (Cambridge: Polity, 2014).

Chapter 8   Above and Beyond the Market

1   Georges Bataille, 'The Notion of Expenditure', in *Visions of Excess: Selected Writings, 1927–1939* (Minneapolis: University of Minnesota Press, 1985), p. 129.

2   Yann Moulier-Boutang, *L'Abeille et l'Économiste* (Paris: Carnets Nord, 2010), p. 123.

3   See also Gustavo Just da Costa e Silva, *Interpréter les théories de l'interprétation* (Paris: L'Harmattan, 2005).

4   Moulier-Boutang, *L'Abeille et l'Économiste*, p. 123.

5   Ibid., p. 126.

6   See Gilbert Simondon, *Du mode d'existence des objets techniques* (Paris: Aubier, 2012).

7   See McKenzie Wark, *A Hacker Manifesto* (Cambridge, MA and London: Harvard University Press, 2004); and Yves Citton, *Pour une écologie de l'attention* (Paris: Le Seuil, 2014).

8   See pp. 8 and 242.

9   Moulier-Boutang, *L'Abeille et l'Économiste*, p. 126.

10 What circulation of exchange values, through money or otherwise, can then be envisaged?

11 Christian Azaïs, Antonella Corsani and Patrick Dieuaide (eds), *Vers un capitalisme cognitif. Entre mutations du travail et territoires* (Paris: L'Harmattan, 2003).

12 Gorz, *The Immaterial: Knowledge, Value and Capital* (New York: Seagull Books, 2010), p. 108.

13 Moulier-Boutang, *L'Abeille et l'Économiste*, p. 126.

14 See chapter 7, n. 26.

15 Georges Bataille, *The Accursed Share: An Essay on General Economy, Volume 1: Consumption* (New York: Zone Books, 1991).

16 Max Weber, *The Protestant Ethic and the Spirit of Capitalism* (London and New York: Routledge, 1992).

17 The distinction between noetic and cognitive will be a central question in Bernard Stiegler, *Automatic Society, Volume 2: The Future of Knowledge* (forthcoming).

18 Gilles Clément, *Toujours la vie invente. Réflexions d'un écologiste humaniste* (Paris: L'Aube, 2008).

19 See Harold Thibault, 'Dans le Sichuan, des "hommes-abeilles" pollinisent à la main les vergers', *Le Monde* (23 April 2014), available at: http://www.lemonde.fr/planete/article/2014/04/23/dans-les-vergers-du-sichuan-les-hommes-font-le-travail-des-abeilles_4405686_3244.html.

20 Oskar Negt, *Die Herausforderung der Gewerkschaften. Plädoyers für die Erweiterung ihres politischen und kulturellen Mandats* (Frankfurt: Campus, 1989), quoted in André Gorz, *Capitalism, Socialism, Ecology* (London and New York: Verso, 1994), p. 58.

21 See Bernard Stiegler, *What Makes Life Worth Living: On Pharmacology* (Cambridge: Polity, 2013), Introduction and § 28. In Stiegler, *Automatic Society, Volume 2* we will see with Hidetaka Ishida how a new reading of Freud is possible, which does not root the unconscious in language. On this point, see Ishida's contribution to the 2014 summer academy of pharmakon.fr, 'À propos du *Wunderblock* de Freud', available at: http://pharmakon.fr/wordpress/academie-dete-de-lecole-de-philosophie-depineuil-le-fleuriel/academie-dete-2014/.

22 This is also highlighted by Richard Sennett, who in *The Craftsman* (New Haven and London: Yale University Press, 2008, p. 287) cites the analyses of Dewey, who wrote in *Democracy and Education*: 'Both work and play are equally free and intrinsically motivated, apart from false economic conditions which tend to make play into idle excitement for the well to do, and work into uncongenial labor for the poor.'

23 *Translator's note*: For Donald Winnicott, the transitional object, such as the cuddly toy referred to above, is what opens up a space that is neither the external world of the mother's breast nor the interior world of the child's mind, but that *involves* the child's imagination as what the mother *facilitates*. Winnicott writes (*Playing and Reality* [Abingdon, Oxon: Routledge, 2005], p. 19): 'Transitional objects and transitional phenomena belong to the realm of illusion which is at the basis of initiation of experience. This early stage in development is made possible by the mother's special capacity for making adaptation to the needs of her infant, thus allowing the infant the illusion that what the infant creates really exists.' For Stiegler, this means that the mother, *through* the transitional object, teaches the child that life is worth living, and does so through a *pharmakon* that opens up what does not exist yet 'holds' together. On the first page of *What Makes Life Worth Living*, Stiegler writes: 'The transitional object has a distinct virtue: it does

not exist. Certainly, something exists that enables it to appear – for example, a teddy bear or cuddly toy. But what makes this teddy bear or cuddly toy *able* to open up "transitional space" – which Winnicott also called "potential space" – in which the mother *can* encounter *her* child; what makes this teddy bear or cuddly toy able to become the transitional object, is that, beyond that part of the object that exists in external space, beyond or beneath this piece of cloth, there holds something that is precisely neither in exterior space, nor simply internal to either the mother or the child.' This 'holding' of what does not exist is what Stiegler means by 'consistence', as he goes on to explain below.

24 Gorz, *Capitalism, Socialism, Ecology*, p. 55.

25 Ibid., p. 56.

26 Gorz takes for granted that we have entered into a post-industrial era that he also calls a society of the immaterial, and this is where his analysis reaches its limit. This view, which he takes, disastrously, from Alain Touraine, prevents him from being able to think grammatization – or its pharmacological dimension.

27 Gorz, *Capitalism, Socialism, Ecology*, p. 57.

28 Maurice Godelier, *The Metamorphoses of Kinship* (New York: Verso, 2012), p. 553.

29 Linus Torvalds, preface to Pekka Himanen, *The Hacker Ethic and the Spirit of the Information Age* (New York: Random House, 2001), p. xiv. *Translator's note*: In the French translation of Himanen's book, *L'Éthique hacker et l'esprit de l'ère de l'information* (Paris: Exils, 2001), these are 'la "survie", la "vie sociale" et le "plaisir"' (p. 16).

30 This assertion, which may seem somewhat surprising, formed the theme of the 2014 summer academy of pharmakon.fr, under the title 'Rêves, cinéma, cerveaux', available at: http://pharmakon.fr/wordpress/academie-dete-de-lecole-de-philosophie-depineuil-le-fleuriel/academie-dete-2014/.

31 See p. 199.

32 'Anthropocène', entry in French Wikipédia (accessed August 2014).

33 It is therefore a matter of rethinking différance as a process of individuation, and the process of individuation as cosmic concrescence in the sense of Whitehead.

34 Christophe Bonneuil and Jean-Baptiste Fressoz, *The Shock of the Anthropocene: The Earth, History and Us* (London: Verso, 2016), p. 17. *Translator's note*: The quotation from Paul Crutzen and Will Steffen has been corrected: see Crutzen and Steffen, 'How Long Have We Been in the Anthropocene Era?', *Climate Change* 61 (2003), p. 253, available at: http://stephenschneider.stanford.edu/Publications/PDF_Papers/CrutzenSteffen2003.pdf.

35 Bonneuil and Fressoz, *The Shock of the Anthropocene*, pp. 24–5.

36 Whitehead, quoted in E. R. Dodds, *The Greeks and the Irrational* (Berkeley and London: University of California Press, 1951), p. 179. *Translator's note*: This quotation is originally from Alfred North Whitehead,

Symbolism: Its Meaning and Effect (New York: Fordham University Press, 1927), p. 88.

37 Jean François Billeter, in *Chine trois fois muette: essai sur l'histoire contemporaine et la Chine* (Paris: Allia, 2000), refers to a 'chain reaction', beginning with the Renaissance and colonization, in the wake of Karl Polanyi.

38 Georges Friedmann, *Où va le travail humain?* (Paris: Gallimard, 1967), p. 360.

39 Ibid., p. 365.

40 And as an aristocracy to come (understood as a melioristic power belonging to everyone).

41 Peter Glotz, quoted in André Gorz, 'Bâtir la civilisation du temps libéré', *Le Monde diplomatique* (May 1993), my italics, available at: https://www.monde-diplomatique.fr/1993/03/GORZ/45105. *Translator's note*: Gorz previously used this quotation by Glotz, a German politician who became secretary general of the SPD, in Gorz, *Critique of Economic Reason* (London and New York: Verso, 1989), p. 190.

42 Gorz, 'Bâtir la civilisation du temps libéré'.

43 In 2003: that is, ten years after the generalization of internet access via the world wide web. Gorz returned to these questions by integrating his understanding of what today Volle calls the universal programmable automaton and that to which its reticulation gave rise, namely, 'internet-based virtual communities [where the] separation between the workers and their reified work [is] virtually abolished, as is the block on producers appropriating the means of production for themselves and self-managing them' (Gorz, *The Immaterial*, p. 14). It is these communities that in the eyes of Gorz form positive externalities that should become the principal sources of wealth and constitute what Yann Moulier-Boutang today calls the pollen economy. These externalities are made possible by an organological transformation in which the 'computer emerges here as the universal and universally accessible tool through which all forms of knowledge and all activities can theoretically be pooled' (ibid., p. 14), and with software, that is, with the algorithm, 'knowledge, separated from any product in which it has been, is or will be incorporated, can carry out a productive action, in and of itself, as software [...]. It can organize and manage complex interactions between a large number of actors and variables [...]. Since the marginal cost of software is either very small or even negligible, knowledge can save much more work than it cost and can do so on a massive scale that was unimaginable just a short time ago. [...] And this means that, though it is a source of value, *it destroys vastly more "value" than it serves to create*. In other words, it saves immense quantities of paid social labour' (ibid., pp. 53–4). Through all these analyses, Gorz paraphrases and comments on *Vers un capitalisme cognitif*, a collective work edited by Christian Azaïs, Antonella Corsani and Patrick Dieuaide. I myself owe much to these analyses of Gorz and

all the authors of that book. I realized this afterwards, in writing this book, and I am deeply thankful: they 'pollinated' me.

44   Julie Bort, 'People Don't Realize How Many Jobs Will Soon Be Replaced By Software Bots', *Business Insider* (13 March 2014), available at: http://www.businessinsider.com/bill-gates-bots-are-taking-away-jobs-2014-3; and see pp. 7 and 59.

45   See in particular the blog by Paul Jorion, 'Piqûre de rappel. *Le Monde*: La Grande Transformation du travail', available at: http://www.pauljorion.com/blog/2014/10/27/piqure-de-rappel-le-monde-la-grande-transformation-du-travail-lundi-21-mardi-22-avril-2014/ – a piece I discovered at the very moment I was finishing this book, and I thank Arnauld de l'Épine for drawing it to my attention.

46   Bort, 'People Don't Realize How Many Jobs Will Soon Be Replaced By Software Bots'.

47   See William Lazonick, 'Profits Without Prosperity', *Harvard Business Review* (September 2014), available at: https://hbr.org/2014/09/profits-without-prosperity, which poses the question, 'Where did the money from productivity increases go?' It is again Arnauld de l'Épine who drew my attention to this article. *Translator's note*: Another version of this article by William Lazonick, entitled 'Profits Without Prosperity: How Stock Buybacks Manipulate the Market, and Leave Most Americans Worse Off', is available at: http://ineteconomics.org/uploads/papers/LAZONICK_William_Profits-without-Prosperity-20140406.pdf.

48   His statements on this subject are astounding: 'In the current crisis, it is clear that it is the indebted poor who are driving finance to its fall.' Moulier-Boutang, *L'Abeille et l'Économiste*, p. 132.

49   I have myself contested this opposition, in Bernard Stiegler, *Ce qui fait que la vie vaut la peine d'être vécue* (Paris: Flammarion, 2010), pp. 165–6. *Translator's note*: The chapter from which this reference is taken is included not in *What Makes Life Worth Living* but in *For a New Critique of Political Economy*. The particular sentence to which the author refers, however, is not included in the latter volume (being based on an earlier version of the text, prior to the publication of *Ce qui fait que la vie vaut la peine d'être vécue*). It reads: 'In this regard, it is illusory or demagogical to oppose a "real" economy to a "virtual" economy: any economy requires investment and therefore virtualization.' This is followed by a lengthy footnote on p. 166:
   'No human reality, no human real is without virtuality. The virtual is what meant that the hunter-gatherer of the Amazonian jungle saw in the greenery an immense wealth while I see only green. The question of the virtual as articulated with the real is of key importance in any human affair – and refers to the way in which secondary retentions virtualize primary retentions in Husserl. The possible is what constitutes the possibilities of the virtual itself in its encounter with the real, in its real projection as concrescence. The virtual is what opens possibilities. But the virtual is not the possible.

'What Marx called fictitious capital should therefore not be called virtual capital or the virtual economy – just as it is meaningless to speak of the productive economy as the "real" economy. Capitalism is *based* on the virtualization of the real at all levels of production and of consumption. The virtual is anything but fictitious capital: it is what gives power to the real, what allows it to *realize itself*, to transform itself. The fictitious is an artefact that aims to capture the virtual and to organize it in a way that may obviously de-realize productivity – the apparatus of production – capital being in general a virtuality that contributes to realizing productivity as investment.'

50 Alfred North Whitehead, *Process and Reality: An Essay in Cosmology* (New York: Macmillan, 1929). To enter this complex but fundamental philosophy in order to understand the questions of our age, see Bertrand Saint-Sernin, *Whitehead. Un univers en essai* (Paris: Vrin, 2000), and from Whitehead himself, see Alfred North Whitehead, *The Function of Reason* (Princeton: Princeton University Press, 1929).

51 See Bernard Stiegler, *Technics and Time, 3: Cinematic Time and the Question of Malaise* (Stanford: Stanford University Press, 2011), ch. 2.

52 The role played by the screen (both as what supports and as what conceals) in the projection in which the imagination consists has led me to describe the faculties of reason as projections of an arche-cinema. On the screen in this sense, see the symposium, 'Vivre par(mi) les écrans', at the Université Jean-Moulin de Lyon-3, organized by Mauro Carbone (September 2014), available at: https://www.youtube.com/watch?v=ALBre0fAT-E. *Translator's note*: See also Bernard Stiegler, 'The Organology of Dreams and Arche-Cinema', *Screening the Past* 36 (2013), available at: http://www.screeningthepast.com/2013/06/the-organology-of-dreams-and-arche-cinema/; and Bernard Stiegler, 'The Writing Screen', a lecture delivered at the Centro Nacional de Las Artes Cenart, Mexico City, on 30 September 2015, available at: https://www.academia.edu/17374065/Bernard_Stiegler_The_Writing_Screen_2015_.

53 Unless we refer, like Jean Hyppolite, to a 'transcendental field without a subject'. *Translator's note*: Jacques Derrida refers to a 'subjectless transcendental field' in his *Edmund Husserl's Origin of Geometry: An Introduction* (Lincoln and London: University of Nebraska Press, 1978), p. 88, and in n. 91 ascribes this to a comment by Jean Hyppolite. According to Derrida, for Hyppolite this would refer to a field in which 'the conditions of subjectivity would appear and where the subject would be constituted starting from the transcendental field'. Derrida then writes (ibid., p. 88): 'Writing, as the place of absolutely permanent ideal objectivities and therefore of absolute Objectivity, certainly constitutes such a transcendental field. And likewise, to be sure, transcendental subjectivity can be fully announced and appear on the basis of this field or its possibility. Thus a subjectless transcendental field is one of the "conditions" of transcendental subjectivity.' The phrase '*champ transcendantal sans sujet*' used by Hyppolite, however,

can already be found in Jean-Paul Sartre, *Being and Nothingness* (New York: Washington Square Press, 1992), p. 318, precisely in the course of a discussion about the *conditions* in which Husserl and Kant could escape solipsism, in which context Sartre refers to the condition of *knowledge* (of the Other: that is, of the relationship between two processes of psychic individuation, or between a process of psychic individuation and a process of collective individuation) without, of course, ascribing the conditions of such knowledge either to writing or, it goes without saying, to tertiary retention (that is, to a process of technical individuation).

54 Gottfried Wilhelm Leibniz, *Opuscules et fragments inédits* (Paris: Alcan, 1903), pp. 98–9.

55 Jacques Derrida, *Of Grammatology* (Baltimore and London: Johns Hopkins University Press, 1997, corrected edition), p. 78. *Translator's note*: Derrida also discusses this quotation from Leibniz in 'Psyche: Invention of the Other', in *Psyche: Inventions of the Other, Volume I* (Stanford: Stanford University Press, 2007), p. 41.

56 I have endeavoured to show this in 'D'une pharmacologie positive', *Rue Descartes* 82 (2014), pp. 132–5, available at: http://www.ruedescartes.org/articles/2014-3-d-une-pharmacologie-positive/; and also at: http://arsindustrialis.org/d-une-pharmacologie-positive.

57 Georges Canguilhem, *Knowledge of Life* (New York: Fordham University Press, 2008), p. 19, translation modified.

58 Ibid., p. 21. *Translator's note*: It would of course also have been possible to retranslate this as 'knowledge and *technics* are indissolubly linked', as could have been done with Mauss's techniques of the body or Foucault's techniques of power, or of the self.

59 See Alain Supiot, 'The Grandeur and Misery of the Social State' (29 November 2012), available at: http://books.openedition.org/cdf/3093.

60 Jean-Michel Rey, *Le Temps du crédit* (Paris: Desclée de Brouwer, 2002).

Conclusion: Noetic Pollination and the Neganthropocene

1 Claude Lévi-Strauss, *Tristes Tropiques* (Harmondsworth, Middlesex: Penguin, 1976), p. 543, translation modified.

2 Georges Bataille, *The Accursed Share: An Essay on General Economy, Volume 1: Consumption* (New York: Zone Books, 1991), p. 12, translation modified.

3 Karl Marx, *Capital, Volume I* (New York: Vintage, 1977), pp. 283–4, translation modified.

4 Ibid., p. 283.

5 Ibid.

6 Karl Marx and Friedrich Engels, *The German Ideology* (Moscow: Progress Press, 1976), p. 37, translation modified.

7   Maurice Godelier, *The Metamorphoses of Kinship* (New York: Verso, 2012), p. 229. We will return to this text in Bernard Stiegler, *Automatic Society, Volume 2: The Future of Knowledge* (forthcoming).

8   It sometimes used to be said to a child who made a mistake, as a threat intended to correct them, 'I'll put lead in your head.' *Translator's note*: This expression more or less means 'I'll knock some sense into you.' In the continuation of the sentence the author obviously relates lead [*plomb*] to plumb line [*fil à plomb*].

9   See Christian Jacob, *The Sovereign Map: Theoretical Approaches in Cartography Throughout History* (Chicago and London: University of Chicago Press, 2006).

10 Yann Moulier-Boutang, *L'Abeille et l'Économiste* (Paris: Carnets Nord, 2010), p. 127.

11 Ibid.

12 Ibid., p. 128.

13 These words themselves, oralized after having been interiorized (what we call learning language), are also equally technical, but this is not so easily appreciated. It was because he did succeed in making this apparent that Derrida was obliged to reconsider, alongside it, the entire 'history of metaphysics', through what we called his deconstruction – which starts from this Archimedean point.

14 Moulier-Boutang, *L'Abeille et l'Économiste*, p. 128.

15 Bernard Stiegler, *Symbolic Misery, Volume 1: The Hyper-Industrial Epoch* (Cambridge: Polity, 2014), p. 45.

16 Godelier, *The Metamorphoses of Kinship*, pp. 446 and 468–70.

17 Aristotle, *Politics* 1253a7–18.

18 Thomas Hobbes, *Leviathan* (Oxford and New York: Oxford University Press, 1998), ch. 17, § 6.

19 Ibid., ch. 18, § 20, and as Gérard Mairet commented in his translation of Hobbes, *Le Léviathan* (Paris: Gallimard, 2000), p. 285.

20 According to Hobbes, this power is required because, while people may constitute themselves into a unified group after being able to 'obtain a victory by their unanimous endeavour against a foreign enemy; yet afterwards, when either they have no common enemy, or he that by one part is held for an enemy, is by another part held for a friend, they must needs by the difference of their interests dissolve, and fall again into a war amongst themselves'. Hobbes, *Leviathan*, ch. 17, § 5.

21 Ibid., ch. 17, §§ 7–12.

22 Ibid., ch. 17, § 13.

23 Gaston Bachelard, *L'Activité rationaliste de la physique contemporaine* (Paris: Presses Universitaires de France, 1951).

24 The im-mense exceeds understanding – and summons reason.

25 On this concept, see, for example, the advertisement for a webinar hosted by the Aberdeen Group, 'How the Digital Worker is Transforming Manufacturing Information' (no longer available online): 'The convergence of cloud, business analytics, social and mobile technology

have fundamentally changed how businesses operate. Employees can access information, launch a Web conference, share know-how, and collaborate in a team environment from just about anywhere. However, few of these technology advances have found their way to the shop floor. The reality is that employees as consumers are already very familiar with today's collaborative, social, and mobile technologies. *Given the popularity of applications such as Skype, Hotmail, Instant Messenger, social and smart phone applications, it's only logical that employees could quickly adapt to a digital manufacturing environment.'* This means that 'vocational training' is now carried over into 'leisure time'. 'Best-in-class manufacturers are actively moving toward a digital manufacturing environment which will enable enterprises to:

- Manage operations through a role-based lens (plant manager, supervisor, operator) in a uniform, secure environment with global deployment capabilities.
- Enable work teams to monitor performance metrics and operational information, facilitate continuous improvement workshops, access know-how and share best practices, and communicate across production shifts.
- Facilitate instant, real-time collaboration across the organization (Engineering or Manufacturing) and across the supply base to identify, understand, and resolve operational issues.
- Enhance training and regulatory compliance levels.

'Please join Microsoft and Aberdeen Group as we discuss how best-in-class manufacturing companies are leveraging cloud, business analytics, social, and mobile technologies on the shop-floor and demonstrate some of these technologies that can drive fundamental change. You'll come away from the webinar being able to benchmark your own organization against your peers, and better understand how these technologies can help you transform shop-floor operations for improved performance.'

26 See the call by the New School of Social Research for papers announcing 'the third in The New School's Politics of Digital Culture Conference Series Sponsored by The New School and The Institute for Distributed Creativity. Over the past decade, advancements in software development, digitization, an increase in computer processing power, faster and cheaper bandwidth and storage, and the introduction of a wide range of inexpensive, wireless-enabled computing devices and mobile phones, set the global stage for emerging forms of labor that help corporations to drive down labor costs and ward off the falling rate of profits. Companies like CrowdFlower, oDesk, or Amazon.com's Mechanical Turk serve as much more than payment processors or interface providers; they shape the nature of the tasks that are performed. Work is organized against the worker. Recent books included

The Internet as Playground and Factory (Scholz, 2013), *Living Labor* (Hoegsberg and Fisher) based on the exhibition Arbeitstid that took place in Oslo in 2013 and *Cognitive Capitalism, Education, and Digital Labour* (Peters, Bulut, et al, eds., Peter Lang, 2011). In 2012, the exhibition The Workers was curated by MASS MOCA in the United States. Christian Fuchs' book *Digital Labor and Karl Marx* is forthcoming with Routledge.' Available at: http://www.wired.com/2014/02/call-proposals-digital-labor-sweatshops-picket-lines-barricades/.

27 See Yves Citton, *Pour une écologie de l'attention* (Paris: Le Seuil, 2014), p. 101.

28 On this point, see pp. 35–6 and 139–41.

29 The speed of lightning is 100,000 kilometres per second.

30 See the Entretiens du nouveau monde industriel 2009, available at: http://www.iri.centrepompidou.fr/evenement/entretiens-du-nouveau-monde-industriel/?lang=fr_fr.

31 Bruce Sterling, *Shaping Things* (Cambridge, MA and London: MIT Press, 2005).

32 See Bernard Stiegler, 'The Indexing of Things', in Ulrik Ekman (ed.), *Throughout: Art and Culture Emerging with Ubiquitous Computing* (Cambridge, MA and London: MIT Press, 2012).

33 Olivier Landau, internal document of Ars Industrialis.

34 Every region or territory is hypomnesic: it is for this very reason that it constitutes a territory – that is, a space symbolized and inhabited by those who participate in and from this symbolic milieu, which is nevertheless obviously not locked or enclosed within this territory.

35 This concept, proposed on the basis of Amartya Sen's 'capabilities', is explained in Bernard Stiegler, *Pharmacologie du Front national*, followed by Victor Petit, *Vocabulaire d'Ars Industrialis* (Paris: Flammarion, 2013), pp. 319 and 326.

36 Evgeny Morozov, *To Save Everything, Click Here: The Folly of Technological Solutionism* (New York: Public Affairs, 2014).

37 Chris Anderson, *Makers: The New Industrial Revolution* (New York: Crown Business, 2012).

38 Chris Anderson, *The Long Tail: Why the Future of Business is Selling Less of More* (New York: Hyperion, 2006).

39 Anderson, *Makers*, pp. 23–6.

40 Ibid., pp. 16–18.

41 Olivier Landau, internal document of Ars Industrialis.

42 David F. Noble, *Forces of Production: A Social History of Industrial Automation* (New York: Oxford University Press, 1986).

43 Johan Söderberg, 'Means of Production: The Factory-Floor Knowledge Economy', *Le Monde diplomatique* (March 2013), available at: http://mondediplo.com/2013/03/10makers.

44 Ibid.

45 Ibid.

46 Marcel Mauss, 'La nation', in *Oeuvres, tome 3: Cohésion sociale et divisions de la sociologie* (Paris: Minuit, 1969). And see also Mauss, 'La nation et l'internationalisme', in ibid.

47 See the article on 'Phéromones' in the French Wikipédia (accessed November 2014): 'Pheromones (or *phérormones*, or again, *phérohormones*) are chemical substances emitted by most animals and certain plants, and which act as messengers between individuals of the same species, transmitting to other organisms information that plays a role in, especially, sexual attraction.

'Extremely active, they act in minute quantities, so they can be transported and detected across many kilometres. In mammals and reptiles, pheromones are mainly detected by vomeronasal organ, while insects generally utilize their antennae.

'Pheromones are chemical substances comparable to hormones. But whereas *classical* hormones (insulin, adrenalin, etc.) are produced by the endocrine glands and circulate only within the organism as part of its metabolism, pheromones are generally produced by exocrine glands, or secreted with urine, and act as chemical messengers between individuals. They can be volatile (perceived by smell), or act by contact (cuticular compounds for insects, for example, perceived by taste receptors). They play a primary role during mating periods, and in some social insects, such as ants and bees. These pheromones are essential to the functioning of the group. The sexual pheromones of insects contribute to the reproductive isolation between species, thanks to their specificity.'

48 Lévi-Strauss, *Tristes Tropiques*, pp. 542–3, translation modified. I would like here to thank Benoît Dillet, who reminded me of this text during the General Organology conference he organized at the University of Kent along with the Noötechnics group, in November 2014.

49 Cf. the entry on 'avenu' in Alain Rey (ed.), *Dictionnaire historique de la langue française* (Paris: Le Robert, 2012).

50 This is why Lévi-Strauss says that the only time man is not entropic is 'when he has been engaged in self-reproduction'.

51 It is with this organological disturbance of the organic that Bertrand Bonello begins his film *Tiresia*.

52 André Leroi-Gourhan, *Gesture and Speech* (Cambridge, MA and London: MIT Press, 1993), p. 26.

53 Lévi-Strauss, *Tristes Tropiques*, p. 543, translation modified.

54 René Descartes, 'Discourse on the Method of Properly Conducting One's Reason and of Seeking the Truth in the Sciences', § 6, in *Discourse on Method and the Meditations* (London: Penguin, 1968), p. 78.

55 Georges Canguilhem, *Knowledge of Life* (New York: Fordham University Press, 2008), p. 21.

56 Alfred North Whitehead, *The Function of Reason* (Princeton: Princeton University Press, 1929).

57 Lévi-Strauss, *Tristes Tropiques*, p. 543, translation modified.

58   Claude Lévi-Strauss, *Introduction to the Work of Marcel Mauss* (London: Routledge and Kegan Paul, 1987). And see also Marcel Hénaff, *Claude Lévi-Strauss and the Making of Structural Anthropology* (Minneapolis and London: University of Minnesota Press, 1998), p. 134.

59   We will return at length to these questions in Stiegler, *Automatic Society, Volume 2*.

60   Georges Bataille, 'The Notion of Expenditure', in *Visions of Excess: Selected Writings, 1927–1939* (Minneapolis: University of Minnesota Press, 1985), p. 116.

61   Ibid., p. 118.

62   Ibid., p. 119.

63   On the unknown, see Pierre Sauvanet, *L'insu: une pensée en suspens* (Paris: Arléa, 2011).

64   Lévi-Strauss, *Tristes Tropiques*, p. 543.

65   Bataille, 'The Notion of Expenditure', p. 125.

66   Ibid., p. 126.

Index